THE
RISE AND FALL
OF CIVILIZATIONS

THE LAW OF HISTORY

First published by O Books, 2008
O Books is an imprint of John Hunt Publishing Ltd., The Bothy, Deershot Lodge, Park Lane, Ropley, Hants,
SO24 0BE, UK
office1@o-books.net
www.o-books.net

Distribution in:	South Africa
	Alternative Books
UK and Europe	altbook@peterhyde.co.za
Orca Book Services	Tel: 021 555 4027 Fax: 021 447 1430
orders@orcabookservices.co.uk	
Tel: 01202 665432 Fax: 01202 666219 Int. code (44)	Text copyright Nicholas Hagger 2008
USA and Canada	Design: Stuart Davies
NBN	
custserv@nbnbooks.com	ISBN: 978 1 84694 010 1
Tel: 1 800 462 6420 Fax: 1 800 338 4550	
	All rights reserved. Except for brief quotations in
Australia and New Zealand	critical articles or reviews, no part of this book may
Brumby Books	be reproduced in any manner without prior written
sales@brumbybooks.com.au	permission from the publishers.
Tel: 61 3 9761 5535 Fax: 61 3 9761 7095	
	The rights of Nicholas Hagger as author have been
Far East (offices in Singapore, Thailand,	asserted in accordance with the Copyright, Designs
Hong Kong, Taiwan)	and Patents Act 1988.
Pansing Distribution Pte Ltd	
kemal@pansing.com	A CIP catalogue record for this book is available from
Tel: 65 6319 9939 Fax: 65 6462 5761	the British Library.

Printed by Chris Fowler International
www.chrisfowler.com

THE
RISE AND FALL
OF CIVILIZATIONS

THE LAW OF HISTORY

NICHOLAS HAGGER

BOOKS

Winchester, UK
Washington, USA

For thus hath the Lord said unto me, Go, set a watchman, let him declare what he seeth....Watchman what of the night? Watchman what of the night? The watchman said, The morning cometh, and also the night.

Isaiah, 21.6, 11-12

In our time, the writing and publication of universal histories is an important public service. We are living in an age in which, for the first time in history, the whole human race, over the whole surface of our planet, is growing together into a single world-society.... We have been, first and foremost, adherents of some local nation, civilisation or religion. In future, our paramount loyalty has to be transferred to the whole human race.... If and when the unification of man is achieved...local histories will be seen... as preludes to a universal history of mankind as a whole.

Our time is the first in which it has been possible to take a literally universal view of human history, because this is the first time in which the whole human race all round the globe, has come within sight of coalescing into a single society. In the past, a number of empires, and a smaller number of missionary religions, have aimed at universality. None of them, so far, has ever attained to universality in the literal sense....

These previous attempts at unification on a world-wide scale have inspired some of the great historians of the past to look at our history in universal terms.... These perceptive spirits have been aware that the goal of human and social endeavours is the unification of the human race which we, in our time, may be on the eve of achieving at last.

If these partial unifications of the human race (i.e. under the Persians, Mongols and Timurids) had power to awaken the historical imagination, our present age ought, *a fortiori*, to produce universal historians of even greater stature. It is one of the paradoxes of the present age that the prevalent school of contemporary historians is still working under the spell of parochial nationalism.... The issue between universalism and nationalism is one of life and death for the human race; and the victory of universalism cannot be taken for granted.

Arnold Toynbee, Foreword to the English edition of the
Larousse Histoire Universelle, Paul Hamlyn, 1967

The development of culture and the development of religion, in a society uninfluenced from without, cannot be clearly isolated from each other....The culture (is) essentially, the incarnation (so to speak) of the religion of a people.

T. S. Eliot, *Notes Towards the Definition of Culture*

ACKNOWLEDGMENTS

This book's precursor is my work *The Fire and the Stones*. Researched during the 1970s and 1980s, that work predicted the end of Communism in the USSR and East Europe, and a United States of Europe. I am grateful to the historian Asa Briggs for calling it, when speaking at its launch, "the most powerful *tour de force* I have come across in my entire academic life"; and to the then Poet Laureate Ted Hughes, who wrote to me on March 19, 1994: "I'm sure you've seen a genuine historical pattern and law." In the companion volume to the present work, *The Light of Civilization*, I acknowledged a number of eminent thinkers, most now dead, with whom I discussed my outlook. (Sir Laurens van der Post told me: "What a pity Toynbee, Eliot and Jung are not here now, they would be so interested in your view of history. You are now carrying the torch that they have handed on to you.")

Once again I am grateful to Michael Mann for his continuing interest in my work, and to John Hunt, who very quickly saw how my view of history should be presented.

BOOKS PUBLISHED BY NICHOLAS HAGGER

The Fire and the Stones
Selected Poems
The Universe and the Light
A White Radiance
A Mystic Way
Awakening to the Light
A Spade Fresh with Mud
The Warlords
Overlord
A Smell of Leaves and Summer
The Tragedy of Prince Tudor
The One and the Many
Wheeling Bats and a Harvest Moon
The Warm Glow of the Monastery Courtyard
The Syndicate
The Secret History of the West
The Light of Civilization
Classical Odes
Overlord, one-volume edition
Collected Poems 1958 – 2005
Collected Verse Plays
Collected Stories
The Secret Founding of America
The Last Tourist in Iran

CONTENTS

The Breakdown of Civilizations

The New People's Renewal of Civilizations

The Decline of Civilizations

The Decay and Demise of Civilizations

PART TWO: LESSONS AND PREDICTIONS

**3. Civilizations as Light-Bearers: The Process of Growth,
Breakdown and Decay**

PROLOGUE

In the precursor and companion volume to this work, *The Light of Civilization*, I saw that religion is about more than hymns and prayers. It is an inner experience of the soul opening to God, who is experienced as Light. Different religions interpret the experience in different ways, but all who open to God as Light are having the same experience.

I focused on 25 Light traditions from different parts of the world, spanning the last five thousand years, and established that the experience of God as Light is the basis of religion and all religions.

I saw that during the five thousand years of recorded history there were many periods of high civilization which have left behind stone monuments and exquisite art, and I identified the principle that has stirred different peoples from nomadic, pastoral culture to the heights of civilization that we still admire today.

I maintained that civilization is based on religion and that religion is based on an experience of the mysterious Light which is interpreted differently in different religions. I identified 25 different civilizations that have reached high civilization through their religions. To recap, the civilizations are, in broadly chronological or geographical order:

1. Indo-European Kurgan (perhaps builders of megaliths in Old Europe)
2. Mesopotamian (Sumerian-Akkadian and later Babylonian)
3. Egyptian
4. Aegean-Greek (including Minoan and Mycenaean)
5. Roman
6. Anatolian (including Hittite)
7. Syrian
8. Israelite (Judaistic)
9. Celtic (including Irish-Celtic and Druid)
10. Iranian
11. European } together forming Western civilisation (now
12. North-American } centred in Europe and USA)
13. Byzantine-Russian (Christian Orthodox)
14. Germanic-Scandinavian

15. Andean (including Peruvian)
16. Meso-American (including Mexican and North-American Mississippian)
17. Arab (Islamic)
18. African
19. Indian (Hindu)
20. South-East-Asian (mainly Mahayana and later Theravada Buddhist)
21. Japanese
22. Oceanian (including Polynesian and Australian)
23. Chinese
24. Tibetan
25. Central-Asian (including Mongolian) from c.500 BC

Of these 25 civilizations the first ten and no. 14 are dead, and the other fourteen are still living. Between them, these 25 civilizations were based on, and reached high civilization through, 21 different religions/distinctive gods, which I saw as:

Civilization	Distinctive god
1. Indo-European Kurgan and Megalithic in Old Europe	Dyaeus Pitar/Magna Mater (Sky Father/Earth Mother)
2. Mesopotamian	Anu/Ogma/Utu Shamash/Tammuz/Marduk Shuqamuna/Ashur
3. Egyptian	Ra/Amon/Aton Horus/Osiris/Apis
4. Aegean-Greek (Minoan/Mycenaean)	Zeus/Apollo Anat/Athene (or Athena)
5. Roman	Jupiter/Apollo Gnostic God as Light

6.	Anatolian	Mistress of Animals/Storm and Weather
	Hittite	god Tarhun or Teshub/Sharruma/ Arinna
	Phrygian	Cybele/Attis

7.	Syrian	
	Canaanite	El/Dagon/Baal/Mot/Resheph/ Molech (or Moloch) Koshar/Astarte/Anath (or Anat)
	Phoenician	Baal/Astarte/Adonis
	Philistine	Dagon/Ashtoreth/Baal
	Aramaean	Hadad/Rammon/Atargatis

8.	Israelite (Judaistic)	El Shaddai/Yahweh

9.	Celtic	Du-w ("Yoo-we", cf "Yahweh")/Lug/ Beli (cf Baal)/Taran/Yesu

10.	Iranian	Mithras/Zurvan (of Medes)/Ahura Mazda/Mani
	Elamite	Inshushinak/Kiririshna (cf Indian Krishna)/Nahhunte/Huban

11.	European (Christian)	God as Light
	* North-American	God as Light
	* Byzantine-Russian	God as Light
	(offshoots from Christian)	

12.	Germanic-Scandinavian	Wodan/Odin

13.	Andean	Smiling god ("El Lanzon" "the Great Image")

	Sun-gods:
	Inti/Quetzlcoatl/Kukulan/
14. Meso-American	Kinich Ahau (or
	Itzamna)/Huitzilopochtli
15. Arab (Islamic)	Allah
16. African	Mwari/Nzambi/Cghene/Ngai/
	Leza/Ndjambi Marunga/
	Raluvhimba/Olodumare
17. Indian	Agni/Brahman/Atman
	Siva/Sakti
	Visnu/Rama/Krishna
	Om Kar
	The Buddha
S.-E.-Asian (Mahayana Buddhist)	The Buddha
18. Japanese	
Shinto	Kami/Amaterasu
	The Buddha
19. Oceanian (Polynesian and Melanesian) (offshoot from Indian/ Andean)	The Buddha?/ Andean Smiling god/Inti? Io (Maoris)
20. Chinese	*Shang Ti*/*T'ien Ti*/The *Tao*
21. * Tibetan	The Buddha
* Central-Asian (including Mongolian)	The Buddha

Four civilizations (see asterisks) have related religions.

I now carry the argument forward by showing in detail how civilizations rise and fall through their religions and Light. We will consider the genesis, growth, arrest of growth, breakdown, renewal, decline, decay and demise of the 25 civilizations in terms of the Light which inspired their religions. When their Light is strong they rise; when their Light dims and fades, they turn secular and begin to fall. As with all patterns, the devil is in the detail; the evidence has to be presented before it can be said that the patterns work, the proof of the pudding is in the eating. Much of the detail can be found in the respective Light traditions and subtradition presented in *The Light of Civilization*. I now give, in summary form, historical detail for the progress of civilizations which should be read in conjunction with *The Light of Civilization*. I give the evidence for my thesis. I show that the Light – the experience of what has been called the divine Light – inspired the religions within 25 civilizations and propelled their growth. In the eleven dead civilizations, when the Light was dimmed the civilization declined. The same may now be true of the fourteen living civilizations, including Western civilization.

In *The Light of Civilization*, we saw that Western civilization is an amalgam of two civilizations: the European civilization, which goes back to the Germanic tribes who sacked the Roman Empire; and the North-American civilization, which, despite its discovery by Columbus in 1492 really began with the founding of the Jamestown settlement, the first English-speaking settlement to survive, in 1607 (the date on which the US has based its observance of its 400th anniversary). One of my conclusions in this book is that the European civilization is old and may need a recovery of the Light if it is to survive and flourish. The North-American civilization, however, is relatively new and young, and contains within it the Light that it needs to survive – and, indeed, expand.

We will see that each civilization goes through the same 61 stages. By overlaying the living civilizations on the dead ones we can anticipate the coming stages of living civilizations, including our own. This will enable us to make some predictions. We shall see that the dead civilizations pass into other living civilizations with different gods and continue their flow; thus, the Egyptian and Mesopotamian peoples woke one day to find that their civilizations had come to an end and that they had passed into the Arab civilization, that their religions and gods had been replaced by Islam and Allah. We can thus grasp that the flow of history is endless in the sense that it is without end until human history ends. By looking at the past of living civilizations and considering what happened to the dead ones as we chart the rise and fall of 25 different civilizations, we shall be treading in the footsteps of Gibbon, Spengler and Toynbee, whose works I taught in Japan where I first glimpsed this fourth way of approaching Western and world history more than forty years ago.

My fourth way is a Universalist way. For Universalist history focuses on the history of all mankind as a whole in relation to the universe, and not on regional parts. It seeks to reveal the pattern of history. By offering the endless rise and fall of 25 civilizations based on religions I am able to offer a Grand Unified Theory of Religion and World History, which to my knowledge has never been attempted before and which is surely timely now that globalism is on the verge of creating a world government that will view us primarily as world citizens.

Nicholas Hagger
August 2007

PART ONE

THE 61 STAGES IN THE RISE AND FALL OF CIVILIZATIONS

1. The Light and History

The twentieth-century historian Arnold Toynbee, whose vast twelve-volume *A Study of History* spanned four decades, wrote near the end of his life: "I have been searching for the positive factor which within the last five thousand years, has shaken part of Mankind...into the 'differentiation of civilization'.... Now that these manoeuvres have ended, one after another, in my drawing a blank, I am led to consider whether my successive failures may not point to some mistake in method."[1] Toynbee had examined each civilization in turn and then made deductions. He postulated Challenge-and-Response as the solution to his problem, although that raises the question: what sort of challenge?

From the evidence of *The Light of Civilization* we are now in a position to see, that what has "shaken" man into civilizations is his vision of the Light, the one galvanising force which different cultures interpret in relation to their own roots and their own image. This escaped Toynbee's notice because the evidence for it is not to be found in history books, but in works of religion, mysticism and poetry.

I hold that civilizations rise and fall in terms of the response of their peoples to visions of the Light. *The Light of Civilization* gives instances of how a vision of the Light has enabled a religion, and therefore a culture and civilization, to grow (for example, the visions of Christ and Mohammed) or to be renewed (for example the visions of Mani and St Bernard). When the tradition of the Light extends over five thousand years, can we believe with the sceptics that although the Light was an issue of the past, in the days of the Romans and of the Templars, it is not an issue today? Can we ignore the tradition, the pattern, of five thousand years? In the dead civilizations, as we shall see, absence of the Light is a symptom (cause?) of decline. When it is to be found in past civilizations can we believe that it is not to be found in our own European or North-American civilizations today? We live in a world of American Presidents and British Prime Ministers, of economic forecasts and trade figures and live television link-ups, and the Light is ignored in the media. Yet the Christian vote put Bush Jr back in power for a second term in 2005. Can we – when the tradition, the pattern, indicates otherwise – avoid connecting the widespread ignoring of the Light in Europe with the state of our European Christian civilization today?

A civilization's response, or lack of response, to the Light will affect its outcome according to my view. What evidence is there in history for this view, and for the view that civilizations rise and fall in terms of their response to the Light?

EVIDENCE FOR A LIGHT-BASED UNIVERSALIST VIEW OF HISTORY

Although there is an obvious difficulty regarding the limited amount that is known about the early civilizations of c.3000 BC, the general outlines are clear and the evidence can be dealt with under four headings:

(1) The evidence of those who have experienced the Light. This "eye-witness" evidence occurs in every culture and civilization and at every time. This "eye-witness" evidence has already been presented very fully in *The Light of Civilization*, which reveals evidence from the culture of all times and ages. The "eye-witness" accounts of those who have expressed it testify to the existence of the Light just as eye-witness accounts of the sun testify to its existence (which may be denied by those who have been born blind). In view of the evidence of the five-thousand-year-old tradition, scepticism about the experience of the Light is more revealing about the limited experience of the sceptics than about the Light, whose existence is so comprehensively attested.

This can be expressed as a universality: the universality in all cultures and civilizations of the written evidence of those who have experienced the Light during the last five thousand years, and whose eye-witness accounts testify to the Light's impact on their religions.

(2) Evidence that history is a pattern of civilizations, each of which grows out of a religion that is inspired by a vision of the Light. I established at the end of *The Light of Civilization* (pp502-506) that, far from being chaotic, history is both linear and cyclical: cyclical because the Light recurs in different rising and falling civilizations; and linear because (like a spiral staircase) it spirals in a linear direction towards one world-wide civilization based on the Light, which all civilizations have in common. My linear-cyclical (i.e. spiralling) Universalist approach can be classified as falling within the philosophy of history.

This can be expressed as a universality: the universality with which past civilizations reveal order, design and pattern through their distinctive religions, and the inadequacy of views which deny pattern and regard history as chaotic.

(3) Evidence that a civilization's life cycle is like a parabola. A civilization is formed when visions of the Light create a religion and grows through its followers, and ceases to grow when the religious vision fades. It is then in decline. All civilizations go through the same stages.

This can be expressed as a universality: the universality with which all past civilizations reveal the pattern of a complex parabola which includes:

(a) the universality of the presence of religions/the Light before the growth of past civilizations;

(b) the universality of the central importance of the presence of the Light in the creation of the religions (through migrations);

(c) the universality of the Light of the religions as the central idea that created, unified and sustained past civilizations, and the inadequacy of alternative central ideas (see pp36-46);

(d) the universality of the central importance of the Light in the continuing growth of past civilizations and its inspiration of their monuments or "stones";

(e) the universality of the breakdown of civilizations when their religion/Light is modified and when their State dominates their religion and weakens their central idea;

(f) the universality of instances of the Light renewing the religion of, and therefore saving, past civilizations, and the universality of periods of renewal when the religion and therefore the civilization is renewed, and the Light is present;

(g) the universality of the link between weakness of the Light and times of decline in past civilizations and the universality of periods of decline when the religion and therefore the civilization is in decline and the Light is weak;

(h) the universality of the absence of the Light in the continuing decay of civilizations, the destruction of the stones;

(i) the universality of the absence of the unifying central idea and of consequent cultural disintegration during the decay of past civilizations;

(j) the universality of the central importance of the absence of the Light in the decay of the religions;

(k) the universality of the absence of religions/the Light at the end of past civilizations;

(1) the universality with which a religion's loss of Light causes the final demise (in the sense of "conveyance or transfer by demising", "transmitting title through death") of its civilization, which is marked by the end of the civilization's religion and the civilization's adoption of another civilization's religion.

(4) Evidence that in consequence, a civilization grows when the vision of the Light is strong and decays when the vision of Light is absent.

This can be expressed as a universality: the consequent universality of the connection between the presence or absence of the vision of God as Light and the growth or decay of civilizations, which should be seen as Light-bearers.

I established (1) and (2) in *The Light of Civilization*. This book establishes (3) and (4). The evidence for (3) will be presented in the rest of *Part One*. The evidence for (4) will arise from this and will be reviewed in *Part Two* (see pp376-443).

CAVEAT

History, like a river, is experienced as a flow, and those living through the dates probably had little idea that they were involved in the transition of one period into another, although they would have been aware of the issues (just as today we have been aware of a change in the (then) Soviet Union under Gorbachev and of the rise of China).

I have always felt that all schemes can always be criticised. The designation of civilizations, which I arrived at in the companion volume *The Light of Civilization*, will be open to debate. Should not the European, Byzantine and Russian – indeed the American – civilizations be regarded as one because they share Christianity? The same applies to dates of stages or phases. The stages, too, are selective.

I am not claiming that there is any numerological or occult significance in the 61 stages I shall identify in each civilization. It is interesting that Taoists saw in the Chinese *I Ching* sixty-four possible permutations of the two opposing forces in the Taoist universe (the force of darkness/inactivity and the force of light/activity) which proceed from the Supreme Ultimate (*T'ai Chi*), and some may consider that my 61 stages, when added to the two forces of darkness and light (the *Yin* and *Yang* – or more strictly, the *Yang* and *Yin* – of growth and decay) and the One Light from which they emerged, may total the number 64: 61+2+1=64. However, it would be possible to diagnose many more stages than my 61 (e.g. the transitional phases between stages, more economic details, more attention to civil wars), and I am aware that I am only offering the main stages, and at that, those that are most relevant to our theme. Some stages occur during the mists of prehistory; although details are lacking there is enough archaeological evidence to confirm that the event in the stage (a migration, for example) took place. Some stages overlap, some run parallel. Tendencies or potentialities that will become later stages are to be found in the time of earlier stages.

The variations in the length of the stages and dates can be attributed to the atrophy or the vitality of the civilizations, but should this date not be slightly earlier, that one slightly later? It is very difficult to be certain about events at the time they happened; and it is only with hindsight that we really see what an administration, regime, or dynasty was like, what the significance of this withdrawal or that conquest was. I have always been the first to point to the danger that we may impose a pattern on history, impose stages and periods that are not really there. I have often argued that different patterns may work equally well, depending on where we take the start of our civilizations to be.

For all these reasons it is wise to be cautious and to look very carefully at philosophies of history that offer a linear-spiralling pattern in place of a chronological flow of events.

TABULATION METHOD

Nevertheless, in spite of this caveat, the prime criterion of the validity of any philosophical scheme is whether it corresponds to reality, and my view of history is based on one fundamental premise: that I can best approach the reality or essence of history by seeing the Light in religions as a force that attracts heterogeneous peoples and as the unifying principle of their civilizations, rather than by merely recording the wars of their kings and the legislation of their parliaments. I have said in the Prologue (pxi) that the historical evidence has to be presented before it can be said that the pattern of each civilization works, that my pattern works; and that the devil is in the detail. As I am reviewing the whole of history, a vast terrain Toynbee could not survey in less than twelve volumes, I have to devise a method which can present the detailed evidence for the patterns of 25 civilizations, and the ensuing whole pattern, in one volume. My method must necessarily be succinct, and some of the detail must be read in conjunction with the Light traditions and subtradition presented in *The Light of Civilization*.

My goal and therefore my priority is to understand the underlying reason for civilizations' growth and decay. Therefore, after much reading, pondering, deliberating, meditating, musing, mulling over, gazing out of the window, and solitary walking in fields, through woods and by the sea, scuffling through autumn leaves and dashed by booming spray, probing and seeing round and through and behind civilizations in the manner of an intelligence chief – in short, after long and profound reflection on forty years' puzzling and searching in the Far East, Middle East and in the West, by the Pacific, Mediterranean and Atlantic, seeking the unifying principle within phenomena – having glimpsed the common pattern behind all our civilizations, I have felt it right to summarize the evidence for each stage of each civilization in a way that can be easily assimilated by the reader, with the maximum clarity, and in a way that can be readily checked by the reader. This involves giving stages and dates.

Summarising each stage of each civilization requires 25 entries for 61 stages, i.e. 1,525 entries. There is no space to say how I arrived at each of the 1,525 entries, to justify each entry in relation to all the possible alternatives (e.g. for the arrest of growth, breakdown etc.) or explain why the many alternatives are less satisfactory than my entry. That exercise (involving the discussion of perhaps ten alternatives for each entry, some 15,250 possible entries in all) belongs to another work. For my present theme and purposes there is only space to present the result of my findings on a take-it-or-leave-it basis, to show the *similarities* of civilizations' progress through comparable stages and to demonstrate how civilizations develop away from – i.e. by secularizing – the Light.

For the checking of the stages and their dates I need to refer the reader to one source rather than to hundreds of books, to an independent and authoritative account which is widely available and unlikely to go out of print, a common currency in our culture which gives full summaries of each of our civilizations, which is full enough to corroborate our entries and which can readily be consulted without cost on both sides of the Atlantic. The *Encyclopaedia Britannica* is such a standard work, combining authoritative, scholarly detail with popular accessibility in public libraries. As my research was done during the reign of the 15th edition, which did not change each year and which is still abundantly available in libraries throughout the world, I give page references in the *Notes and References to Sources* (see pp550–555) for the volumes in the *Encyclopaedia Britannica* where my factual information can be checked. Amplified information for each of my 1,525 entries can be gleaned from the *Encyclopaedia Britannica* (in whatever edition is ready-to-hand); the concept of my 25 civilizations and the Light-based pattern of my 61 stages will of course be lacking, as will the significance I attribute to each stage (e.g. the military blows which caused arrest of growth or breakdown). The facts about the events are in the *Encyclopaedia Britannica*, the interpretation and allocation of significance to them are entirely mine.

As there is a lot for the reader to absorb and retain I have given considerable thought as to how our information should be presented, and I have concluded that it is right to choose the method which makes it the most easy for the reader to assimilate our information at a glance.

I therefore introduce an entirely new view of history – I have said that I think of it as my *prolegomena*, a few notes at the beginning of a vast, hitherto unwritten work that would, if written, run to many thousands of pages – by taking comparative tabulation as my method (i.e. I tabulate the civilizations and the details of each stage so that the reader can compare stages in different civilizations). Through this method the reader can at first reading absorb the main point of each stage, then glance at or skim each table. Later the reader can return to each table and spend time scrutinising the details, which are given with a balanced regard for precision, economy and clarity. At that point I invite the reader to use my tables (in conjunction with the summary chart 3) as a basis for his (or her) own research into or search through civilizations, working *down* for a clear and comprehensive statement of each stage of each civilization, or *across* through the 61 tables for a clear, concise and flinty statement of the 61 successive stages of each civilization, and to check my solution against his (or her) own solution. It could be that the reader can come up with a better or fuller solution for some stages, improve the edges here or there or add important detail, possibly through his (or her) superior knowledge of the detailed history of a particular civilization.

I have endeavoured to keep abreast of current archaeological developments, have made visits to archaeological sites and subscribed to *Current World Archaeology* and other publications. Many of the dates will no doubt have to be revised in the light of forthcoming archaeological discoveries and where appropriate they should be regarded as being approximate. I am confident that some stages of the early civilizations will receive further confirmation as a result of forthcoming archaeological discoveries. But in the final analysis let us remember that quibbling over detail is secondary to the overriding theme, which is the hitherto unacknowledged role of the Light in the history of the last five thousand years.

I will review the universality of the evidence that civilizations have a Light-based life cycle by examining the evidence of each stage in turn, using – to save space and reduce a vast subject to manageable proportions – my method of comparative tabulation of each of the 61 stages and comparing similarities to demonstrate the universality of the pattern.

A rainbow has seven bands (red, orange, yellow, green, blue, indigo and violet). In the same way, the entire rainbow-parabola of each of our 25 civilizations will be seen to have seven bands which are all present simultaneously to some degree (some pronounced and some faded) at each of the 61 stages. The seven bands are:

1. the Light/Central Idea;
2. the alternatives (which are present throughout each civilization's development) to the Light as the Central Idea;
3. the civilization's religion, which degenerates into coteries;
4. the monuments ("the stones") which are inspired by the Light and later destroyed;
5. the heterogeneous peoples who join the civilization and make for cultural unity/the seceders who later cause cultural disintegration;
6. a foreign military threat/foreign cults; and
7. the secularizing State which expands into empire.

These bands run throughout the life of each of our 25 civilizations' parabolic rainbow, and as in a rainbow in the sky, some bands are more visible on the rising side than on the falling side, more visible in growth than in decay, and vice versa.

Bearing all this in mind, I will now review these stages and the evidence for a Light-based Universalist view ("universalist" in the sense that *gnosis* of a universal God perceived or experienced as Light is central to all civilizations, and determines their growth and decay). The concept is such that I am inevitably presenting nothing short of a Grand Unified Theory of world history which integrates religion and the metaphysical vision and reunifies historical knowledge.

2. The Rise-and-Fall Pattern

I have classified civilizations with an eye to their distinctive religions. *The Light of Civilization* has established that the Light is central to religions, which transmit it socially from generation to generation and preserve their civilizations.

The Genesis of Civilizations

Each civilization's Light originated in an earlier civilization and migrated to a new culture, which it conquered and absorbed. It created a new religion through a religious unification and a central idea to which peoples were attracted. This sustained a growing civilization. The Light has preceded the civilization's genesis.

To see this we need to look at the origin of each Light. If I list each civilization in relation to its distinctive god and religion, we can consider where the Light that inspired it originated.

1. The Origin of the Light in an Earlier Civilization

The result is very interesting, for it shows that all the religions of my civilizations have immediately derived from earlier religions and civilizations, and it is fair to assume that there was a carry-over: that if a Light existed, for example, in c.2250 BC in Iran, then when Iranians migrated to India c.1500 BC and created a new religion they took the Light with them, as the texts we have quoted in *The Light of Civilization* bear out. (We saw that Iran and India share the Light, or Fire, of Mitra, Varuna and Indra.) I can tabulate the process as follows:

New civilization	New civilization's new religion in terms of distinctive god/Light	Old civilization in which Light originated before it created the new religion of the new civilization
1. Indo-European Kurgan	Dyaeus Pitar known to Kurgans (i.e.	Central-Asian civilization's Altaic Shamanism from

	& Megalithic in Old Europe	"tumuli- builders") in Central Asia c.4500-3700 BC before they reached the Danube: supplemented by Kurgans who took Shamash from Akkad c.2400-2300 BC (& whose barrow shafts face the rising sun & Sky Father)	c.50,000 BC; known to Neolithic settlers who farmed, domesticated animals, fired pottery & used polished tools from c.10,000 BC & spread from the Near East (e.g. Jericho, which they settled c.8500 BC) to Anatolia, Crete, C. Europe & Britain c.6000-4000 BC, building megaliths as the Cortaillod culture from c.3000 BC
2.	Mesopotamian	Anu/Ogma/Utu	Indo-European Kurgan civilization, from which Sumerians were an offshoot c.3500 BC
3.	Egyptian	Ra & pantheon	Indo-European Kurgan/ Mesopotamian civilizations, from which Egyptians were probably an offshoot c.3400 BC & certainly before c.3100 or 3032/2982 BC (& before the Pyramid- culture began 27th C BC), perhaps via hunters and herders in the eastern desert
4.	Aegean-Greek (including Minoan/ Mycenaean)	"Mistress of animals"/ Zeus	Indo-European Kurgan civilization, from which the Pelasgians were an offshoot c.3500 BC; Achaeans

			probably via Anatolia (from Baltic?) c.2200 BC; & Minoans, who came from Anatolia c.2200 BC
5.	Roman	Jupiter	Indo-European Kurgans who entered Etruria from Anatolia, possibly as far back as the late Bronze Age c.1600-1200 BC – archaeological support for a trading colonization of Latium around Rome in the 12th C BC fits in with the legend of the Trojan Aeneas – & certainly c.800 BC, when they became the Etruscans, before their contact with Greek culture during the colonization of Italy between 800 & 500 BC
6.	Anatolian	"Mistress of animals"/ Storm & Weather god Tarhun or Teshub	Indo-European Kurgan civilization which succeeded Neolithic farmers who were in Anatolia c.6000 BC; from which Hittites (who probably came from Thrace) were an offshoot c.2000 BC
7.	Syrian	El/Dagon/Hadad	Indo-European Kurgan/ Mesopotamian civilizations which c.3000 BC succeeded

			Neolithic farmers who were in Jericho c.8500 BC; from which the Phoenicians derived – they probably originated in the Persian Gulf as Kena'ani (Akkadian Kinahna), and were hence known as Canaanites
8.	Israelite (Judaistic)	El Shaddai	Indo-European Kurgan/ Sumerian Mesopotamian civilizations, from which Hebrews of Ur were an offshoot as a result of the first Amorite expansion c.19th-18th C BC
9.	Celtic	Lug/Du-w	Indo-European Kurgan (Celto-Ligurian)/ Anatolian (Hittite)/Israelite civilizations, which were absorbed by some Celts after the rise of the Urnfield Celts from the Celto-Ligurians c.1200 BC
10.	Iranian	Mithras	Indo-European civilization, from which Iranians were an offshoot probably via Akkad through Elamites c.2250 BC (Akkadians dominated Elam after c.2334 BC)
11.	European	God as Light	Israelite civilization/Jesus

Christ's vision of the Light
before AD 26; Celtic
civilization in Britain;
Roman civilization of 1st C
AD with Christian
community in Rome

12.	North-American	God as Light	European civilization's voyages of discovery after Columbus's second voyage (no settlers having survived from his first voyage), from c.1494 (Spanish/English/ French), culminating in Jamestown settlement of 1607, before the Puritan migration c.1620-1649
13.	Byzantine-Russian (Eastern Orthodox)	God as Light	Roman civilization under Constantine's Christian rule which created the Byzantine civilization
14.	Germanic-Scandinavian	Odin	Indo-European Kurgan civilization, from which Germanic & Scandinavian (i.e. Teutonic) peoples were an offshoot c.2000 BC, the Germanic civilization emerging c.500 BC; Byzantine civilization whence the Light entered the civilization of the Germanic-

Scandinavian Varangian
Vikings in 988

15.	Andean	Sun-gods	Central-Asian civilization's Altaic Shamanism which arrived in Latin America across the Bering Strait c.30,000 BC & was cut off when the ice melted & the sea rose, submerging the land bridge of the Bering Strait/Indo-European Kurgan civilization(?) before c.2600-2100 BC (when the Milesian Tuatha were perhaps expelled from Ireland) before their Pyramid-culture of c.1500-1200 BC
16.	Meso-American	Sun-gods	as Andean
17.	Arab (Islamic)	Allah	Israelite civilization of 8th C BC when the Lost Ten Tribes were dispersed c.721 BC, giving rise to pre-Islamic Arabian monotheism AD c.325& certainly from 5th C AD – Dhu-Samawi (Lord of Heavens) in S. Arabia (cf Celtic Druid Du-w from Samaria) & El or Ilah in N. Arabia (cf later Allah) – long before Mohammed's vision of the

18.	African	African gods	Central-Asian civilization's Altaic Shamanism/Egyptian civilization before c.2000 BC
19.	Indian	Agni/Siva/Brahman	Iranian civilization c.2250 BC/Indo-European Kurgan civilization from which Hindus were an offshoot c.1500 BC
20.	S.-E.-Asian	The Buddha (Mahayana Buddhism)	Indian civilization of 1st C AD
21.	Japanese	Kami/Amaterasu (Shinto)	Indo-European Kurgan & Chinese (Taoist) civilizations before c.250 BC
22.	Oceanian	New Guinea god?/ the Buddha?/Inti?	Central-Asian civilization's Altaic Shamanism c.3000 BC/Indo-European Kurgan civilization through settlers on New Guinea associated with Lapita pottery c.1300-1100 BC/Indian Hindu civilization/South-East Asian civilization's Buddhism c.1st C AD?/ Andean civilization c.300/c.1100?

23.	Chinese	Heaven/*Tao*	Central-Asian/Indo-European civilizations, from which the Chinese were an offshoot before c.2205 BC (from Altaic Central Asia or Eurasia)
24.	Tibetan	Bon/the Buddha	Indian civilization (& to a lesser degree Chinese civilization) before c.200 BC
25.	Central-Asian (including Mongolian)	Shamanism/ Confucianist Taoism/Turkic Allah	Origin before c.50,000 BC unknown, later became Indo-European Kurgan civilization

It is immediately apparent that all the Lights originated in the Indo-European Kurgan civilization, and ultimately in the Central-Asian civilization from which the Indo-European Kurgan civilization descended, from which all civilizations ultimately derived their Light, even those civilizations which look back to the Israelite (Judaistic) civilization (which also had Indo-European origins). In other words, there was a flow of civilization from culture to culture (see chart on pp534-535 *The Light of Civilization*), and it is fair to assume that the Light went with it.

2. THE MIGRATION OF THE LIGHT TO A NEW CULTURE

When one culture migrated to another place and settled it, its religion took on some of the characteristics of the religion of the new place. Where documentary evidence is lacking it is fair to assume that the new religion that grew up (a blend of the culture's old religion and the local religion of the new place) contained the Light that was transmitted from the old culture; and that the Light commanded assent from the local peoples of the new place as a new civilization grew. Such a movement can be seen in Italy where Indo-Europeans brought Dyaeus Pitar who became Jupiter,

Father Ju (compare the Celtic Du-w), Father Jove.

We can see how a Light originating in one civilization migrated to another, if I list the migration which carried an old Light into a new religion in each of our 25 civilizations:

1. Following the Neolithic migrations of megalith-builders from the Near East to C. Europe and Britain (c.6000-4000 BC), the Kurgans migrated from Central Asia to the Danube c.3700 BC; and there was religious unification under Dyaeus Pitar.

2. The Kurgan Anannage(?) migrated from Kharsag (?) – for a full account of the Anannage, see *The Light of Civilization*, 'The Mesopotamian Light' – to Sumeria c.3500 BC and created the Sumerian Light of Anu.

3. Sumerians migrated to Egypt at an early time (c.3400 BC) and influenced the Egyptian religion when Menes or Aha – some books say Menes was the first Pharaoh and Aha the second, some say that Menes's real name was Aha – united the Lower and Upper Kingdoms c.3100 or 3032/2982 BC, building a new capital near Saqqara at the modern Memphis and uniting the earlier Sumerian influence on the Lower Kingdom with the religious tradition of the Upper Kingdom (whereby he became Horus the hawk).

4. Indo-Europeans migrated to Greece c.3500 BC as Pelasgians and c.2200 BC (probably via Anatolia) as Achaeans and created the Light of Dyaeus Pitar as Zeus/Apollo. Anatolians migrated to Crete as Minoans before c.2200 BC and recreated the Minoan Light of the Mistress of animals (a naked goddess with upturned hands), Anat and Athene (or Athena).

5. Indo-Europeans (possibly early Lydians under Tyrsenos, the ancestor of the Tyrrhenians which Herodotus says was the Greek name for the Etruscans) migrated to Italy possibly c.1200 BC and certainly before c.800 BC and created the Light of Dyaeus Pitar as Jupiter, while Greeks migrated to Italy between 800 and 500 BC and created the Light of Zeus Pater (or Father) as Jupiter.

6. The Hittites migrated to Anatolia probably from Thrace (and possibly including displaced Pelasgians) c.2000 BC and in the 19th C BC turned an Assyrian colony into the "kingdom of Hatti" and, absorbing the indigenous "Mistress of animals" (the nude mother goddess who dominated Anatolia from c.6500 to the 19th C BC), created the Light of the Zeus-like Storm and Weather god Tarhun or Teshub.

7. The Phoenicians migrated from the Sumerian region c.3000 BC and created the Light of Anu as El (cf the N. Arabian El).

8. The Hebrews migrated from Mesopotamian Ur to Canaan c.19th-18th century BC and created the Light of El Shaddai, and some (under Joseph when the Egyptian Hyksos ruled Palestine and the Delta c.1674-1570 BC) later migrated to, and from, Egypt, whence they brought the post-Akhenaton, relatively monotheistic Egyptian Light.

9. The Celts migrated from north of the Alps through France, S. Germany and Bohemia to much of Europe, including Britain, c.1200 BC. They seem to have absorbed a migration from Samaria in Israel to Britain after 721 BC during the time of the Hallstatt Celts (7th-6th C BC), which created the Light of Du-w (compare the S. Arabian Dhu-Samawi of the 5th C AD) or Lord Lug, the Celtic god of light. They also seem to have absorbed the Anatolian Tarhun as Taran probably earlier than did their eastern neighbours, the Cimmerians, who overthrew the Phrygian Empire of Midas c.696 BC.

10. The Iranians migrated from Akkad (?) to Iran c.2250 BC and created the Iranian Light of Mithras.

11. The Christians migrated from Palestine to Britain in the 1st C AD and blended with British Druidism and created the Christian Light before they moved to Rome, and the Christian Light developed Celtic and Roman religions simultaneously throughout Europe, which passed into the European civilization of the Germanic tribes.

12. Europeans migrated to America in voyages soon after 1494 – Columbus's second voyage, all Spanish left behind during his first voyage having been wiped out by Indian chiefs – from the early 16th C and culminating in 1607, bringing the Christian Light. European Puritans migrated to America c.1620-1649 and recreated the Protestant European Light as the American Puritan Light.

13. Romans migrated from the Roman West to the Byzantine East after AD c.330 – the "New Rome" was established in 324 on the site of Byzantium and dedicated in 330 – and created the Christian Roman Light as the Byzantine Orthodox Light which emphasised transfiguration.

(Later the Varangian Vikings, followers of Rurik the Viking, migrated to Russia c.860 and recreated the Germanic Light, and the Byzantine Light migrated to join it in 988.)

14. Indo-Europeans migrated to Germany and Scandinavia as Teutons/the Baltic Battle-Axe culture c.2000 BC and later, c.500 BC, and created the Light of Tiwaz or Tiw. Indo-Europeans migrated to Germany and Italy in 102 BC.

15.&16. American Indians from Central Asia developed a culture with mathematics and astronomy, while the Tuatha (?) perhaps migrated to South America with their pyramid-culture c.2600-2100 BC and created the Light of the Sun-gods in both the Andean and Meso-American civilizations.

17. Israelites migrated to Arabia after 721 BC, and influenced the monotheism of the South Arabian Dhu and North Arabian Ilah which were known AD c.325 in Petra, Palmyra, Characene, Mesene and al-Hirah before the Persians attacked the Arabs and which culminated in Mohammed's move into Mecca, when his opponents gave up their local deities for the new Light of Allah.

18. Egyptians and Nubians migrated to the Sahara c.2000-1000 BC and created the Light of the African sun-gods.

19. Indo-Europeans migrated from Iran to India c.1500 BC and created the Hindu Light.

20. Indian traders migrated to South-East Asia from 1st C AD and recreated the Light of Mahayana Buddhism in terms of the new countries (Thailand, Vietnam, Cambodia etc.).

21. Chinese migrated to Japan via Korea c.250 BC and created the Taoist Light as the Light of Shinto.

22. South-East Asians migrated via New Guinea to the Melanesian Solomon Islands (c.1300-1100 BC), New Caledonia, Marianas and Fiji (by 1000 BC), Tonga and Samoa (c.500 BC), and to the Polynesian Marquesas (AD c.500), which seem to have known the Mahayana-Buddhist Light, and thence to Easter Island, Hawaii (c.800) and New Zealand (c.850). Andeans migrated to Oceania c.1100 (if not before), bringing the Light of the Andean sun-god Inti.

23. Indo-Europeans migrated from Central Asia or Eurasia to China in Neolithic times and probably c.2205 BC and certainly before c.1766 BC. The *Shang* dynasty moved to Yin by the Huan river c.14th century BC and developed the ancestor worship of *Ti* which prepared for the Chou religious unification of much of China under *Ti* after c.1122 BC.

24. Indians migrated to Tibet c.200 BC and created the Light of Tibetan

Buddhism in place of Shamanistic Bon.

25. Central Asians received their Light from Altaic Shamanism, which goes back to c.50,000 BC, c.500 BC, and the Mongolians migrated as the *Hsiung-nu* or Huns in the 4th C BC after which there were many Central-Asian nomadic migrations.

3. Migrating Light Conquers and Absorbs New Culture

In each civilization the migrating culture swiftly conquered and absorbed the new culture, as we can see from the following pattern:

	Civilization	Conquerors	Area conquered/ absorbed	Date of conquest/ absorption
1.	Indo-European Kurgan/ Old European	Neolithic megalith-builders from Near East	Anatolia/Crete/ C. Europe/Britain	c.6000-4000 BC
		Kurgans	Danube	c.3700 BC
2.	Mesopotamian	Anannage?	Sumeria	c.3500 BC
3.	Egyptian	Sumerians? of Egypt	Lower Kingdom	c.3400-3100 BC
4.	Aegean-Greek	Achaeans	Mainland Greece	c.2200 BC
5.	Roman	Etruscans	Rome	c.1200/800 BC
6.	Anatolian	Hittites	North Anatolia	c.2000 BC
7.	Syrian	Canaanites/ Phoenicians	Canaan/Syria	c.3000 BC

8.	Israelite	Hebrews under Abraham	Canaan/Palestine	c.19th-18th C BC
9.	Celtic	Urnfield Celts from Germany, S. France & Bohemia	S. Europe	c.1200 BC
10.	Iranian	Indo-Europeans, Akkadians (?), Iranians (dominant after c.1300 BC)	Iran	c.2250-1700 BC
11.	European	Teutonic barbarians	Europe (England, France, Germany, Italy)	1st-5th C AD
12.	North-American	Europeans (Spanish/English/ French/Dutch)	N.-American east coast	c.1494-1650
13.	Byzantine-Russian	West Romans who settled in Byzantium	Anatolia	AD c.330-395
14.	Germanic-Scandinavian	Germanic tribes	Germany, Scandinavia	c.500 BC
15.	Andean	Descendants of Tuatha?	Area of later Chavin culture, Central Andes	c.2600-1200 BC
16.	Meso-American	Descendants of Tuatha?	Area of later Olmec culture, N.E.	c.2600-1150 BC

		Mexico/ Zapotec culture, Monte Alban, S. Mexico	c.1000 BC
17. Arab	Israelites	Arabia	c.721 BC-AD 325
18. African	Egyptians	Nubia (Sudan)	c.2000 BC
19. Indian	Indo-European Iranians	Ganges valley	c.1500 BC
20. S.-E.-Asian	Indian traders	S.-E. Asia	1st-4th C AD
21. Japanese	Yayoi culture	Jomon Japan	c.250 BC
22. Oceanian	Indian-influenced S.-E. Asians	New Caledonia, Fiji, Marianas, Tonga, Easter Island	c.1000 BC- 1st C AD
23. Chinese	Central Asians	Huang Ho China	c.2205-1122 BC
24. Tibetan	Indians	Tibet	c.200 BC
25. Central-Asian	*Hsiung-nu* (Huns)	Mongolia	c.500 BC

In each case, the migrating culture's conquest gave it a secure base in which the Light it had brought with it could begin to operate in the new place.

4. The Light's Creation of a New Religion through Religious Unification

All the migrations swiftly resulted in the creation of a new Light religion through a religious unification in the new place. This would of course have pleased the political leaders of each new civilization, as they would have seen religious influence as aiding their political, centralizing influence. For clarity I can tabulate the process:

Civilization	Migration	Date of migration from old civilization	Religious unification of local peoples in new place, leading to new religion that blended Light with religion of new place in the form of:
1. Indo-European Kurgan/Old European	Kurgans from C. Asia to Danube	c.3700 BC	Magna Mater/ Sky Father
2. Mesopotamian	Anannage (?) from Kharsag to Sumeria	c.3500 BC	Sumerian Anu/Utu
3. Egyptian	Sumerians from Mesopotamia to Egypt (?) (north)/Seth (south)	c.3400 BC	Ra pantheon under Menes'/Aha's religious unification in c.3100 or 3032/2982 BC: religion of Horus
4. Aegean-Greek Minoan	Anatolians	before	Minoan pantheon of

	Mycenaean	from Anatolia to Crete Indo-Europeans to Greece as Pelasgians, Achaeans	c.2200 BC c.3500 BC c.2200 BC	Mistress of animals/ Anat/Athene Zeus pantheon
	Greek	Dorians to Greece	c.1100 BC	Apollo
5.	Roman	Indo-Europeans to Italy Greeks to Italy	c.800 BC c.500 BC	Etruscan Tin/ Jupiter (Dyaeus Pitar) pantheon
6.	Anatolian	Hittites from Thrace (?) to Anatolia	c.2000 BC	Mistress of animals/ Zeus-like Storm & Weather god Tarhun or Teshub (sometimes represented as a sacred bull)
7.	Syrian	Phoenicians from Persian Gulf to Canaan	c.3000 BC	El/Dagon
8.	Israelite	Hebrews from Ur to Canaan From Canaan to Egypt From Egypt to	c.19th- 18th C BC c.17th- 16th C BC c.1230 BC	El Shaddai Yahweh (taken from Midianites by Moses,

		Canaan		who married the daughter of the Midianite priest-leader, & invested Yahweh with Akhenaton's monotheism)

9.	Celtic	Urnfield Celts from France, S. Germany, Bohemia throughout Europe, Anatolian Tarhun-worshippers,	after c.1200 BC	Du-w/Lug
		Israelites from Samaria (?) to Britain during Hallstatt period	after 721 BC & during 7th/6th C BC	
10.	Iranian	Indo-Europeans from Akkad (?) to Iran	c.2250 BC	Iranian pantheon of Mithras from c.1700 BC
11.	European	Hebrews from Palestine to Britain, thence Rome	1st C AD	Roman Catholicism's Christian God as Light (blended with British Druidism) in 5th & 6th C AD
12.	North-American	Protestants, Puritans from Europe to	1607 c.1620- 1649	Protestant Christianity's Christian God as Light (e.g. brought by Pilgrim

	America		Fathers to Plymouth, Massachusetts)
13. Byzantine-Russian	Romans from Roman West to Constantine's Byzantium	AD c.330	Greek Orthodox Christian God as Light, known by the East Roman *oikoumene* (the one universal Christian society of which the Byzantine Emperor was head) from AD c.395
14. Germanic-Scandinavian	Indo-Europeans from C. Asia to Germany & Scandinavia	c.2000 BC/ c.500 BC	Tiwaz/Tiw
15. Andean	Tuatha (?) Ireland to S. America	from c.2600 BC	Andean Sun-god
16. Meso-American	Tuatha (?) Ireland to S. America "	from c.2600 BC "	Meso-American Sun-god

Zapotec jaguar/temple-pyramids |
| 17. Arab (Islamic) | Israelites from Israel to Arabia | c.721 BC | Monotheistic Dhu, El or Ilah as Dhu-Samawi between c.721 BC & AD c.325; expanded from S. Arabia to Central Arabia in the 5th C AD |

18. African	Egyptians & Nubians to Sahara	c.2000 BC	African gods
19. Indian	Indo-Europeans from Iran to India	c.1500 BC	Hindu pantheon of Vedic Brahmanism
20. S.-E.-Asian	Indian traders to S.-E. Asia	1st C AD	The Buddha
21. Japanese	Chinese to Korea whence Chinese influence reached Japan	c.250 BC	Shinto Kami c.250-108 BC
22. Oceanian	S.-E. Asians to Oceania (Andeans to Oceania)	c.1000 BC AD c.1100	The Buddha? between c.1000 BC & 1st C AD Inti?
23. Chinese	Indo-Europeans from C. Asia to China/ *Shang* to *Yin*	c.2205 BC (before *Shang*); 14th C BC	*Ti*
24. Tibetan	Indians to Tibet	c.200 BC	The Buddha
25. C.-Asian (Mongolian)	*Hsiung-nu* or Huns to Mongolia	c.500 BC	Shamanistic Light

This pattern of migrations which carried old Light into new religions began shortly before the beginning of recorded history when the Kurgans surfaced after over 45,000 years of Shamanism c.4500 BC and moved to the Danube c.3700 BC with their Fire-temples and eastward-facing barrow tombs. The pattern may then already have been over 45,000 years old – we have no means of knowing – but ever since then visions of the Light have created each new religion at the start of each new civilization.

5. THE LIGHT/RELIGION PRECEDES THE GENESIS OF A CIVILIZATION

Each religion and Light was in a position to contribute to the creation of its civilization because it was founded before the genesis of its civilization. We can see this at a glance if I list the civilizations and their religions, and the dates when they were founded:

	Civilization	Date civilization was founded	Religion	Date religion was founded
1.	Indo-European Kurgan/Old European	by c.3700 BC	Dyaeus Pitar	Before c.3700 BC, probably c.4500 BC among Indo-Europeans
2.	Mesopotamian	c.3500 BC	Sumerian pantheon	Anu before c.3500 (the pre-Sumerian Anannage were "the people of Anu")
3.	Egyptian	c.3100 or 3032/2982 BC (Menes or Aha)	Ra	Before 3100 or 3032/2982 BC as Ra was then united with Osiris

4.	Aegean-Greek			
	Minoan	c.2200 BC	Anat/Athene	In Anatolia (cf Anat) before c.2200 BC
	Mycenaean	c.2200 BC	Zeus	Before c.2200 BC as Dyaeus
	Greek	c.1100 BC	Zeus	Before c.1100 BC as Zeus
5.	Roman	c.750 BC (Rome founded 8th C BC)	Jupiter	Before c.750 BC Jupiter was introduced by Indo-Europeans (perhaps by Etruscans who came from Asia Minor c.1200 BC or c.800 BC)
6.	Anatolian	c.2000 BC	Storm & weather god (Tarhun in Luwian & Hittite, Taru Teshub in Hattic, in Hurrian)	In Thrace before c.2000 BC
7.	Syrian	c.3000 BC	El/Dagon	Before c.3000 BC
8.	Israelite	19th-18th C BC 13th C BC	El Shaddai Yahweh/ Judaism	Before 19th C BC Yahweh was revealed to Moses but Yahweh was the god of the

			Midianites (Moses' wife Zipporah was a Midianite) & the name was known to Moses' tribe of Levi & probably goes back to before 19th C BC
9. Celtic	c.1200 BC	Lug/Du-w	Lug of Tuatha De Danaan (cf Canaan) before 1200 BC
10. Iranian	c.1300 BC	Mithras	In Akkad before c.2250 BC, & religion of Mithras founded by c.1700 BC, long before the rise of the Medes, the first Iranians to achieve empire, c.850 BC
11. European	5th C AD	God as Light/ Christianity ,,	In Palestine, Britain, Rome from 1st C AD
12. North-American	1607 (Jamestown)/ c.1650 N.-American colonies		In Europe (Spain, Britain & Holland) before 1494 (Columbus's second voyage)
13. Byzantine-Russian	AD c.330/by AD c.395	,,	In Roman Empire before AD 330
14. Germanic-	c.500 BC	Tiwaz/Tiw	Among Celts before

Scandinavian			c.500 BC
15. Andean	c.1200 BC	Sun-god/ Smiling god	In S. America from c.2000 BC
16. Meso- American	c.1150 BC	Sun-god/ Jaguar/ Feathered Serpent	"
17. Arab (Islamic)	AD c.325	Dhu/El/Ilah	Ilah in pre-Islamic Central Arabia before AD c.325, later taken over by Mohammed (610-632) as Allah
18. African	c.2000 BC	African gods	In Egypt before 2000 BC
19. Indian (Hinduism)	c.1500 BC	Agni, Siva	Agni in Iran before 1500 BC, Siva probably in Mohenjo- daro & Harappa before 1500 BC
20. S.-E.-Asian (Mahayana Buddhism)	1st C AD	The Buddha	The Buddha began Buddhism in 6th C BC
21. Japanese Shinto	c.250 BC 4th/7th C AD	"	Taoism in China in 6th C BC
22. Oceanian	c.1st C AD	The Buddha?	Buddhism in S.-E. Asia from before 1st C AD

23. Chinese	by c.1766 BC (*Shang*)	*Ti*	*Ti* was in China before c.2205/c.1766 BC
24. Tibetan	c.200 BC	Bon/Tibetan Buddhism	Bon & Buddhism before c.200 BC
25. C.-Asian (Mongolian)	c.500-220 BC	Shamanism of *Hsiung-nu*	Shamanism before 500 BC

This table shows that religions were in a position to help create new civilizations.

6. THE LIGHT OF THE NEW RELIGION CREATES THE CENTRAL IDEA OF A GROWING CIVILIZATION

Each of my civilizations stands for a Central Idea which early on in its growth it endeavoured to carry out into the world. My view is that the Central Idea of a grow-ing post-migrational civilization has always been expressed through its distinctive god who embodied the vision of the Light and inspired works of architecture and art (the stones) which the heterogeneous peoples admired. The Central Idea thus attracted the heterogeneous peoples, who supported the growing civilization, and it therefore inspired the creation and evolution of a high cultural tradition. The Light of the religions has therefore created the Central Idea of the civilizations that suc-ceeded them.

However, historians have offered alternative theories which bypass the theolog-ical-metaphysical-Providential model. In response to the question, "What created civilizations, gave them their central idea, united the heterogeneous peoples into admiring support and created the conditions for cultural evolution?" historians have given various answers. Some historians have isolated racial dominance. Positivists (like Comte) have asserted that civilization is the result of progress through three phases of cultural evolution: theological, metaphysical and scientific phases, the scientific (or positivist) phase being the goal of the process. Evolutionary anthro-pologists (like Tylor) have held that social man is the result of progress through various evolutionary phases (seven according to Morgan). (Columbus's voyages had put Europe in touch with primitive peoples, and from Hobbes to Rousseau philosophers puzzled over the connection between savagery, barbarism and civilization.) Some historians have regarded cultural evolution as a consequence of economic benefits and benefits of affluence. Social Darwinists have seen the process in terms of Spencer's "survival of the fittest", while the "new evolutionists" (such as White, Sahlins, Steward and Service) have attributed cultural evolution to a mixture of planning, accident and invention. Marxists have seen the Central Idea of civilizations in terms of the class struggle between a patrician capitalists' ruling class and the working class which aim to overthrow it and establish a proletarian culture. Some sociologists have seen natural selection in the animals as being replaced by purposive behaviour in man, which led civilizations to progress through bureaucracy (Weber), specialisation (Tönnies) or the division of labour (Durkheim). Diffusionists (such as Graebner, Schmidt and McNeill) have seen civilization as passing from culture to culture by trade, a view we have already commended. Some historians (like Childe) have linked the birth of civilization to the emergence of urban centres that dominate agricultural villages and have technological and economic control over food-production. Some (like Boas) have rejected all idea of cultural evolution, regarding each culture as unique, and some (notably Spengler and Toynbee) have proposed cyclical "rise and fall" views of civilizations as we have already seen. (Spengler saw civilizations as passing through a life cycle from youth to old age, while Toynbee saw civilizations as growing in response to the challenge of a difficult environment.)

Each of these alternative views may seem impressive, and as they have attracted followers who make claims for their exclusiveness, they all embody widely held beliefs. To preserve a perspective of appropriate complexity, we need to fit them into our pattern before we consider the Light-based Central Idea, and we can do this by summarising them, and codifying them, as 16 different views which each make the exclusive claim that civilizations spontaneously arise and unite their peoples because of:

1. the racial dominance or militaristic power of one people over another people (the military view);

2. their political unification or centralization (the political view);

3. their manipulation of Nature and development of higher living standards and

superior technology (the technological view);

4. their trading links and the guaranteeing of trade routes, which brought valuable goods and wealth (the commercial view);

5. the promise of economic benefits, affluence and funding (the economic view);

6. their mobilization of material resources from their economic base in relation to military commitments, which can lead to "imperial overstretch" (a combination of the military and economic views);

7. their benefits of citizenship and freedom under the law (the legal view);

8. their drive to secularism and scientific materialism (the Humanist and Positivist view);

9. their social organization and evolutionary drive to the social man (the evolutionary anthropological view);

10. their cultural survival of the fittest by analogy with Darwin's biological theory (the "old evolutionary", Darwinian view);

11. their planning, accident and invention (the "new evolutionary" view);

12. their proletarian overthrow of the priestly ruling class (the Marxist view);

13. their purposive rationalization, bureaucratizing, specializing drive to progress through the division of labour (the rationalizing view);

14. their contact with other cultures (the diffusionist view);

15. their creation of cities (the urban view);

16. their life cycle from youth to old age, or from the first challenge of a difficult geographical environment to their final exhaustion (the cyclical view of Spengler and Toynbee).

THE INADEQUACY OF ALTERNATIVES TO THE LIGHT AS CENTRAL IDEA

Let us briefly examine each theory in turn and demonstrate its inadequacy as the exclusive Central Idea that created civilizations while acknowledging its subordinate role in our complex pattern. For although the 16 theories lack credibility as theories in their own right, they all contain points which undoubtedly need to be included in my Universalist view.

1. If racial dominance or militaristic power was the sole central idea that created civilizations and united their heterogeneous peoples, then we must believe that all the peoples were intimidated into joining each new post-migrational civilization: the Danubians and other European peoples into joining the Kurgan civilization; the Mesopotamian peoples into joining the Sumerian civilization; the heterogeneous Egyptian and African peoples into joining the Egyptian civilization; the Aegean and colonial peoples into joining the Greek civilization; the Italian and colonial peoples into joining the Roman civilization; the Anatolian peoples into joining the Anatolian civilization; the Syrian people into joining the Syrian civilization; the Jewish tribes into joining the Israelite (Judaistic) civilization; the Iranian peoples into joining the Iranian civilization; the Germanic tribes into joining European civilization; the North-American peoples into joining the North-American civilization; the Byzantine peoples into joining the Byzantine civilization; the Russian peoples into joining the Russian civilization; the Germanic-Scandinavian peoples into joining the Germanic-Scandinavian civilization; the Andean and Meso-American peoples into joining the Andean and Meso-American civilizations; the Middle Eastern peoples into joining the Arab (Islamic) civilization; the African peoples into joining the African civilization; the Indian peoples into joining the Indian civilization; the South-East-Asian peoples into joining the South-East-Asian civilization; the Japanese peoples into joining the Japanese civilization; the Chinese peoples into joining their new civilization; the Tibetan and Central-Asian peoples into joining their civilizations.

In fact, although there were conquests near the start of civilizations (stage 3, as we have seen), many of these peoples joined willingly – the Jewish tribes were clearly united under El Shaddai/Yahweh and the Islamic peoples under Allah – and the descendants of the Western barbarians who succeeded to the Roman Empire turned Christian because they were converted and not because they feared the Christians. Undoubtedly there is an element of domination in the spread of civilization, but by itself the militaristic explanation is inadequate as it does not account for the benefit that attracted the heterogeneous peoples to the new civilization.

2. If political unification or centralization was the sole central idea that created civilizations and united their peoples, then we must believe that all the civiliza-

tions began with acts of political unification. All civilizations did have political unifications near their beginning (stage 11): for example, the Egyptian civilization which effectively began with Menes'/Aha's union of the Lower and Upper Kingdoms in c.3100 or 3032/2982 BC, and the Arab (Islamic) civilization, which effectively began with Mohammed's political unification in the 7th century AD. (Both these unifications were also religious unifications.)

The trouble is, the Israelite political unification was effected by David by c.950 BC, relatively late in the history of the Israelite civilization, and the European (Christian) political unification was anticipated by Charlemagne in AD 800 and completed with the establishment of the Holy Roman Empire in AD 962, whereas both the Israelite and the European civilizations began long before those dates (in the 19th/18th century BC, and the 5th century AD respectively).

In fact, political unifications and centralizations also happen towards the end of the history of a civilization: both Russia and China were unified and centralized under the Communists in the 20th century, for example. Undoubtedly, there is an element of political unification in the spread of civilization, but by itself the political explanation is inadequate as it is often a feature of a maturing civilization rather than a feature of the beginning of a new civilization.

3.   If the manipulation of Nature and the development of higher living standards and superior technology was the sole central idea that created civilizations and kept the heterogeneous peoples united, then we must believe that all the peoples were impressed into joining each new civilization: the Indo-European peoples were impressed by the Kurgan metallurgy, wheeled chariot and observation of the heavens; the Mesopotamian peoples by the Sumerian hieroglyphics, metallurgy, high buildings and observation of the heavens; the Egyptian peoples by the Egyptian engineering which raised the pyramids and obelisks, stonemasonry and astronomy; the Minoan and Mycenaean Aegean Greeks by the engineering and architecture of the Knossos throne room and the Lion Gate at Mycenae; the Greek, Celtic and Hittite peoples by the prevailing Iron Age weaponry; the Roman peoples by the Roman engineering and technology; the Phoenician peoples by Phoenician ships which traded throughout the Mediterranean; the Jewish tribes by the skills which built the Temple; the Iranian peoples by Iranian technology; the European peoples by European

church-building and architecture; the North-American peoples by the settlers'
technology; the Byzantine and Russian peoples by Orthodox technology and
architecture; the Andean and Meso-American peoples by the technology of the
temple-mounds (and later, the Meso-American peoples by the Mayan calendar
and architecture); the Arab peoples by the Muslim knowledge of mathematics
and architectural skill; the African peoples by their leaders' building skills; and
the Indian and S.-E.-Asian peoples by the prevailing scientific and technological progress; the Japanese peoples by Japanese temple technology; the Oceanian
people by the engineering skill that raised gigantic statues; the Chinese peoples
by Chinese technology; the Tibetan and Central-Asian peoples by the technology in their regions.

In fact, some of the peoples joined their new civilizations without much
hope of greater material standards – the early European and Arab peoples, for
example – and although living standards and technology improved as the civilizations progressed, they were not the initial central idea. As we can see from
our modern Western (European and North-American) civilization, technology is
a side-benefit; the sophisticated computers which can accurately propel a rock-
et to the remoter reaches of our galaxy fill non-Westerners with wonder, but do
not represent the European or North-American civilization's central idea. There
is undoubtedly an element of development and technology in the spread of civilization, but by itself the technological explanation is inadequate as it does not
explain the initial crusading spirit that moved heterogeneous peoples to support
the new civilization. (This is the objection to Comte's Positivism. Comte
believed that a scientific phase is the crowning glory of a civilization which has
already passed through theological and metaphysical phases, but the relative
absence of advanced technology in the early stages of a civilization means that
technology cannot be the central idea that created the civilization and attracted
peoples to it.)
4.   If trading links and the guaranteeing of trade routes was the sole central
idea that created civilizations and kept the heterogeneous peoples united, then
we must believe that all civilizations, and their aspirations, fine art and high
ideals, began and developed for the sole purpose of promoting and maintaining
trade. In that case we must believe that the Kurgan, Mesopotamian, Egyptian,
Aegean-Greek, Roman, Anatolian and Syrian civilizations were solely motivat-

ed by mercantile commercialism, as were the Yahweh-following Israelite, Celtic, Iranian and European civilizations; the North-American, Byzantine and Russian civilizations; the Germanic-Scandinavian, Andean, Meso-American, Allah-following Arab and African civilizations; and the Reality-seeking Indian, S.-E.-Asian, Japanese, Oceanian, Chinese, Tibetan and Central-Asian civilizations.

There is archaeological evidence that all the ancient civilizations traded with each other (that 14th century BC British beads were found in Egypt, for example), and a network of trade routes clearly did criss-cross the ancient world. Trade is undoubtedly present during all stages of a civilization's life, and undoubtedly certain stages of expansion were trade-led, as was the case with the British Mercantile Empire of the 17th century AD and the Assyrian westward expansion of the 9th century BC (tribute lists show that the Assyrians were after iron, copper, silver and gold), although we shall see that these stages of expansion are a substitute for growth which may actually have contributed to their civilizations' decline.

However, the idea that the civilizations rose merely in order to produce goods and indulge in materialistic trade and be capitalist is shallow and unsatisfactory, for man is more than a commercial animal, and it seems that trade may equally as well have been a consequence of the civilizations' existence. Trade is important to the development of a civilization but by itself the commercial explanation is inadequate as it does not account for the central idea of a civilization in all its stages of growth and decay, and does not explain the crusading spirit, aspirations and ideals that inspired the Israelite and Arab civilizations to rise and gather heterogeneous peoples round their stones.

5.   If the promise of economic benefits, affluence and funding was the sole central idea that created the civilizations and attracted the heterogeneous peoples, then we must believe that all the peoples were attracted by money when they joined the new civilization: the Indo-Europeans found it financially rewarding to support the Kurgan civilization; the Mesopotamian peoples to support the Sumerian civilization; the Egyptian peoples to support the Egyptian civilization; the Aegean-Greek and Roman peoples (including the colonies) to support the Aegean-Greek and Roman civilizations; the peoples of Anatolia and Syria,and the Jewish, Celtic and Iranian peoples to support their civilizations;

the Teutonic barbarians to support the European civilization; the North Americans, Byzantines and Russians to support their civilizations; the Germanic-Scandinavian, Andean and Meso-American peoples to support their civilizations; the Arab and African peoples to support their civilization and the Indian, South-East-Asian, Japanese, Oceanian, Chinese, Tibetan and Central-Asian peoples to support their civilizations.

In fact, money played little part in the establishment for example, of the European and Arab civilizations, and although economic strength invariably leads to expansion and the creation of empire, a moment's thought confirms that it was the idea of Christ and God, of Mohammed and Allah, rather than desire for money that created those two civilizations. Undoubtedly there is an element of funding in the spread of civilization, and undoubtedly the promise of affluence attracts outsiders to an economically thriving civilization – we see this process happening today as Third World citizens are attracted to the West (Europe and North America) by the promise of wealth and the material benefits of Western Welfare States – but by itself the economic explanation is inadequate as it does not explain the initial crusading spirit that moved heterogeneous peoples to support each new civilization.

6.   If the mobilization of material resources from their economic base in relation to military commitments was the sole central idea that created civilizations and kept their heterogeneous peoples united, then we must believe that all the peoples joined each new civilization because the material resources in its economic base led it to take on military commitments: in that case, the Indo-European Kurgans had a strong economic base which led them to take on military commitments, as did the Mesopotamians and Egyptians, the Greeks and Romans, the Anatolians and Syrians; the Israelites were motivated by economic militaristic considerations and not by El Shaddai/Yahweh, as were the Celts, the Iranians, the early Europeans and North Americans, the Byzantines and Russians; the Germanic tribes expanded as a result of a strong economic base, as did the Andean and Meso-American civilizations; the Arab civilization expanded as a result of economic militaristic considerations and not as a result of Allah; the African, Indian, S.-E.-Asian and Japanese civilizations were all driven by economic-military considerations, as were the Oceanian, Chinese, Tibetan and Central-Asian civilizations.

Undoubtedly the economic-military explanation is helpful in understanding one or two stages in the life of a civilization – those of counterthrust or expansion into empire, when "imperial overstretch" is undoubtedly a contributing factor in the petering out of such a stage – but by itself the economic-military explanation is inadequate as it does not explain the initial crusading spirit that moved heterogeneous peoples to support the new civilization and develop a sound economic base. The economic-military explanation is, then, helpful regarding expansive phases in specific regions within a civilization (e.g. the "great power" expansion of the Habsburgs 1516-1659, the French in the 18th century, the British in the 19th century and the Americans in the 20th century) but it cannot be applied to the genesis, growth, breakdown, renewal, decline, decay and disintegration of a civilization from start to finish.

7.   If the benefits of citizenship and freedom under the law was the sole central idea that created the civilizations and attracted the heterogeneous peoples, then we must believe that all the peoples were attracted by the legal system of the new civilization. All our civilizations had outstanding legal systems for their time at differing periods in their history. We can immediately think of the codes of Hammurabi in Mesopotamia and of Justinian in the Byzantine civilization, and of the Roman arrangements for citizenship.

Undoubtedly legal benefits did attract as the civilization grew in influence. But in fact these legal benefits were not available at the beginning of the civilizations, and were a feature of their maturity, a consequence of their success; and they therefore do not comprise the central idea that created the civilizations and attracted the heterogeneous peoples to support each new civilization. They were one element in the spread of civilization, not the central idea.

8.   If a drive to secularism (in the sense of "this worldliness" instead of "other worldliness") and scientific materialism was the sole central idea that created the civilizations and kept their heterogeneous peoples united, then we must believe that all the peoples were attracted by the Humanism and science of each civilization.

But Humanism and science did not exist until the mature stage of our civilizations. (It is true that the European civilization was technically secular between the times of Constantine and Charlemagne as the Church was subordinated to the State and the Pope was subject to the Emperor of the East, but the whole tone of the 5th-8th centuries AD was far more religious than our 20th century secularism.) Were the religions strong at the beginning of the civilizations so that they could usher in Humanism and science later on? Did each religion have as its goal its own non-existence in the face of spreading Humanism and science? Are we to believe that the Kurgans propagated a religion of Dyaeus Pitar so that the non-existence of Dyaeus Pitar could follow? Did the Christians propagate a religion of God so that the non-existence of God could follow, and did the first Muslims spread a religion of Allah so that the non-existence of Allah could follow?

Such a view smacks of what Vico warned against, a tendency to impose interpretations from the historian's own time rather than to enter into the attitudes of the past. The same criticism can be made of Comte's siding with civilizations' secular-scientific phase, which can also be regarded as a regression or symptom of decay. Undoubtedly very mature civilizations do go secular, but Humanistic or Positivistic secularism does not explain the initial crusading spirit that moved heterogeneous peoples to support each new civilization, for secularism did not exist on a wide scale at the outset of civilizations.

9.   If social organization and the evolutionary drive to the social man was the central idea that created civilizations and attracted their peoples, then we must believe that the peoples were attracted by a latent society, the refinement and perfection of which was the goal of history. We must believe that the Kurgans, Sumerians, and Egyptians all gave primacy to their concept of society in which the social man was the most important idea.

The concept of the social man was certainly strong in the Greek and Roman societies and in the development of Greek and Roman Classicism, and also in the Christian view of society as it appears in the letters of St Paul. It was thus strong at the outset of the European, North-American, Byzantine and Russian civilizations. Was it equally important to the Hittite, Syrian, Israelite, Celtic, Iranian, Germanic-Scandinavian, Andean, Meso-American and Arab societies, and to the societies of Africa, India, South-East Asia, Japan, Oceania, China, Tibet and Central Asia? Certainly the Chinese social man features strongly in Confucianism.

But once again, the social man is a consequence of a mature civilization. Undoubtedly he is an element in the spread of civilization, but he was not there at the civilization's outset, and he is not the central idea of each growing civilization which was dominated by its religion. He was not the central idea that drew the heterogeneous peoples to support the new civilization.

10.   If the ability to survive culturally ("the survival of the fittest") was the sole central idea that created our civilizations and attracted their peoples, then we must believe that each civilization began as a culture that was in competition to survive. We must believe that Darwinian natural selection and the ability to survive explain the rise of the Kurgan, Mesopotamian, Egyptian, Aegean-Greek, Roman, Israelite (Judaistic), Iranian, European, Arab and our other civilizations.

However, the civilizations survived because they attracted the support of the heterogeneous peoples, and the Darwinian theory does not elaborate on what this support was. Darwinism is an incomplete theory which was devised to explain the animal world and which is ill at ease in the world of men, who, unlike animals, exhibit "telic" purpose. The Darwinian theory may touch on an element in the spread of civilization, but it is not the central idea.

11.   If a mixture of planning, accident and invention was the sole central idea that created civilizations and attracted the heterogeneous peoples, then we must abandon any clear explanation as to how civilizations were created and how they attracted their peoples. In place of such an explanation is a confusion of stimuli, some orderly and some chaotic; and on this view civilizations have advanced in fits and starts, partly creatively and partly at random.

In effect, the mixture or new evolutionary theory declines to explain or look for a pattern, but it is no doubt an element in the spread of civilization. It is certainly not the central idea that accounts for the attraction of heterogeneous peoples to a civilization.

12.   If the proletarian overthrow of a priestly ruling class was the central idea that created civilizations and attracted heterogeneous peoples, then we must believe that all our civilizations were conquered by proletariats.

As there was no working-class revolution in, for example, the Greek or Roman civilizations (although there were secessions of the plebs, and military dictatorships and proletarianization certainly increased with advancing decay) the question is: how loosely do Marxists define "proletariat" in our 25 civilizations? The question then becomes: why, if a civilization's goal and central idea is the triumph of its proletariat, did the priestly ruling class come to be in power in the first place? It would seem that the priestly ruling class has more claim to embody the central idea of the civilization as it was there at the outset.

There is no evidence that proletarian rule is either a goal of history – this would be a matter of faith – or inevitable, and the proletarian phase of the Russian and Chinese civilizations can be regarded as a decay from patrician origins as easily as progress towards a proletarian ideal. Proletarianism is not the central idea that explains the creation of civilizations and the support of their peoples.

13. If purposive rationalization, bureaucratizing, specializing and the division of labour form the sole central idea that created civilizations and attracted their peoples, then we must believe that all our civilizations grew through the enlargement and refinement of their administrative systems (something all civil servants might like us to believe).

We can certainly see evidence of this in China, and probably in the Roman Empire, but increasing bureaucratisation is a symptom of a mature civilization. It is an element in the spread of civilization and not the central idea that created our civilizations and attracted their peoples.

14. If contacts with other cultures was the sole central idea that created civilizations and attracted their peoples, then we must believe that no culture had its own pre-civilizational central idea as it acquired it from another culture in the course of trade links.

As can be seen from the chart on pp534-535 of *The Light of Civilization*, there may be some truth in the diffusionist view, but our account shows that each civilization was capable of originating its own central idea. The diffusionist theory is less complete than our own view, and although it can co-exist alongside our Universalist view, by itself it is inadequate.

15. If the creation of cities was the central idea that created civilizations and attracted their (presumably agricultural) peoples, then we must believe that all our civilizations began with the creation of cities.

This may be true of Mesopotamia, but it is not true of the European (Christian) and Arab (Islamic) civilizations, which inherited cities. The urban view is therefore an incomplete theory which makes a valid point about certain primitive cultures,but which does not include the more sophisticated civilizations. Urbanism is a symptom of a certain type of new civilization; it is not the central idea for all civilizations.

16.   If the cyclical rise and fall view of civilizations is the central idea that has explained the creation of civilizations, whose rise attracted their peoples, and if Spengler and Toynbee's view of the cycles apply, then we must believe that all our civilizations age "like a mallow in the field" (Spengler) or pass from a response to the challenge of adverse geographical or environmental conditions to a state of eventual exhaustion (Toynbee).

In fact, there is no evidence that all civilizations inevitably age and die organically like flowers or people – the two most ancient civilizations, the Indian and Chinese civilizations, should have died long ago according to this view, yet they are still alive – and the particular rise-and-fall cycle championed by Toynbee ultimately fails to convince because, as we have seen on p2, by his own admission Toynbee never located the "positive factor which within the last five thousand years, has shaken Mankind...into the 'differentiation of civilization'" (*Reconsiderations*), i.e. the central idea which creates civilizations. The cyclical views of Spengler and Toynbee offer elements of truth but they do not finally convince because they do not take us within the central idea of each civilization. In other words, in our terms they missed the Light.

I have demonstrated the inadequacy, for varying reasons of incompleteness, of the alternatives to our Light-based Universalist view. In fact, with so many conflicting and flawed theories one could almost be forgiven for asserting with Henri Frankfort (whose Sumerian-Egyptian hypothesis I quoted in *The Light of Civilization*) that the forces behind civilizations and cultures may never be known, and that they lead a man "astray in the direction of quasi-philosophical speculations, or tempt him to give pseudo-scientific answers" (*The Birth of Civilization in the Near East*, 1951).

This would be a mistake, for it is unfair to write off the philosophy of history (the search for pattern in historical events) – and, for that matter, cultural history – as "quasi-philosophical speculations", although Frankfort's feeling regarding patterned views of history is typical of the prevailing empirical rejection of Universalist views. The truth is that although the alternatives are, for one reason and another, less satisfactory than the Universalist view, they do all have a place in, and strengthen, the Universalist view.

How the Light of the Religions Unifies and Sustains each Growing Civilization

Although the alternatives do not convince as sole theories, then, they all offer useful insights and should be woven on to our Central Idea as subordinate ideas. It is the advantage of a Universalist view that many alternatives have a place in the complex whole it expresses. Nothing is simple, and by presenting the Light within the context of the alternatives I will achieve the sense of a complex whole. The image is of a carpet in the centre of which glows the Light, and the main design shows 25 rainbows, each with seven bands; each rainbow has 16 faint, alternative bands stitched round it and each band becomes pronounced at a certain point in the curve. Each alternative is emphasised at a different stage in each civilization's life. But the overall pattern shows that the Light of the religions "created civilizations, gave them their central idea, united the heterogeneous peoples into admiring support, and created the conditions for cultural evolution".

With this view of the Light in mind, I can summarize the emergence of civilizations in relation to the alternatives. A civilization is created round a distinctive god who is associated with an old culture's vision of the Light. The god is carried to a foreign territory and new culture by a migration, and may be guarded by a priestly class or associated with a prophet such as Christ or Mohammed. This vision of the Light is symbolized in the religion of the new place and heterogeneous peoples round the new place are attracted to it.

As the civilization grows the influence of the distinctive god widens and the god affects the everyday life as it is believed to make the crops grow. The influence of the growing civilization spreads among the peoples. There may be racial dominance as the power of the new civilization increases. There is a development in living standards and technological advance, which are consequences of the growing influence. Wealth increases initially through conquest and plunder, which is justified on religious grounds – the wealth is sent back to the Holy City – and later perhaps through commerce or trade, and this in turn attracts foreigners who detect a promise of affluence. There may be funding of sympathetic groups and the founding of colonies.

As the new civilization's hold on its peoples increases, so a legal code is developed, with benefits of citizenship and freedom under the law. As the economic machinery matures, secularism appears (State control of religion), and the religious vision that first attracted diverse peoples becomes less intense although it is still the backbone of the civilization, a permanent reminder of its foundation. A concept of society emerges, and of the social man, and therefore of Classicism. The new civilization is inventive and determined to survive. There may be political unification, and there is certainly increasing centralization. Bureaucracy grows, there is specialization and division of labour. Cities are created and they regulate food-production.

A rise-fall pattern has begun. But all these features of the new civilization take place round the central idea of its religious Light, which penetrates every aspect of the new civilization's life, uniting its art and architecture and all its disciplines. The Light affects the lives of the many peoples in the civilization.

Let us see how this complex Light-centred growth process works out in detail by observing it in each of our civilizations. I record the bare facts; the sourced details (for which we have no space) can be found in *The Light of Civilization* and in reference and history books. All facts can be checked in the *Encyclopaedia Britannica* (see pp550-555).

1. In the Indo-European Kurgan civilization, after the migration of the Kurgans to the Danube c.3700 BC the Light of Dyaeus Pitar, which apparently made the crops grow and therefore commanded assent, was carried about by the wandering Kurgans as they dominated the territories and peoples they settled, and their technological development led to the building of eastward-facing kurgan barrows and to Stonehenge III, which was probably a Fire-temple. There was wealth, judging by finds in graves. A social organization evolved, there was contact with other cultures and city-like settlements were established. But Dyaeus, and the religious rites and ceremonies that were celebrated in Indo-European Fire-temples and which were connected with Dyaeus, remained the Kurgan central idea as the Kurgan religion guaranteed the continuing progress of the Kurgan civilization.

2. In the Mesopotamian civilization, after the migration of the Anannage (?) from Kharsag (?) to Sumeria, the Sumerian pantheon appeared to make the crops grow, and in Sumerian times the Light was celebrated through the Royal Sacred Marriage (see *The Light of Civilization*). The Sumerians dominated the peoples in their new land, commanding assent because their gods apparently

made the crops grow, and they developed relatively high living standards for their time. Their technological advance included metallurgy, the building of the ziggurats and the discovery of writing by scratching cuneiform on clay. There was considerable wealth judging by the gold in the graves of Ur, and there was a relatively advanced social organization in cities with specialised food-production and a legal code, and instruction in mathematics and astronomy. There were contacts with other cultures. But the Light of Utu/Shamash remained the Sumerian-Akkadian central idea as religious rites and ceremonies guaranteed the continuing progress of the Mesopotamian civilization and made daily life go on.

3. In the Egyptian civilization, after the Sumerian migration to Egypt and the political and religious unification under Menes or Aha c.3100 or 3032/2982 BC, Ra apparently made the Nile flood and the crops grow, and the Pharaoh was Ra through the divine Light. Egypt drew together various peoples (proto-Arabs and Africans) and developed buildings suggesting high living standards, including the pyramids, and there was considerable wealth as is evidenced from the magnificence of the temples and the contents of the pre-20th-dynasty tombs. There was an advanced, centralized social organization, and there were inventions. There was a highly efficient administrative bureaucracy, and eventually there was proletarianization. There were contacts with other cultures. But the Light of the *akh* remained the Egyptian central idea as the Egyptian religious rites and ceremonies guaranteed the continuing progress of the Egyptian civilization and made daily life go on.

4. In the Aegean-Greek civilization, after the migrations of the Pelasgians to the Greek mainland c.3500 BC and of the Achaeans c.2200 BC, and of Anatolians to Crete before c.2200 BC, the fundamentally Indo-European Zeus or Apollo apparently made the crops grow, initially through the Light that was received at sacred sites like the Delphic Oracle. As a result first the Mycenaeans and later the Athenians dominated the peoples of Greece (the Ionians, Aeolians and Dorians). They developed relatively high living standards and developed their own writing. The Cretans worked in bronze, but later the Greeks were known for their Iron Age smelting of weapons. There was considerable affluence as is evidenced by the splendour of the public buildings, and there was an elaborate system of citizenship and social organization with a democratic concept of soci-

ety. There was considerable centralization. There was proletarianization: Greece saw demagogues like Cleon. There was administrative bureaucracy and specialized labour in cities. There was trade with other cultures. But the Light of Zeus, to whom smoke sacrifices were made, remained the Greek central idea as religious rites and ceremonies guaranteed the continuing progress of the Greek civilization (with reduced conviction as secularization and Hellenization gathered force).

5. In the Roman civilization, after the migrations of the Indo-Europeans to Italy c.800 BC and of the Greek colonizers between 800 and 500 BC, the Light of Jupiter apparently made the crops grow and commanded the assent of the Roman peoples. As a result the Romans dominated the peoples of Italy, achieved political unification and developed high living standards, a sound economy and good laws. There was affluence, as is evidenced by the public buildings and social organization, and an efficient bureaucracy and division of labour in cities. There was considerable centralization and a huge empire was administered. There was proletarianization. (The plebs seceded in 5th century BC Rome, beginning a process that culminated in the reforms of the Gracchi.) There was trade with other cultures. But the Light of Jupiter to whom sacrifices were made remained the Roman central idea as religious rites and ceremonies guaranteed the continuing progress of the Roman civilization (with reduced conviction as secularization gathered force).

6. In the Anatolian civilization, after the migration probably from Thrace of c.2000 BC the Light of the Hittite Storm and Weather god Tarhun or Teshub appeared to make the crops grow and commanded assent. Tarhun took over from the nude mother goddess/mistress of animals who was dominant from c.6500 to the 19th C BC. The Hittites were able to dominate the Anatolians, Mitannians and Syrians, and their living standards developed. Their great technological advance was their almost exclusive development of iron, which brought in the Iron Age, and of the light war chariot. There was wealth in cities and a social organization with law codes, and an administrative bureaucracy. There was contact with other cultures. But the Indo-European Light of the Hittite god remained the Hittite central idea as religious rites and ceremonies guaranteed the continuing progress of the Anatolian civilization.

7. In the Syrian civilization, after the migration of the Phoenicians probably

from the Persian Gulf region near Sumeria to Canaan c.3000 BC, the Light of El and Dagon apparently made the crops grow and commanded the assent of the Canaanite peoples. As a result the Canaanite Phoenicians dominated Syria and reached a high point at Ugarit, later colonizing the Mediterranean. Their boats reflected advanced technology for the day, and they created cities and traded with other cultures. There was affluence within contemporary terms, and social organization. But the Light of El and Dagon, and later Baal, remained the Syrian central idea as religious rites and ceremonies guaranteed the continuing progress of the Syrian civilization into the time of Jezebel.

8. In the Israelite civilization, after the migrations from Ur to Canaan in the 19th-18th centuries BC and to and from Egypt, ending with Moses' return to the Promised Land c.1270-1230 BC, the Light of El Shaddai/Yahweh, who had covenanted with the Israelites, came down into the tabernacle and affected the destiny of the nation and everyday life, and apparently made the crops grow. It commanded assent from all the Jewish tribes who respected Moses. The Jews developed high living standards and showed advanced architectural skill in building the Temple. There was affluence and social organization, and political unification under Saul and David. There was centralization and there was a strong administrative bureaucracy. There were contacts with other cultures. But the Light of Yahweh remained the Jewish central idea as the Jewish religious rites and ceremonies guaranteed the continuing progresss of the Israelite civilization.

9. In the Celtic civilization, after the migrations from France, Germany and Bohemia to Europe and Britain from c.1200 BC, and from Samaria following the Assyrian conquest of Israel in 721 BC, the Light of Taran or Du-w, which came down into oak-grove Fire-temples, apparently made the crops grow (including the acorns which were made into cakes). The Celts developed their living standards and in Britain there were large Druid universities, suggesting a high level of social organization. But the Light of Taran or Du-w remained the Celtic central idea as the Druid religious rites and ceremonies guaranteed the continuing progress of the Celtic civilization.

10. In the Iranian civilization, after the migration of Indo-Europeans to Iran c.2250 BC the Light of first Mithras and later of Ahura Mazda came down into the Fire-temples and actually made the universe go round and the crops grow.

The Iranians dominated the various Persian peoples, including, later, the Medes, and developed high living standards and sophisticated methods of building. They had social organization in cities, and an administrative bureaucracy. They had contacts with other cultures. But the Light of Mithras remained the Iranian central idea as the religious rites and ceremonies guaranteed the continuing progress of the Iranian civilization.

11. In the European civilization, after the migration in the 1st century AD which blended with Druidism, the Light of God came down and affected everyday life, and through prayer apparently made the crops grow. (Hence our Harvest Thanksgiving Festival.) Christ, the Light of the World, was illumined by the Light and guarded it like the priestly class of other civilizations. The European civilization began as a break-away sect within Judaism and developed a religion whose vision of the Light commanded assent from increasing numbers of peoples (first in Britain, then in Rome, and finally, after it was adopted as the Roman religion by Constantine, in the far-flung corners of the Roman Empire). It was adopted by the Teutonic barbarians who conquered Rome, and living standards rose during the Middle Ages. There was affluence and technological advance, social organization in cities, political unification under Charlemagne, and, as the feudal system broke down, increasing proletarianization. There was considerable centralization and a strong administrative bureaucracy that involved the Papacy and the European states, and there was contact with other cultures. But to this day the Light of God is the central pentecostal Christian idea which religious rites and ceremonies attempt to perpetuate (with increasing difficulty) and which guarantees the continuing progress of European civilization even in this late secular phase.

12. In the North-American civilization, after the migration of the Spanish after 1494, of the early European voyagers which culminated in the founding of Jamestown in 1607 and of the European Puritans c.1620-1649, the Light of God affected everyday life and through prayer apparently made the crops grow and commanded the assent of the North-American peoples. The settlers dominated North America (including Canada) and achieved political unification. Living standards and technology developed, there was increasing affluence and after 1776 human rights were guaranteed by the law. There was social organization and an effective administrative bureaucracy. But throughout, the Light of God

(which had taken on a peculiarly American Puritan individualism and self-sufficiency) was the North-American central idea, and religious rites and ceremonies guaranteed the continuing progress of the young North-American civilization.

13. In the Byzantine-Russian "offshoot" civilization, the Light of God also came down into the care of Christ, the Light of the World, and through prayer made the crops grow. This civilization also developed knowledge and living standards, monastic and social organizations, legal codes and administrative systems. But throughout, the Light of God was the Byzantine/Russian central idea and religious rites and ceremonies guaranteed the continuing progress of this civilization.

14. In the Germanic-Scandinavian civilization, after the migrations of c.2000 BC and c.500 BC the Light of Odin came down into the Fire-temples and affected everyday life. Odin commanded the assent of the Germanic and Scandinavian tribes and peoples, and there was a development in living standards. Boat-building and weaponry improved, and there was affluence to be had from plundering other countries, from which the Vikings in particular collected protection money. There was a social system, but it was not as permanent as in some of the other civilizations. This lack of permanence was reflected in the wooden architecture of the Saxons and Vikings. There were frequent contacts with other cultures, and there were settlements abroad (as at the English Viking Jorvik in modern York). But the Light of Odin remained the Germanic-Scandinavian central idea as the Germanic-Scandinavian religious rites and ceremonies in their wood-and-stone temples guaranteed the continuing progress of the Germanic-Scandinavian civilization.

15&16. In the Andean and Meso-American civilizations, after the migration of c.2600-2100 BC, which probably took place from Ireland, the Light of the Sun-gods affected everyday life and different South-American centres at different times dominated other regional South-American peoples. There was a development in living standards and in the architectural skill that built the stone temple-pyramids. There was affluence when these cities flourished, there was social organization and an administrative capacity that could formulate the Meso-American Mayan calendar. There was contact with other cultures. But the Light of the Sun-gods remained the Andean and Meso-American central idea and the religious rites and ceremonies guaranteed the continuing progress of the New World civilizations.

17. In the Arab civilization, after the migration of Israelites in the 8th century BC which culminated in Duh and Ilah and in Mohammed's political and religious unification under Allah, the Light of Allah was involved in everyday life through Mohammed, and the Muslims of Mecca were able to dominate all the Arab peoples from the Atlantic to Central Asia. Living standards developed, plundering Arabs sent back their booty to the Holy Cities, which grew wealthy, and Muslim scientific, literary, medical, mathematical and astronomical knowledge was renowned in the West, notably translations from Latin which had been lost to the West and which surfaced in Spain. Mosques show the architectural skill of the Muslims, and there was affluence and social organization in cities, and an administrative bureaucracy. There were contacts with other cultures. But the Light of Allah remained the Muslim central idea as the Muslim religious rites and ceremonies guaranteed the continued progress of the Islamic civilization.

18. In the African civilization, after the migration from Egypt to Nubia c.2000 BC the Egyptian Light apparently made the Nile flood and the crops grow and commanded the assent of the African peoples, and the shamanistic African king was the divine Light. Egyptian architecture spread across the Sahara and down the east coast, which was also visited by Phoenician ships from c.820 to 480 BC (when Phoenicia was under Persian influence), and in due course Phoenicia had shaped an indigenous African architecture that was unaffected by contact with the Arabs (the Zimbabwean stone walls, for example). In isolated areas where cultures rose and fell there were small cities, and living standards were relatively high. Social organization, however, remained tribal over most of Africa. But throughout, the shamanistic Light of the African gods was the African central idea, and religious rites and ceremonies guaranteed the continuing progress of the African civilization.

19. In the Indian civilization, after the migration of c.1500 BC the Light of Agni, Siva and Brahman, and later the Enlightenment of the Buddha, provided the way to Reality and commanded the assent of all the various peoples of the Indian subcontinent. In India living standards developed very early on, and sophisticated drainage systems can be seen at Mohenjo-daro and Harappa.

There were advances in building under the Hindus, and affluence. There was social organization in cities, and an administrative bureaucracy. There were contacts with other cultures. But the Light of Reality or Enlightenment remained the Indian central idea as the varying religious rites and ceremonies guaranteed the continued progress of Indian civilization.

20. In the South-East-Asian civilization, after the migration of Indian traders from AD 100 to 400, the Light of Agni, Siva and Brahman, but especially the Mahayana Enlightenment of the Buddha apparently made the crops grow and commanded the assent of the South-East-Asian peoples. Living standards rose, there was some degree of political unification in the South-East-Asian territories. But throughout, the Enlightenment of the Buddha remained the South-East-Asian central idea as the varying religious rites and ceremonies guaranteed the continuing progress of the South-East-Asian civilization.

21. In the Japanese civilization, after the migration from China to Korea after c.250 BC and the resulting Chinese influence, via Korea, on Japan, the Shinto Light (and later, the Enlightenment of the Buddha) apparently made the crops grow – hence the modern Shinto rites involving rice in paddy fields – and commanded the assent of the Japanese peoples. There was dominance and political unification, and relatively high living standards. There was affluence in certain centres. But throughout, the Shinto Light (later reinforced by the Enlightenment of the Buddha) remained the Japanese central idea as the religious rites and ceremonies guaranteed the continuing progress of the Japanese civilization.

22. In the Oceanian civilization, after the migrations from Asia AD c.400-500, and from South America c.1100, the Light of *manas*, which was reinforced by the Enlightenment of the Buddha (?) and later by the Light of the Andean Smiling god ("El Lanzon") or the Andean Sun-god Inti (?) – see *The Light of Civilization*, 'The Oceanian Light' for these possible influences – apparently made the crops grow and commanded the assent of the Oceanian peoples. There was technological development as huge sculptures were erected. Throughout, the Light of *manas* remained the Oceanian central idea as the religious rites and ceremonies guaranteed the continuing progress of the Oceanian civilization.

23. In the Chinese civilization, after the migration from Central Asia (Sinkiang/Xinjiang and Mongolia) before the Hsia dynasty (c.2205 BC if not legendary) the Light of *Ti* and of Heaven (*T'ien*) was involved with the

Emperor, and therefore with the Chinese people. *Ti* apparently made the crops grow – *Ti* was invoked for good harvests – and the Light of *Ti* commanded the assent of the peoples of the autonomous Chinese regions. Living standards developed and discoveries were made. There was political unification and centralization under the Chou dynasty, a strong bureaucracy and social organization which expressed themselves in Confucianism, and there was considerable affluence. But the Light of *Ti* and of Heaven remained the central Chinese idea, resurfacing in the *Tao*, as the Chinese religious rites and ceremonies guaranteed the continued progress of the Chinese civilization, and the mandate of the Emperor, the Son of Heaven.

24. In the Tibetan civilization, after the migration of peoples from Central Asia, the shamanistic Light of Bon (later reinforced by the Enlightenment of the Buddha) apparently made the crops grow and commanded the assent of the Tibetan peoples. There was dominance and technological development as temples and monasteries were built on mountain slopes. There was affluence in the religious centres and a degree of political unification. Throughout, the Light of Bon, reinforced by the Enlightenment of the Buddha, remained the Tibetan central idea as the varying religious rites and ceremonies guaranteed the continuing progress of the Tibetan civilization.

25. In the Central-Asian civilization, after the migration of the *Hsiung-nu* or Huns c.500 BC, the shamanistic Altaic Light, and the Light of Huna, apparently made the crops grow and commanded the assent of the Central-Asian peoples. There was dominance and a degree of political unification; there was some affluence and there were benefits of citizenship as the Mongols plundered and extended their empire. But throughout, the Altaic Light reinforced by Huna remained the Mongolian central idea as the religious rites and ceremonies guaranteed the continuing progress of the Central-Asian civilization.

7. THE LIGHT ATTRACTS, CONVERTS AND UNIFIES PEOPLES ROUND CENTRAL IDEA/STONES

The Light, the Central Idea which creates and sustains each civilization through its distinctive gods and religion, now unites the heterogeneous peoples. In each civilization the peoples are attracted by the Light, are converted to the new religion, and are unified round the Light and its "stones": the various religious sites which embody the Light and on which each civilization's religion is based.

Thus after their migrations the Danubian and other European peoples were attracted to the megalith-based Kurgan religion; the Mesopotamian peoples to the ziggurat-based Sumerian-Akkadian religion; the Egyptian peoples to the pyramid-based Egyptian religion; the Aegean and colonial peoples to the temple-based Minoan-Greek religion; the Italian peoples to the temple-based Roman religion; the peoples of Anatolia to the temple-based Hittite religion; the Syrian peoples to the temple-based Syrian religion; the Jewish tribes to the Temple-based Judaistic religion; the Celtic peoples to the oak-grove Fire-temples of the Druid religion; the Iranian peoples to the Fire-temples of the Zoroastrian religion; the Teutonic barbarian peoples to the church-based Christian religion; the North-American peoples to the church-based Puritan religion; the Byzantine peoples to the Orthodox church-based Byzantine religion; the Russian peoples to the Orthodox church-based Russian religion; the Germanic-Scandinavian peoples to the Fire-temples of the religion of Odin; the Andean and Meso-American peoples to the pyramid-temples of the Andean and Meso-American religions; the Arab peoples to the mosque-based Islamic religion; the African peoples to the stone temples of the African religion; the Indian, South-East-Asian and Japanese peoples to the temple-based Hindu and Buddhist religions; the Oceanian peoples to the statue-based Oceanian religion; the Chinese peoples to the temple-based religion of *Ti* or Heaven; the Tibetan peoples to the temple-based religions of Bon and Tibetan Buddhism; and the Central-Asian peoples to the shamanistic Central-Asian religion.

In each case the Light of each religion dominates each civilization for the rest of its growth, and its centrality is evidenced by the importance given to the religious sites in each civilization: "the stones" which enshrined the central idea of each civilization, the Light.

We can see how the Light of each religion attracts, converts and unifies peoples round the new Central Idea, and thus creates and sustains its civilization, if I list the peoples that have been attracted to each civilization and the Central Idea of the Light that has attracted them:

Civilization	Heterogeneous peoples attracted to the new civilization's religion	Date peoples supported religion (to political unification)	Central Idea of new civilization's new religion that united peoples through distinctive god
1. Indo-European Kurgan/Old European	Europeans, Danubians, British (Also Iranians, Indians, Greeks, Celts, Germanic tribes)	c.3700-2700 BC	Dyaeus Pitar's effect on crops & everyday life through the Light, which was probably received in ceremonies in Fire-temples
2. Mesopotamian	Mesopotamian peoples attracted to Sumerian pantheon, e.g. Ubaidians, Akkadians	c.3500-2350 BC	Anu/Sumerian gods' effect on crops through Royal Sacred Marriage & the Light
3. Egyptian	Egyptian peoples including Africans	c.3100 or 3032/ 2982 (Union of Upper & Lower Kingdoms)- 2686 BC	African Ra's effect on flooding of Nile, growth of crops & everyday life through the Pharaoh (who was divine by 2750 BC) & the Light
4. Aegean-Greek	Indo-European	c.3500 BC	Zeus/Apollo's effect on

		Pelasgians, Kurgan Achaeans attracted to Pelasgian Zeus/ Apollo;	c.2200-1800 BC	everyday life through the Light, which was received in ceremonies in Fire-temples & Oracles
		Cretan colonists & settlers;	from c.2200 BC	
		Mycenaeans who probably invaded from the north;	c.1900 BC	
		Dorians;	c.1200-1100 BC	
		Greeks & Greek colonies;	8th C BC	
5.	Roman	Romans & Italian city-states & Roman colonies	c.800-509 BC	Jupiter's effect on every-day life through the Light, which was received in ceremonies in Fire-temples
6.	Anatolian	Hittites, expelled Anatolians, Phrygians, N. Syrians attracted to Hittite god	c.2000-1700 BC	Effect of Tarhun/ Teshub (Storm & Weather god) on crops & everyday life through the Light
7.	Syrian	Canaanites, Phoenicians, Philistines, Neo-Hittites	c.3000-2000 BC	Effect of El/Dagon/ Hadad/Baal on crops & everyday life through the Light
8.	Israelite (Judaistic)	Twelve Tribes of Canaan	19th C- c.1200 BC	El Shaddai's defence of the Israelites which

			became Yahweh's covenant with & defence of the Israelites through the Light of the tabernacle (after Yahweh ceased to be the god of the Midianites & became the God of the Hebrews, replacing El Shaddai)
9. Celtic	Urnfield & Hallstatt Celts, Britons & Gauls attracted to Celtic religion, Irish peoples, Anatolians	c.1200-450 BC, 8th C BC/3rd C BC 1st-2nd C AD	Du-w's covenant with Celts (e.g. British in Hallstatt period) & effect on crops & every-day life through the Light of Taran/Yesu (later Esus/Jesus)
10. Iranian	Iranian peoples attracted to Mithras (by 850 BC Medes attracted to Zurvan, existed separately from Persians)	c.1700-550 BC	Mithras/Iranian pantheon's effect on crops & everyday life through Fire-temples
11. European	Teutonic barbarians & Northmen: Angles & Saxons (England, Germany), Franks (Germany & France),	5th C-900	Roman Catholic God the Father's effect on & involvement in everyday life through the Light of Christ

	Lombards & Ostrogoths (Italy), Visigoths (Spain, Portugal) Vikings (England, Ireland & Normandy). Also: Magyars (Hungary)		
12. North-American	North-American & Canadian peoples	1607/c.1620-1787	Puritan God the Father's effect on & involvement in everyday life through the Light of Christ
13. Byzantine-	Anatolian, Greek, Macedonian, Serbian, Bulgarian, Syrian, Palestinian, & Egyptian peoples	c.395-540	Greek Orthodox God the Father's effect on & involvement in everyday life through the Light of Christ
Russian	Russian peoples of Finnic & Slavic tribes, Varangians/ Vikings, peoples of Kievian Rus, Mongol Tatars	from 988	Russian-Greek Orthodox God the Father's effect on & involvement in everyday life through the Light of Christ
14. Germanic- Scandinavian	Germanic tribes, Angles, Saxons, Jutes, Frisians, Danes, Norwegians,	c.500-150 BC	Wodan/Odin's effect on crops & everyday life through the Light

Swedes

15.	Andean	Peoples of Andes	c.2600-1000 BC	Sun-god's effect on crops & everyday life through the Light
16.	Meso-American	Peoples of Mexico, Mayan, Aztec & other South-American peoples	c.2600-1100 BC, AD c.600, c.950	"
17.	Arab	Arabian peoples	c.721 BC-622	The effect of the Light of monotheistic Dhu/ El/Ilah & later Allah on crops &involvement in everyday life (later through Mohammed)
18.	African	African peoples of Sudan & later of Ghana, Nigeria & Zimbabwe	c.2000-750 BC	The effect on crops & everyday life of the shamanistic post-Egyptian Light of the African gods
19.	Indian	Peoples of Indian subcontinent	c.1500-325 BC	Attainment of Reality through the Light of Agni, Siva
20.	S.-E.-Asian (Mahayana Buddhist)	Peoples of S.-E. Asia from: Burma (Mons, Pyu) – Theravada; Thailand –	1st C AD-400 3rd-9th C 9th C	Attainment of Reality through the Enlightenment of the Buddha

	Mahayana (also China, Korea, Japan, Tibet); Vietnam (Cham) – Hindu	2nd C	
	W. Java & Borneo – Hindu	5th C	
	Cambodia (Khmers, Chenla) – Saivism;	6th-9th C	

21.	Japanese			
	Shinto	Japanese peoples	c.250 BC-AD 420	Kami's effect on crops & everyday life through the Light
	Buddhism	"	7th C	Attainment of Reality through the Enlightenment of the Buddha

22.	Oceanian	Polynesian & Melanesian peoples	c.1000 BC-500	Attainment of Reality through the Enlightenment of the Buddha?/Light of the Sun-god (Andean?)

23.	Chinese	Peoples of autonomous regions of China	c.2205-221 BC	The Light of *Ti*/Heaven's effect on crops & involvement in every-day life through the Emperor

24.	Tibetan	Tibetan peoples	c.200 BC-AD 608	Attainment of Reality through the Enlightenment of the

			Buddha
25. Central-Asian	Central-Asian & Mongolian peoples	c.500-220 BC	The Light's effect on crops & involvement in everyday life through shamans (& later, the Buddha)

The attraction of the peoples to a Central Idea of the Light gives a more complete explanation for the creation and survival of a civilization than any of the alternative views, which make a subordinate contribution without being exclusive.

THE GROWTH AND ARRESTED GROWTH OF CIVILIZATIONS

During a civilization's growth, the Light is strong and expresses itself in enduring monuments. Its supporters achieve a political and religious unification. Doctrinal controversies lead to schism; and a foreign threat delivers a military blow that arrests growth for some 50 years, during which the civilization becomes secularized. The civilization achieves a counter-thrust through territorial expansion, and is celebrated in epic poetry.

8. THE LIGHT IS STRONG DURING THE GROWTH OF CIVILIZATIONS

I would expect the Light to be strong during the growth of a civilization, and I can confirm this pattern if I return to our revised list of civilizations and relate the growth of our 25 civilizations to our dating of the Light in each. We have seen that the growth of a civilization is a complex process involving many "alternatives" to our central Light-based idea but for the sake of convenience we can now ignore the alternatives.

Although information is obviously scanty about some of the earlier civilizations, I can again give an approximate date when each civilization started, state its metaphysical vision in terms of its religion, and list when the vision of the Light was known to be strong according to our findings in *The Light of Civilization*. Our view of the growths of our 21 distinctive and four related civilizations will then look like this:

Civilization	Date civilization is known to have started	Metaphysical vision vision of God as Light in terms of religion of:	Vision of Light known to be strong:
1. Indo-European Kurgan & Megalithic in Old Europe	before c.3700 BC	Altaic Shamanism Dyaeus Pitar/ Magna Mater (Sky Father/ Earth Mother)	c.3700-750 BC
2. Mesopotamian	c.3500 BC	Utu/Shamash/ Ogma Tammuz/Marduk/ Anu Inanna/Ishtar	c.3500-11th C BC
3. Egyptian	c.3100 (or 3032/2982) BC	Ra/Amon/Aton/ Horus/Osiris/ Apis	c.3100 (or 3032/ 2982) BC -11th C BC
4. Aegean-Greek Minoan/	c.2200 BC	Mistress of animals/ Anat/Athene/	c.2200-1500 BC
Mycenaean &	c.1800.BC	Zeus/Apollo	
Greek	c.1100 BC	Zeus/Apollo	c.1100-5th C BC
5. Roman	c.750 BC	Jupiter/Apollo	c.800-50 BC

			Gnostic God as Light	1st-3rd C AD
6.	Anatolian			
	Hittite	c.2000 BC	Storm & Weather god Tarhun or Teshub/ Sharruma/Arinnitti	c.2000-1500 BC
	Phrygian		Cybele/Attis	c.2000-700 BC
7.	Syrian	c.3000 BC	El/Dagon/Hadad	c.3000-1000 BC
			Baal/Astarte/ Adonis	c.2000-700 BC
8.	Israelite	19th-18th C BC	El Shaddai Yahweh	c.1800-600 BC
9.	Celtic	c.1200 BC	Lug/	c.1200 BC-2nd C AD
			Du-w	8th-7th C BC
			Beli/(cf Baal)/Taran/ (or Taranis)/ Yesu or Esus	3rd-1st C BC
		1st-2nd C AD	Jesus/God as Light	5th-7th C AD
10.	Iranian	c.1300 BC		c.2250-4th C BC
			Mithras	c.2250-1500 BC
			Zurvan	c.750-550 BC
			Ahura Mazda	7th-4th C BC
			Anahita	c.250 BC-AD 226
			Mani	3rd-8th C AD
11.	European	5th-6th C	Catholic God as Light	5th-17th C

12.	North-American	c.1650	Puritan God as Light	c.1620-present
13.	Byzantine- Russian	c.395	Orthodox God as Light	c.395-1000
		c.1000	Orthodox God as Light	c.1000-19th C
14.	Germanic- Scandinavian	c.500 BC	Wodan/Odin	c.500 BC-5th C AD 7th C AD (known 1st-2nd C/7th C AD)
15.	Andean	c.1200 BC	Sun-gods	c.1200 BC-AD 1300
16.	Meso-American	c.1150 BC		c.1150 BC-AD 1200
			Quetzlcoatl/	c.600-800 (Mayan)
			Kukulcan (or Kukulan)/ Kinich Ahau (or Itzamna)	c.950-15th C
			Huitzilopochtli Aztec)	(pre-Aztec/
	American	c.800	Sun-god	c.800-1500
17.	Arab	AD c.325	Allah	5th-17th C
18.	African	c.2000 BC	African gods	c.2000 BC- 16th C AD

19. Indian	c.1500 BC (Hindu)		c.1500 BC-20th C AD
		Agni/	c.1500-1200 BC
		Brahman/ Atman	c.6th C BC
		Siva-Sakti	2nd C BC-16th C AD
		Vishnu/Rama/ Krishna	9th C-16th C
		19th-20th C	
Buddhism		The Buddha	from 6th C BC
Jainism		Jinas e.g. Mahavira	from 6th C BC
Sikhism		Om Kar	from 16th C
20. S.-E.-Asian (Mahayana Buddhist)	1st C AD	The Buddha	1st-16th C
21. Japanese	c.250 BC		
Shinto		Kami/ Amaterasu	4th-19th C
Buddhism		The Buddha	6th-19th C
22. Oceanian	1st C AD?	The Buddha?/ Smiling god?/ Sun-god (Andean?)	c.380-1680
23. Chinese	c.1766 BC (*Shang*)		c.2000-3rd C BC/2nd-4th & 9th C AD:
		Shang Ti	from c.1766 BC
		T'ien Ti	from c.1122 BC
		The *Tao*	6th-3rd C BC/ 2nd-4th & 9th C/17th C

| 24. | Tibetan | c.200 BC | Shamans | from c.200 BC |
| | | | The Buddha | 8th-18th C AD |

25.	Central-Asian	c.500 BC	Shamans	from c.500 BC
			The Buddha	13th-14th C,
				1690s

It is immediately apparent from the above pattern that the Light was strong during the growth of each of my 25 civilizations. In view of my detailed analysis of each civilization's Light, and in view of the evidence for my Universalist view to date, it is reasonable to conclude that just as each civilization was created by the Light of its religion, so there *is* a connection between the growth of a civilization and the continuing appearance of the vision of the Light in its religion. This raises a question of cause and effect (which we will leave to one side for now) as to whether a civilization grows because of the energy created by visions of the Light which pass by migration from an old culture into its religion, and then continue to appear; or whether the visions of the Light continue to appear in its religion after the migration as a result of the inner *élan* that is felt when a civilization is growing.

9. THE LIGHT INSPIRES ERECTION OF STONES DURING GROWTH

As the civilization grows round the central idea of the Light, the peoples are moved to erect buildings – "stones" – which celebrate the Light.

In all churches and cathedrals, for example, the stone spire, like the Egyptian obelisk and *Axis Mundi*, represents the vertical descent of the Light intersecting the horizontal everyday world of the congregation in the nave, and its vertical ascent back up to the sun which symbolizes the Light of Heaven. This process is symbolized by the vertical-horizontal cross. The stained glass, pictures with haloes, the eternal lamp before the sacrament, the monstrance and candles further represent the Light.

In all mosques, the stone minaret – the Arabic root *nar* means "fire" – like an obelisk and *Axis Mundi* represents the descent of the Light. The stucco inside, transforming stone into light as "Allah is the Light of the heavens and the earth". The Light then ascends back up the minaret to the sun, which symbolizes the Light of Heaven. The Islamic crescent represents the Light of Allah breaking through the inner dark like a crescent moon.

All Hindu temples are stone pyramid-mountains down which a descending shaft of Light widens. It enters the soul of those who worship images of Siva or Visnu inside. The Light ascends back up the pyramid-mountain to the sun, which symbolizes the Light of Reality.

All Buddhist temples have a pinnacle which is often golden, a world axis or obelisk joining earth and Heaven, down which the Light descends into a hall where there is either an image of a meditating Buddha, very often with an aura of flames, whose enlightenment is to be imitated; or a *stupa* which contains relics of the historical Gautama the Buddha. A statue of the Buddha symbolizes the attainment of the Light.

Taoist temples symbolize the Light when the priest lights an incense burner to symbolize the Light in his own body, which he mirrors to the community.

Let us now relate my 25 growing civilizations to the stones that have been inspired by the vision of the Light. I have referred to most of them in the course of *The Light of Civilization*, and I can now extract and list the main stones of each civilization and give them a date. We can then compare the dates of the stones of each civilization, which began to be erected around the time of this ninth stage, with the dates when the vision of the Light was known to be strong in each civilization (see foregoing table). We can then confirm the link between the Light and the stones. My view of the stones in relation to their civilizations looks like this:

Light of Civilization	Stones inspired by Light	Date of stones
1. Indo-European Kurgan & Megalithic in Old Europe	Temples to bull-god in Anatolia	c.6700-5650 BC
	Caucasian burial mounds with eastward looking shafts	c.4500 BC-3500 BC
	Fire-temples to Dyaeus Pitar, Sky Father, & to Earth Mother	c.4000-1750 BC
	Wessex farmers (Anannage/Tuatha?):	c.3500-3000 BC

		Stonehenge I	c.3000 BC
		Proto-Indo-European Funnel-Neck Beaker folk/Milesians: Stonehenge II, Newgrange, Silbury Hill, Avebury, Glastonbury Tor, Wandlebury, Long Man of Wilmington	c.2600-2100 BC
		Battle-Axe: Stonehenge III, Cerne Abbas Ogma/Herakles	c.2000-1500 BC
2.	Mesopotamian	Ziggurats, e.g. Etemenanki (Hanging Gardens of Babylon)	c.2600-2200 BC
		Temples or shrines to:	
		Anu	from c.3500 BC
		Ogma	c.3500-1500 BC
		Utu	c.3000-2400 BC
		Shamash	from c.2400 BC
		Tammuz	from c.2600 BC
		Marduk	18th-11th C BC
3.	Egyptian	Pyramids including Great Pyramid	27th-18th C BC
		Sphinx	26th C BC
		Temples to Ra/Amon/Aton/Horus/ Osiris	from c.3100 (or 3032/2982) BC
		Temples to Sun-bull (Apis who was begotten by a ray of Heavenly Light)	from c.3100 (or 3032/2982) BC
		Temple of Ptah at Karnak	c.1450 BC
		Paintings in tombs of Valley of Kings	16th-11th C BC
		Obelisks e.g. Cleopatra's Needle	26th-15th C BC
		Glastonbury Chalice Well (?)	c.1991-1786 BC
		Temple of Isis, On	from 7th C BC

4.	Aegean-Greek		
	Minoan	Minoan Fire-temples & open-air sanctuaries to Zeus Minotaur/Apollo/ Anat/Athene	c.2200-1400 BC from c.1600
	Mycenaean	Greek temple at Eleusis, temples to Dionysus/Orpheus	from c.1800 BC
	Greek	Delphic Oracle	14th C BC-4th C AD
		Parthenon	5th C BC

5.	Roman	Roman Temples of Jupiter & Apollo	from c.500 BC
		Roman Fire-temples of Vesta	from c.500 BC
		Roman Temples of Astarte, Cybele & Mithras	3rd C BC-2nd C AD
		Roman Temples of Isis	1st C BC-3rd C AD
		Roman Temples of Sol Invictus	3rd C AD
		Temple of Serapis at Alexandria	3rd C BC-AD 391
		"Churches" to the Gnostic God as Light	1st-2nd/7th-8th C

6.	Anatolian		
	Hittite	Temples to Storm & Weather god, temples to Tarhun or Teshub/ Sharma/Arinna	c.2000-1225 BC
	Phrygian	Temples to Attis/Cybele	c.1000-c.700 BC

7.	Syrian		
	Canaanite- Phoenician	Temples to El/Dagon/ Hadad at Ugarit	c.2000-1100 BC
		Temples to Baal/Astarte	c.1200 BC-700 BC
		Temples to Adonis	from c.2000 BC

8.	Israelite	Stone of Israel (Stone of Scone)	c.1800 BC?
		Temple of Solomon	c.950-586 BC
		Second Temple & Wailing Wall	c.516 BC-AD 70
		Qumran jars	2nd C BC-AD 68

		Synagogues	from AD 70
		(Kabbalistic schools	from 11th C)
9.	Celtic	Fire-temples to Lug/Du-w	9th C BC-2nd C AD
		Fire-temples to Belenus (or Beli, cf Baal)/Taran/Yesu	3rd C BC-2nd C AD
		Late Stonehenge trilithons	9thC BC-2nd C AD
10.	Iranian	Persian Mithraeums	from c.1700 BC
		Zoroastrian Fire-temples to Ahura Mazda, e.g. Takt-i-Taqdis at Shiz & Naqsh-i-Rustam near Persepolis	7th C BC-4th C AD
		Manichaean churches	3rd-8th C AD
11.	European	First churches to God as Light, e.g. Glastonbury, Rome	1st-2nd C/ from 5th C
		European churches & cathedrals to God as Light (for symbolism, see p69), e.g. Canterbury, Chartres, Notre-Dame	from 1st C/ from 5th C
		European monasteries & abbeys	from 529
		Sistine Chapel & St Peter's, Rome	15th C-16th C
		St Paul's Cathedral, London	17 C
		Irish churches, cathedrals & monasteries to God as Light e.g. Clonmacnoise & Clonard	5th-9th C
		Iona	from 563
12.	North-American	Cathedrals & churches in America	17th C-present
13.	Byzantine-	Eastern Orthodox cathedrals & churches to God as Light, e.g. Hagia Sophia	6th-12th C
		Icons & murals on church walls	
	Russian	Russian Orthodox cathedrals & churches	c.1000-19th C

to God as Light, e.g. Cathedral of St Sophia, Kiev,		12th C
Cathedral of the Archangel, Moscow		16th C
Icons & murals on church walls		

14.	Germanic/	Fire-temples & shrines to Wodan/Odin,	? 1st-5th C
	Scandinavian	e.g. Temple at Uppsala	5th C
		Stone of Harald Bluetooth at Jelling	c.960

15.	Andean	Temple-pyramids to Sun-gods	from c.2500 BC/from c.900 BC
		Temples to Inti and predecessor, e.g. Temple-Pyramid of Cuicuilco, Mexico	c.200 BC-AD 600
		Huaca del Sol, Peru	c.200 BC-AD 600
		Gateway of the Sun, Tiahuanaco, Bolivia	c.500-1000
		Temple-pyramids of Chan Chan, Peru	c.1200-1400
		Temple of the Sun, Cuzco, Peru	c.1200-1500

16.	Meso-American	Temple-pyramids to Sun-gods	from c.2500 BC/ from c.900 BC
		Mayan: Temples to Quetzlcoatl/ Kukulcan/Kinich Ahau (or Itzamna), e.g.:	
		Temple-pyramids at Tikal, Guatemala	c.300 BC-AD 900
		Temple of the Sun, Palenque, Mexico	c.600-900
		Pre-Aztec & Aztec: Temples to Huitzilopochtli, e.g. Temple of the Sun, Teotihuacan, Mexico	1st C-c.650/c.950-15th C
	American	Mississippian: Temple-pyramids, e.g. Monk's Mound, near Cahokia, Illinois	c.800-1500

17.	Arab	The Black Stone at Ka'bah, Mecca	5th C

	Mosques to Allah in every Muslim territory (for symbolism , see pp69/70)	from c.630-17th C
18. African	Stone temples	c.1000 BC-16th C
	Stone walls at Great Zimbabwe, Rhodesia	11th-15th C
19. Indian	Temples to early Siva (? horned cross-legged figure) at Mohenjo-daro & Harappa	c.2500-1500 BC
	Hindu temples to:	c.1500-1200 BC
	Agni	
	Brahman (e.g. at Elura)	after c.600 BC
	Atman	
	Tantric Hindu temples to Siva-Sakti in India, Nepal, Bhutan, Tibet	5th-11th C
	Temples to Visnu-Lakshmi/Rama/Krishna, e.g. temple at Khajuraho &	10th-11th C
	Temple of the Sun at Konarak	13th C
	Hindu World Mountain at Angkor Wat, Cambodia (for symbolism , see p70)	9th-13th C
	Buddhist temples (halls, *caityas*), e.g. at Sanchi & Ajanta (for symbolism , see p70)	3rd C, 1st C BC
	Buddhist *stupas* & pagodas (architectural diagrams of the cosmos, World Mountains with several storeys), e.g. the	
	Buddhist *stupa* at Sanchi (adorned with	3rd C BC
	lantern) & pagoda at Peshawar	1st C AD
	Tantric Buddhism	2nd-4th C
	Jain temples & stone conquerors, e.g. stone replica of Gommatesvara at Mount Abu, Sravana Belgola, Southern India	

	Islamic mosques	12th-18th C	
	Sikh temples, e.g. Golden Temple, Amritsar	1604/19th C	

20.	S.-E.-Asian Mahayana Buddhist/ Theravada Buddhist	Buddhist temples in Korea, Java, Sumatra, Sri Lanka, Vietnam, Cambodia & Thailand, e.g. Temple of the Emerald Buddha, Bangkok	1st C – 9th C/ from 10th C 19th C
		Mahayana- & Theravada-Buddhist temples & monasteries in S.-E. Asia	6th-11th C

21.	Japanese	Buddhist temples including Zen temples, e.g. the Ryoanji stone garden (how existence looks to the enlightened gaze)	7th-19th C
		Statues of enlightened Buddhas, e.g. at Nara Shinto temples & shrines to Kami/Amaterasu, & *torii*	1st-9th C AD/752 from 4th C

22.	Oceanian	Temples to Polynesian/Melanesian god (the Buddha?/Smiling God?)	c.300-17th C
		Statues of enlightened men, e.g. the Easter Island giants	c.1100-1680

23.	Chinese	Temples to *T'ien* (Heaven) where the Supreme Ruler (*Shang Ti*) sent down the Light of *Tao*, e.g. the Temple of Heaven, Peking	from 18th C BC- 17th C AD 15th-16th C
		Confucian temples in China, Korea & Japan, e.g. the Confucian temple in Peking	from 2nd C BC
		Monasteries to *T'ien*/the *Tao*, e.g. T'ai-ch'ing-kung monastery, Shenyang	
		Stone (jade) representations of the *Tao*	

24.	Tibetan	Buddhist & Tantric Tibetan-Buddhist temples & monasteries in Lhasa/Tibet	7th-18th C
25.	Central-Asian	Buddhist & Tibetan-Buddhist temples in Mongolia & Central Asia	3rd C BC-14th C AD

By comparing the dates of the stones with the dates when the vision of the Light was known to be strong we can see that in each civilization the stones were erected, as we would expect, during times when the Light was known to be strong and the civilization in question was growing. The stones have acted as hearthstones for past Fires (i.e. Lights), some of which have gone out and some of which are still burning.

10. DOCTRINAL CONTROVERSY SURROUNDING LIGHT

The Light is now interpreted in conflicting ways and a doctrinal controversy energises the growing civilization's religion. This questioning of the established religion is expressed by one god's challenge to an existing god. Some of the peoples side with the existing god (the status quo) while others side with the rising god, who takes on a new importance. The effect is not to loosen the unification of the civilization round the Central Idea of the Light but rather to develop the Central Idea, as the god of the Light develops a less primitive and more sophisticated identity and the religion therefore evolves. It is the difference between the Canaanite El Shaddai and the Mosaic Yahweh, or between the Etruscan Tin and the Roman Jupiter. We can see the pattern in our 25 civilizations:

Civilization	Existing god	Rising god who assumes new importance	Date
1. Indo-European Kurgan/ Old European	Neolithic Earth Mother	Neolithic Moon-goddess	c.3000 BC

2.	Mesopotamian	Anu of Sumerians	Utu	c.2750 BC
3.	Egyptian	Horus (falcon) in Northern Kingdom (Union of Northern & Southern kingdoms in c.3100 (or 3032/2982) BC led to Peribsen calling himself a Seth-king & not a Horus-king)	Seth in Southern Kingdom of Naqadah	c.2800 BC
4.	Aegean-Greek	Mistress of animals from Anatolia, naked with up-turned arms (cf Anat in Ugarit)/Mother goddess/Potnia/ Demeter (Eleusis)/ Athene & Shield Goddess (Mycenae)	Zeus (at Cretan Ida & at Mycenae)	c.1800 BC
5.	Roman	Tin or Tinia of Etruscans	Jupiter	c.550 BC
6.	Anatolian	"Mistress of animals", a nude mother goddess with bearded consort & child who dominated Anatolia from c.6500-19th C BC & was identified with the	Tarhun (Hittite) or Taru (Hattic) or Teshub (Hurrian), identified with & perhaps even represented by a sacred bull (cf Etruscan Tarquin)	c.1750 BC

		lion, whom the Hittites absorbed (cf the Lion Gate at Hattusas c.1370-1290 BC, & the earlier Lion Gate at Mycenae)		
7.	Syrian	El (the Bull)	Dagon (Ugaritic "grain")	after c.2500 BC
8.	Israelite	El Shaddai of patriarchs (see *Exodus* 6.3, "God Almighty" being "El Shaddai")	Canaanite epithets El/El Elyon/El Olam/ El Bethel/El Ro'i (after entry into Canaan)	from c.1275 BC
9.	Celtic	Lug ("Light" or "Shining One", of the Tuatha De Danann)	Teutates king	c.5th C BC?
10.	Iranian	Mithras	Zurvan of Medes	c.720 BC
11.	European	Christ with image (Western Christ)	Christ without image of Iconoclastic controversy (Eastern Orthodox Christ over whom Pope claimed control)	c.727
12.	North-American	Puritan God/Christ known through mysticism of	Protestant revivalist (Calvinist, Congregationalist,	c.1725-1750

	intellect and forms	Presbyterian & Baptist) God/Christ known through emotions & heart as in the Great Awakening & later modified by reason in Deism inspired by the Enlightenment	
13. Byzantine-Russian	West Roman fully divine Christ with two natures of St Athanasius (Dyophysitism/ Nestorianism/ Chalcedonian view of Nicene creed)	East Roman Christ with one nature, inferior to God the Father, of Arius; preached by Byzantine missionaries (Arianism/Mono-physitism)	c.400-451
14. Germanic-Scandinavian	Tiwaz or Tiw (or Tyr or the Saxon Saxnot?) (cf Dyaeus/Zeus/Du-w)	Wodan (Germanic) or Woden (English)	c. 200 BC
15. Andean	Feline god	Jaguar	c.1100 BC
16. Meso-American	Feline god	Jaguar	c.1150 BC
17. Arab	Pre-Islamic Dhu/ El or Ilah	Allah of Mohammed	c.610-632
18. African	Shamanistic Light	Egyptian Light (in Nubia or Sudan)	c.1000 BC

19.	Indian	Hindu Vedic Brahman Reality	Buddhist Enlighten-ment (began c.525 BC)	4th C BC
20.	S.-E.-Asian	Theravada-Buddhist Enlightenment	Mahayana-Buddhist Enlightenment	3rd C AD
21.	Japanese	Shinto Chinese	Confucianist Taoism	c.400
22.	Oceanian	Religion of *mana*	Sun-god (Andean?)	c.380
23.	Chinese	Reality of *Ti* in Heaven (later taken up by Confucius & still vital in 31 BC when supporters of *Ti* restored sacrifices to Heaven & Earth at Ch'ang-an city)	Lao-Tze's Reality of the *Tao* (from which religious Taoism spread throughout China)	6th-5th C BC
24.	Tibetan	Reality of Shamanistic Bon introduced from China & Central Asia several generations prior to AD c.630)	Chinese Buddhist Enlightenment (first	6th C
25.	Central-Asian	Reality of Shamanism	Confucianist-Taoist Reality from China	3rd C BC

We can see that in each civilization the rising god is a more advanced version of the existing god, who is identified with the civilization's Central Idea of the Light. The Central Idea and thus the civilization are therefore carried forward.

11. POLITICAL UNIFICATION

The growing civilization's religious unification in terms of its Light and its religious development in terms of its rising god are now formalised into a political unification, which is on a scale that awakens within the civilization a Universalist awareness of all known mankind, as we see from the following pattern:

Civilization	Date of political unification	Details of political unification
1. Indo-European Kurgan/ Old European	c.2700 BC	Implied through spate of simultaneous advanced megaliths in Switzerland, N. France (e.g. Carnac), Britain (e.g. Stonehenge, Glastonbury Tor) & Iberia, built by Wessex farmers & contemporaries with Sumerian help or Sumerian knowledge (Communal megalithic tombs were made from huge stone blocks packed round with small stones & held in place by mounds, & their laborious construction suggests a social effort akin to church-building, a new belief-system regarding the Sky Father & sunrise, which the barrow shafts faced, & a profound awareness of religious emotion)
2. Mesopotamian	2350 BC	Sumerian city-states unified under Akkad, where Sargon ruled from Agade; the Gutians overran Akkad c.2200 but were expelled by the Sumerians of Erech c.2100, after

which the third dynasty at Ur re-
established Sargon's state

3.	Egyptian	c.2686 BC	Unification of the Old Kingdom after Menes' union (c.3100 or 3032/2982 BC) of Upper& Lower Egypt which founded the Egyptian civilization & created a kingdom (with capital at Memphis) 750 years before the Sumerian city-states became united, & which, in view of Egypt's geographical isolation, lasted 1,000 years without external threats or colonial wars
4.	Aegean-Greek	c.1800 BC	Cretan unification:Minoan-type cities with palaces on mainland (Mycenae, Tiryns, Pylos) which recall Hittite palaces
5.	Roman	c.509 BC (traditional) c.475 BC (archaeo- logical)	After the expulsion of Etruscan kings & the establishment of the Republic, the Latin League unified the Italians around Rome
6.	Anatolian	c.1700 BC	Old Hittite Kingdom or Empire with capital at Hattusas
7.	Syrian	from c.2000 BC	Amorites from Arabia occupied Babylonia, Syria & Palestine, where they were known as East Canaanites; they set up a network of small kingdoms which had Mycenaean -type cities & palaces

8.	Israelite	c.1250 BC	Moses' tribal Covenant league after the Exodus (probably c.1270-1230 BC), which settled in Gilead (east of the Jordan) & in central Palestine, the Promised Land, & then competed with the Canaanites & Philistines under the judges (e.g. Barak who defeated the Canaanite confederacy at Esdraelon & Gideon, who defeated the nomadic Midianites)
9.	Celtic	c.450 BC	Celtic princes of La Tène Culture from Oder to Rhône (whose network imported Etruscan wares by 6th century) settled in Italy, Greece, Spain, W. France (including Brittany) & E. Europe
10.	Iranian	c.550 BC	After the Empire of the Medes, which was checked by the Lydians 590-585 BC after it had obliterated Assyria, the Persian Empire of Cyrus stretched from India to Macedonia & Libya, & included Lydia & Mesopotamia
11.	European	c.800	Charlemagne, king of Franks, united the French, Germans & Italians; Alfred united Kingdom of Wessex
12.	North-American	c.1787	Creation of United States' federal Constitution for east coast states (the original 13 colonies becoming states) following Declaration of

Independence from Britain in 1776; this led to the creation of the United States following wars with Britain (1812-14), the ratification of the Canadian boundary (1818-1846) & the addition of many states especially after the Mexican war of 1848-1850 until the Civil War of 1861-5 checked American expansion for a while

| 13. | Byzantine-Russian | c.540 | Justinian's expansion which left an empire stretching from France to Persia, & including Italy, the Balkans, Greece, Anatolia, Palestine, Egypt & N. Africa |

| 14. | Germanic-Scandinavian | c.150 BC | Germanic tribes migrated from S. Sweden & N. Germany to the south Baltic (Vandals, Gepidae & Goths) & to W. Germany & the Danube, confining the Celtic Helvetii to Switzerland; the Belgae (a mixture of Germans & Celts) crossed the Rhine c.200 BC & from 115 BC the Cimbri & Teutones (Celtic tribes from Jutland & Frisia in Germany – the Romans did not distinguish the Germans and Celts until Caesar's time) pressed back the Celts, invaded Gaul & attacked the Romans |

| 15. | Andean | c.1000 BC | At Chavin |

16. Meso- American	c.1100 BC c.1000 BC	Olmec culture Zapotec culture
17. Arab	c.622	Mohammed's founding of the *ummah*, the Muslim community, which was the basis for his political unification of Arabia; this led to the Caliphate's conquest of Syria, Persia, Mesopotamia & Egypt (632-661), & to the Ummayad conquest of Byzantine Africa (696), Spain where Berbers created al-Andalus (711), Armenia, Iberia & Lazica (717) & of the Khazars' Khanate (737), which unified the Arabs from Spain to Iran in an empire ruled from Damascus
18. African	c.750 BC	Kush/Meroe (in Nubia or Sudan) invaded Egypt c.730 BC & brought Egypt under its control between 716 and 656 BC, & influenced the interior, unifying what was then known of Africa in a culture that would last 1,000 years
19. Indian	c.325 BC	Mauryan Empire (Asoka's Empire covered all modern India, Pakistan & Bangladesh, except for S. India)
20. S.-E.-Asian	c.300-400	Kingdoms of the Mon people (then the dominant Austro-Asiatic race in S.-E. Asia) in Burma, Thailand & Cambodia/Hindu kingdoms in W.

Funan had links with India & China from c.250, & dominated the Malay-Mekong shipping lanes until c.800

21.	Japanese	c.420	Unification of the Yamato court (which advanced into Korea until 663) through the *tenno* (Emperor of Heaven); the Yamato court expanded to control virtually the whole of Japan from Kyushu to the north & traded with T'ang China, whose culture it borrowed (Nara eventually imitating the Chinese capital of Ch'ang-an & Buddhism becoming the State religion)
22.	Oceanian	c.400-500	Unification on Marquesas/Easter Island while settlers left for Hawaii & New Zealand
23.	Chinese	c.221 BC	Ch'in's domination & unification of China, with borders wider than any previously known, under the first Ch'in Emperor, Shih Huang Ti, today known as Shihuangdi (who burned religious books, executed 400 Confucians & was buried with a pottery army), after the *Hsiung-nu* formed a tribal confederation & attacked China, causing the completion of the Great Wall

24. Tibetan	c.608	Slon-brtsan-sgam-po's unification of Ch'iang tribes on the Chinese border & creation of a centralized kingdom – in 763 Tibet took tribute from China & captured Ch'ang-an, its capital, & also invaded N. India – which disintegrated into chieftans' territories after c.842 & by c.889, after which Tibet was disunited until the 14th C (despite the revival in W. Tibet of the 10th-11th C)
25. Central-Asian	c.220 BC	*Hsiung-nu* formed a tribal confederation in Mongolia under a *shan-yu* ("Son of Heaven"), hence Great Wall of China built to resist their threat

The political unification of course makes use of the rising god of the doctrinal controversy, to whom the peoples are attracted and by whom they remain unified. Thus after c.3100 (or 3032/2982) BC Ra takes over from Horus in the Egyptian civilization and becomes the national god; and the political unification is strengthened by this religious development.

12. SCHISM

The growing civilization's religion now undergoes a schism, which first weakens and then develops the Central Idea. It is vital to grasp the ambivalence. The schism first blurs the existing god but then renews the Central Idea in terms of a new god. For a while there is a confused lull as the schism anticipates an arrest in the civilization's growth, but then it carries forward the Central Idea with new energy. During the confusion there is allegiance to conflicting gods, creeds or beliefs, as we see from the following pattern:

Civilization	Supporters of existing god	Supporters of new god	Date
1. Indo-European Kurgan/ Old European	Neolithic matriarchal Earth Mother/Moon-goddess	Indo-European patriarchal Sky Father,e.g. Sumerian Anu of Tuatha	c.2650 BC
2. Mesopotamian	Utu	Shamash	c.2300 BC
3. Egyptian	Horus/Seth	Ra (god of 5th dynasty)	c.2400 BC
4. Aegean-Greek	Zeus	Poseidon (Mycenaean Poseidaon), especially at Pylos; god of maritime Cretans	c.1750 BC
5. Roman	Jupiter	Hellenising Juno (alias Moneta or "Warner", a Hera-like figure who pro-tected the Roman State)	c.430 BC
6. Anatolian	Tarhun	Istanu (Hittite)/ Ertan (Hattic)/ Tiwat (Luwian)/ Shimegi (Hurrian)/ the male sun-god represented in the	c.1600 BC

robes of the king,
whose title was
"My Sun"

7.	Syrian	Dagon	Baal or Hadad (chief god of Ugarit, the "cloud-rider" who influenced Yahweh)	c.1600 BC
8.	Israelite	Canaanite El/El Elyon/El Olam/ El Bethel/El Ro'i	YHWH or Yahweh (taken from the Midianites) (Yahweh was the god of the Midianites; Jethro, their priest & leader, had a daughter, Zipporah, who was married to Moses, & Yahweh was later revealed to Moses as the God of the Hebrews; the Midianites became camel-riding raiders during the 12th-11th C BC & were defeated by Gideon)	after c.1230 BC
9.	Celtic	Teutates	Belenus or Beli ("Bright One", god of the May 1st fire-festival Beltane or	c.400 BC

"Bright Fire")

10.	Iranian	Zurvan of Medes	Anahita & Mithra of Persians (gods not accepted by Zoroaster but worshipped in West Persia)	c.500 BC
11.	European	Western Roman Christ of pro-West Roman Iconophiles (who believed with Heraclians like Justinian III & with the Council of Trullo, 691-692, that Christ's incarnating nature should be shown in symbolic images or icons, including coins)	Eastern Orthodox Christ whose divine incarnating nature should not be shown in symbolic images or icons (Iconoclasm of 730-787, 815-843), over whom the Pope claimed control despite the rejection of the Pope's supremacy; Photian Schism of 867 in which Photius was deposed as patriarch & then reinstated	867 (formalised in 1054)
12.	North-American	Puritan God/Christ brought in by first European immigrants	American (as opposed to German & English) Protestant revivalist (Calvinist, Congregationalist,	c.1860

	Presbyterian & Baptist) new radical Evangelical God/Christ, & church of Protestant individualism & evangelical salvation of souls that opposed slavery in the lead-up to the Civil War		
13. Byzantine-Russian	Christ with one nature: Monophysitism & Monotheletism (i.e. union of God-Man in Christ's will, which was one divine-human energy), Heraclius' compromise between Christ with one nature/Christ with two natures, designed to win back Syrians, Armenians & Egyptians after Persian conquest	Christ with two natures, one divine, one human, which should not be shown in symbolic images or icons, e.g. coins (pre-Iconoclastic Christ)	c.638
14. Germanic-Scandinavian	Wodan/Woden/Wotan	Odin	c.75 BC
15. Andean	Jaguar	Smiling god	between c.900 &

c.600 BC

16. Meso-American	Jaguar	Feathered Serpent	between c.900 BC (when stone statues were destroyed) & c.600 BC
17. Arab	Allah/Mohammed of Sunni Ummayad Caliphate (which ruled from Baghdad)	Allah/Mohammed of Ali's Shi'ite Caliphate (eventually the Buyid Shi'ites who captured Baghdad in 945 & controlled the Abbasid Caliphate, & Fatimid Shi'ites who captured N. Africa & ruled from Cairo from 969)	from 661
18. African	Egyptian Light	African Light which eventually focused round the Bantu god Mwari	after 656 BC
	(In 656 BC the 25th dynasty of Egypt retired to Meroe before the Assyrians & began a Nubian culture that emphasised "God's Wife of Amon" & lasted 1,000 years)		
19. Indian	Mahayana-Buddhist/ Jain Enlightenment	Hindu Saivism	1st C AD

20.	S.-E.-Asian	Mahayana Buddha/ Brahmanistic Reality	Tantric/Saivist/ Vaisnavist Reality	c.500
21.	Japanese	Chinese Confucianist Taoism/Shinto	Buddhism (Heian Tendai & Shingon Great Sun Buddha)	after c.550
22.	Oceanian	Sun-god (Andean?)	Mahayana Buddha? (from S.-E. Asia)	after c.600?
23.	Chinese	Taoist Reality (affected by the suppression of religious Taoism in AD 184)/Tibetan Buddhist-Enlighten- ment	Indian Buddhist Enlightenment	before c.300
24.	Tibetan	Chinese Buddhism	Indian Tantric Buddhist Enlightenment (e.g. Padmasambhava)	8th C
		(In 763 Buddhist teachers were invited to Tibet from China & India, & c.800 the ensuing doctrinal dispute was decided in favour of India)		
25.	Central-Asian	Chinese Confucianist- Taoist Reality	Buddhist Enlightenment, which spread along the Silk Route through Central Asia	c.100 BC

The schism releases energy and appears to be a manifestation of progress like the doctrinal controversy but in fact, with hindsight, it can be seen to move the Central Idea further away from the god with which it began the new civilization. On balance, therefore, the schism promotes the cessation of a civilization's growth.

13. FOREIGN THREAT DEALS A MILITARY BLOW

An occupying or confining military threat now deals the growing civilization a dramatic military blow, soon after (sometimes within 100 years of) the political unification, as we see from the following pattern:

	Civilization	Foreign threat	Military blow	Date
1.	Indo-European Kurgan/ Old European	Funnel-Neck Beaker Folk	Occupation of N. Europe & Britain by Indo-European Funnel-Neck Beaker Folk	c.2600 BC
2.	Mesopotamian	Elamites	Elamites' conquest of the third dynasty at Ur (Ur III) ended the Sargonid unification, after pressure from Amorites & Gutians	c.2004 BC
3.	Egyptian	First Hyksos (?), influential infiltrators across border from Canaan who settled in the Delta; also Bedouins & Nubians	Indo-European use of Hittite-style light war chariot causing collapse of Old Kingdom	c.2160 BC

4.	Aegean-Greek	Luwian-speaking Anatolians	Luwian-speaking Anatolians con-quered Minoan Crete (which was ahead of mainland Greece at this time)	c.1700 BC
5.	Roman	Celts (i.e. La Tène Gauls)	Celts (i.e. La Tène Gauls)besieged the Etruscan town Veii, which had hegemony over Rome c.399-396 BC, obliterated Etruscan colonies in Po valley & captured Rome c.390 (see Livy book V for the shock Rome felt)	c.390 BC
6.	Anatolian	Hurrians, Mitanni, Egypt	Hittite abandonment of North Syria after Hurrian conquest of Cilicia, during reign of Telepinus, the last king of the Old Kingdom	c.1520 BC
7.	Syrian	Mitanni	Mitannian conquest of Syria from capital of Wassukkanni (pro-bably the modern Tell al-Hawa in N. Iraq); the Mitannians arrived from Central	c.1520 BC

or Western Asia
c.1600 BC

| 8. | Israelite | Sea Peoples, mainly the Philistines (formerly Minoan Sea Peoples, now Palestinians) | The Sea Peoples destroyed many sites in the Egyptian-ruled Levant, e.g. Enkomi, Ugarit, Alalakh, Carchemish, Hamah, Tell Abu Hawam, & Ashkelon, & the Philistines (who wore helmets with a circlet of feathers or reeds which seem to have represented the Light as Fire, like the Red Indian's head-dress) set up a federation of 5 city-states (Gaza, Ashkelon, Ashdod, Gath & Ekron); in the course of their military invasion of Palestine they delivered a military blow against the new Israelites | c.1190 BC |
| 9. | Celtic | Romans | Celts driven back | c.387 BC |

from Rome to
Alpine foothills

10. Iranian	Macedonians	Alexander the Great's Greek Macedonians conquered the Achaemenian Empire & burned the palaces at Persepolis in 330 BC	c.330 BC
11. European	Vikings/Spanish Muslims/Magyars	Invasions of N., S. & E. Europe: Viking invasions of England & France (Normandy was ceded by the French King in 911); Spanish Muslim invasions of Burgundy (c.898), Corsica & Sardinia; Magyar invasion of Hungary & Empire of Great Moravia (after being driven out of Russia by the Patzinaks in 893)	c.900
12. North-American	Confederacy	Invasions of expansionist Washington-based North by	c.1861

"foreign" government
of the Confederacy
under Lee in 1861 &
1862 led to 360,000
Unionist-Federalist
deaths; (the
Confederacy
President,
Jefferson Davis,
sought foreign aid
& intervention &
was regarded by the
North as a foreign
threat)

| 13. | Byzantine-Russian | Persians, Avars & Arabs | Persians, Slavs and Avars, then Arabs took much of Justinian's Empire; Persians took Syria, Palestine & Egypt (616) but surrendered them in 629; Arabs seized the recovered territories 636-642, adding Tripolitania in N. Africa, causing the Byzantine Empire to shrink | c.626 |
| 14. | Germanic-Scandinavian | Romans | Caesar's military campaign against the Germans in 55 BC, during which | c.55 BC |

		he massacred two German tribes (the Usipetes & Tencteri)	
15. Andean	Invaders	Invaders ended Chavin culture, leaving Paracas culture to continue	c.400 BC
16. Meso-American	Invaders	Invaders ended Olmec La Venta culture	c.400 BC
17. Arab	Byzantines	Byzantines under Leo III won a major victory over the expanding Arabs at Acroinon, shortly after the Franks under Charles Martel halted the expanding Arabs at Poitiers in 732; the Arabs became less active	740
18. African	Aksum or Axum (Ethiopia)	Aksumites under King Ezana defeated Meroe; in the 8th & 7th C BC Minaeans & Sabaeans from Saba (the Biblical Sheba) in S. Arabia had migrated to	AD c.320

Ethiopia, bringing
the Israelite Yahweh
& making possible
the rise of Aksum,
which became
Christian soon
after AD c.340

19. Indian	Sakas or Scythians/ C.-Asian Yueh-chih	Sakas swept through India, Yueh-chih conquered N. India which was ruled by Kaniska (dated to AD 78 or 248)	AD c.70/ c.240	
20. S.-E.-Asian	Nanchao	Nanchao, a union of 6 Tai kingdoms (now in S. China), invaded the Indianised Buddhist Burmese Pyu kingdom c.800 & Annam (N. Vietnam) in 850	c.800	
21. Japanese	Chinese & Koreans	Chinese & Korean (T'ang & Silla) armies defeated Japan at Pak River; the Japanese Empress Saimei personally directed the battle from N. Kyushu, & so the defeat was felt as a great blow	663	

22. Oceanian	Settlers from S.-E. Asia (Hotu Matua?) who crossed the Pacific & may have reached Peru	S.-E.-Asian invaders probably caused the expansion from the Marquesas NW, SW & SE c 800; legendary invader arrived at Easter Island & Polynesian Maoris arrived in New Zealand	c.800
23. Chinese	*Hsiung-nu* (or Huns)	Sinicised *Hsiung-nu* broke through the Great Wall & conquered N. China with nomadic hordes from AD c.304 & established 16 barbarian kingdoms	AD c.304
24. Tibetan	Mongols	Mongolia forced Tibet to become a vassal to Genghis Khan	c.1207
25. Central-Asian	China	Chinese attacks split the *Hsiung-nu* Empire (or con-federation) in half c.51 BC; these eastern & southern horde Mongolian tribes submitted to	c.51 BC

the Chinese & were
later settled in
China & the western
& some of the
northern tribes mi-
grated westward
(probably to
appear as Attila's
Huns in the
5th C AD)

The blow comes as a shock to each growing civilization and has consequences.

14. ARREST IN GROWTH OF SECULARIZED CIVILIZATION

The blow is a reverse which leads to an arrest in the growth of the civilization. Defence becomes paramount, and the State widens its powers and escapes from the control of its religion, and even assumes control over the religion, and therefore of the Light. As a result the civilization undergoes secularization during a period of decline, as we can see from the following pattern:

	Civilization	Details of State's control over religion/the Light	Date of arrest of growth
1.	Indo-European Kurgan/ Old European	As the round-headed & stocky Funnel-Neck Beaker Folk arrived (traditionally from Iberia but equally possibly from the Rhine-Elbe region of Germany) with their metallurgy, the indigenous builders of Stonehenge I would have been awe-inspired by their bronze-making & the local shamanistic priests would have	c.2600-2550 BC

welcomed them as chiefs of their
communal society; as rulers, the Beaker
invaders would have controlled the local
religion, their interest in which is confirmed by their addition of the bluestones
to Stonehenge I

2.	Mesopotamian	After the fall of Ur III there was political fragmentation & small States escaped the control of the old Sumerian-Akkadian religion	c.2004-1950 BC
3.	Egyptian	In the First Intermediate period, centralized government & the State religion of Ra broke down; except for Akhtoy (c.2160), local rulers' states escaped from the control of religion during this disturbed period	c.2160-2110 BC
4.	Aegean-Greek	Following the invasion of the Luwian-speaking Anatolians(?), the palaces at Knossos & Mallia were damaged & the State took control of Minoan religion; hence the flowering of a secular Minoan art from c.1600 BC	c.1700-1650 BC
5.	Roman	Roman religion was Hellenised after the Celts' siege of Veii c.399 BC & after the Celtic capture of Rome c.390 BC, & the State then controlled religion	c.390-341 BC
6.	Anatolian	Following the Mitannians' Hurrian invasion of the Hittite civilization, & their alliance with Egypt, the Hittite	c.1520-1471 BC (until treaty between Hittite

State, which was embodied by the king who was not divine, escaped the control of its religion & indeed controlled the religion when Suppiluliumas defeated the Mitannians c.1370 BC & put his son, Telepinus "the Priest" (a different Telepinus from the Old Kingdom King) in charge of Syria

king – Zidantas or Huzziyas – & Egyptian pharoah Thutmose III during inter-regnum between Old and New Kingdoms)

7.	Syrian	Following Mycenaean influence, the Ugarit kings' "State" seems to have escaped the control of its religion as did the Mycenaean kings, leading to the golden age of Ugaritic art; there was Egyptian dominance from 1471 to 1450 BC	c.1520-1471 BC
8.	Israelite	Following the Sea Peoples'/Philistines' invasion c.1190 BC, the Philistines, who had iron weapons, ruled as a military aristocracy over the Canaanite people from 5 cities (but not over the Cannaanite people under Phoenician rule), & checked Israelite growth in Palestine; as a result the Israelites demanded a secular earthly king who would conquer the Philistines, in place of the kingship of God, & the State escaped the control of the Israelites' religion	c.1190-1140 BC
9.	Celtic	After the Celts plundered Rome in 387 & after their defeat at the hands of the Romans, the Celts withdrew probably into Central Europe & the Celtic princes	c.387-337 BC

regrouped in a period when competing tribes were giving way to States led by kings; flat (i.e. unmounded) military cemeteries containing men buried with weapons now appeared, replacing the Hallstatt chamber graves & suggesting that local militarised states controlled the religion

10. Iranian	As a result of the Macedonian invasion, the ranian State was completely Hellenised under the Seleucids & escaped the control of the Iranian religion which was totally submerged under Greek religion; the Greek Seleucids resisted Anahita as Seleucus I hoped to Hellenise Asia, regarding Greeks & Macedonians as a superior race	c.330-280 BC
11. European	Following the intensification of Viking, Spanish Muslim & Magyar raids which put Europe under non-Christian pressure & arrested its growth – when the Vikings occupied England & Normandy, the Muslims occupied Burgundy & took Corsica & Sardinia, & the Magyars occupied Hungary & the Empire of Great Moravia – the German State annexed N. Italy (951-961) & in 962 became a 1806 & in which the Pope was nominated by the Holy Roman Emperor, thus secularizing the religion	c.900-951
12. North-	Following the invasions of the secessionist	c.1861-1913

American	Confederacy in 1861-2, the Federalist North under Lincoln defeated the South; defence became paramount as central control was jeopardised, religion was secularized by the State to justify the Abolition of Slavery, & there was economic depression in the South until the 1890s; the arrest in the growth of the United States began to be reversed in 1898 when after a brief war with Spain over Cuba, the Americans took Puerto Rico, Hawaii, Guam & the Philippines	
13. Byzantine-Russian	Following the invasions of the Slavs & Avars (a Turko-Mongol people) in the Balkans, Justinian's successors abandoned Italy & lost Syria, Palestine & Egypt (616) to the Persians, who besieged Constantinople with the Avars in 626 (when the defenders celebrated their deliverance in Greek by singing Romanos' Akisthistos hymn); in 629 Heraclius defeated the Persians who evacuated the captured territories & surrendered the True Cross in 630, after which the character & language of the administration of the Empire became Greek (in recognition of which it is called the Byzantine Empire, Byzantion being the old Greek for Constantinople); the Byzantines became Greek rather than Latin, & heirs to the Greek world, which had a secularizing effect; the Arabs swiftly moved in on the recovered territories, capturing Syria &	c.626-677

Palestine (636-8), Egypt (640-2), &
Tripolitania in N. Africa (642), before
halting before Constantinople in 677, &,
struggling to survive, the State escaped
the control of the Byzantinist religion

14. Germanic-Scandinavian	After Caesar's foray across the Rhine in 55 BC, Augustus pacified Germany between 12 BC & 9 BC; a revolt led to Germanicus's campaign in AD 14-16, & a rudimentary German State evolved between the times of Caesar and Tacitus, with a permanent connection between leader & retainers or companions (*comites*) in a developed *comitatus* system; the State escaped the control of its religion & indeed controlled religion	c.12 BC-AD 38
15. Andean	After the fall of Chavin, when temple platforms & the Smiling god were discontinued, the State seems to have escaped the control of its religion	c.400-350 BC
16. Meso-American	During the Olmec colonization, the land-owning class & army grew in the San Lorenzo time & the State seems to have escaped the control of its religion before the fall of San Lorenzo, when temple mounds & "Colossal Heads" were discontinued (c.900 BC), & again after the fall of La Venta (c.400 BC), when the Olmec culture ended	c.400-350 BC
17. Arab	After the Arabs' defeat by the Byzantines,	c.740-790

the Ummayad Caliphate of Damascus collapsed, expansion was replaced by internal dissension, & the Abbasids took over in 750, founding a new capital in Baghdad in 763 & declaring for Sunnite Islam despite having received support from the Shi'ites; they escaped the control of their religion, emphasising the Abbasid Caliphate's political functions at the expense of its religious functions

18. African	After the Aksumites (S. Arabian Semites) defeated Meroe, the centre of Kush in Nubia for 600 years, in AD c.320, the Nubian State escaped the control of its religion & the Sudan became Christian, as did Ethiopian Aksum	c.320-370
19. Indian	After the Sakas' & Yueh-chih's migratory invasions of India, the old Asoka-ist Mauryan concept of the State escaped the control of the old Brahmanistic religion	AD c.70-120 or c.240-290 (depending on dating)
20. S.-E.-Asian	After the Nanchao invasions of S.-E. Asia, the threatened Khmer State controlled religion, changing it from Saivism to Vaisnavism & then to Mahayana Buddhism as it suited, while the Burmese State controlled Theravada Buddhism, the national religion	c.800-850
21. Japanese	After the Chinese & Korean defeat of Japan, the Japanese State built fortifica-tions in Kyushu in anticipation of a T'ang	c.663-710

& Silla invasion & escaped the control of its religion in the course of preserving its independence; soon after Japan adopted Buddhism at the beginning of the Nara period in 710

22. Oceanian	After the arrival of settlers from S.-E. Asia in the Marquesas (?) c.800, the ruler of Easter Island (according to legend, Hotu Matua) began the Vinapu *ahu* (or burial monument) & archaic, realistic pre-Inca statues, suggesting that the State/ruler had control over the religion he brought	c.800-850
23. Chinese	After the Sinicized *Hsiung-nu* conquered N. China with nomadic hordes & established 16 barbarian kingdoms, S. China fell into chaos under 5 dynasties; the Southern State escaped the Confucian religion, which had failed to save the Han Empire, & encouraged Taoism & Buddhism which had a secularizing effect on the first half of the 4th century	c.304-354
24. Tibetan	After becoming a Mongolian vassal Tibet failed to pay tribute & was raided by Genghis Khan; the Tibetan State escaped the control of Tibetan religion until the Sa-skyas became rulers on behalf of the Mongols	c.1207-1247
25. Central-Asian	Southern Mongolian tribes surrendered to China & were settled within China, northern Mongolian tribes migrated to	c.51 BC-AD 1

Europe, probably emerging eventually
as Attila's Huns, whose secular
organization escaped the control of its
religion

The arrest in each civilization's growth, then, coincides with increasing secularization, when the State exerts greater control over the civilization's religion.

15. COUNTER-THRUST: EXPANSION INTO EMPIRE AND LIGHT-LED RENEWAL OF GROWTH

The arrest in its growth has come as a shock to the civilization. It revives by reversing the military blow through a territorial expansion that can last 200-500 years, and
it recovers its previous growth round a new Universalist interpretation of the
Central Idea of the Light.

Thus, Europe recovered from the Viking, Muslim and Magyar invasions by
founding the Holy Roman Empire in 962, Christianizing the Vikings and Normans
and conquering England in 1066, winning back Spain from the Muslim invaders
and launching the First Crusade to guarantee access to Jerusalem. The Normans
won Sicily from the Muslims (c.1030-1091) and later conquered Ireland (from
c.1166). In 1099 the Crusaders (Frankish and Norman, then German and English)
won the Frankish Crusader Kingdom of Jerusalem (that guaranteed pilgrimage to
Jerusalem denied by the Seljuq Turks after 1071) and the Crusader states of
Antioch, Tripoli & Edessa; and a confident Europe produced the Gothic Cathedrals
(c.1140-1240). Europe's new interpretation of the Light of Christ/God involved a
cult of Mary, which was brought back from the Crusader Kingdom of Jerusalem.

The North-American civilization, after the confederacy's invasion that led to the
Civil War, began to expand in 1867 (Alaska and Midway), 1898-9 and 1903 (the
acquisition of Panama), and continued with Woodrow Wilson's accession in 1913
and the US role in the First World War when Wilson loaned the Allied government
$2,000m to buy American food, raw materials and ammunitions. He then helped
defeat the German submarine war in 1917 and supplied an Expeditionary Force of
1,200,000 men in September 1918 which tipped the balance in favour of the Allies

and produced the Armistice. Wilson sent troops into Russia, set up the League of Nations under American leadership and kept Germany undivided. During the Second World War American influence spread throughout the world and America developed the atomic bomb. After the end of the War, in which America was the chief victor, America established a Jewish colony in Israel; the Truman Doctrine led the free world; Marshall Aid reconstructed Europe, and America founded the beginnings of the EEC as a bastion against the Cold War USSR. In the 1960s America's world role increased through NATO and through her conquest of the moon, but was checked by defeat in South Vietnam and the Watergate scandal (both 1973). The rival world powers Japan, the ex-USSR and the EU have adopted American systems of government, and, like Rome after the Punic Wars, following two world wars, in the aftermath of the September-11 Muslim attacks and wars against terror in Afghanistan and Iraq America now dominates the world and can be expected to formalise this domination in an empire. America's new interpretation of the Light of Christ/God involved a radical American ecumenical world Protestantism which funded the World Council of Churches.

The expansion renews the civilization's growth. Once again the Light is strong, as we can see from the following pattern:

Civilization	Expansion	Universalist Light-led renewal of growth under:	Date of expansion & growth
1. Indo-European Kurgan/ Old European	Funnel-Neck Beaker Folk (Milesians) spread to Ireland, Kurgans expanded to land of N. Pontians, Anatolia, Greece, Scandinavia	Indo-European Sky Father/Dyaeus Pitar (by 2200 BC)	c.2550- 2200 BC?
2. Mesopotamian	Old Babylonian Empire of Amorites or Amurrus (Arabian	Marduk (national god of Babylonia)	c.1950- 1750 BC

nomads) which
absorbed the Sumerian
city-states & reached
its height under
Hammurabi (c.1792-
1750 BC)

3.	Egyptian	Empire of Middle Kingdom beginning c.2110 BC with the 50 year reign of Intef II, the first Theban to be called "King of Upper & Lower Egypt", before Mentuhotep II ruled from Thebes	Osiris-Ra	c.2110-1786 BC
4.	Aegean-Greek	Minoan empire on mainland Greece & mainland empire in the Cyclades	Cretan bull-cult (originated in Anatolia) of Dionysus (at Mycenae), especially in 15th C BC; (the name Dionysus seems to have had a Minoan-Mycenaean origin)	c.1650-1450 BC
5.	Roman	Rome conquered Campania in 341 BC, dissolved the Latin League in 338 BC & controlled the former Etruria & all Italy down to the	Hellenising Apollo (who was first imported by Cumae in 431 BC & who was strengthened when Roman religion was Hellenised after	c.341-218 BC

	Greek cities in the south by 290 BC; the Roman Empire then expanded its Republican Empire in Carthage, Macedonia, Greece & Spain as a result of the Punic Wars	c.400 BC)		
6.	Anatolian	Hittite Empire in Anatolia, Syria/ Canaan & Babylon	Arinnitti (sun goddess of Arinna to whom king & queen were high priest & priestess) & Nerik (weather god) in time of Hurrian influence (Hebat & Sharruma in Hurrian)	c.1471-1300 BC
7.	Syrian	Ugaritic hegemony in Canaan	Baal (c.1500 BC)	c.1471-1360 BC
8.	Israelite	The Israelites' slow expansion against the Philistines saw reverses (e.g. the battle of Ebenezer c.1050 BC, when the ark of the Covenant was captured, Israelite towns were destroyed, & the Philistines dominated Israel from	National God of Israel (linked to chosen dynasty of David & chosen city of Jerusalem)	c.1140-960 BC

the hills; & the battle
of Mount Gilboa in
the plain of Esdraelon
c.1000 BC, after which
Saul killed himself);
it culminated in
David's expansion
into empire from
Aqaba to Damascus
& a united Israel
(Canaan, including
Jerusalem, Aramaean
S. Syria & E. Jordan)
after his defeat of the
Philistines c.980 BC

9.	Celtic	Celtic La Tène (Gauls') expansion through France to Spain, Britain, C. Europe, Adriatic, Italy, Balkans, Greece (raiding Delphi in 279 BC), & Anatolia (where they became the Galatians)	Taran (cf Hittite Tarhun, influenced by Delphic Zeus)	c.337-250 BC
10.	Iranian	Expansion of Parthian Empire especially during its Phil-Hellene period (c.231 BC-AD 10), most notably under Mithradates I, Phraates II & Mithradates II	Anahita	c.280 BC-AD 10

("King of Kings")

11. European	Europe's first expansion as Germany conquered Italy & founded the Holy Roman Empire (962); the Vikings & Normans were Christianized (c.962-1000), and Christian Normans conquered Danish Viking-Saxon England (1066) ; the Spanish *Reconquista* won most of Spain from the Muslims (c.1000-1212); Crusaders won the Kingdom of Jerusalem and Crusader states (p111); Europe produced Gothic Cathedrals (c.1140-1240)	Cult of Mary (Black Virgin) taken from Crusader Kingdom of Jerusalem & Crusader states	c.951-1244
12. North-American	America's world expansion through two world wars and the Cold War, and the war against terror in Afganistan and Iraq to superpowerdom or hyperpowerdom (see	Christ of radical American Ecumenical Protestantism, which led world Protestantism after 1945 (e.g. the USA funded the World Council of Churches	c.1913-present

p111-112)		& African churches), supported from home by massive donations as 38% of the United States' population attend church; in due course blending with the Universalist New Age vision of the metaphysical Light (see pp510-512)	
13. Byzantine-Russian	The Byzantine Empire, which AD c.700 was reduced to Greece, Anatolia, Italy/Sicily & the Balkan coast, slowly expanded into Crete (961), Cyprus (965), Eastern Bulgaria (972) & the Western Bulgarian Empire (1018), Crimea (1016) & the Armenian Kingdom of Vaspurakan (1022), & reduced the Serbs to vassalage until they revolted (in 1043); 1071 saw a dual set-back as the Seljuq Turks destroyed the Byzantine army at	Iconoclastic Christ whose divine incarnat-ting nature could not be shown in symbolic images or icons (730-787/815-843), quietly followed by Iconophile Christ focusing on transfiguration; especially after St Symeon the New Theologian & following the Greek-Latin Schism of 1054	c.677-1071

Manzikert, capturing
the Byzantine Emperor
Romanus IV Diogenes
& sweeping through
Anatolia to the
Bosphorus, & as the
Normans took S. Italy
at Bari, permanently
dividing the Greek
East from the Latin
West

14.	Germanic-Scandinavian	Expansion of Germanic tribes to Germany, France & Italy	Thor (equated with Jupiter at this time, Jove's day becoming Thor's day or Thursday)	AD c.38-170
15.	Andean	Nazca (south)/Moche (north) cultures' expansion	Staff god	c.350 BC-AD 300
16.	Meso-American	Post-Olmec (La Venta) Late Formative Expansion	Fire Serpent	c.350 BC-AD 100
17.	Arab	Abbasid Caliphate's expansion, beginning with the 782 victory over the Byzantines of later Caliph Harun ar-Rashid (786-809), in Crete, Sicily, Sardinia & Corsica	Sunni Allah	c.790-1055

	(823-850) until in 945 the Abbasid Caliph's political power was devolved by the Shi'ite Buyids, which strengthened the Fatimids who captured N. Africa & ruled from Cairo from 969; the Seljuq Turks (foreign Oğuz Turkmen migrants led by the Seljuq family) captured Baghdad in 1055, controlling the Abbasid Caliphate, & defeated the Byzantines in 1071, after which they controlled Asia Minor		
18. African	Aksum (or Axum) trading Empire in N. Ethiopia which dominated Southern Arabia, the Yemen & the Red Sea until the 10th C, & which is linked to the legend of Prester John	Christ (Aksumite kings were Christianised in 4th C AD & were linked to Byzantine Egypt)	c.320-540
19. Indian	The Gupta Empire in N. India (AD 320-540), the Calukyas in the	Siva/Visnu through Guptas' Vaisnavism & the Buddha; Tantric	AD c.120 or c.290- 750

	Deccan (6th C) & the Pallavas in S. India; temple-building for all cults & expansion of Indian Hinduism & Buddhism into S.-E. Asia despite the invasion of the C.-Asian Huns or Hunas AD c.450 which devastated the Gupta Empire & Buddhism	cults	
20. S.-E.-Asian	Indianised kingdoms:	Localised Indian religions:	c.800-1100
	Thalassocracy of the Srivijaya Empire in Sumatra/Malay Archipelago, which controlled the Strait of Malacca;	Mahayana Buddhism	c.800-1300
	Khmer Empire in Java, Cambodia, S. Thailand & S. Vietnam;	Siva (later Visnu & later still, AD c.1150, Mahayana Buddha)	9th- 14th C
	1st Burmese Empire at Pagan;	Theravada Buddha	9th- 12th C
	Dai Viet Empire (N. Vietnam);	Mahayana Buddha/ Confucianist Taoist Reality	10th C
	Champa Empire (S. Vietnam, slowly absorbed by Dai Viet);	Hindu-Buddhist Reality	11th- 15th C

	Thai-Lao-Shan Empire (expanded southwards); Mons Empire of Thaton & Duravati	Theravada Buddha	11th-12th C 11th C 7th-13th C
21. Japanese	Empire of Japanese islands ruled from first Nara & then Kyoto, closely linked to T'ang China until c.900 (Nara was based on the T'ang capital Ch'ang-an); by 1000 Emperors were cloistered Buddhist priests surrounded by wealth	Chinese Buddhism (which had been introduced c.538); Great Vairocana Buddha of Nara	c.710-1000
22. Oceanian	S.-E.-Asian/ Polynesian expansion from the Marquesas Islands to Hawaii, Society Islands, Tahiti, Cook Islands & New Zealand, & towards the rising sun to Easter Island (Polynesian short ears)	God of the *moai* (the Buddha?)	c.800-950
23. Chinese	Sui/T'ang Empires, during which China recovered from the	Religious Taoism/ Chinese Buddhism whose schools	c.589-907

	invasion of the *Hsiung-nu*	upplanted Indian Buddhist schools, e.g. the Inner Light school which can be traced back to Tao-sheng (died 434) & his "thesis of sudden enlightenment"	
24.	Tibetan	Tibetan expansion through Sa-skya lamas who ruled Tibet as the Mongols' viceroy in the Chinese court after 1247, & after 1358 throughthe Phag-mo-gru-pa line	The Buddha taught by Atisa/Indian Tantric Tibetan Buddhism	c.1247-1481
25.	Central-Asian	Expansion under some of the northern Mongolian *Hsiung-nu* (AD c.1-304) & some of their descendants: the Mongolian Huns who invaded Europe c.370-455, the T'u-chueh or Mongolian Orkhon Turks c.618, then Uighurs & then Manchurian Khitan	Allah (of Turks)/ Chinese T'ang Taoist & Confucianist Reality & Chinese Buddhist Enlightenment Khitan)	AD c.1-950

The Light is now symbolized in a different god from the one with which the civilization started, but the civilization has undergone a revival of its inner energy in the course of its reversal of the military blow.

16. THE GOD OF LIGHT-LED GROWTH IN HEROIC EPIC LITERATURE

The god of the Light-led renewal of growth appears in heroic epic literature, in the genre of the long narrative poem which describes heroic deeds, and which is set (if not written down) in times of growth, as we can see from the following pattern:

Civilization	God of Light-led growth	Heroic epic literature (religious parables of suffering & salvation transmitted from early times)	Date written
1. Indo-European Kurgan/ Old European	Dyaeus Pitar	Dyaeus mentioned in Indian *Rig Veda*	c.1500 BC
2. Mesopotamian	Shamash/Marduk	Sumerian epic: *Gilgamesh and Agga of Kish,* Akkadian epic: *Epic of Gilgamesh*	first written c.1900 BC
3. Egyptian	Osiris-Ra	Heroic deeds of soul in: *Pyramid texts, Coffin texts, Book of the Dead*	c.2345-2181 BC c.2040-1786 BC from c.1570 BC
4. Aegean-Greek	Zeus, Poseidon & Dionysus	Homeric epic (*Hymn to Dionysus* began Homeric	c.800 BC

collection)

5.	Roman	Apollo (first imported by Cumae in 431 BC)	Virgil's *Aeneid* on the foundation of Lavinium (parent town of Alba Longa & Rome)	c.29-19 BC
6.	Anatolian	Arinnitti/Nerik	Heroic deeds of soul in cuneiform texts found at or near Boğazköy	from c.1700 BC
7.	Syrian	Baal	The Baal epic	early 2nd millenium BC
8.	Israelite	God of Israel	*Psalms* of David/ Mosaic epic (Pentateuch)	c.1000-960 BC 10th-5th C BC
9.	Celtic	Taran	Irish & Welsh epics, Druid bardic epics	from 1st C AD/ Oral
10.	Iranian	Mithra, Ahura Mazda & Anahita	Iranian epic, *Shah-nameh* (Iran's national epic)	c.550 1009/10
11.	European	Mary	Arthurian Grail romances coloured by crusades, French epic *Chanson de Roland* (about	c.1190- 1225

		Charlemagne),	c.1100
		Roman de la Rose	c.1240
12. North-American	Radical, ecumenical Protestant God	(not yet written or not yet emerged; American epic poetry about heroic deeds in Second World War/ war against terror can now be expected)[1]	21st C?
13. Byzantine-Russian	Christ/Mary through icons	Byzantine Greek epic e.g. *Digenis Akritas*	10th C
	Byzantinism after 988	Russian heroic ballads of Varangians	from 10th C
14. Germanic-Scandinavian	Thor	Teutonic epic, e.g. *Beowulf*; Icelandic sagas, e.g. *Elder Edda*	8th C c.1270
15. Andean	Staff god	Oral	?
16. Meso-American	Fire Serpent	Oral	?
17. Arab	Fraternal Sufi orders/ Sunni Allah/ Shi'ite Allah	Persian epic e.g. Ferdowsi's *Shah-nameh*	11th C
18. African	Christ	Oral	?
19. Indian	Siva/Visnu & the Buddha	*Rig Veda* Sanskrit epic e.g. *Ramayana*	c.1500 BC c.300 BC

		& *Mahabharata* (which includes the *Bhagavadgita*)	c.400 BC- AD 200
20. S.-E.-Asian	Siva/the Buddha	Indian epics	from 1st C AD
21. Japanese	The Buddha	Japanese epics e.g. *Koji-ki & Nihon shoki*	c.712
22. Oceanian	God of the *moai*	Oral	?
23. Chinese	Religious Taoist Reality	Heroic deeds of soul in *Shih Ching* compiled by Confucius (poems going back as far as c.1766 BC, burned in Shih Huang Ti's (Shihuangdi's) burning of the books & as a result now in 4 versions)	compiled c.5th C BC
24. Tibetan	The Buddha	*Rgal-po Ge-sar* (The Great Deeds of King Gesar)	Oral
25. Central-Asian	Allah/Chinese Taoist-Confucianist Reality, & Chinese Buddhist Enlighten- ment	Kirgiz-Kazakh heroic ballads (e.g. *Manas*) Mongolian *Üligers* (orally transmitted verse epics)	Oral Oral

"Oral" means that a written version has either not been preserved, or that it is impossible to date it as it was written down in the course of a long oral tradition.

THE BREAKDOWN OF CIVILIZATIONS

The pattern of breakdown concerns a transfer of power from the people who have hitherto ruled the civilization to a new people, who follow a heresy. The turning point is a military blow which destroys the confidence of the people who have hitherto ruled and secularizes their religion, their Light. The new people seize the limelight and their heresy carries forward the Light, but in a less intense, more worldly context in which the power generated by the Light clearly shows signs of running out of steam.

17. CREATION OF LIGHT-BASED HERETICAL SECT

Nothing stands still, the unwinding of civilizations is a process of perpetual development. The Light-led renewal of growth through a change of emphasis in the civilization's religion (stage 15) is now the orthodoxy, and in each civilization a new rising people throws up a new Light-based sect, which is deemed heretical. The orthodox religion is now in decline. Whether the throwing up of the heretical sect is a cause or an effect of the decline is debatable. It is probably both. The orthodoxy begins to weaken and petrify (i.e. "turn to stone", in the sense that as the Light recedes attention is focused on the religious buildings it has created, the stones); as a result a new heretical movement comes into being which has more energy within it than the petrified orthodoxy and which can also be seen as the effect of a decline in the orthodoxy's Light. We can best understand these heresies in the context of the orthodoxies that preceded them, as follows:

Civilization	"Change of Beginning orthodoxy (stage 4)	emphasis" orthodoxy (stage 15)	Heretical god	Date
1. Indo-European	Magna Mater	Dyaeus Pitar	Ogma	c.2250 BC

	Kurgan/Old European		(Zeus in Greece)	(Herakles of Battle-Axe Kurgans in Greece)	
2.	Mesopotamian	Anu/Utu	Marduk	Ashur of Assyrians (under Shamshin Adad I)	c.1800 BC
3.	Egyptian	Horus/Seth	Ra/Osiris-Ra	Amon	c.1991 BC
4.	Aegean-Greek	Minoan Mistress of animals/ Anat/ Athene	Dionysus	Hittite Apollo of Asia Minor, Crete & Dorians of N. Greece	c.1500 BC
5.	Roman	Tin	Jupiter/Apollo	Deification of leader's "genius" or avatar within pagan cults; began with Alexander the Great becoming the son of Zeus-Amon after encountering the god in the Syrian desert, & continued with Scipio Africanus,	c.204 BC

who communed
with Capitoline
Jupiter at night
& was reputed to
be the son of the
god; after
Hannibal's
invasion of Italy
(219-204) when
he took Capua &
Tarentum &
ravaged &
terrified Italy
without
marching on
Rome, pagan
Delphic Oracle

6.	Anatolian	"Mistress of animals"/ Tarhun or Teshub	Arinnitti/Nerik	Cybele/Attis (of the Phrygians)	c.1350 BC
7.	Syrian	El/Dagon	Baal	Melqart* or Baal Hammon (i.e. the Egyptian Amon)/Astarte (an Egyptian heresy that may have originated when the Phoenician	c.1450 BC

				Byblos was controlled by Egypt during the Old Kingdom, 2686-2160 BC)	
8.	Israelite	El Shaddai	Yahweh	Elohim after (borrowed from Canaan, Canaanite plural "gods" made singular in this use)	c.1050 BC (Gideon)
9.	Celtic	Du-w/Lug	Taran	Esus (Yesu) Taruos Trigaranus	from 3rd C BC 1st C AD
10.	Iranian	Mithras	Zurvan/Anahita (introduced by Artaxerxes II, 404-359 BC)	Ahura Mazda, god the heretical of Zoroaster under the Persian kings Darius I & Xerxes I, 522-465 BC, who possibly worshipped him among other gods; & now the god of the Persians who	1st C BC (when Iranian religion resurfaced after Hellenism, e.g. Zeus Oromazdes)

			opposed the expansionism of Parthia and supported the Macedonian Seleucids, especially under Vologases I, AD 51-77/78, who compiled the *Avesta*	
11. European	Roman Catholic Christ	Mary	Personal Church-free God of Templars, Cathars & Reformers (Lollards/ Hussites)	from c.1130
12. North-American	Puritan God	Christ of radical Ecumenical Protestantism	Coming New Age Universalist God anticipated by 1776 Freemasonic Deistic Illuminatists who influenced the founding fathers of the USA (see pp500-508); (the heretical nature of the New Age	21st C? (has already started)

from the Christian point of view can be judged from the fact that the Archbishop of Canterbury has called on Anglican Christians to "engage" the New-Age belief that the Christian Age is ending)

| 13. Byzantine-Russian | Byzantine or Greek Orthodox God/ Christ known directly by the East Roman *oikoumene* (the one universal Christian society) | Eastern Orthodox Christ/Mary venerated through icons, focusing on the transfiguration (following St Symeon the New Theologian & the Schism of 1054) | Russian Light: the Varangian Vikings, followers of Rurik the Viking, migrated to Rus c.860, took over Kiev's Finnic & Slavic tribes & recreated the Germanic Light which was replaced by the migrating Byzantine Light in 988 when the Kievian prince Vladimir I was | after c.988 |

converted to
Byzantine
Orthodoxy &
married a sister
of the Byzantine
Emperor, Basil
II; the Kievian
princes now
followed the
Byzantine
imperial
tradition, even-
tually creating
the heretical
Russian
Orthodox
Byzantine Christ
of Moscow as
"Third Rome"
(in contrast to
Constantinople,
second Rome)

| 14. | Germanic-Scandinavian | Tiwaz/Tiw | Thor (Saxons) | Human Christ (later Arianism after 325) | c.120 |
| 15. | Andean | Smiling god (El Lanzon at Chavin) | Staff god | Doorway god (from Gateway of the Sun, Tiahuanaco) – Viracocha? (who first appeared during Nazca | c.200 BC |

			influence on Ica & Huari)	
16. Meso-American	Feathered Serpent (god of Cuicuilco)	Fire Serpent who bears sun across sky (at Teotihuacan)	Mayan Kinich Ahau, alias Itzamna, Lord of the Fire (i.e. Light)	AD c.50
17. Arab	Allah	Sunni Ayyubid Allah	Theosophical Sufi al-Haqq (a Sufism mixed with Neoplatonism & Gnosticism, later inspired by the Persian Suhrawardi & the Spanish Ibn al-Arabi & still later associated with Shi'ite Iran & taken up by some of the Mamluk rulers in Egypt, who followed the Ahmadiyah Sufi order, the Ottomans, & the Indian Moghul Empire under Akbar)	c.900-1000

18.	African	Shamanistic African gods	Egyptian Light	Pre-Islamic Allah	before c.540
19.	Indian	Vedic Brahmanism	Visnu (under Hindu Gupta Empire 320-540)	Islamic Allah	8th C
20.	S.-E.-Asian	Mahayana Buddhism/ Brahmanism	Mahayana Buddha/ Tantric Buddha/ Tantric Hindu Reality/ Vaisnavist Reality	Theravada Buddha	c.1056-1100
21.	Japanese	Chinese Confucianist-Taoist/Shinto Reality	Chinese Buddhism	Personal enlightenment of Chinese Ch'an which focused on the experience of the Buddha's enlightenment & Sudden Enlightenment as taught by Tao-sheng (died 434); introduced from China in 7th C & flowered in Japan as Zen Buddhism in 1191 (shock	from c.750

enlightenment of
Rinzai)/1227
(quiet sitting or
zazen
enlightenment of
Soto)

22.	Oceanian	Sun-god (Andean)	God of *moai* (the Buddha?)	Doorway god from Tiahuanaco (Peru/Bolivia) or precursor of Peruvian Incas' Inti?/Io of Maoris	c.850?
23.	Chinese	*Ti*	Taoist Reality/ Buddhist Enlightenment	Neo-Confucianism	8th C
24.	Tibetan	Shamanistic Bon	Tantric Reality (second generation before 632): Indian Tantric Tibetan Buddha	Following Atisa's missionary journey from India c.1042, Atisan Tantric Tibetan-Buddhist sects were established; first the Karma-pa & Bka'brgyud-pa, & later the heretical Dge-lugs-pa c.1400	after c.1409

25.	Central-Asian	Shamanism	Orkhon Turkic	Tibetan Buddha	after
			Allah/Chinese	(Chinese	c.900
			Taoist	Buddhist leaders	
			Confucianist	were invited to	
			Reality &	Tibet in 763, &	
			Chinese-	Tibetan ideas	
			Buddhist	were taken to	
			Enlightenment	Mongolia by the	
			(Khitan)	Mongol	
				Manchurian	
				Khitan, who	
				founded the	
				Liao Empire in	
				947 & controlled	
				most of	
				Mongolia; later	
				still Mongols &	
				Tibetans drew	
				together before	
				Tibet submitted to	
				Genghis in 1207)	

(*The Phoenician Melqart was brought into Israel by Ahab's wife Jezebel, while Baal was brought in by his sister or daughter Athaliah, who married Jehoram of Judah. Ahaz was compelled to raise an altar in the Temple to the Assyrian god Ashur when he was a vassal of the Assyrians)

We can see that in each case the heretical sect enshrines a god who is quite different from the god of the recent change of emphasis, which has become the new orthodoxy. The god of the heresy is important to the civilization as he (or she) will become a still newer orthodoxy in the near future.

18. RESISTANCE TO/PERSECUTION OF HERETICAL SECT

The heretical sect is resisted or persecuted, as the following pattern shows:

Civilization	Heretical movement	Date of persecution	Details of resistance/persecution
1. Indo-European Kurgan/ Old European	Ogma/Herakles	c.2200-2150 BC	Resistance by Funnel-Neck Beaker Folk before they were conquered by Battle-axe Kurgans who spread from North, Central & Eastern Europe
2. Mesopotamian	Ashur	c.1800-1650 BC	Resistance by Babylonians who opposed the rise of Assyria
3. Egyptian	Amon	c.1900-1850 BC	Resistance by supporters of Ra/Osiris-Ra & by supporters of the cult of Sebek, the crocodile god, in Shedet & a few miles south of Thebes
4. Aegean-Greek	Apollo	c.1200 BC	Resistance by supporters of Zeus & Dionysus
5. Roman	Cults of Cybele/ Mithras	c.186 BC	Resistance by supporters of Jupiter: worried about the defence of Italy against the Gauls (e.g. the Ligurians & Boii) who pressed into N.

				Italy from 200 to 166 BC, causing panic in Rome, the Senate suppressed the worship of Dionysus in 186 BC & for a long while disapproved of the other cults
6.	Anatolian	Cybele/Attis	c.1300 BC	Hittite Teshub dominant over Cybele (the goddess of the Phrygians)
7.	Syrian	Melqart or Baal Hammon	c.1360 BC	Hittite Tarhun dominant over Egyptian-inspired Melqart or Baal Hammon when Hittites occupied Syria (including Ugarit)
8.	Israelite	Elohim	after c.1050-900 BC	Resistance by supporters of Yahweh to the Canaanite heresy of Gideon
9.	Celtic	Esus (or Yesu)	3rd C BC	Esus is of unknown origin, appearing on the Paris & Trier altars as cutting a tree; the cult of Esus seems to be a new cult connected with oak-trees and druids, & can be expected to have been resisted by the traditional worshippers of Taran, the Tarhun-like or Zeus-like god of the sky & thunder who may have arrived in Britain

from Israel with the Levites
(who left Samaria after 721
& entered Britain in the
Hallstatt period, 7th-6th C
BC, & who worshipped Baal
– cf the Celtic Belenis or
Beli – & therefore the Hittite
Tarhun as the Hittites had
dominated Canaan)

10.	Iranian	Ahura Mazda (or Auramazda)	1st-2nd C AD	Supporters of Anahita resisted Ahura Mazda
11.	European	Church-free God of Templars, Cathars, Lollards & Hussites	c.1244/ c.1312 c.1380-1430	Roman Catholic Church sup-pressed Cathars in Albigensian Crusade & Templars, banned Wycliffe's writings, Hus was burned at the stake
12.	North-American	—		— —
13.	Byzantine-Russian	Russian "Third Rome" believers	c.1204-1261	Byzantine resistance to Russian "Third Rome" & misgivings regarding the "heretical" pro-Vatican policy of second Rome (i.e. Constantinople) during the Venetian Latin occupation of Constantinople (1204-1261), before the Mongol invasion of Kiev in 1240, & later under the Tatar Oz Beg who permitted Moscow to

maintain contact with
Constantinople through the
Crimea c.1340

14. Germanic- Scandinavian	Christ	AD c.150	Pagan Germanic tribes living outside Roman frontier & following Odin persecuted German Christians in their midst
15. Andean	Doorway god	after c.200 BC	Doorway god resisted by supporters of Smiling god or Staff god
16. Meso- American	Kinich Ahau (or Itzamna)	AD c.50	End of post-Olmec Late Formative culture of Feathered Serpent & Fire Serpent, beginning of Mayan cultures of Kinich Ahau – transition resisted by some mystics of the Late Formative Period culture
17. Arab	Theosophical Sufism	c.900-1000	Sunnis executed Al-Hallaj in Baghdad in 922, which led to persecution of Sufis
18. African	Pre-Islamic Allah	c.540	Resistance by supporters of the old Christian Light (e.g. an unsuccessful expedition to destroy Mecca AD c.540 by Abraha, viceroy of the Ethiopian emperor Ella-Asbeha or Caleb)

19. Indian	Islamic Allah	8th C	Resistance to Arabs by Hindus
20. S.-E.-Asian	Theravada Buddhism/ Hinduism	c.1056-1150	Resistance by the Mahayana monks & by Saivists/ Vaisnavists
21. Japanese	Japanese Zen Buddhism	9th C	Resistance by Tendai & Shingon monks
22. Oceanian	Andean Doorway god?	c.900?	Resistance by the supporters of the god of *moai* (the Buddha?)
23. Chinese	Neo-Confucianism	from 8th C	Resistance by Taoists & by Buddhists (until a fanatical Taoist suppressed Buddhism in 843-845, closing 4,600 temples & 40,000 shrines & returning 260,000 monks to lay life); government persecution of Chu Hsi's school & banishment of leaders (before 1200)
24. Tibetan	Dge-lugs-pa	c.1430	Karma-pa resisted the new Dge-lugs-pa monasteries
25. Central-Asian	Tibetan Buddhism (Buddhism flourished under the Uighurs)	c.925	Tibetan Buddhism resisted by supporters of Turkic Islam

19. DECLINE OF RELIGION/CHURCH, AND
20. ATTEMPTED RENEWAL BY MYSTICS/REFORMERS WHO RESIST DECLINE

Between the end of the counter-thrust (stage 15) and the breakdown of the civilization (stage 22) the organized religion goes into a decline that is caused partly by the heretical sect and partly by a foreign influence.

Thus, the European religion declined following the advance of the Mongols in Europe and the Muslims in the Crusader states, the Byzantine empire and Spain. The heretical Templars had opened themselves to Muslim influences and further weakened European religion despite escorting pilgrims to Jerusalem. The Black Death (1348-51) reduced Europe's population by a third and perhaps even a half, and destroyed the manorial system on which Christianity had been based. The English Peasants' Revolt of 1381 further loosened the feudal system and the hold of religion. The so-called "Great Schism" (1378-1417) rent the Church, which saw two and eventually three competing Popes, after the Papal States were recognised as independent by the Holy Roman Emperor, giving a temporal basis for temporal power and secularizing the religion.

The Byzantine religion declined following the Schism of 1054 and the Norman invasion of Sicily, which separated the Greek East from the Latin West during the time of the Crusades. The Crusaders invaded the Seljuq Sultanate, whose capture of Antioch and Jerusalem had caused the First Crusade, and founded the crusading states of Antioch, Tripoli, Edessa and Jerusalem (1097-9), pushing the Seljuqs back into Anatolia. From 1099 the Byzantine Empire expanded again, conquered the Serbs and Patzinaks (1122), and recovered Antioch. Religion declined when the Fatimids fought back from Egypt, briefly capturing Jerusalem from the Seljuqs, and an empire was founded at the expense of the Crusader states, first under Zangi, the Shi'ite Seljuq regent in Mosul who halted the Crusaders' advance c.1121-2 and overran the Crusader state of Edessa in 1144; and then under the Sunni Ayyubids, founded by Saladin, son of Ayyub. A Kurdish officer from Seljuq Mosul, Saladin overthrew the Shi'ite Fatimid dynasty for the Zangid Sultanate in 1171, set up his own Ayyubid Sultanate after the death of the last Zangid, Nur-ad-Din in 1174, ruled North Iraq, Syria, the Yemen and Egypt, reduced the Crusader Kingdom of Jerusalem to Tyre (1187) and reduced the principalities of Antioch and Tripoli, leaving only Acre still in Crusader hands.

After the bankrupting trade monopoly granted to Venice, and later Pisa and Genoa, in return for aid against the Normans and Turks, the Venetians and Crusaders under Baldwin I, Count of Flanders, occupied the Byzantine Empire (draining its remaining wealth) as a new Frankish Empire to compensate for the loss of the Frankish kingdom of Jerusalem to Saladin in 1187. In 1261 the Palaeologi-ruled Empire of Nicaea (a Byzantine Empire and church in exile) recaptured Constantinople and the Byzantine Empire in Thessalonica from the Venetian Latins. Emperor Michael VIII resisted Charles of Anjou's plan to re-establish the Latin Empire by submitting the Church of Constantinople to the see of Rome (1274), thus saving the Empire – for which he was reviled as a heretic and traitor. (It was left to his son Andronicus II to isolate himself from the Papacy and the West and to restore Orthodox Byzantinism.)

Religion further declined when Turks crossed Anatolia c.1282, pushed by the Mongol Khanate of Persia. In 1293 the Jalayrid Sultanate in Iran who ruled from Baghdad defeated the army of the Seljuq Sultanate of Iconium, splitting S.W. Anatolia into six Emirates and leaving N.W. Anatolia to the newly arrived Ottoman or Osmanite clan under Osman I, who defeated the Byzantine Army in 1302 at Nicomedia and advanced towards the Bosphorus, threatening Constantinople.

The decline caused by foreign influence and internal heresy is one decline which mystics/reformers attempt to resist, as we see from the following pattern:

Civilization	Date of decline	Details of decline (stage 19)	Resistance by mystics/ reformers (stage 20)
1. Indo-European Kurgan/Old European	c.2200- 2000 BC	Decline of Funnel-Neck Beaker religion before invasion of Battle-Axe Kurgans	Sun-swirls at Newgrange
2. Mesopotamian	c.1750- 1595 BC	Decline of Babylonian religion before the invasions of the Kassites	Creation of *Enuma Elish* in 14th C BC, the story of Marduk which was recited for

3.	Egyptian	c.1786- 1674 BC	Second Intermediate Period, decline of Egyptian religion under Hyksos domination. (The Hyksos came from Canaan – the Biblical Joseph and the Hebrews migrated to Egypt with them – & *hekaukhasut* or *hikkhoswet* means "princes or chiefs of foreign uplands")	Texts from Egyptian *Book of the Dead.*
4.	Aegean-Greek	c.1450- 1200 BC	Decline of Minoan & Mycenaean religion following the eruption of Thera c.1500 BC & the conquest of Crete after c.1450 BC (which led to a mixture of Mycenaean & Minoan culture & religion) & with the Sea Peoples' invasion of mainland Greece c.1200 BC	Cults of Demeter & Kore at Eleusis & of Athene
5.	Roman	c.218- 113 BC	Decline of Roman religion in the face of foreign cults following the Carthaginian invasion under Hannibal & the agrarian agitation of the	2nd & early 1st C BC, Stoics' belief that the human soul is part of the divine, universal spirit

6.	Anatolian	c.1300-1225 BC	Decline of Hittite religion after Mursilis II at the hands of Anatolian revolts, Egyptian revival & the rise of Phrygia	Following the rise of Assyria Hattusilis III's daughter married Ramesses II in the 1260s, & Hattusilis & his wife Pudukepa rebuilt the old capital Hattusas & restored the traditional Hittite religion
7.	Syrian	c.1360-1225 BC	Decline of Syrian religion under Hittite & Egyptian rivalry; Ugarit fell under Hittite sway	Under Hittite influence Baal took on the Storm & Weather characteristics of the Hittite Tarhun, & there were attempts to restore Baal as a fertility god when Syria revolted against the Hittites at the time of the death of Mursilis II's brother (the king of Carchemish) towards the end of the 14th C BC
8.	Israelite	c.960-841 BC	Decline of Hebrew religion under Solomon, who based his Temple on Phoenicia (Ahiram) &	9th C BC prophets Elijah & Elisha denounced northern Israel's defection to

			Canaan (concept of the priest-king); after the invasions of Judah & Israel c.930-924 BC by the Libyan Pharaoh of Egypt Shishak I (alias Sheshonk I) who supported Jeroboam against Rehoboam, & after the division between north & south as a result of the unwise policies of the reputedly wise Solomon in 922 BC, the north declined under Baal/ Melqart, the south under foreign cults sponsored by the King	Canaanite Baal (e.g. under Ahab's Phoenician queen, Jezebel or Jeze-baal, daughter of Ethbaal or Ithobaal, the high priest of Astarte & king of Tyre and Sidon)
9.	Celtic	c.250-58 BC	Decline of Celtic religion as Romans reached Gaul & began to subdue the Gallic tribes one by one	Information is scanty but the Romans created an anti-Roman nationalistic attitude in the Celts, & it is likely that there was an attempt to revive Celtic religion
10.	Iranian	AD c.10-114	Decline of Iranian religion of Anahita following Macedonian Hellenism & the Romans' invasion of Parthia; the Parthians sought to drive Rome out	Magi revived Iranian religion during this decline

11.	European	c.1244-1453	Decline of European religion following the Mongolian victory (by Khanate of the Golden the Horde) against Poland, the Teutonic Knights & Hungary (1241-2); the defeat of the Crusaders (the loss of Jerusalem to Khwarezmians fleeing from Mongol-occupied Iran in 1244, Antioch in 1268, Tripolis in 1289 & Acre in 1291); & the Venetian Latins' loss of Constantinople in 1261; the revolt of the reconquered Moors in Spain in 1263 (see p143)	The 14th C & later medieval mystics, Wycliffe's Lollards c.1380 & Hussites c.1410-30
12.	North-American	—	—	—
13.	Byzantine-Russian	c.1071-1354	Decline of Byzantine religion following the Schism of 1054 & the Norman invasion of Sicily, as a result of which the Greek East was separated from the	Resistance to foreign influence during this Crusading period by monastic mystics who c.1260-1320 revived Hesychasm (seeing God "the Uncreated

			Latin West during the time of the Crusades; (for details of decline during the Crusades, see p143)	Light" as Light in quiet) & the Byzantine mystical tradition, e.g. on Mount Athos, as the Greeks re-emphasised their Greek identity after the Latin occupation
14.	Germanic-Scandinavian	c.170-270	Germanic religion declined as Germanic invasions (e.g. those of the Marcomanni & Quadi c.170) were resisted by the Romans	The Roman religion influenced the Germanic tribes as they became less nomadic & more settled, the Germanic gods had Roman equivalents, & Latin became more wide-spread among the tribes; & it seems there was resistance & a movement to return to the Germanic gods
15.	Andean	c.300-500	Decline of Andean religion as the Early Horizon unity of cultural style gave way to the Middle Horizon cultural style of invaders	Reformers supported Smiling god & Shaft god before Doorway god triumphed
16.	Meso-American	AD c.100-200	Decline of Meso-American religion as post-	Reformers supported Feathered Serpent &

		Olmec Late Formative culture decayed into Mayan culture	Fire Serpent before Kinich Ahau (or Itzamna) triumphed
17. Arab	c.1055-1258	Decline of Islamic religion before the advance of the Seljuq Turks who conquered the Buyid ex-Abbasid lands in 1055, & before the Mongols who conquered the ex-Seljuq Shahdom of Khwarezm (1220-1 & again in 1231) & Georgia (1239), made vassals of the Seljuqs (1243), & destroyed the Abbasid Caliphate in Baghdad (1258)	11th-12th C Sufis sought to restore the purity of Islamic religion in Seljuq & Mongol times, e.g. Suhrawardi, the philosopher of *ishraq* or "illumination" who was executed in 1191, & Ibn al-Arabi, who was attacked by orthodox Sunnis on the grounds that monism excludes morality
18. African	c.540-640	Decline of African religion under the spreading influence of Allah, the Persian invasion of Ethiopian colonies near Aden in 572, & the Arab invasions of the Aksumite Empire	Reformers supported the purity of African Christian culture & religion
19. Indian	c.750-1150	Decline of Indian religion in the face of the spreading influence of Islam (Arabs and Turks)	Reformers supported the purity of Indian religion, e.g. the Bhakti mystics

20. S.-E.-Asian	c.1100-1177	Decline of traditional S.-E.-Asian religion under new Indian Islamic influence	Reformers supported traditional Indian religion
21. Japanese	c.1000-1274	Decline & secularization of Japanese religion during the time of cloistered Emperors, worldly religious factionalism, the rise of the *samurai* & the Heiji War	Amidist sects & Zen *samurai* supported the purity of Japanese religion
22. Oceanian	c.950-1100?	Decline of Oceanian religion of *mana*/Andean Sun-god/Buddha(?) under S. American influence?	Reformers supported the purity of the Oceanian religion of *moai*?
23. Chinese	c.907-1271	Decline of traditional Chinese religion of *Ti*, of Buddhism (except for Ch'an which drew on Taoism as well as Buddhism) & of religious Taoism as North Sung was ended by the Juchen in 1126, & South Sung by the Mongols in 1279 (all of which was reflected in the Mannerism of Sung sculpture)	Neo-Confucianist scholars & philosophers, supporters of *Ti*, restated the metaphysical superstructure of Confucianism as sudden enlightenment, & kept Chinese religion alive
24. Tibetan	c.1481-	Decline of Tibetan	The Dge-lugs-pa kept

		1565	Buddhism following the fall of the Sa-skya lamas at the time of the collapse of the Yuan dynasty	the purity of Tibetan Buddhism alive in monasteries
25.	Central-Asian	c.950-1125	Decline of Turkic Islam under the Khitan, a Mongol people whose homeland was in Manchuria & who were Chinese Buddhists	Resistance to Chinese influence by Mongol supporters of Islam

21. FOREIGN THREAT'S MILITARY BLOW BEFORE BREAKDOWN
22. BREAKDOWN OF CIVILIZATION

As a result of its phase of decline, the hitherto growing civilization is now confronted by a foreign threat. Just as the arrest of the civilization's growth was caused by a military blow, so a military blow (stage 21) heralds in the civilization's breakdown (stage 22), as the following pattern shows:

Civilization	Foreign threat's military blow (stage 21)	Date of breakdown (stage 22)
1. Indo-European Kurgan/ Old European	Battle-Axe Kurgans' (or Bell-Beaker Indo-European Celto-Ligurians') invasion of Greece, Scandinavia, France, Britain c.2000 BC	c.2000-1900 BC
2. Mesopotamian	Hittites destroyed Babylon in c.1595 BC, & Kassites from NE Zagros Mountains invaded	c.1590-1490 BC

Babylonia & replaced the
Hittites there, destroying
Hammurabi's dynasty

3.	Egyptian	Hyksos captured Memphis c.1674 BC	c.1674-1576 BC

4.	Aegean-Greek	Sea Peoples invaded mainland Greece & destroyed Mycenaean centres by fire from c.1200 BC; Dorian invasions of Peloponnese brought in Dark Age c.1100 BC	c.1200 BC-1100 BC

5.	Roman	Cimbri & Teutones invaded N. Italy & destroyed a Roman army in 113 BC	c.113-30 BC

6.	Anatolian	Sea Peoples c.1225 BC (probably Achaean Greeks displaced by Dorians), Phrygians	c.1225-1125 BC (Trojan War)

7.	Syrian	Sea Peoples (probably Anatolian Luwians including Etruscans & Sardinians displaced by Phrygians, & some Achaean Greeks or Cretans, such as the Philistines, displaced by Dorians) c.1225-1190 BC, who ruled as a military aristocracy over the people of Canaan	c.1225-1125 BC

8.	Israelite	Assyrians exacted tribute from Israel: the Assyrians under Shalmaneser III inflicted heavy	c.841-732 BC c.841-732 (Israel) c.841-782 (Judah)

losses on the armies of Israel,
Aram, Phoenicia & Hanath at
the battle of Karkar or Qarqar in
853 BC; & then reached Damascus
in 841, from where Shalmaneser
marched through Israel to Mount
Carmel, as a result of which Jeho
is shown on an obelisk paying
tribute; the Assyrians made Israel
a vassal in 804, & attacked again
in 738, & in 733-2 the Assyrian
Tiglath-pileser III took Gilead &
Galilee from Israel & placed
Israel under his nominee &
vassal Hoshea

9.	Celtic	Romans under Julius Caesar defeated the Helvetii & the Germans in Gaul in 58 BC, & Gaul was Romanized by 50 BC	c.58 BC-AD 52
10.	Iranian	The Roman Emperor Trajan invaded Armenia in 114 & captured Babylonia & Ctesiphon, & carried off the golden throne of the Parthian kings & a daughter of Osroes, the Parthian king; which led to the dissolution of the Parthian State into small countries	c.114-226
11.	European	Ottomans conquered the Christian Byzantine civilization in 1453, ending the union of the Greek & Latin churches (1438-9) & causing	c.1453-1555

Christendom to lose the Greek
Church (to Russia), which, coming
after the Europeanization of
Constantinople during the Crusades
in the 13th C & after a European
crusade organized by Hungary &
Venice in 1444, when
Constantinople was under the
protection of the Roman Church,
was felt as a tremendous blow
throughout Christendom; the
Ottomans retained their Danube
frontier, & having conquered
Serbia (1439), extended their
European conquests by taking
S. Greece (1456-8), Bosnia (1463)
& Wallachia (1475); in view of
the Ottomans' pressure on Europe,
the fall of Christian Constantinople
continued to be felt as a military
blow throughout Christendom for
the rest of the 15th C

12. North-American	Future military blow?	?
13. Byzantine-Russian	Ottomans took over the opposition to the Byzantines after the defeat of the Seljuqs in 1293, occupied Gallipoli in 1354 & gained a foothold in Europe, directly threatening Constantinople at a time when Thrace, Macedonia, Serbia &	c.1354-1462

Bulgaria had won an independence
that would soon be destroyed by
Ottoman invasions

| 14. | Germanic-Scandinavian | Romans (Roman recovery under Aurelian 270-272) | c.270-375 |

| 15. | Andean | Middle Horizon invaders (who destroyed Nazca & Moche cultures) c.500 | c.500-600 |

| 16. | Meso-American | Mayan invaders c.200 | c.200-300 |

| 17. | Arab | Il-Khanate Mongols destroyed the Abbasid Caliphate in Baghdad in 1258, & converted to Islam c.1300; were succeeded by the Mongol Jalayrid Sultanate after the Il Khan line became extinct | c.1258-1358 |

| 18. | African | Arabs who invaded parts of Africa (including the Sudan), tamed the camel & opened up the Sahara | c.640-740 |

| 19. | Indian | Turks' Islamic invasion of part of India, beginning with the Ghurids' defeat of the Ghaznavids in 1150-1151 | c.1150-1236 |

| 20. | S.-E.-Asian | Chams' capture of Khmer capital, Angkor, which began Khmer decline in 1177; Mongols' invasion of Annam (1257-8 & | c.1177-1287 |

1285-8), Champa (1283), &
Burma (1277, 1287); Mongols'
conquest of Burmese Pagan in
1287

21. Japanese	Mongol & Korean army invaded & occupied part of Japan before their ships were destroyed by a typhoon; the same happened in 1281 when a Mongol, N.-Chinese & Korean army, & a S.-Chinese army, invaded but were destroyed by a *kamikaze* (divine wind)	c.1274-1391
22. Oceanian	S. American migration to Polynesia c.1100	c.1100-1200
23. Chinese	1271, Mongol conquest of China which was completed in 1280 & which led to China being occupied by the Mongol Yuan dynasty	c.1271-1398
24. Tibetan	After the secular Gtsang kings conquered the Rin-spungs princes in 1565, the Tumed Mongol leader Altan Khan invaded Tibet in 1578 in support of the third Dge-lugs-pa leader, a military blow that threatened all except the Dge-lugs-pa	c.1565-1642
25. Central-Asian	Juchen-Chin (*Chin* = "Golden"), a Tunguz people north of the	c.1125-1206

23. SECULARIZATION OF BROKEN-DOWN CIVILIZATION, WHEN DEFENSIVE STATE RULES RELIGION

The military blow is a reverse which paralyses the civilization. Defence again becomes paramount and in response to the blow and the ensuing unsettled, disorderly period when order breaks down, the State widens its powers and again acts independently of the religion, and therefore the Light. The military blow causes the civilization to break down because it allows the secular organization of the State to escape from the control of the civilization's religion. This control was weakened by the arrest in the civilization's growth (stage 14), but it had been re-established by the counterthrust (stage 15).

A religion's control over its civilization's secular organization is weakened when, despite the efforts of its mystics, its religion ceases to reflect the Light which is its Central Idea. Preoccupied with its outer situation, the civilization loses its inward vision of the Light and turns worldly. The State thus wins an ascendancy over the civilization's church and the civilization's religion undergoes a secularization. A civilization therefore breaks down when its religion ceases to reflect the Light which is its Central Idea. We can see the process in the following pattern:

Civilization	Process of breakdown during which as a reaction to the foreign threat secular organization (State) dominated metaphysical vision & religion ("Church") (stage 23)	Date after which secular State ruled religion/ "Church" after breakdown
1. Indo-European Kurgan/ Old European	In response to the invasions of the Battle-Axe Kurgans, the Funnel-Neck Beaker Folk's military organization	c.2000-1900 BC

seems to have developed from tribal chiefdoms to embryonic States with tribal assembly places (e.g. Stonehenge) by c.1900 BC, & each "State" seems to have controlled & therefore secularized the religious rites; as the Kurgans intermingled with native cultures, e.g. Beaker culture in France & Britain, the vision of Dyaeus Pitar seems to have become lost

---

2. Mesopotamian

After the Hittite sack of Babylon & the Kassite conquest of Babylonia, the Kassite god of Shuqamuna was made the equal of Marduk, & the State escaped the control of Babylonian religion; Babylonia had secularized the temples c.1962-1600 BC, when the State sold priestly offices with income to individuals & the State was therefore happy to allow itself to be bound by religious ceremonies

c.1590-1490 BC

---

3. Egyptian

In response to the invasions of Hyksos the New Kingdom saw the rise of a new military class, the divine king embodied the State but increasingly texts treated him as human, so that a human held a divine office; the State controlled religion thus secularizing the divine kingship, with the result that after 1085 BC the king ceased to be divine

c.1674-1576 BC

4.	Aegean-Greek	Dorian invasions plunged Greece into its Dark Age; the Peloponnesian palaces were overrun & although literacy temporarily disappeared, the Mycenaean culture continued in a depressed form; there was a change of emphasis & city-states escaped the control of their religious life & became more secularized; by c.900 BC Athens became the cultural centre of Greece	c.1200-1100 BC
5.	Roman	In response to the impending threat from the Germanic tribes, absolute dictators arose & the Roman State escaped the control of its religion, &, indeed controlled Roman religion	c.113-30 BC
6.	Anatolian	In response to the invasion of the Sea Peoples the Phrygian migration of 12th-11th C BC escaped the control of the Hittite religion in the course of settling Western Anatolia & establishing a conquering State	c.1225-1125 BC
7.	Syrian	In response to the invasion of the Sea Peoples & the Philistines, the Canaanite State seems to have escaped the control of its religion in the course of reorganising itself into Canaanite enclaves in N. Palestine, from which grew the Phoenician culture	c.1225-1125 BC
8.	Israelite	In response to the Assyrian invasions	c.841-732 BC

which made Israel a vassal, the State
of Israel escaped the control of the
Israelite religion under Jeroboam II
(who defeated Aram, subjugated
Damascus & extended Israel's
authority to Lebo-hamath in the
north & in Transjordan as far as
the Dead Sea) & fell under corrupt
pagan influences prior to the Assyrian
conquest of Israel (738-721 BC) &
annexation of Israel in 722 BC, while
Judah rose under Uzziah

9.	Celtic	In response to the Roman invasions of Gaul & Britain under Julius Caesar the Gallic & Celtic British States escaped the control of Celtic religion in the course of resisting the Romans	58 BC-AD 52
10.	Iranian	As a result of the Roman invasion, the Iranian State was mobilized & Trajan was driven out in 117; the Kushan Empire then threatened from the east, & the Romans returned in 161 & recaptured Armenia & again destroyed Ctesiphon; there was a new Roman invasion under Caracalla c.213; during this troubled time the Parthian State escaped the control of the Iranian religion	c.114-226
11.	European	In response to the Ottoman invasion of Constantinople, which was under	c.1453-1555

the protection of the Roman Church,
the Holy Roman State escaped the
control of its religion & Popes
became more secular; the Reformation
(c.1510-1550) detached States from
Rome & gave rise to secular States
in charge of their Church (like Henry
VIII's after his dissolution of the
monasteries & appropriation of their
proceeds); the Renaissance secularization of 1500-50 strengthened in the
17th century when scientific
materialism replaced the Reformation
outlook & when the British Divine
Right of Kings was ended by
Cromwell's execution of Charles I

12.	North-American	Has not happened yet	
13.	Byzantine-Russian	In response to the Ottoman invasions of the Byzantine Empire, as a result of which the Byzantine Empire became a Turkish vassal state in 1373, paying tribute – the Ottomans occupied Gallipoli in 1354 at a time when the Serbs had revolted under Dushan, & between 1363 & 1389 they conquered Thrace, Macedonia, Serbia & Bulgaria (all independent in 1354) & in 1444 Hungary, controlling the Balkans – the Byzantine State escaped the control of its religion; alarmed that Western Popes refrained from sending	c.1354-1462

help as the Byzantine Church was in schism from Rome from 1054, it accepted the authority of Rome in 1439 to obtain Western support; & was rejected by the Byzantine (& Russian) people & clergy, it had a further secularizing effect before the Ottoman capture of Constantinople in 1453

14.	Germanic-Scandinavian	In response to the Roman recovery of c.270-272, when Aurelian defeated the Alamanni and Juthungi who had invaded N. Italy, the Germanic tribes' *comitatus* States escaped the control of their religion in the course of preparing for worldly hegemony over the Romans, & the resultant secularization led to their widespread adoption of Arianism in the 4th C	c.270-375
15.	Andean	In response to the Middle Horizon invaders the Nazca/Moche States escaped the control of their religion in the course of growing the new Huari culture	c.500-600
16.	Meso-American	In response to the Mayan invaders, the Meso-American States escaped the control of the defunct Late Formative religion in the course of growing the new Mayan culture	c.200-300
17.	Arab	In response to the Mongol invasion,	c.1258-1358

the Ottoman State in Bithynia escaped
the control of its religion in the course
of its worldly military onslaught on
Mongol & Byzantine territories which
eventually led to the Ottoman capture
of N.W. Anatolia & Gallipoli

18. African	In response to the Arab invasions, the African States that were penetrated by Muslims escaped the control of African religion in the course of becoming Muslim & preparing to build worldly trading empires, notably the Kumbi trading empire	c.640-740
19. Indian	In response to the Turks who set up a Delhi Sultanate, the Indian States escaped the control of their religion in the course of attempting to cope with the secular threat	c.1150-1236
20. S.-E.-Asian	In response to the Cham & Mongol invasions the S.-E.-Asian States escaped the control of their religions in the course of restoring their worldly independence	c.1177-1287
21. Japanese	In response to the Mongol & Korean invasions, the Kamakura State raised its military expenditure, which under-mined its economic stability; & escaped the control of its Buddhist religion in the course of fighting for its life, which had a further secularizing	c.1274-1391

effect

22.	Oceanian	In response to the S. American invasions, the Oceanian States escaped the control of their religion in the course of establishing a new Oceanian culture	c.1100-1200
23.	Chinese	In response to the invasion of the Mongols, the Chinese escaped the control of their religion as the Mongols encouraged first Taoism & then Tibetan (not Chinese) Buddhism & thereby alienated & secularized Chinese support for what came to be known as these "Mongol religions"	1271-1398
24.	Tibetan	In response to the Mongol invasion, the Gtsang Tibetans escaped the control of their religion in the course of recovering their worldly independence from the Mongols, & in 1642 the Dge-lugs-pa became both spiritual & temporal rulers of Tibet, with secularizing consequences	c.1565-1642
25.	Central-Asian	In response to the Juchen-Chin invasions, the Mongols escaped the control of their religion in the course of uniting All the Mongols into a secular State that was poised for empire	c.1125-1206

24. REVIVAL OF ANOTHER CIVILIZATION'S PAST CULTURE

Having lost its confidence as a result of the military blow, the civilization now turns away from its own culture and revives the past culture of another civilization, which is either that of the deliverer of the military blow or a civilization the deliverer of the blow has been in contact with or one that contrasts with what is perceived as the "uncivilised" values of the deliverer of the blow; as we see from the following pattern:

	Civilization	Revival of past culture	Date	Civilization from which culture is revived
1.	Indo-European Kurgan/Old European	Battle-Axe Kurgans had acquired Sumerian-Akkadian ideas c.2400 BC, & revived Ogma	c.2000-1900 BC	Mesopotamian
2.	Mesopotamian	Following the Hittite invasion of Babylon in c.1590 & Hittite penetration into Assyria, there was a revival of Anatolian Hittite culture in Assyria, & in due course Assyria won free from the Mitanni with Hittite help (c.1350); the Kassites looked towards Hyksos Egypt (the Kassite Ulamburiash negotiated with Egypt c.1450, & Kadashman-Enlith & Burnaburish II corresponded	c.1590-1490 BC	Anatolian

with Amenhotep III &
Akhenaton, importing the
Egyptian styles & Light)

3.	Egyptian	Following the invasion of the Canaanite Hyksos, who ruled from Avaris (the nearest coastal Egyptian city to Canaan), there was a revival of Syrian Canaanite culture with Baal-like Egyptian bulls, & Egypt, Palestine & Syria became one kingdom	c.1674-1576 BC	Syrian
4.	Aegean-Greek	Following the invasion of Luwian-speaking Anatolians (?) (Sea Peoples) c.1200 BC & the migration of Greeks from Attica to Ionia c.1100 BC, there was a revival of Anatolian Hittite culture	c.1200-1100 BC	Anatolian
5.	Roman	Following the invasion of the Germanic tribes there was renewed interest in the more civilised values of Greece, which the Romans had absorbed & by 146 BC there was a revival of Greek culture which later led to the Greek Renaissance of the Augustan Age (c.31 BC-AD 14) in which Virgil, Horace & Livy imitated the writing of classical Greece	c.113-30 BC	Aegean-Greek

6.	Anatolian	The Mycenaean settlement of Aeolia & Ionia brought a revival of Mycenaean culture which affected the Luwians & Phrygians	c.1225-1125 BC	Aegean-Greek
7.	Syrian	The Hittite rule in Syria before 1225 & the setting up of Neo-Hittite states after 1180 brought a revival of Anatolian culture	c.1225-1125 BC	Anatolian
8.	Israelite	As the Phoenicians & Aramaeans were allies against the Assyrians from 853 BC, there was a revival of Syrian culture & the religion of Baal/Melqart spread in the north & through royally sponsored cults in the south; the Canaanite Elohim of the Torah spread under Uzziah (783-742) when Judah re-established the Red Sea trade with Phoenician help	c.841-732 BC	Syrian
9.	Celtic	Following the Celts' conflict with the Romans in Gaul & Britain, there was a revival of Roman culture in the Celtic lands & the Celts became increasingly Romanized	c.58 BC-AD 52	Roman
10.	Iranian	The Roman conquest of Iran	c.114-	Aegean-Greek

	brought a revival of interest in Macedonia, Rome's traditional enemy, & therefore of Hellenistic Greek culture which had swamped Iran after 330 BC	226		
11. European	The Ottoman conquest of Constantinople sacked the libraries & a flow of Roman & Greek manuscripts (sent by Byzantine Humanists) reached the West, notably Italy, which revived interest in classical learning & brought about the Humanist Renaissance & Classicism; there had been an earlier trickle of Arabic translations of Greek & Roman texts seized when the Muslimss conquered Alexandria and transported to Spanish al-Andalus, notably Toledo, whence some of which reached Oxford	c.1453-1555	Aegean-Greek & Roman
12. North-American	Revival of European culture in the future?		European?
13. Byzantine-Russian	The Ottoman invasions brought appeals for Western help &, in 1444, a new Latin crusade, & with memories of the Venetian Latin rule in	c.1354-1462	European (Italian)

Constantinople (1204-1261)
there was a revival of interest
in Italian Rome & Byzantine
Greece & of its religious
culture within an Orthodox
Byzantine context, especially
in Greece (at Mistra & Mount
Athos where Gregory Palamas
was a monk & where there had
been a revival of Hesychasm,
the perception in quiet of God
as Light) from 1260-1320;
Greek Byzantine painting &
philosophy influenced the
Slavs & Russia, especially
after the fall of Constantinople
in 1453, until Greece was
Ottomanised in 1456-8

| 14. | Germanic-Scandinavian | The Roman recovery after c.270 brought a revival of Roman culture that led to the Germanic tribes becoming Arians & achieving the status of *foederati* | c.270-375 | Roman |
| 15. | Andean | The Middle Horizon invasion of c.500 brought a revival of Tiahuanaco which may have been inspired by the Oceanian civilization from Easter Island or by re-discovering the Andean civilization's Egyptian | c.500-600 | Oceanian(?)/ Egyptian (?) |

origins

16. Meso-American	The Mayan invasion of c.200 brought a revival of Teotihuacan, whose Avenue of the Dead & Pyramid of the Sun may have been inspired by the Egyptian civilization (see *The Light of Civilization*, pp37, 252-253)	c.200-300	Egyptian(?)
17. Arab	The Mongol invasion by the Khanate of Persia led to a Central-Asian renaissance & after the Il-Khanate's conversion c.1300, to a Muslim cultural revival, which saw a golden age of Sufism & which spread from Spain & Morocco & reached Malaya, sub-Saharan Africa, India, Southern Russia & Nubia	c.1258-1358	Central Asian, Iranian
18. African	The Arab conquests brought a revival of Arab culture	640-740	Arab
19. Indian	The Turkish conquest extended Islam into India & brought a revival of Arab culture	c.1150-1236	Arab
20. S.-E.-Asian	The Indianised Cham invasion of 1177 & the Mongol invasion of N. China in 1211	c.1177-1287	Indian

& of Theravada Burma in 1277 & 1287 brought a revival of interest in Indian culture & in Burmese Theravada Buddhism (as opposed to Chinese Mahayana Buddhism)

---

21. Japanese — The Mongol & Korean invasions brought a revival of traditional, pre-Mongol Chinese culture from the Sung, Yuan & Ming periods, & anti-Mongolism expressed itself among the military *samurai* as Chinese Ch'an (which had survived the Chinese suppression of Buddhism of 843-845 & which was introduced in Japan in 1191 as Zen) in the five Zen monasteries of Kyoto — c.1274-1391 — Chinese

---

22. Oceanian — The S. American invasion of Oceania led to a revival of interest in the Andean culture of Peru — c.1100-1200 — Andean

---

23. Chinese — The Mongol conquest opened up trade routes to the Near East & brought a revival of Arab culture, particularly in science & technology — c.1271-1398 — Arab

24.	Tibetan	The Mongol interventions of 1578 & 1640 brought a revival of interest in Mongolian culture, & in the Central-Asian civilization; the title Dalai ("Oceanwide") Lama, conferred by the Tumed Mongol leader Altan Khan, was a Mongol title	c.1565-1642	Central Asian
25.	Central-Asian	The Juchen-Chin who inherited China from the Khitan supported the Tatars, not All the Mongols, but there was still a revival of interest in Buddhist China which was linked to an interest in Tibetan Buddhism	c.1125-1206	Chinese

25. FURTHER RESISTANCE TO HERESY LEADS TO CIVIL WAR

The heresy rose to prominence with the rise of a particular people or dynasty within the civilization. This heresy now meets further resistance from the established rulers in whose hands the civilization has broken down. As they struggle to reverse the effects of the military blow with their new secularization, they are aware that their own religion and Light have lost power, and they try to suppress the growing influence of the heresy, which is beginning to look like an alternative religion. They fight a civil war with the new people or dynasty, who win.

In Europe Roman Catholics resisted new Protestants. The Inquisition, which began in Spain after the *Reconquista*, spread and imposed Catholicism by torture and *autos-da-fé*. In Russia, pro-German, pro-Roman Catholic Muscovite princes who had turned against the Mongols opposed a new heresy that arose with Ivan III.

The Kievian Rus had been converted to Byzantine Christianity in 988 and had been united into a single State c.1000 by Vladmimir I. In 1240 the Mongols overran the southern Principalities, sacked Kiev and established a Mongol commercial empire under the Khanate of the Golden Horde, whereas the Novgorodian north (where the emphasis of Russian life had already shifted following the sack of Kiev by Asiatic nomads, the Polovtsy in 1093) remained intact and merely became a Mongol vassal. It became a flourishing German trade centre, and the grand duchy of Moscow collected tribute for the Mongols. When the Turkic Central-Asian Timur or Tamerlane destroyed Tatar rule in 1395-6, and weakened the Mongol hold, the Muscovite princes gradually expelled the Mongols, taking their domains along with the Novgorodian north. In the conflict for the Muscovite succession the pro-German and therefore pro-Roman (as Germany was within the Holy Roman Empire) commercially-minded claimants or *boyars* resisted the Byzantinist "Moscow first" heresy that surfaced with Ivan III.

After the fall of Constantinople to the Ottomans in 1453, when Hagia Sophia became a mosque (as a result of an Anatolian civil war that at first sight replaced the Byzantines in Anatolia by the Ottomans), the old Byzantine Turkish nobility were executed or exiled, many to Russia, and the grand duchy of Moscow continued the Byzantine Light. In the long civil war for the Muscovite succession Vasily II's pro-Byzantine house triumphed over Vasily I's brother, Yuri of Galich (who led the Muscovite princes or *boyars*), and Ivan III succeeded him in 1462. From 1453 members of the Byzantine imperial family arrived from Constantinople as refugees, and Ivan III married Sophia, the neice of Constantine Palaeologus, the last Byzantine Emperor who was killed in 1453, to express his continuation of the Byzantine civilization from Moscow which he called "the third Rome" (the first Rome being "heretical", and Byzantine, now Ottoman-occupied, Constantinople being the second Rome).

The victory of the new people – the Protestants in Europe, the Byzantine Russians within the Byzantine-Russian civilization – ensures that they inherit the limelight from the now eclipsed established rulers, who swiftly slide into oblivion. I can summarize this stage in the following pattern:

Civilization	Date & details of further resistance to heresy (see stage 18)	Civil war: new people named first (stage 25)
1. Indo-European Kurgan/ Old European	c.2000 BC Funnel-Neck Beaker Folk resisted the Battle-Axe Kurgan god, Ogma	c.1900 BC? Battle-Axe Kurgans replaced Funnel-Neck Beaker Folk
2. Mesopotamian	From c.1590 BC the Kassites, whose god Shuqamuna was made the equal of Marduk, resisted Ashur, the god of the Assyrians	c.1490 BC, the Assyrians seem to have fought and replaced the Kassites & the Assyrian Puzur-Ashur III made a border treaty with Babylonia
3. Egyptian	From c.1650 BC Hyksos resisted Theban Amon	c.1580 BC, Thebans replaced Hyksos
4. Aegean-Greek	11th C BC resistance to Dorian Apollo by the native Mycenaean Greeks or by the first invaders who had settled	c.1100 BC, Dorian Greeks overran and replaced Mycenaeans/Sea Peoples invaders
5. Roman	2nd-1st C BC, after Scipio Africanus, the later Republic resisted deification for pagan sun-worship & the foreign cult of Mithra (imported during the Second Punic War)	49-30 BC, pro-posthumous deification Caesarians resisted the Republic which was overthrown and replaced by the Caesarian Principate; the outlawed Julius Caesar's civil war against the Republican Senate's Pompey was followed by the civil war

of his heir, the pro-Apollo Octavian, against the pro-Dionysus Mark Antony, who allegedly committed suicide with Cleopatra (who embodied Isis) in 30 BC

6.	Anatolian	13th C BC, Hittites & Sea Peoples resisted Cybele of the Phrygians	After c.1225 BC, (& the Trojan War) & by c.1125 BC Phrygians from Macedonia & Thrace) swept aside and replaced Hittites/Sea Peoples
7.	Syrian	13th C BC, Hittites & Sea Peoples resisted Baal of the Canaanites	By c.1125 BC, Phoenicians replaced Hittites/Sea Peoples, & continued Canaanite culture, freeing themselves from the military aristocracy of the Sea People Philistines who settled further south, while the Aramaeans (inner Syrians) spread into Mesopotamia
8.	Israelite	From c.841 BC Assyrians menaced the northern kingdom of Israel & the Israelites became Assyrian vassals & resisted the *Deuteronomy*-based Torah of	733-732 BC, Jews of Judah replaced the Assyrians: Ahaz of Judah invoked Assyrian help against an anti- Assyrian

	the Jews of Judah		Aramaean- Israelite coalition (2 *Kings* 16.6-7) & in the ensuing civil war the Assyrians conquered Israel & made the coastal, northern & Transjordanian parts of Israel into Assyrian provinces, leaving the Jews of Judah supreme
9.	Celtic	1st C BC-1st C AD, Esus/ Jesus of Celts/Christian Celts resisted by Romans underCaesar/ Claudius	AD 42-52, Christian Celts (Culdees) & British Silures resisted Roman British (as a result of which Caractacus lived in Rome), withdrew and replaced Romans in their fringe areas
10.	Iranian	2nd C AD, the Parthians, who followed Anahita, resisted Ahura Mazda	213-226, the Zoroastrian Sasanians from Persis (modern Fars) replaced the Parthians in Iran when Ardashir, whose ancestors had kept the Anahid Fire (i.e. Light) at a fire-temple, defeated the Parthian Artabanus V in battle
11.	European	After the Spanish *Reconquista* (1492), which counterbalanced	1546-1555, Renaissance Humanists and German

the fall of Constantinople to Islam, Isabella and Ferdinand set up the Inquisition to eliminate heresy, burn non-Catholics and expel Muslims who would not convert; Catholic Europe was divided by the French invasion of Italy under Charles VIII, 1494-5, & in 1495 the Pope formed a Holy League which included Venice & Aragon (Spain); wars lasted from 1494 to 1517 & spread Italian Renaissance Humanism throughout Europe, & as Protestantism (belief in a personal God outside the Catholic Church and adoption) of Graeco-Roman heretical ideas) developed out of Humanism, from 1520 Roman Catholics resisted Protestantism, e.g. in 1535 princes' Protestantism split the Holy Roman Empire (which included Italy) & resisted Spanish Catholicism, which permitted Protestantism at the Religious Peace of Augsburg, 1555: Protestant Humanism replaced Catholicism in some countries

12.	North-American	Has not yet happened	
13.	Byzantine-Russian	The Muscovite Russian princes or *boyars*, having broken away from their former Mongol Masters, resisted the Byzantinist "Moscow-first as third Rome" heresy that surfaced with Ivan III and which declared Roman Catholicism to be heretical (See pp173-174)	1453-1462, Byzantine Russians under Vasily II replaced Muscovite Russians under Vasily I's brother, Yuri of Galich; in 1462 Ivan III succeeded, having married Sophia, the niece of Constantine

			Palaeologus, the last Byzantine Emperor to express his continuation of the Byzantine civilization from Moscow, "the third Rome" (See pp173-174)

| 14. | Germanic-Scandinavian | The Romans resisted Arianism (that Christ was human & not divine) from 325-350, & again from 364, when, despite Valens' Arianism, there was persecution of Arians in the east | c.350-380, Germanic tribes displaced by Huns replaced Romans in some territories: during the civil war between Constantine's sons, the main Germanic tribes invaded each others' territories c.350, e.g. the Alemanni (who went on to ravage Gaul), the Burgundians & the Franks; & from 372-375, the Huns expanded, occupying territory of Germanic tribes, crushing the Visigoths & enslaving the Gepidae |

| 15. | Andean | Before 500 the Doorway god with rayed headdress, who is found everywhere at Middle Horizon sites, is not found, suggesting that he belonged to the Middle Horizon people & would have been resisted by the | c.575-600, Peruvian Middle Horizon people replaced Early Intermediate Period people at Tiahuanaco & Huari (Middle Horizon were presumably a new |

		Early Intermediate Period people	people who triumphed in a civil war)
16.	Meso-American	Before AD 200 the Mayan Fire Serpent/Kinich Ahau (or Itzamna) would have been resisted by the Late Formative Feathered Serpent, & both Serpents alternate in the Temple of Quetzlcoatl at Teotihuacan	c.275-300, the Early Classic Mayan replaced Late Formative culture in S.-E. Meso-America & at Teotihuacan (a new people triumphing in a civil war)
17.	Arab	The militant orthodox Abbasid-Seljuq Islamic faith of the Ottomans was inspired by Sufi orders, e.g. the Turkish Shi'ite Bektashiyah & the Mawlawiyah, whose leader invested the Ottoman sultan with a sword & which inspired classical Turkish poetry, music & art; this Sufism was resisted by the Byzantines, the Mongols & by the Mamluk Sultanate, which traditionally followed the Ahmadiyah Sufi order	c.1331-1358, Orhan, the Ottoman Sultan, took much of N.W. Anatolia from and re-placed the Byzantines & Mongols in what was in geographical terms a civil war, & eventually captured Gallipoli (& married Theodora, daughter of the Byzantine Emperor)
18.	African	Arabian invasions of N. Africa began c.640, & Arabs soon crossed the Sahara; Islam was resisted by the Africans at first	c.740, Muslim Africans dominated and replaced Africans of indigenous religion in the north & to the south of the Sahara
19.	Indian	Islam was first resisted in the	1206-1236, Turkish

	8th century, before c.998-1030 when Turkish Abbasids moved into Ghazna (now in Afghanistan) & attacked N. India	Ghurids (Shansabanis of Ghur, rivals of the Ghaznavids) defeated and replaced the Ghaznavids/ Abbasids after fighting a civil war against many Hindu chiefs in the course of setting up a Delhi sultanate in 1236
20. S.-E.-Asian	In the 11th C there was resistance to Burmese Theravada Buddhism in much of S.-E. Asia, which was Hindu or Mahayana Buddhist	c.1250-1287, Indianized S.-E.-Asians/Indian-Burmese Theravada Buddhism replaced Hinduism & Mahayana Buddhism in Thai king-doms, Cambodia, Laos & S. Vietnam after civil wars
21. Japanese	There was resistance to military *samurai* Zen Buddhism by the two rival Emperors	c.1378-1391, the Ashikaga shogun Yoshimitsu imposed his bakufu (military dictator-ship) after a split in the imperial family created rival Emperors in Kyoto & Yoshino; he replaced the Emperors & erected the Golden Pavilion & declared himself to Ming China as King of Japan

22.	Oceanian	The S.-American Sun-god would have been resisted at first by the Polynesians	c.1175-1200, S. Americans (long ears) dominated and replaced Polynesians (short ears) presumably after a civil war
23.	Chinese	The Mongols resisted Neo-Confucianism	c.1368-1398, Ming dynasty expelled and replaced the Mongol Yuan dynasty after a civil war
24.	Tibetan	Tibetan Buddhism of the Dge-lugs-pa began c.1409 & was resisted by their rivals the Kar-ma-pa sect, & after 1565 repressed by the Gtsang kings	c.1620-1642, Dalai Lamas gained Mongol recognition & armed support in 1578, & in 1642 replaced the Gtsang kings & their Karma-pa supporters when Gushi Khan, a Khoshotd Mongol, invaded Tibet at the appeal of the fifth Dalai Lama's minister & enthroned the fifth Dalai Lama as the temporal (i.e. secular) ruler of Tibet
25.	Central-Asian	Tibetan Buddhism was resisted in 12th C by the Khitan & Juchen-Chin	c.1185-1206, Genghis Khan wrested power from other clans in a civil war; All the Mongols replaced the Khitan & Juchen-Chin

26. New People or Dynasty/Power now Hold Limelight
27. Heresy is Grafted on to Central Idea

The disappearance of the Light in this worldly time reflects itself in a major shift of emphasis in the civilization's religion, in which a new people or dynasty or power takes over the heresy and grafts it onto the civilization's Central Idea. The pattern is as follows:-

Civilization	New people or dynasty/power who now hold limelight (stage 26)	New religious focus of civilization: heresy grafted on to Central Idea (stage 27)
1. Indo-European Kurgan/ Old European	Battle-Axe Kurgans or Bell-Beaker Folk (who built Stonehenge III & perhaps came from the Rhine-Elbe region of Germany & had links with Greece as amber bead spacers from Wessex have been found in the shaft graves of Mycenae)	Ogma or Herakles, e.g. at Cerne Abbas c.1900 BC if the giant was originally Kurgan & not one of the following:Corina, the companion of a Trojan prince expelled from Italy; an Iron Age fertility god; or a Roman-British celebration of the Emperor Commodus (AD 180-192), who entered the gladiatorial arena & took the title of the divine Hercules Romanus; or a Roman-British celebration of the triumph of the Heraclii through Constantine (c.324)
2. Mesopotamian	Assyrians	Ashur c.1490 BC
3. Egyptian	New Kingdom rulers in Thebes	Amon (rock tombs/Egyptian *Book of the Dead*)
4. Aegean-Greek	Dorian Greeks	Dorian Apollo

(from Balkans?)

5.	Roman	Caesarian Principate	Cult of posthumous deification of Emperors as *divi*, not *dei* like the Olympian gods: e.g., Augustus as avatar of laurelled Apollo/*Sol Indiges*; Claudius of Cybele; Vespasian of Serapis; Domitian of Osiris; & Commodus of Hercules; (the Emperor had spiritual power as Pontifex Maximus as well as temporal power)
6.	Anatolian	Phrygians (in N. Anatolia, while Luwian Neo-Hittites held S. Anatolia)	Cybele
7.	Syrian	Phoenicians	Melqart/Astarte or Ashtoreth (liberated from Hittite control)
8.	Israelite	Jews of Judah	Torah Elohim of the Pentateuch (source E)
9.	Celtic	Christian Celts (who withdrew to the fringes of Roman Britain & Gaul & who were in touch with Ireland)	Esus (or Yesu) as Jesus
10.	Iranian	Sasanians	Ahura Mazda/Zoroastrian Fire-cults (The ancestors of Ardashir had kept the *Adur-Anahid*, the Anahid Fire, at the fire-temple at

Istakhr or Istaxr)

11. European	Renaissance Humanists (e.g. Ficino, Erasmus)	Protestantism (belief in a personal God outside the Catholic Church and adoption of Graeco-Roman heretical ideas) within a context of Classicism
12. North-American	?	Coming Universalism? (from New Age roots which were anticipated by the 1776 Illuminatists, see pp500-508): gnosis of a universal God perceived or experienced as Light is central to all civilizations
13. Byzantine-Russian	Byzantinist Russian Grand Duchy of Moscow	Byzantine Christ of "third Rome" (i.e. Moscow, the last bastion of true Orthodoxy); Ivan III took his architectural style from Rome, e.g. the Italianate Kremlin churches with their catacomb-like murals & haloed Light, a style his Byzantine wife knew from the Byzantine Italian revival (see stage 25), & created an Italianate Byzantinism
14. Germanic-Scandinavian	Germanic tribes displaced by Huns & fleeing into Roman Empire	Arian Christianity (adopted from Romans)
15. Andean	Peruvian Middle Horizon (Huari in Peru/Tiahuanaco)	Doorway god (with rayed headdress)

16.	Meso-American	Mayans	Kinich Ahau, alias Itzamna, Lord of the Fire
17.	Arab	Ottomans from Central Asia	Islamic Allah based on Iranian Theosophical Sufism/Sunnism
18.	African	Muslims	African Allah
19.	Indian	Muslims (Turkish Ghurids)	Indian Allah
20.	S.-E.-Asian	Indianised S.-E. Asians	Sinhalese Theravada Buddhism/ Indian Tantrism/Islam (brought by merchants from India)
21.	Japanese	Ashikaga/Muromachi	Zen Buddhism
22.	Oceanian	S.-American Long Ears	S.-American Sun-god (prototype of Inti, the ancestor of the nearby Peruvian Incas from c.1460?)
23.	Chinese	Chinese Ming ("Brightness") dynasty	Neo-Confucianism (Ch'eng-Chu School of Nature & Principle)
24.	Tibetan	Dge-lugs-pa's Dalai Lamas	Atisan Tibetan Buddhism of Dge-lugs-pa in which the mind (*sems*) was Light, with succession based on the reincarnation of the Living Buddha as the Dalai Lama
25.	Central-Asian	All the Mongols after Genghis Khan & his successors	Tibetan Buddhism

28. New People's Heretical Renewal of the Light and Central Idea

When the Light is strong it is renewed every generation, and when it is no longer renewed the civilization suffers a decline. The new people's renewal of the Light gives it – and the civilization – a new lease of life (see pp191, 394-412 for further discussion) but whereas the heresy they graft onto the Central Idea brings freshness the change brought about by the heresy weakens the Central Idea, which can now be restated as follows:

Civilization	Dates of new people's renewal	How heresy renewed Light & civilization's Central Idea
1. Indo-European Kurgan/ Old European	c.1900-1750 BC	Ogma linked Heaven & Earth & affected crops & everyday life through the Light in Fire-temples
2. Mesopotamian	c.1490-1000 BC	Ashur affected growth of crops & everyday life through the Light
3. Egyptian	c.1576-1085 BC	Amon affected flooding of Nile, growth of crops & everyday life through the Light
4. Aegean-Greek	c.1100-750 BC	Apollo affected growth of crops & everyday life through the Light in Fire-temples
5. Roman	c.30 BC-AD 270	Cult god through divine Emperor's "genius" or avatar affected growth of crops & everyday life through the Light in Fire-temples
6. Anatolian	c.1125-900 BC	Cybele affected growth of crops &

everyday life through the Light

7.	Syrian	c.1125-980 BC	Melqart/Astarte affected growth of crops & everyday life through the Light
8.	Israelite	c.732-640 BC	Elohim affected growth of crops & everyday life through the Light
9.	Celtic	AD c.52-313	Esus/Jesus affected growth of crops & everyday life through the Light in Druid oak-grove Fire-temples
10.	Iranian	c.226-364	Ahura Mazda affected growth of crops & everyday life through the Light in Fire-temples
11.	European	c.1555-1778	Personal Protestant God/Christ affected growth of crops & everyday life through the Light during individual prayer outside the authority of the Catholic Church; Classical writings of Protestant Metaphysical poets, Counter-Reformation's renewal of the Light in Classical/Baroque art c.1600-1750
12.	North-American	Has not happened yet	
13.	Byzantine-Russian	c.1462-1689	Russian Orthodox Christ affected growth of crops & everyday life through the Tsar ("Emperor",

"Caesar")/Russian Light (which had
arrived from the Byzantine Light via
Mount Athos) in monasteries

14.	Germanic- Scandinavian	c.375-476	Arian (human) Christ affected growth of crops & everyday life through the Light of Odin (now Arianized)
15.	Andean	c.600-1200	Doorway god affected growth of crops & everyday life through the Light (faded c.1000)
16.	Meso- American	c.300-900	Kinich Ahau (or Itzamna) affected growth of crops & everyday life through the Light
17.	Arab	c.1358-1683	Sufi/Sunni Allah affected growth of crops & everyday life through the Light known in prayer in mosques (The Abbasid-Seljuq Islamic faith of the Ottomans turned Sunni in the face of anti-Ottoman attacks by the Iranian Safavids)
18.	African	c.740-1500	African Allah affected growth of crops & everyday life through the Light known in communal prayer
19.	Indian	c.1236-1526	Indian Allah affected growth of crops & everyday life through the Light known in prayer in mosques
20.	S.-E.-Asian	c.1287-1550	Theravada-Buddhist Enlightenment gave oneness with growth of crops

& everyday life through the Light

21.	Japanese	c.1391-1573	Zen-Buddhist Enlightenment gave oneness with the growth of crops & everyday life through the Light
22.	Oceanian	c.1200-1500	The Sun-god affected growth of crops & everyday life through the Light
23.	Chinese	c.1398-1644	Neo-Confucianism drew on Ch'an's Sudden Enlightenment & held that "Principle is one but its manifestations are many" (Cheng I); Principle & Nature gave oneness with the crops & everyday life through the Light
24.	Tibetan	c.1642-1720	Tibetan-Buddhist Enlightenment gave oneness with the growth of crops & everyday life through the Light
25.	Central-Asian	c.1206-1370	Tibetan-Buddhist Enlightenment gave oneness with the growth of crops & everyday life through the Light

THE NEW PEOPLE'S RENEWAL OF CIVILIZATIONS

The new people expand into empire and renew their civilization, but are challenged when a sect secedes – and is persecuted and crushed. Scientific materialism weakens the new people's vision and further expansion into empire overstretches them.

29. GEOGRAPHICAL EXPANSION AS SUBSTITUTE FOR GROWTH/RELIGION

The military blow has come as a renewed shock to the civilization, which seeks to reverse it through a territorial expansion. The new people, with a new heretical emphasis on their religion, seek to recover their former growth round a renewed heretical interpretation of the Central Idea of the Light. This is accompanied by a revival in the Universalist outlook. The new people find that their outer expansion is a substitute for growth and for the inner religion, and there is classicism in art in which the mind and soul are in balance. It overextends the civilization and has a cosmopolitanizing and therefore secularizing effect. The pattern of expansion is as follows:

Civilization	Date of new people's attempt at renewal of Light through heresy grafted onto Central Idea (see stage 27), & details of geographical expansion (substitute for growth) & overextension
1. Indo-European Kurgan/ Old European	c.1900-1750 BC?, Battle-Axe expansion (post-Saxon Thuringian) in W. Europe e.g. to Britain, Spain, Sardinia, Corsica & Italy
2. Mesopotamian	c.1490-1000 BC, growth of the First Assyrian Empire (founded c.1350 BC by Ashur-uballit, the first to name Assyria the Land of Ashur) at the expense of the Mitannians, Urartu, the Hittites & Babylon while the Aramaeans of S. Syria spread into Mesopotamia, absorbed the Kassite Kingdom of Babylon (which had been established c.1450 BC) & destroyed the Elamites c.1155, & some Aramaean tribes settled in the south as Chaldeans; Second Assyrian Empire founded by Tiglath-pileser I (c.1115-1077 BC) expanded to Syria, Babylon, Palestine & Egypt, wiping out the Aramaeans

3.	Egyptian	c.1576-1085 BC, New Kingdom Egyptian Empire to South & in Asia which began with Ahmose's imperialism & Thutmose III's expansion into Syria, as a result of which culture became cosmopolitan & secular
4.	Aegean-Greek	c.1100-750 BC, Greek colonizing after the Trojan War in the ruins of Hittite Empire in Anatolia (Ionia to south & Aeolia to north) by refugees displaced by Dorians from Pylos & Boeotia who gathered in Attica & founded Miletus & Ephesus; & in the Mediterranean (including the Achaeans who migrated to Cyprus & the Philistines who migrated from Minoan Crete to Palestine & became the Palestinians); the colonies lasted through the Early Archaic (Proto-Geometric & Geometric) period
5.	Roman	c.30 BC-AD 270, the early Roman Empire under the Julio-Claudians, Flavians, Antonines & Severans until disintegration of 235-270; expansion after Caesar's campaigns into Gaul, Britain, Dacia, Armenia, Assyria & Mesopotamia, reaching its greatest extent under Hadrian; the Empire was not seriously threatened until the Germanic Marcomanni & Quadi & the Sarmatian Iazyges crossed the Danube into N. Italy from 167 to 175, & expansion made Rome cosmopolitan
6.	Anatolian	c.1125-900 BC, Phrygian Empire with Luwian Neo-Hittites in S. Anatolia until the Assyrians pushed westwards
7.	Syrian	c.1125-980 BC (to David's defeat of the Philistines), Phoenicians, hemmed in by Neo-Hittites, Aramaeans, Philistines & Israelites colonized westwards, especially in N. Africa, under Melqart or Baal Hammon, the god of Tyre, while the Aramaeans spread from inner Syria into Mesopotamia under Baal-Hadad

8.	Israelite	c.732-640 BC, Judah's counterthrust which had begun under the expansionist Uzziah (who defeated the Arabs, Meunites, Ammonites & Philistines & restored the Red Sea trade) continued under the pro-Assyrian Ahaz (who introduced an Assyrian altar in the Temple at Jerusalem) & under his son Hezekiah (who purged the Jewish religion of Assyrian, Aramaean & Canaanite contamination), after which Judah became an Assyrian vassal
9.	Celtic	AD c.52-313, withdrawal of Celts before Romans, expansion of Culdees' Celtic Christian Empire on Celtic fringes of Roman Britain, Gaul & Ireland, & conversion of Roman Britain in 156; persecuted by the Romans until Constantine's conversion c.313 BC
10.	Iranian	c.226-364, expansion of Sasanian Empire which conquered & enlarged the Parthian Empire including Oman, part of India & Armenia; it expanded into the western part of the Kushan Empire & expanded through conflicts with Rome until Jovian abandoned much of Mesopotamia & Armenia to the Sasanians
11.	European	c.1555-1778, expansion of Renaissance Humanist Europe after the Reformation: from c.1500, voyages to discover new lands; from c.1600, early colonial settlements founded a trade empire in N. America (including Canada), W. Indies & India; from c.1680 Western capitalism created Industrial Revolution & a Mercantile Empire; England's union with Wales and Scotland, Habsburg rule in Bohemia, Polish Commonwealth
12.	North-American	Has not happened yet
13.	Byzantine-Russian	c.1462-1689, expansion of Byzantinist Russian Empire as Republic of Novgorod's trading empire became the Great

Principality of Moscow under Ivan III, who finally expelled the Mongols from Central Russia & annexed the Novgorodian territories, & under Ivan IV, who annexed the Mongol domains from the Cossack lands to Siberia; the Byzantine-style *tsar* (from the Latin *Caesar*) was first used in 1510 of Basil III & first adopted by Ivan IV in 1547, recalling the Roman Emperors & suggesting "Emperor of the third Rome", & Tsar absolutism or "caesaropapism" followed the Byzantine pattern of Emperor absolutism, with the metropolitan & (after the creation of the first Russian patriarch in 1589) the patriarch submitting to the Tsar; from 1611 there was a Time of Troubles with Polish-Swedish invasions, one of which captured the Kremlin & set up a new dynasty (the Romanovs)

14.	Germanic-Scandinavian	c.375-476, Germanic hegemony as, displaced by Huns (especially 372-453), Germanic tribes expanded to S. Germany (Burgundians), France (Franks), Ukraine (Goths), N. Transylvania (Gepidae), Italy (Ostrogoths & in 568 Lombards), Spain (Alani, Suevi), England (Angles & Saxons), & Africa (Vandals) & set up kingdoms; the Germanic tribes appealed to the Romans & many were allocated lands in the Danube region to act as a buffer between the Huns & the Roman frontier; as the Huns established their Empire on German land, many Germanic tribes were displaced, & this led to their becoming Romanized; the *foederati* adopted Roman Arianism to counter the Empire of the Huns, e.g. the Visigoths (382-395), the Vandals (409-429), the Burgundians (412-436), the Ostrogoths (456-472), the Rugii (by 482) & the Franks under Clovis (496); the Huns returned to the Russian steppe in 470
15.	Andean	c.600-1200, Huari Empire based on Tiahuanaco, faded c.1000

16.	Meso-American	c.300-900, Mayan Empire (Early & Late Classic periods) until Nahua invasions from north which began c.850 & included the Toltecs
17.	Arab	c.1358-1683, Ottoman Empire's early rapid expansion briefly checked by Timur's Turkic Central-Asians who ravaged Syria in 1401 & conquered & captured the Ottoman Bayezid I in 1402; from 1453 the Ottoman Empire's new capital at Istanbul & expansion to the peak of its power in Anatolia, Greece, the Balkans, Serbia, Bosnia, Wallachia, Hungary (which was surrendered to Austria in 1699), Crimea, Mesopotamia, Syria, Palestine & Egypt (which it took in 1516-7 from the Mamluk Sultanate, a dynasty of slave soldiers of the last Ayyubid who took power at his death in 1250), the Yemen (including Mecca), N. Africa, the Persian Gulf & Black Sea; Islam's parallel expansion in India under the Moghul Empire, & in Iran under the Sufi Shi'ite Safavids (1502-1736)
18.	African	c.740-1500, first African Muslim trading empires grew up slowly in desiccated, remote Saharan conditions: the Muslim trading empires in Ghana (at Kumbi, which had begun in the 8th C, had an iron-weaponed army of 20,000 by AD 1000, turned Muslim when the King of Ghana was converted to Islam c.1100, & which was destroyed c.1230); at Lake Chad (in the 9th-10th C at Kanem-Bornu, where the Bantu may have learned to work iron from the royal family of Meroe who seem to have fled to Darfur c.325, & which subjugated the Fezzan end of 13th C – end of 14th C); the Arab Swahili settlements in Kenya; also in the Kukiya & Gao kingdoms (8th-9th C), & Igbo-Ukwu (from 9th C) where wax casting was practised, an art since lost; & in the Kisalian culture (10th-14th C); the Almoravid Empire in Morocco 1050-1140; the Almohad Empire along the N.-African coast 1140-

1250; the Fatimid, Ayyubid & Mamluk Empires in Egypt, 960-1517; the Muslim trading empire in the 13th & 14th C in Mali (at Niani & Songhai, near Timbuktu) & Benin (the 14th C Empire of Jolof); & Christian Ethiopia (which claimed descent from Solomon through the Queen of Sheba) dominated Muslim Africa from c.1270 to c.1470

19. Indian	c.1236-1526, expansion of Muslim Turkish Ghurids & successors until Timur's conquest of Delhi in 1398, & of Muslim Bahmani State in south (1347-1527); & Hindu expansion in south during Bhakti age in Vijayanagar Empire (1336-1646)
20. S.-E.-Asian	c.1287-1550, Majapahit Empire in Java ended the Srivijaya Empire & ruled as an Indianised kingdom until Islam reached Indonesia; c.1300-1550, Thai Empire of Ayutthaya (from c.1350, Thai conquest of Khmers 1431); Mons Pegu Empire (14th-16th C); Arakan's Islamic Empire (14th-15th C); Burmese Ava Empire (14th-16th C)
21. Japanese	c.1391-1573, Ashikaga/Muromachi family restored old imperial regime based on aristocracy, expanded into a trading empire in China & Korea, & created a Zen-Buddhist *samurai* culture for warriors which brought in a Golden Age in which scholarship & the arts flourished in the five Zen monasteries of Kyoto
22. Oceanian	c.1200-1500, S. American influence dominated in Polynesia & spread from island to island
23. Chinese	c.1398-1644, Ming Empire's expansion, particularly under Admiral Cheng Ho who headed Chinese maritime exploration from 1405 to 1433, reaching India, Africa & Arabia

24.	Tibetan	c.1642-1720, expansion under Dalai Lamas through Mongol Overlordship (in 1653 the Dalai Lama visited China's court as an independent ruler, & later invaded Bhutan)	
25.	Central-Asian	c.1206-1370, Mongol Empire from Yellow Sea to the Euphrates & Genghis's four sons' khanate successor states after 1259: the Empire of the Great Khan of Kublai Khan; the Chagatai Khanate; the Khanate of the Golden Horde, which attacked Russia; & the Il-Khan Empire	

30. Seceders from New People

There are now seceders from the religion of the new people. This development suggests that the Light in the new people's religion is not strong; the purpose of the secession is to create a stronger Light. The secession does not re-form the Central Idea of the civilization but it can become the Central Idea of a later civilization. (Thus the seceding Roman Christians made it possible for Christ to be the Central Idea of the Byzantine civilization, and the seceding European Puritans made it possible for the Puritan Christ to be the Central Idea of the North-American civilization.) The pattern is as follows:

Civilization	New people's god	Date & details of seceders from new people	God of seceders
1. Indo-European Kurgan/ Old European	Ogma	From c.1875 BC Mycenaeans? (Greece) Hittites (Anatolia) Hyksos (Egypt) Kassites (Babylonia) Aryans (India)	Ogma-Herakles Teshub Seth Shuqamuna Indra
2. Mesopotamian	Ashur	c.1400 BC	Mitra, god of the

		Mitannian Assyrians		Iranian Mitanni (along with Varuna & Indra)
3.	Egyptian	Amon	c.1379-1361 BC Akhenaton (whose innovations shocked the Egyptian soul into a Mannerist art with lengthened bodies)	Aton
4.	Aegean-Greek	Dorian Apollo	c.950 BC Ionians (who migrated from Attica to Ionia, e.g. Miletus & Ephesus)	Ionian Athene/Artemis
5.	Roman	Posthumously deified Emperor as avatar of a cult	AD c.30-251 Christians	Christ
6.	Anatolian	Cybele	c.1100 BC Luwian Neo-Hittites in Cilicia (protected by mountains from Sea Peoples & Phrygians)	Luwian Tarhun
7.	Syrian	Melqart or Hammon/ Astarte	c.1100 BC Neo-Hittites in N. Syria	Cybele
8.	Israelite	Elohim	c.720 BC Ahaz's pro-Assyrian	Asherah

supporters

9.	Celtic	Christ	From AD c.90 Romanized pagan Hercules Celts of Belgic stock	Jupiter (for Jovii)/ (for Herculii)
10.	Iranian	Ahura Mazda	AD c.240-274 Manichaeans who followed Mani	Mani
11.	European	Protestant Christ	c.1600-1680 Puritans (including the English Puritan Revolution of the 1640s)	Puritan Christ
12.	North-American	Has not happened yet		
13.	Byzantine-Russian	Byzantine "third Rome", Tsar absolutist Christ of Ivan III	c.1596-1620 Polish Catholics: under Polish pressure (as Poland supported the False Dmitry & eventually invaded Muscovy in 1609) the metropolitanate of Kiev accepted union with Rome in 1596; this lasted during the Time of Troubles until the Poles were expelled from Moscow	Roman Catholic Christ

		& Michael Romanov was elected tsar	
14. Germanic-Scandinavian	Arian Christ	c.380-410 Germanic pagans (soon after Roman pagan Sun-worship returned under Julian from 361)	Thor
15. Andean	Doorway god	c.800 & later Temple-oracle at Pachacamac	Eagle-headed griffin
16. Meso-American	Kinich Ahau (or Itzamna)	c.600 Maya who borrowed Kukulcan from the Itza of Yucatan (after c.250)	Kukulcan (meaning "Feathered Serpent")
17. Arab	Allah	c.1502-1514 Safavids (Iranian Sufi Shi'ite missionaries spread religious heresy throughout Anatolia)	Sufi Shi'ite Allah
18. African	African Allah	c.1200 Bantu Zimbabweans: Bantu stone "temple" & acropolis of the Mwene Mutapa) Empire at Great Zimbabwe (or "Enclosures"), which	Bantu god Mwari/Bird of bright plumage (the sacred fish -eagle revered as guardian by the Shona, perhaps an echo of Horus

had long been
inhabited, was now
intensively occupied
until it declined
c.1430 when there was
a shortage of salt &
the king, Nyatsimba
Mutota, led a
migration to the salt-
mines in the Dande
area of the Zambezi
valley, & took the
title Mwene Mutapa
("Master Ravager")
(Great Zimbabwe was indigenous,
although the knowledge may have come
from the Bantu of Lake Chad who were
perhaps taught by the royal family of
Meroe, the descendants of the 25th or
"Ethiopian" dynasty of Egypt which
retired there after 656 BC & therefore
possessors of the Egyptian Light of the
Saite revival of the Old Kingdom)

the hawk)

19.	Indian	Turkish Allah	c.1290-1316 The Khaljis (Turks of impure stock allied to Indian Muslims)	Allah of Khaljis

20.	S.-E.-Asian	Buddha	c.1350-1480 Asokaist Theravada Buddhist in Burma (& elsewhere in S.-E. Asia); after	Asoka's Buddha (Burma)

		c.1431 Brahmanic Khmer tradition in Thai kingdom at Ayutthaya	
21. Japanese	Zen-Buddhist Enlightenment	After 1400 Shinto secession from Shinto-Buddhist amalgamation (e.g. Watarai or Ise Shinto), Shinto shrines free from Buddhist control	Japanese Kami/ Amaterasu
22. Oceanian	S.-American sun-god	14th C Bird-man (Quetzl?) on Easter Island	Makemake (god incarnated in sea-birds)
23. Chinese	Neo-Confucian *Ti*	c.1500-1529 Wang Yang-ming followed Lu Hsiang-shan (12th C) in championing Mind rather than thePrinciple of the Ch'eng brothers (11th C) & Chu Hsi (12th C), & in founding a Chinese Idealism which had many followers	Mind as Reality
24. Tibetan	Dge-lugs-pa Buddha	c.1696-1705 Rejection of rightful Dalai Lama	Dalai Lama as mature lama rather than infant

25.	Central-Asian	Buddha	c.1230-1396 Islam of the Golden Horde (in which Turks outnumbered Mongols or Tatars, & the Turkish language replaced Mongol)	Allah

31. NEW PEOPLE PERSECUTE SECEDERS

The new people now persecute the seceders. As a result of the persecution, the religion of the new people prevails, and the new people are confirmed as the new orthodoxy, as the following pattern shows:

Civilization	Date of persecution of seceders	Details of resistance to or persecution of seceders
1. Indo-European Kurgan/ Old European	c.1850 BC?	Late Unetice chieftans in W. Europe & Wessex farmers clashed with Western seceders
2. Mesopotamian	c.1375 BC	Supporters of Ashur resisted Mitra, especially in the capital Ashur which was semi-independent of the Mitanni
3. Egyptian	c.1358 BC	Tutankhamon's rule purged the Aton-ites
4. Aegean-Greek	c.900 BC	Dorian Apollonian Greeks opposed to Ionian religion

5.	Roman	AD c.30-251 (especially in 64 under Nero, 111 under Trajan, 202 under Severus, 251 under Decius & 303-5 under Diocletian)	Persecution of Christians by Roman State
6.	Anatolian	c.1050 BC?	Phrygians resisted Neo-Hittite Tarhun & c.850-700 BC passed Cybele on to the Neo-Hittites as Kubabas-Cybele, just as c.1100-838 BC they passed Cybele on to the Anatolianised Greek colonies in Aeolia & Ionia as Artemis (The Phrygians always divided them-selves culturally from the Luwian Neo-Hittite states east of Phrygia & in N. Syria)
7.	Syrian	c.1075 BC	Phoenicians & Aramaeans resisted the Neo-Hittites & in due course conquered some of the Neo-Hittite principalities & city-states before the Aramaeans were overrun by the Assyrians
8.	Israelite	from c.715 BC	Jews under Hezekiah began to purge Assyrian/foreign elements from the religion of Judah
9.	Celtic	c.150	Christian Celts opposed Romanized Celts & Jupiter/ Hercules

10. Iranian	c.274-300	Sasasians persecuted the Manichaeans after putting Mani to death
11. European	c.1620-1700	Persecution of Puritans/Huguenots in Europe (in Britain after 1620 & in France from 1572 to 1715)
12. North-American	—	
13. Byzantine-Russian	from c.1620	Michael Romanov restored Orthodoxy in 1620 & persecuted Catholics; in 1620 the patriarch Philaret pronounced an anathema on Lithuanian (i.e. secular) books
14. Germanic-Scandinavian	from c.392	Germanic paganism proscribed by Theodosius & opposed by *foederati*
15. Andean	c.800	Huari Empire suppressed independence of religious ceremonies at Pachacamac
16. Meso-American	after c.600	Orthodox Maya resisted the Itza Kukulcan (who was identified with Quetzlcoatl, the Feathered Serpent)
17. Arab	c.1502-1554	Bayezid II & Selim I drove Safavids to Iran & massacred thousands of pro-Safavids in Anatolia; in Iran after 1514 the

Ottomans mounted several
expeditions against the Safavids
& turned from Sufism to Shi'ism
to obtain Persian support for a
Turkish dynasty there; as a
reaction against the Shi'ite
Safavids, the hitherto Sufi-Shi'ite
Ottomans championed the Sunni
cause elsewhere

18. African	c.1300-1350	Bantu Zimbabwe attacked by Muslim Africans?
19. Indian	c.1316-20	The Tughluqs resisted Allah of Khaljis
20. S.-E.-Asian	c.1400	Sinhalese Theravada Buddhism established by the monastery of Mahavihara triumphed over the Asokaist variety in Burma and elsewhere in S.-E. Asia
21. Japanese	from c.1420	Zen temples (e.g. Enryaku-ji) persecuted seceders
22. Oceanian	14th C	Resistance to new cults by Long Ears? (Makemake still dominant in 15th C)
23. Chinese	from c.1500	Resistance to Idealistic Confucianism by the Ch'eng-Chu School of Principle, which became the Ming orthodoxy

24.	Tibetan	c.1720	Dzungars (Western Mongols) invaded Tibet & punished seceders until they were driven out by the Chinese
25.	Central-Asian	c.1260-1294	Tibetan Buddhism of Kublai Khan resisted Islam of the Golden Horde

32. SCIENTIFIC MATERIALISM WEAKENS RELIGION

The further bout of expansion brings the civilization back from its preoccupation with the past, and its sense of religion weakens in a bout of scientific materialism. This is derived from another civilization, but the acquiring civilization makes it its own and the new trend lasts getting on for 100 years. New scientific skills prepare the civilization for still further expansion, as the following pattern shows:

	Civilization	Scientific materialism	Date
1.	Indo-European Kurgan/ Old European	Metallurgy inspired by Battle-Axe culture, exploitation of gold, copper & tin, bronze-making	c.1850-1750 BC
2.	Mesopotamian	Mitannian & Babylonian-inspired architecture; scientific writings, medical diagnosis & recipes, astrological signs; Babylonian astronomers	c.1250-1150 BC
3.	Egyptian	Hyksos-inspired war-chariots, building of temples & palaces under Ramesses II-VI	c.1250-1150 BC
4.	Aegean-Greek	Ionian-inspired science, eastern	c.850-750 BC

bronze & iron metalwork &
jewellery in graves

5.	Roman	Greek-inspired Roman scientific materialism produced concrete & cross-vaults in soaring bridges & aqueducts, & thermal baths	c.138-235
6.	Anatolian	Advanced Phrygian building & fortification, bronze metalwork, ivory carving & textiles influenced by Assyria	c.1000 BC
7.	Syrian	Phoenician boat-building, textiles & dyes, metallurgy (iron, copper, silver, gold), masonry (including Solomon's Temple) & ivory-carving (Phoenician ports were busy when the Egyptian envoy visited Byblos c.1075 BC)	c.1050-980 BC
8.	Israelite	Assyrian-inspired building & military technology was made available to the pro-Assyrian Judah during Manasseh's reign of 55 years	from c.697 BC
9.	Celtic	Roman-inspired building methods made available to Gallic & British Celts	c.170-270
10.	Iranian	Hellenistic-inspired science continued; Sasanian architecture & metalwork	c.280-360
11.	European	Industrial Revolution's machines	c.1680-1778

inspired by Arab science in Spain
which passed to Europe with the
Reconquista, and by the scientific
outlook of the Renaissance following
the fall of Byzantine Constantinople
to the Ottomans

12.	North-American	—	
13.	Byzantine-Russian	Following the fall of Constantinople in 1453 & the end of the Byzantine Empire, Moscow, conscious of being the last bastion of Orthodoxy, a "third Rome", had consciously inherited Roman-Byzantine science by looking to the West & the Renaissance; now European-inspired science was let in by the Romanovs	from c.1630
14.	Germanic-Scandinavian	Roman-inspired barbarian weaponry	c.400-500
15.	Andean	Oceanian-inspired (?) use of bronze with textile-derived patterns, advanced irrigation systems	c.900-1000
16.	Meso-American	Oceanian-inspired (?) advanced building (Toltecs were the first Latin-American city-builders)	c.900-1000
17.	Arab	After the Ottoman capture of Constantinople with firearms, Mehmed II rebuilt the city's streets, bridges &	c.1560-1660

aqueducts with advanced technology
& made use of Iranian scientific
learning; the Ottoman expansion into
Europe 1520-6, when Hungary was
attacked, resulted in the absorption of
European military science, & the
Ottomans remained in contact with
the Habsburgs for the next 150 years

18. African	Arab-inspired building & scientific skills which came with the Muslim trading empires, e.g. in Mali (see stage 29)	c.1350-1450
19. Indian	Arab-inspired scientific skills originally funded by Ala-ud-Din who raided the wealth of Central India	c.1400-1500
20. S.-E.-Asian	Arab-inspired scientific skills first introduced from India c.1300	1450-1550
21. Japanese	Chinese-inspired science led to growth of cities & trade	c.1450-1570
22. Oceanian	S. American migration of c.1100 brought Andean-inspired scientific skills	c.1375-1475?
23. Chinese	Arab-inspired science & technology (astronomy, medicine, mathematics & geography) had been introduced during the Mongol rule; the intellectual & aesthetic ferment of late Ming times included encyclopaedias on scientific	c.1540-1640

knowledge; e.g. one on industrial technology (1637); the Ming Age threw up incipient capitalism which might have led to an industrial revolution but for the Manchu conquest & European imperialism, & China exported silks & porcelains while trying to remain free from foreign "barbarian" customs

| 24. | Tibetan | Scientific skills introduced from China, especially after 1653 when the Dalai Lama visited the Chinese Emperor, & from Jesuit scholars who brought mathematics & astronomy to Lhasa in 1661 | c.1650-1720 |

| 25. | Central-Asian | After conquering China, the Mongols abolished State trade controls & encouraged trade in silk & ceramics; they imported Arab-Persian science & technology (e.g. astronomy, mathematics, medicine & geography), which pleased Islamic Mongolian Turks | c.1270-1370 |

33. ARTISTIC REACTION AGAINST SCIENTIFIC MATERIALISM

There is a reaction within the arts against scientific materialism. This reaction is inspired by a return to an earlier, pre-scientific stage of the civilization's art, or by influence from another civilization. In either case, the reaction emphasises the vital spirit as opposed to mechanism, and shows Nature as a living being rather than as a materialistic process, as the following pattern shows:

Civilization	Literary/artistic reaction	Date
1. Indo-European Kurgan/ Old European	Bronze & tin artefacts influenced from Ugarit & Mycenae; the bronze came from C. Europe (e.g. Unetice), the tin from Cornwall	c.1760 BC?
2. Mesopotamian	Poetry from Kassite time; Babylonised Kassite epics & poems about Marduk	from c.1150 BC
3. Egyptian	Late Ramesside piety in serene art from Ramesses VI to Ramesses XI	from c.1150 BC
4. Aegean-Greek	Classical style replaced Geometric style, art influenced from Egypt, & Near East, geometric designs became animal-friezes (sphinx, griffin)	c.760 BC
5. Roman	After Greek Renaissance of 2nd C AD, in which art & religion were influenced from the East, e.g. introduction of Helios (who became Aurelian's *Sol Invictus*) & Hercules (from whom Constantine claimed descent), first Israelite-inspired Christian art resisted Roman scientific worldliness from c.230 & prepared for Christianized Rome after 313	from AD c.230
6. Anatolian	Art influenced from Luwia (e.g. polychrome pottery known as Early Phrygian or Alisar IV, Phrygian sculptures found at Ankara)	c.950 BC

7.	Syrian	Phoenician art influenced by Imperial Hittite traditions in 11th & 10th C BC as well as from Assyria; animals carved on ivory & bowls	c.1000 BC
8.	Israelite	Art influenced by anti-Assyrian movement which brought Josiah to power & purged Israelite religion of foreign elements	c.650 BC
9.	Celtic	Art influenced by independent Celtic Empire including Gaul, Spain & Britain, which was governed from Trier from 260 following invasion by the Germanic Franks; it revived the old Celtic tradition against Roman materialism	c.260
10.	Iranian	Art revived old Iranian Zoroastrian tradition under the Mazda-worshipping Shapur II, whose 70 year long reign won 5 provinces & Armenia from the Romans, persecuted Christians & forcibly converted them to Zoroastrianism, & took the Sasanian Empire to its zenith; a rock-cut relief sculpture at Bishapur shows him among nobles, soldiers & captives	c.350
11.	European	Romanticism in literature, art & music (which began in Germany with Goethe, spread to England in the 1790s & lasted until c.1840); emphasised the Gothic vision of the	c.1770

12.	North-American	—	
13.	Byzantine-Russian	European-inspired classical/baroque art rejected science but replaced Russian icons during New Believers' "Greek first" restoration of supremacy of patriarch over tsar by Nikon who forced Tsar Alexis Romanov to submit to the Church, & the Russian liturgy to comply with the Greek liturgy; causing schism in the Russian Church as millions of Old Believers continued to believe that Russia, not Greece, was the last refuge of Orthodoxy	c.1650
14.	Germanic-Scandinavian	Pre-Christian, Arian art & frescoes of barbarian tribes until conversion to Catholic Christianity of Clovis, king of Salian Franks in 496	c.450
15.	Andean	Early Chimu pots show humans holding moons or cats, & have stirrup spouts on which sit monkeys	c.1175
16.	Meso-American	Art of Tula shows sun-worship & is religious & anti-scientific (& was taken up by the Aztecs)	c.1175
17.	Arab	Ottoman art combined Persian-Islamic, Byzantine & old Turkish culture, & after the early Ottoman frontiersmen's	c.1650

thrusting, worldly attitudes, there was
an Iranian mystical movement against
science under Shah Abbas the Great
(died 1629), which influenced Ottoman
art

18.	African	African art turned against Arab science & rediscovered its tribal roots, e.g. the Bantu art of Rozwi occupation of Great Zimbabwe from c.1450 (human figures & birds on soapstone)	c.1450
19.	Indian	New feeling of impartiality regarding Muslims & Hindus turned against Arab science & in 1526 found expression in the Moghul disestablish-ment of Islam; Moghul art turned against Arab science	c.1490
20.	S.-E.-Asian	Art influenced by Indian Moghul art which turned against Arab science	c.1540
21.	Japanese	Neo-Confucianism introduced in Zen art, haiku, Nō play & tea ceremony, counteracting arrival of Portuguese & Jesuits (e.g. St Francis Xavier in 1549)	c.1560
22.	Oceanian	Oceanian sculptures at their height c.1470, according to carbon-dating; artistic Golden Age	c.1470
23.	Chinese	Iconoclasm of the art of the final Ming decades, whose total individual freedom & vitalism anticipated Romanticism	c.1630

24. Tibetan	Influenced by art of China (late Ming & early Manchu)	c.1720

25. Central-Asian	Timurid Renaissance in which the dynasty of Timur & the Samarkand-based successors of Timur reflected Iranian miniature painting, Persian carpets & Seljuq styles, & rejected scientific materialism	from c.1370

34. NEW PEOPLE'S HEIRS' FURTHER EXPANSION INTO EMPIRE OVEREXTENDS CIVILIZATION

The heirs of the new people now undergo a further expansion into empire in a climate that is more secular than was the climate of stage 29. There is a further awakening of Universalist awareness. This expansion is a further substitute for growth and for the inner religion, and it further overextends the civilization. An attempt to renew the Light is made; not by the regimes, which (unlike the early sacred kings) are usually godless, but by people who take their lead from monastic communities or groups. This renewal of the Light is strongly coloured by the artistic reaction against scientific materialism (stage 33), which in retrospect can be seen to have provided a new impetus for the civilization's further expansion in stage 34. This impetus co-exists with a new classicism in art. The pattern is as follows:

Civilization	Date of further expansion into empire	Details of new people's heirs' further expansion into empire & renewal of Light
1. Indo-European Kurgan/Old European	c.1750-1625 BC	Further Battle-Axe Empire in Rhineland, Brittany, Wessex & C. Europe during which bronze-working spread from Europe to Britain & Iberia

2.	Mesopotamian	c.1000-626 BC	After Aramaean counter-attack; growth of Third Assyrian Empire, founded c.910-626 BC in Syria, Cilicia, Babylonia, Israel & Egypt
3.	Egyptian	c.1085-730 BC	Egyptian Empire under Tanite & Libyan dynasties (e.g. Sheshonk I), after temporary loss of Nubia & Asiatic Empire between 1085 & 945
4.	Aegean-Greek	c.750-431 BC	Further Greek colonizing: mercantile Empire in N, S, E, W Mediterranean during Archaic period
5.	Roman	c.270-410	Recovery of Roman Empire under the Illyrian Aurelian as avatar of Sol Invictus (a revival of Elagabalus's solar monotheism) & under the Dominate of sun-emperors with Diocletian as avatar of Jupiter or Jove (he was of the "Jovii" & resisted the oriental Baal of Elagabalus); Maximian of Hercules; & Constantine of Helios (until for political reasons he accepted Christ); resistance to barbarian attacks & recovery of Gaul & Syria as Constantine & his sons ruled the Late Empire from Constantinople (Byzantium), the Eastern Emperor being "Augustus" & the Western Emperor being "Caesar" under him
6.	Anatolian	c.900-696 BC	Phrygian Kingdom with Syrian

border that wiped out the Neo-Hittites
until it was attacked by the Assyrians
& overrun by the Cimmerians,
leaving the Lydian Empire to the
west confronting the Median Empire
(which had absorbed the Cimmerians)
& squeezing the Greek colonies in
Aeolia & Ionia (which had sprung
up c.1100-750 BC)

7.	Syrian	c.980-710 BC	Further Phoenician colonization (including the foundation of Carthage in 814 BC) under Melqart (the god of Tyre & Carthage) as a result of Assyrian invasion & encirclement while Aramaeans were absorbed by Assyrians c.860-804 BC
8.	Israelite	c.640-597 BC	Josiah's attempted restoration of David's Empire as Assyria retreated, enabling Judah to become independent of Assyria in 627, purify & repair the Temple in Jerusalem & control former Israelite territory
9.	Celtic	c.313-446	After Constantine's conversion & the Christianization of the Roman Empire, Christian Celtic expansion as Romans withdrew from Britain in 407-410 to defend Gaul against Germanic invasions; before the British tyrant Vortigern invited the Saxons to defend Britain against the Picts & began the Saxon invasions,

which King Arthur resisted

10.	Iranian	c.364-572	Further Sasanian expansion to the east, at the eventual expense of the Hephthalites (originally Central Asians known to Chinese as Hoa or Hoa-tun) under Khosrow I (a Zoroastrian), who defeated the Hephthalites
11.	European	c.1778-1914	Protestant European Empires (British, German & Dutch Empires); also Catholic Belgian & French Empires; the general European expansion was strongly influenced by the French Revolution of 1789, which led to Napoleon's domination of Europe from 1799 & whose de-Christianizing outlook further secularized European civilization; British union with Ireland in 1801
12.	North-American	—	
13.	Byzantine-Russian	c.1689-1855	Expansion of Westernized Petrine Empire in Europe & Asia, founded on Peter the Great's cultural Europeanism & his religious reforms which made Orthodoxy a Western secular religion; Alexis Romanov's son, Peter, turned against the New Believers, abolishing the patriarchate & emphasising the superiority of the

Tsar & also moved against the Old
Believers, making the Orthodox Church
a department of a secular, Western-
style, post-Renaissance State; Peter
dealt personally with Church affairs &
put and end to "third Rome"
Byzantinist Christianity

| 14. | Germanic-Scandinavian | c.476-596 | After the fall of the West-Roman Empire c.476, Germanic Arian kingdoms of Merovingian Franks (N. France), Burgundians (S. France), Ostrogoths (Italy), Visigoths (Spain), Anglo-Saxons (Britain), Suevi (Spain) & Vandals (N. Africa, Sicily, Sardinia & Corsica) as Germanic leaders waged war against the East Roman puppet Emperor & provincial governors, & established Arian kingdoms in Italy & in the former Roman provinces; the Franks became Catholic under Clovis in 468 & the Frankish Kingdom soon swallowed its neighbours & dominated Europe after the Italian Ostrogoths were reconquered by the East Roman Justinian by c.563 & the Spanish Visigoths became Catholics in 589 |
| 15. | Andean | c.1200-1460 | Peruvian Chimu Empire surfaced c.1300 with capital at Chan Chan (flourished after c.1370), until it was conquered c.1460 by Inca Empire |

with capital in Cuzco Valley from the
12th C

16. Meso- American	c.1200-1428	Mexican Toltec Empire with capital at Tula (c.900-1300) until Aztec Empire with capital at Tenochtitlan (c.1300-1521), conquered Mexico after 1426 by dominating an alliance of three states
17. Arab	c.1683-1798	Sunni Ottoman Empire continued with minor losses until 1798: parallel Islamic Empire in India, & in Iran under the Shi'ite anti-Sunni Safavids (until 1736); the Shi'ite Nader Shah (who captured Delhi & the Moghul Empire's treasure in 1738-9); the Zand dynasty (1750-79); & the Qajars (from 1779)
18. African	c.1500-1835	Rise of African states as Gao took over from the great Songhai Empire in Nigeria & nearby Bornu took over from Kanem & Hausa states; & the Bantu Matapa to the north replaced Great Zimbabwe; Portuguese colonies were established on the east & west coasts & after 1600 there was a slave trade centring on Sudan & W. Africa (the Ashanti & Abomey)
19. Indian	c.1526-1740	Moghul Empire & aftermath until Maratha Empire

20. S.-E.-Asian	c.1550-1786	Second Burmese Empire in 16th C & conquest of Siam (1767); Empire of Luang Prabang c.1707; Vietnamese Empire in Cambodia (19th C) (From 1511 to 1682 there were European rivalries as the English, Dutch, Spanish & Portuguese captured different trading posts in S.-E. Asia from each other)
21. Japanese	c.1573-1863	Empires of Hideyoshi (in Korea) & of Tokugawas, whose shogunate was confined to Japanese islands & who championed Neo-Confucianism
22. Oceanian	c.1500-1840	Further expansion of Oceanian culture from island to island to which Europeans made Oceanic voyages of discovery (1513-1642)
23. Chinese	c.1644-1840	Empire of Manchus or Juchen, the Ch'ing dynasty
24. Tibetan	c.1720-1903	Empire of Dalai Lamas under Chinese Manchu overlordship, but with freedom to run their own affairs
25. Central-Asian	c.1370-1543	Timur Lenk ("Timur the Lame", a Barlas Turk) seized the Il-Khan's Empire; the Empire of Timur & his Timurid successors to 1506, capital at Samarkand, lay between the rivers Oxus & Jaxares (Transoxania),

& eventually stretched from Mongolia
to the Mediterranean after victories
over the Ottomans, the Golden Horde
in Russia, Delhi & a campaign
against Ming China

THE DECLINE OF CIVILIZATIONS

The new people's energy is now dispersed abroad, and the Light weakens and fades from the official religion. As a result, old certainties collapse and the arts become restless and secular. Scientific materialism weakens religion, and the subjects of the new people become sceptical. There is imperial decline and colonial conflict as a rival civilization challenges for colonies. There is a levelling down, a process of proletarianization and egalitarianism. The dominant rival civilization forms a conglomerate, into which the civilization, broken up, passes with loss of national sovereignty. There is syncretism and a yearning for the lost past. The civilization attempts a counter-thrust to restore its glorious past, but fails to renew the Central Idea. It is now in deep decline.

35. THE WEAKNESS OF THE LIGHT DURING THE CIVILIZATION'S DECLINE AS ENERGY IS DISPERSED ABROAD

If, as my evidence suggests, a renewal of the Light of a religion by the people has the effect of renewing its civilization and Central Idea, then is it not logical to suppose that failure to renew the Light of a religion by the people has the effect of failing to renew its civilization and Central Idea? In short, that the weakness of the Light (for whatever reason) precipitates the decline of a civilization which, if it is not reversed by a renewal of the Light, rapidly slides into decay? (See pp412-428 for further discussion.) The evidence supports this conclusion.

As we begin to unravel this theme we shall see that a civilization declines first because it is overextended and its energy is dispersed abroad, and later as the result of a foreign military threat through a colonial conflict which a challenger for the civilization's colonies wins and which results in foreign occupation by the challenger. We shall be identifying the foreign military threats and occupiers in due course, but first it will be helpful to state when the Light weakened in each civilization, and who the main foreign military threats were at the time:

Civilization	Vision of Light weak	Foreign military threat or occupying power
1. Indo-European Kurgan/ Old European	after c.1750-1625 BC	Greeks
2. Mesopotamian	c.1000-626 BC	Egyptians
3. Egyptian	c.1085-730 BC	Libyans
4. Aegean-Greek	c.750-480 BC	Persians
5. Roman	c.270-410	Barbarians/Goths & Ostrogoths
6. Anatolian	c.900-696 BC	Assyrians
7. Syrian	c.980-710 BC	Assyrians
8. Israelite	c.640-597 BC	Assyrians
9. Celtic	c.313-446	Saxons
10. Iranian	c.364-572	Hephthalites, Byzantines
11. European	c.1778-1918	North Americans, who seized British colonies in N. America and took over European oilfields in the

Middle East after Verdun (1916) in return for entering the First World War, a civil war which sapped nation-states' energy (see Hagger, *The Syndicate*); anti-colonialists in Africa (Zulus, Boers), India, Asia

12.	North-American	—	
13.	Byzantine-Russian	c.1689-1855	European French (Napoleon)
14.	Germanic-Scandinavian	c.476-596	East-Roman Empire, British Celts, Avars
15.	Andean	c.1200-1460	Incas
16.	Meso-American	c.1200-1428	Aztecs
17.	Arab	c.1683-1798	Europeans
18.	African	c.1500-1835	European colonizers on African coast
19.	Indian	c.1526-1740	European British
20.	S.-E.-Asian	c.1550-1786	European colonizers
21.	Japanese	c.1573-1863	Portuguese, Americans, British, French
22.	Oceanian	c.1500-1840	European colonizers

23.	Chinese	c.1644-1840	European British
24.	Tibetan	c.1720-1903	Chinese
25.	Central-Asian	c.1370-1543	Uzbek Black Sheep & White Sheep Turks

36. Light disappears from Official Religion

An outside military influence now has a cosmopolitanising effect and causes the Light to disappear from the official religion. The Light can now be contacted in cults more readily than in the existing, established religion, as the following pattern shows:

	Civilization	Date Light disappears from established religion
1.	Indo-European Kurgan/Old European	c.1650 BC? Sumerian influence of Ogma faded before Unetice & Greek influence?
2.	Mesopotamian	c.648 BC, after the Assyrians destroyed Babylon a second time; (in 689 they had levelled the temple & carried off the image of Marduk)
3.	Egyptian	c.760 BC, when the Kushites were pressing into Libyan Egypt & championing a virgin God's Wife of Amon against the Libyan God's Wife of Amon who was the spouse of the King; the Kushite Kashta forced Osorkon III to retire & he challenged the Libyan priesthood causing the Light to weaken; the Kushites (Ethiopians) took power in Egypt in c.730 BC & worshipped God's Wife of Amon
4.	Aegean-Greek	c.510 BC, after the Persian-Spartan expulsion of the

Athenian Peisistratids

5.	Roman	c.380, when the Goths were victorious in the Balkans while Roman paganism weakened under the Christian Theodosius & Arianism was proscribed; Constantine's conversion to Christianity c.324 led to Christianity flourishing in Constantinople but remaining a minority religion in the West where paganism continued especially under the pagan emperor Julian the Apostate (361-3) & the Arian emperors Constantius & Valens (351-381)
6.	Anatolian	c.730 BC, after Assyrian inroads into Anatolia which began the process of destroying the remaining Neo-Hittite states
7.	Syrian	c.750 BC, during the collapse of the Neo-Hittite states, when Syria & Palestine were being pressed by the Assyrians
8.	Israelite	c.620 BC, during the approaching collapse of the Israelite Empire at the hands of the Neo-Babylonians & when Judaism became more Torah-based following the discovery in the Temple c.620 BC of a scroll of Moses' Torah, probably of *Deuteronomy*
9.	Celtic	c.410, around the time of the withdrawal of the Romans from Britain & the fall of Christian Rome at the hands of Germanic tribes
10.	Iranian	c.542, after Iran was pressed by the Hephthalites & Byzantines & Kavadh I had moved from Zoroastrianism to Mazdakism, which thrived until the Mazdakites were massacred by the crown prince Khosrow in 528; Iran was again pressed by the Byzantines from c.540
11.	European	c.1880 when Europe was opposed by & absorbed African &

Indian/Asian influences (e.g. in Theosophy) which challenged Christianity, & after the discovery of electricity following the advance of scientific materialism

12.	North-American	—

13.	Byzantine-Russian	c.1812, after Napoleon's invasion, during the decline of the Romanov Empire & before the rise of revolutionary socialism & terrorism, & of Nihilism; Peter the Great's isolation of the Church brought a revival of monasticism & a renewal of Hesychasm (seeing "the Uncreated Light" in quiet), & the Light remained strong in the monastic Hesychasm of the startsy (elders) of Optino (e.g. Makarius, died 1860, & Ambrose, died 1891) who were visited by the masses c.1900; although the Orthodox Church was suppressed during the State atheism & persecutions of 1918-1943 & 1959-1964, the Light appears to have survived in individual Russians & is now re-emerging under Gorbachev's reforms
14.	Germanic-Scandinavian	c.568, Thor/Odin disappeared from Germanic Saxon religion when the Asian Avars threatened the Frankish eastern frontier & took the Merovingian descendant of Clovis, Sigebert I, prisoner in 568
15.	Andean	c.1430(?), the Chimu Light weakened before the Incas
16.	Meso-American	c.1400, the Toltec Light weakened before the Aztecs
17.	Arab	c.1770, the Arab Light weakened following the Ottoman Empire's pro-European "Tulip Period" (1717-30) when Ottomans dressed like Europeans

18. African   c.1806, the African Light weakened as a result of European trading contacts which had begun with the Portuguese (1446), English (1553) & Dutch (1595), & increased during the Industrial Revolution; & after Mungo Park's two journeys down the Niger (1795, 1805) & other explorations; in 1806 following the Napoleonic Wars South Africa passed to Britain, extending European contact

19. Indian   c.1710, the Indian Light weakened as a result of European trading contacts (e.g. with the British East India Company)

20. S.-E.-Asian   c.1760, during the preliminary conquest of insular S.-E. Asia by Europeans

21. Japanese   c.1840, during the time of the Opium War in China when European ships reopened Japan & Europeans were renewing contact at the end of the Tokugawa Shogunate

22. Oceanian   c.1810? after the European voyages of discovery of 1720-1780 the Light weakened as a result of European trading contacts

23. Chinese   c.1810, near the beginning of the imperial Ch'ing decline & the Opium War (1839-40), when Neo-Confucianism had lost its grip before advancing Westernisation (which emphasised concrete evidence & practical learning)

24. Tibetan   c.1880, during the decline of the Chinese Manchu control of Tibet after contact with the British

25. Central-Asian   c.1490, during the decline of the Timurid Empire as a result of Uzbek Black Sheep & White Sheep Turks

37. BREAKDOWN OF CERTAINTIES

A generation after the Light has faded from the religion, there is a breakdown of certainties following a military event. Absolute values become relative, and the old religious certainties are no more, as the following pattern bears out:

Civilization	Date of breakdown of certainties
1. Indo-European Kurgan/Old European	c.1625 BC? further Battle-Axe invasion & Greek influence as Unetice-Tumulus culture & Mycenaeans sought C.-European & Cornish tin (attested by appearance of faience beads, which were invented in Egypt & made in Mycenaean Aegean, in Unetice & Wessex areas, probably in exchange for C.-European & Cornish tin)
2. Mesopotamian	c.626 BC, when the Chaldean Neo-Babylonians occupied Assyrian Babylon; later in 606 BC together with the Medes they ended the Assyrian Empire
3. Egyptian	c.730 BC, when Libyan Egypt fell to the Kushites
4. Aegean-Greek	c.480 BC, when the Persians achieved victory over the Greeks at the battle of Thermopylae, & delivered both the Spartans & Athenians a great blow
5. Roman	c.410, when Rome was sacked by the Visigoths after invasions by the Ostrogoths, Gauls & Huns
6. Anatolian	c.696/5 BC, when the Cimmerians sacked Gordium, the Phrygian capital, & Assyrian rule had replaced the last Neo-Hittite states
7. Syrian	c.710 BC, when Assyrian rule was replacing the Neo-Hittite states in Syria

8.	Israelite	c.597 BC, when the Neo-Babylonians captured Jerusalem after the Davidic Josiah had died in 609 BC & the Neo-Babylonian Empire had obliterated Assyria by 606 BC
9.	Celtic	c.446, when, following the withdrawal of the Romans from Britain & the fall of Rome & around the time of the murder of St Augustine by the Vandals, & following the British tyrant Vortigern's invitation to the Saxons, the Saxons caused the Celtic British to flee to Brittany
10.	Iranian	c.572, when the Turks & Byzantines conducted a war against Iran (572-9)
11.	European	c.1916, after the First World War began (see Hagger, *The Syndicate*) and after the Liberal legislation of 1910 began a change in relationships between master and servant
12.	North-American	—
13.	Byzantine-Russian	c.1855, when the Crimean defeat by the British & French was followed by the emancipation of the serfs (1861), the outbreak of terrorism & the rise of the Bolsheviks whose roots are in Nihilism (which is portrayed by Bazarov in Turgenev's *Fathers and Sons,* 1862) & after the First World War, by the Bolshevik Revolution
14.	Germanic-Scandinavian	c.596 when the Avars attacked Thuringia & forced Queen Brunhilda to buy their departure
15.	Andean	c.1460, when the Incas overran the Chimu Empire, shortly before the Spanish conquest of Latin America, which followed the civil war over the Inca succession (c.1525-1532)

16. Meso-American	c.1428, when the Aztecs overran the Toltec Empire, shortly before the Spanish conquest of Latin America
17. Arab	c.1798, when Napoleon I invaded Egypt (to be expelled by the British & Ottomans in 1801)
18. African	c.1835, when 12,000 Boers began their Great Trek inland, delivering a blow against the indigenous black Africans shortly before the European conquest of Africa
19. Indian	c.1749, the battle of Ambur after the emergence of the Maratha Empire at the expense of the Moghul Empire, when European French superiority over India was established & the Anglo-French struggle for India began
20. S.-E.-Asian	c.1786, when the British acquired Penang & before the European conquest of S.-E. Asia
21. Japanese	c.1863, when the American, French & British bombardment of Kagoshima & Shimonoseki (repeated in 1864) demonstrated foreign military superiority & led to the defeat of the last Tokugawa shogun at Kyoto, the imperial restoration in 1868 & the Europeanization of Japan
22. Oceanian	c.1840, when the British colonized New Zealand shortly before the French colonized the Marquesas in 1842; Europeans began trading with Oceania & imposing colonial rule & values
23. Chinese	c.1840, when during the Sino-British conflict of the Opium War the West was penetrating commercially & militarily & when unrest & disorder had caused imperial deterioration
24. Tibetan	c.1903, when the Dalai Lama fled to China in 1903/4 after

the British conquest of Tibet

25.	Central-Asian	c.1543, when Central Asia passed under the ascendancy of the eastern Mongols of the Ordos under Altan Khan who reintroduced the Tibetan Buddhism of the Dalai (Mongolian for "Ocean") Lamas & allied with the Manchus

38. Central Idea/Religion weaken, Visual Arts become Restless and Secular

As the Light weakens before an external threat, so there is a restlessness in the visual arts which become concerned with the individual rather than the type. Sculpture becomes tortured, violent and emotional, or realistically down to earth, and in books there is a growing interest in personality as vast libraries are compiled:

Civilization	Date Central Idea & religion weakened & visual arts became restless/secular
1. Indo-European Kurgan/Old European	c.1660-1600 BC? Central Idea & arts of Wessex/European culture weakened on the evidence of archaeological finds in the last Wessex barrows c.1600-1500 BC
2. Mesopotamian	c.658-597 BC, Mesopotamian Central Idea & religion weakened; under Ashurbanipal, after the destruction of Babylon in 648, Assyrian art reached its peak with human figures, camels & icons (e.g. bas-reliefs at Nineveh)
3. Egyptian	c.770-710 BC, naturalism in art, creativity slowly disappearing, Egyptian Central Idea & religion weakened as Kushites (Ethiopians) dominated Egypt
4. Aegean-Greek	c.510-450 BC, Greek Central Idea & religion weakened, art took on human scale as Persians menaced and was influenced

from Persepolis. Pheidias

5.	Roman	c.370-420, Roman Central Idea & religion weakened, pagan themes continued but without the pagan Light, lyrical & poetical styles deteriorated, arts declined
6.	Anatolian	c.510-450 BC, Anatolian Central Idea weakened after Phrygians & Neo-Hittites disappeared before Cimmerians & Assyrians
7.	Syrian	c.760-700 BC, Syrian Central Idea weakened & Neo-Hittite religion passed from the arts under Assyrian rule
8.	Israelite	c.630-587 BC, Israelite Central Idea weakened as the Neo-Babylonian Empire menaced & "traitorous" Jeremiah urged surrender to Nebuchadrezzar
9.	Celtic	c.400-460, Celtic Central Idea weakened as Saxons menaced
10.	Iranian	c.532-592, Iranian Central Idea & religion weakened as the Byzantines menaced
11.	European	c.1870-1930, European Central Idea & religion weakened under pressure from African & Indian/Asian influences & the First World War as the European Empires began to disintegrate; Modernist movement including abstract art & Art Nouveau coincided with loss of Light
12.	North-American	—
13.	Byzantine-Russian	c.1800-1860, Russian Central Idea weakened as socialist terrorists & Bolsheviks menaced & the Russian Light disappeared from the arts

14. Germanic-
    Scandinavian
    c.558-618, Germanic Central Idea weakened together with
    Germanic religion of Thor/Arian Christ in the face of Avar
    attacks & the Spanish Visigoths' conversion to Catholicism

15. Andean
    c.1420-1480, Andean Central Idea & religion weakened as
    the Incas menaced

16. Meso-
    American
    c.1390-1450, Meso-American Central Idea & religion
    weakened as the Aztecs menaced & Motecuhzoma I (crowned
    1440) & his brother Tlacaelel invented a new (Aztec)
    religion, synthesising northern tribal & indigenous religion

17. Arab
    c.1760-1820, Muslim religion & arts weakened as the
    Europeans menaced

18. African
    c.1795-1855, African religion & arts weakened as the
    Europeans menaced

19. Indian
    c.1700-1760, Indian Hindu & Muslim religion & arts
    weakened as the Europeans (notably the British) menaced

20. S.-E.-Asian
    c.1750-1810, S.-E.-Asian Central Idea weakened as S.-E. Asia
    disintegrated before the Europeans

21. Japanese
    c.1830-1890, Japanese Central Idea & religion weakened
    before the Europeans, art declined

22. Oceanian
    c.1800-1860, Oceanian Central Idea, religion & arts
    weakened as the Oceanian culture disintegrated before
    European colonialism

23. Chinese
    c.1800-1860, Chinese Central Idea, religion & arts weakened
    as the Ch'ing dynasty disintegrated before European menace

24.	Tibetan	c.1870-1930, Tibetan Central Idea, religion & arts weakened as the Manchu control of Tibet disintegrated & in the face of British involvement, & Tibet was concerned to preserve its political independence	
25.	Central-Asian	c.1480-1540, Central-Asian Central Idea, religion & arts weakened as Timurids disintegrated before Uzbek Black Sheep & White Sheep Turks	

39. PHILOSOPHICAL RATIONALISM AND SCEPTICISM

Another symptom of the uncertain time is a development in philosophy, which becomes realistic and sceptical, as the following pattern shows:

Civilization	Philosophical rationalism & scepticism	Date
1. Indo-European Kurgan/ Old European	Weakening of Old Europe's religion as Indo-European era weakened with approaching end of Wessex culture	c.1660-1600 BC?
2. Mesopotamian	Scepticism as Assyrian religion weakened during the decline of the Assyrian Empire after AD c.640; (apart from inscriptions of the Assyrian kings, hymns, prayers, oracle texts & histories, no Assyrian or Babylonian literature has survived from the time of Ashurbanipal)	c.658-597 BC
3. Egyptian	Scepticism as Egyptian religion weakened before Kushites	c.770-710 BC

4.	Aegean-Greek	Rationalism of Ionian philosophers (a reaction to the weakening of Assyrian and neo-Babylonian empires and religion & Sophists developed into the rationalism & realism of the Greek Sophists (satirised by Aristophanes in *The Clouds*), Socrates & Thucydides after the Persian menace	c.510-450 BC
5.	Roman	Philosophy dominated by Stoicism & then the Sophists; the universities were still founded on rhetoric & pagan literature, & St Augustine was a teacher of rhetoric; (his *Confessions* challenged the prevailing scepticism)	c.370-430
6.	Anatolian	Rationalism of Ionian philosophers as the Phrygians and Neo-Hittites disappeared	c.725-665 BC
7.	Syrian	Rationalism & scepticism when Phoenician religion weakened as Assyrians destroyed Phoenician coastal cities & deported populations	c.730-670 BC
8.	Israelite	Doom prophecies of Jeremiah & Ezekiel against prevailing rationalism & scepticism as the Neo-Babylonian Empire menaced	c.630-587 BC
9.	Celtic	Scepticism during the collapse of Celtic rule before the Saxons	c.400-460
10.	Iranian	Scepticism as Sasanian religion	c.532-592

weakened during the dissolution of
Sasanian Empire before the Byzantine
menace

11.	European	Scepticism as Christianity weakened during the later Victorian period, under colonial influences and during the First World War; Logical Positivism & Linguistic Analysis of the Vienna Circle	c.1870-1930
12.	North-American	—	
13.	Byzantine-Russian	Following Napoleon's invasion of Russia and during the rise of terrorism, the rationalist, sceptical & atheistic philosophy of the Westernizers which opposed the philosophy of the religious Slavophiles, the contrast being found in the novels of the Slavophile Dostoevsky	c.1800-1860
14.	Germanic-Scandinavian	Germanic scepticism after decline of Germanic religion in Britain, France, Italy & Spain and during Avar attacks; (Saxon philosophy was rationalist & sceptical in *The Wanderer* & *The Seafarer*; both Anglo-Saxon poems probably of the 7th C & certainly from the earlier part of the Saxon period)	c.558-618
15.	Andean	Philosophy of Chimu was rationalistic & sceptical regarding Chimu religion	c.1420-1480

before Inca sun religion

16.	Meso-American	Philosophy of Toltecs was rationalistic & sceptical regarding Toltec religion before new Aztec sun religion	c.1390-1450
17.	Arab	Rationalism & scepticism as a result of the Ottoman Empire's pro-European phase	c.1760-1820
18.	African	Philosophy of pro-European Africans was rationalistic & sceptical regarding African religion as European contacts increased	c.1795-1855
19.	Indian	Rationalism & scepticism during the decline of the Moghul Empire & the advent of the European powers	c.1700-1760
20.	S.-E.-Asian	Rationalism & scepticism during the decline of Hindu-Buddhist S.-E. Asia before the Europeans	c.1750-1810
21.	Japanese	Rationalism & scepticism increased with advancing Westernization	c.1830-1890
22.	Oceanian	Rationalism & scepticism during the decline of Oceanian culture in the face of European colonialism	c.1800-1860
23.	Chinese	Rationalism & scepticism increased with advancing Westernization (which emphasised concrete evidence & practicalities)	c.1800-1860

24. Tibetan	Rationalism & scepticism during the decline of Manchu Tibet & in the face of British involvement	c.1870-1930
25. Central-Asian	Rationalism & scepticism during the decline of Timurids & in the face of Uzbek confederations	c.1480-1540

40. IMPERIAL DECLINE

As a result of overextending itself, the civilization now enters a time of imperial decline. The empire created by the counter-thrust has undergone a decline, and yields to an undefeated inheriting power, as the following pattern shows:

Civilization	Date of imperial decline
1. Indo-European Kurgan/Old European	c.1625-1550 BC, decline of Wessex chieftans' culture before the Unetice-Tumulus culture which brought faience beads to Wessex, probably in exchange for Cornish tin
2. Mesopotamian	c.626-539 BC, decline of Assyrian Empire, then of short-lived Chaldean Neo-Babylonian Empire
3. Egyptian	c.730-664 BC, Kushite Sudan & Asiatic empire lost during Kushite occupation of Egypt (730-671 BC) & Assyrian conquest of Egypt (671-664 BC)
4. Aegean-Greek	c.460-404 BC, end of First Athenian Empire as a result of First & Second Peloponnesian Wars
5. Roman	c.410-476, disintegration of the Roman Empire before the Germanic tribes after Theodosius (died 395) when the Eastern Roman Augustus, ruling from Byzantium, had pre-eminence

over the Western-Roman Caesar & the West-Roman Empire was finally Christian

---

| 6. | Anatolian | c.696-547 BC, following the Cimmerian conquest of Phrygia in 696, occupation of parts of Anatolia by the Assyrians (636) & the Medes (who conquered the Cimmerians, c.590-585), & final conquest of Anatolia by the Persians (547) while the Greek cities of Anatolia were conquered by Lydia |

| 7. | Syrian | c.710-538 BC, collapse of Syrian Empire before Assyria; then Neo-Babylonian Empire; then Persian Empire |

| 8. | Israelite | c.597-538 BC, collapse of Israelite Empire before the Neo-Babylonian Empire, which had wiped Assyria off the map in 609 BC; the fall of Jerusalem (587/6 BC) & the Exile in Babylon (586-538) |

| 9. | Celtic | c.446-540, the Christian Celtic Empire declined before the invading Saxons despite the resistance of King Arthur who opposed the Saxons; in 446 the British appealed to the Romans for help which never came, & many Celtic British emigrated to Brittany as the Romans maintained a protective presence in Gaul |

| 10. | Iranian | c.572-642, the Sasanian Empire declined before the invading Turks, Byzantines & Arabs |

| 11. | European | c.1916-1997?, decolonization, shedding of European empires before North-American challenge & Russian-backed Communist nationalists between the withdrawal of South Africa in 1910 and the British surrender of Hong Kong to China in 1997; ending with final triumph of North-American ideology |

12.	North-American	—

13.	Byzantine-Russian	c.1855-1918, decline of Romanov Empire after Napoleon's invasion of Russia, as a result of colonial conflicts & reform (which was designed to arrest the decline but which further accelerated it by encouraging revolutionary terrorism)

14.	Germanic-Scandinavian	c.596-687, decline of Germanic Frankish & Saxon Empires before the Avars who threatened the Franks, the Arabs who conquered the Germanic Visigothic kingdom in Spain c.711, & Christianizing Celts in Britain

15.	Andean	c.1460-1572, decline of Inca Empire taken from Chimus before Christianizing Spain

16.	Meso-American	c.1428-1542, decline of Toltec Empire under new Aztec rulers before Christianizing Spain

17.	Arab	c.1798-1881, decline of Ottoman Empire before Christianizing Europe (which led to eventual loss of Arabia & Syria to T. E. Lawrence); parallel decline of Iran under Qajars (1779-1925) & Anglo-Russian influence

18.	African	c.1835-1914, decline of African rule before penetration of Christianizing European colonial powers who had now repudiated the slave trade, although the Sokoto Caliphate in Nigeria, the Zulu state in Natal & the rise of Madagascar had provided strong African leadership

19.	Indian	c.1749-1818, decline of Maratha Empire before the advent of the European powers (Anglo-French Seven Years' War) & the triumph of the British Raj

20.	S.-E.-Asian	c.1786-1876, decline of S.-E. Asia as Burma invaded Siam; before the advent of the European powers
21.	Japanese	c.1868-1945, decline of Japanese Empire before Europeans after the Meiji Restoration of 1868 & the revival of Pure Shinto with the Emperor as *tenno* (Son of Heaven) led to Japanese expansion into Manchuria, Inner Mongolia & E. China, Tonkin & French Indo-china, British Malaya, Thailand, Burma, Dutch East Indies & Philippines (at the expense of the European, British & French empires whose decolonization the Japanese expansion assisted); this Empire was eroded 1942-1945 & collapsed abruptly following the N.-American civilization's dropping of atomic bombs on Hiroshima & Nagasaki
22.	Oceanian	c.1840-1900, decline of Oceanian culture following the advent of European colonialism (& more voyages of discovery 1722-1776 & the beginning of trade in 1788), in the course of which there were movements against native religions, e.g. the public desecration of statues of gods in Hawaii in 1819 & on Easter Island in the early 19th C
23.	Chinese	c.1840-1949, decline of Manchu Ch'ing Empire before European colonialism (e.g. the Opium War of 1839-41) & emerging republicanism
24.	Tibetan	c.1903-1951, decline of Chinese control of Tibet following the Chinese invasion of Tibet in 1910 & expulsion of the Chinese in 1911
25.	Central-Asian	c.1543-1644, decline of Empire of Mongols descended from Genghis Khan (Ordos & Chahars)

41. COLONIAL CONFLICT LEADING TO DECOLONIZATION

In the course of its imperial decline, the civilization enters a time of colonial conflict. This coincides with, or starts later than, the onset of the imperial decline, it features loss of the empire's territory to a great power or powers, and/or surrender of colonies (decolonization), and it ends with the winner of the conflict, a civilization that is younger and has not yet reached stage 41, effectively occupying the civilization (in stage 43).The winner of the conflict may not be the great power which has taken territory. Thus in the Mesopotamian civilization the Neo-Babylonians made the running but the Persians proved the winner, inheriting their gains. In the same way, in the European civilization the Byzantine-Russians made the running, challenging many Western colonies, but North America emerged to dominate and manipulate the world into world government.

There are several challenges, both from outside and from within the civilization itself as conflicting great powers within the civilization compete for supremacy (e.g. Athens and Sparta within the Aegean-Greek civilization, Britain and Germany within European civilization). The colonial conflict can produce a civil war and a new absolutist dynasty within one of the conflicting civilizations which may also be a civilization in colonial conflict (e.g. the conflict between the Russian Bolsheviks and Mensheviks that followed war with European Germany, and the conflict between the Chinese Communists and Nationalists that followed war with Japan). The period of colonial conflict always accompanies the imperial decline, always involves loss of territory and/or colonies, and always ends with an undefeated power defeating/conquering or inheriting the civilization and inaugurating a secularizing internationalist rule, as the following pattern shows:

Civilization	Colonial conflict with & loss of territory to undefeated power	Date of colonial conflict
1. Indo-European Kurgan/ Old European	More Battle-Axe settlers in Britain from Unetice-Tumulus culture of the Danube & Battle-Axe settlers from Mycenaean Greece? (who sought	c.1625-1550 BC

C.-European & Cornish tin, &

Danish amber)

2.	Mesopotamian	Chaldean Neo-Babylonians became independent of Assyria (626-539) & with the Medes ended the Assyrian Empire in 606; Persians took Babylonia	c.626-539 BC
3.	Egyptian	Occupation by Kushites (730-671) & Assyrians (671-664)	c.730-664 BC
4.	Aegean-Greek	Persian invasions; Athens' conflict with Sparta & loss of colonies and empire (the shock of which led to a Mannerist art)	c.460-404 BC
5.	Roman	Germanic tribes driven out by Asiatic Huns occupied parts of Roman Empire including colonies; invasions of Visigoths, Ostrogoths, Huns, Vandals & Gauls during decolonization; sack of Rome in 410 (by Visigoths), 455 (by Vandals) & 476 (by Odoacer of the Scyri, Heruli & Rugii)	c.410-476
6.	Anatolian	Following the Cimmerian conquest of Phrygia, occupation of parts of Anatolia by Assyria (636) & Medes (590-585), & final conquest of all Anatolia by Persians (547)	c.696-546 BC
7.	Syrian	Assyrian rule (709-609), then Neo-Babylonian rule (609-538), then Achaemenian Persians (538)	c.710-538 BC

8.	Israelite	Neo-Babylonian rise after Nebuchad-rezzar's defeat of Egypt in 605 BC, Neo-Babylonian invasions in 597 & 586 & the deporting of the Jews of Judah to Babylon (586-538)	c.597-538 BC
9.	Celtic	Saxon invasions of Britain put to flight the Christian Celts under Arthur	c.446-540
10.	Iranian	Sasanian conflicts with the Turks (a new nation), the Byzantines during the reign of Khosrow II (ending with Heraclius' invasion of Iran 622-628) & the Arabs, who sacked Ctesiphon, the Sasanian winter-capital, after the battle of al-Qadisiyed (636-7) & killed Rustam, the Sasanian commander-in-chief	c.572-642
11.	European	Eastern Europe: 1st & 2nd World Wars, Soviet Empire from 1945 until the collapse of the Berlin Wall, with final triumph of North-American ideology	c.1914-1989
		Western Europe: colonial conflict involving North American challenge during 1st & 2nd World Wars (which were civil wars between Germany & other European states that weakened the European empires & made decolonization inevitable), N.-American occupation of Germany and reconstruction and	c.1914-1997 (at least)

dominance through Marshall Aid,
Suez & wars of decolonization with
Soviet-backed Communist nationalists
in Asia & Africa, ending with the
surrender of Hong Kong in 1997 &
final triumph of North-American
ideology

(Following the economic integration &
expansion of the European Community
in 1992, a new European constitution
that was deeply unpopular with donor
nation-states' peoples, if ratified by
four-fifths of the 25 member states,
promised to create a superstate with full
political integration in 2008, in effect a
unified North-American-sponsored
United States of Europe, see stage 43)

12.	North-American	—	
13.	Byzantine-Russian	The Russian defeats by the Anglo-French in the Crimean War led to the creation of Rumania (1854); Russia expanded into Caucasia, the country of Kazaks & Kirgiz & Manchuria, but surrendered Manchuria to Japan (1905); after the First World War against Germany & Turkey (1914-16) & the Bolshevik Revolution of 1917 Russia ceded the Baltic provinces, its part of Poland, the protectorate in Finland & part of the Ukraine to the Central Powers,	c.1855-1918

while British, Canadian, Japanese, American & French troops landed in Archangel, Vladivostock & Odessa to help the Whites; other parts of Russia had seceded from the Bolsheviks; under the Bolsheviks the USSR effectively became a colony of American-German capitalism, its 5 year plans being financed by Western international banks

14.	Germanic-Scandinavian	Avars, Arabs & Christianized Celtic Saxons were in conflict with Germanic kingdoms; decline of Merovingian Franks as Frankish Neustria struggled with Frankish Austrasia	c.596-687
15.	Andean	Inca conflict with N. Ecuador; with occupying Spain & Roman Catholicism	c.1460-1572
16.	Meso-American	Aztec conflict with Toltec Mexico, which it won by dominating the states of Texcoco & Tlacopan; with occupying Spain & Roman Catholicism; (main conflict c.1460-1521)	c.1428-1542
17.	Arab	Conflict between Ottoman Empire, Arabs, & occupying European colonial powers which were carving out empires in Middle East & North Africa; British took Aden in 1839, & influenced Oman in 1853	c.1798-1881

18. African	Conflict with occupying Christian European colonial powers after centuries of trading contact (Portuguese voyages to Africa began as early as c.1434-1553, & Dutch & British voyages c.1553-1600); expansion inland from west by British (Rhodes in Rhodesia, Lugard in Nigeria)	c.1835-1914
19. Indian	Conflict with occupying European colonial powers (including the Anglo/French Seven Years' War)	c.1749-1818
20. S.-E.-Asian	Conflict with occupying European colonial powers, e.g. British occupation of Penang 1786 & Singapore 1819; Anglo-Dutch conflict of 1824; British occupation of coastal Burma 1824-6, 1852, 1876; French protectorate in Indo-china 1853-1867; British protectorate in Malay states 1874	c.1786-1876
21. Japanese	Conflict with European colonial powers following expansion in China, S.-E. Asia & Burma, at expense of British, French & Dutch Empires	c.1868-1945
22. Oceanian	Conflict with occupying European colonial powers, which began shortly before the discovery of Australia in 1788; British colonization of New Zealand 1840; French colonization of Marquesas & Tahiti 1842; British colonization of Fiji Islands 1874;	c.1840-1900

many South Pacific islands colonized
by British, French & Germans in
1880s & 1890s

23.	Chinese	British & other European forces (including French) opened up China to Western penetration during Opium Wars (beginning 1839-1841); Japan made gains (1894); conflict with Japan, which occupied Manchuria & parts of China (1937-1945); Nationalists' struggle against Soviet-influenced Communists (1931-1949)	c.1840-1949
24.	Tibetan	Conflict with European colonial power (Britain) & with occupying China as independence was won & lost	c.1903-1951
25.	Central-Asian	Mongols of Ordos allied with Manchus to conquer the Western Mongols (the Oirat tribes undescended from Genghis Khan)	c.1543-1644

42. AUTHORITARIAN PROLETARIANIZATION AND EGALITARIANISM

Around the end of the imperial decline the civilization undergoes proletarianiza-tion. The prevailing ideology is an egalitarianism, an egalitarianism of bodies under the rule of law, and authoritarian empires that go into decline concede legal and human rights to their citizens, who become genuinely egalitarian before the law. In this stage a benevolent Welfare State concedes lavish benefits, luxuries and pay set-tlements which "egalitarianize" the standard of living of the citizens; and a prole-tarian culture embraces all peoples within the civilization (a process today made possible by television). This egalitarian outlook is encouraged and perpetuated by the hugeness of the coming secular conglomerate, which embraces different cultures and religions and unifies them by the concept of benevolent proletarian egalitarianism under the law, which is the basis for the power's popular support. The proletarianization and egalitarianism further weaken the feudal structure of the civilization, in whose religion the Central Idea was invested.

	Civilization	Date	Nature of proletarianization
1.	Indo-European Kurgan/ Old European	from c.1550 BC	Unetice & Mycenaean egalitarianism (?)
2.	Mesopotamian	from c.539 BC	Persian egalitarianism (with one imperial law for all satrapies or provinces within the Persian Empire)
3.	Egyptian	from c.664 BC	Saite egalitarianism
4.	Aegean-Greek	from c.404 BC	Peloponnesian League's egalitarianism
5.	Roman	from c.476	Germanic barbarian egalitarianism of Ostrogothic Italy with with personal loyalty to monarchs, reinforced by Christian egalitarianism of souls as in Augustine's *De Civitate Dei* (City of God) & equality before the Roman law
6.	Anatolian	from c.546 BC	Persian egalitarianism

7.	Syrian	from c.538 BC	Persian egalitarianism
8.	Israelite	from c.538 BC	Persian egalitarianism acquired by exiled Jews in Babylon
9.	Celtic	from c.540	Christian Celtic egalitarianism of souls at the Round Table (no precendence) gave way to egalitarianism of the Saxon *foederati*, whose ancestors had been invited to Britain c.430 to garrison the east coast against the Picts, & who now joined their brothers
10.	Iranian	from c.642	Arab egalitarianism which was briefly anticipated by Mazdak's egalitarianism (abolition of all social inequalities) under Khavadh c.488-528, before the Mazdakites were massacred in 528
11.	European	from c.1997	American-style Pan-European egalitarianism & democratiz-ation under European Socialism; coming blend of W.-European capitalism & E.-European & ex-Soviet Communism under American free market capitalist ideology (Gorbachev's " common European home")

12.	North-American	—	
13.	Byzantine-Russian	c.1918-1991	Russia's authoritarian absolutism since Peter the Great became the proletarian absolutism of Soviet Communism, with theoretical egalitarianism of bodies under the law (& materialistic denial of souls); however the repressed ex-Soviet people have been deprived of human rights & since the fall of the Berlin Wall and the end of Gorbachev/Communism, may have begun to enjoy genuine egalitarianism under the law
14.	Germanic-Scandinavian	from c.687	Christian Carolingian Frankish egalitarianism in France & Germany; Christian Saxon egalitarianism in Britain, which became Catholic rather than Christian Celtic at the Synod of Whitby in 664
15.	Andean	from c.1572	Christian Spanish egalitarianism
16.	Meso-American	from c.1542	Christian Spanish egalitarianism
17.	Arab	from c.1881	Christian egalitarianism in N.

Africa & Middle East

18. African	from c.1914	Christian egalitarianism in Africa
19. Indian	c.1818-1947	Christian egalitarianism in India
20. S.-E.-Asian	c.1876-1947	Christian egalitarianism in S.-E. Asia, Soviet-backed revolutions in S.-E. Asia
21. Japanese	c.1945-present	American egalitarianism (Christian democracy) introduced in Japan from 1945
22. Oceanian	from c.1900	Christian egalitarianism in Polynesia & Melanesia
23. Chinese	1949-present	Chinese Communist absolutism without human rights which imitated Soviet absolutism, egalitarianism of bodies & materialistic denial of souls following Mao's revolution
24. Tibetan	1951-present	Chinese Communist absolutism without human rights, egalitarianism of bodies
25. Central-Asian	c.1644-1911	Chinese Manchu egalitarianism which used Tibetan Buddhism to rule the Mongols, placing Living Buddha"

43. LOSS OF NATIONAL SOVEREIGNTY TO AN INHERITING SECULARIZING CONGLOMERATE

As a result of the colonial conflict the declining civilization suffers a loss of sovereignty at the hands of the winner of the conflict, which is also a secularizing foreign influence. I can list the winners of each colonial conflict in relation to the stage their own civilization was in at the time as follows, noting that the younger the stage of their own civilization – which is always younger than the stage of the declining civilization – the more vital their Light and the less violent or secularizing the conglomerate will be:

Declining civilization	Winner of colonial conflict & foreign influence	Stage winner's own civilization was in at the time (indicating age of winner's civilization, vitality of winner's Light & therefore potentiality to renew declining civilization)
1. Indo-European Kurgan/ Old European	Neolithic Unetice-Tumulus people of Danube/Mycenaean Greece	? (Unetice)/ 15 (Aegean-Greek)
2. Mesopotamian	Persians (Cyrus's Achaemenian Persian Empire)	11 (Iranian)
3. Egyptian	Assyrian-backed Saite	34 (Mesopotamian)
4. Aegean-Greek	Persian-backed Peloponnesian League	11 (Iranian)

5.	Roman	Germanic tribes	34 (Germanic-Scandinavian)
6.	Anatolian	Persians	11 (Iranian)
7.	Syrian	Persians	11 (Iranian)
8.	Israelite	Persians	11 (Iranian)
9.	Celtic	Saxons	34 (Germanic-Scandinavian)
10.	Iranian	Arabs	11 (Arab)
11.	European	Americans (who via the Syndicate – see Hagger, *The Syndicate* – are set to create a United States of Europe)	15 (North American)
12.	North-American	—	
13.	Byzantine-Russian	American/European-funded Bolsheviks (see pp504-505)	15 (North American)/ end of 34 (European)
14.	Germanic-Scandinavian	Europeans (Carolingians in France & Germany)	7 (European)
15.	Andean	Spanish	28 (European)
16.	Meso-American	Spanish	28 (European)

17. Arab	Europeans	34 (European)
18. African	Europeans	34 (European)
19. Indian	Europeans	34 (European)
20. S.-E.-Asian	Europeans	34 (European)
21. Japanese	Americans	15 (North American)
22. Oceanian	Europeans	34 (European)
23. Chinese	Soviet-backed Chinese Communists	43 (Byzantine-Russian)
24. Tibetan	Chinese	43 (Chinese)
25. Central-Asian	Chinese Manchus	34 (Chinese)

The declining civilization is at the mercy of the winner of the colonial conflict. It passes within the influence of the winner, who inherits it and creates, either directly or indirectly, an expansionist conglomerate in which the declining civilization becomes a province or satrapy or a number of provinces or satrapies. The winner of the colonial conflict can be an undefeated foreign power which adds the declining civilization to its empire (often after another great power has exhausted itself in colonial conflict with the civilization), thus occupying and colonizing it.

In the case of the European civilization, the North-American winner of the Cold War worked for a reunification of Eastern and Western Europe as part of the dismantling of the Soviet Union's East-European empire, and (via a pro-Syndicate puppet British Prime Minister) for the reunification of Ireland, which was set to be a separate state in the coming United States of Europe (possibly along with Wales and Scotland), thus ending the period of IRA terrorism. Western Europe has decolonized with North-American encouragement at least until 1997 (the surrender of Hong Kong). Seventeen former British colonies (including Australia, New Zealand, Canada, Jamaica and Barbados) are considering dumping the Queen as Head of State following the Prince of Wales's marriage to his mistress, to pre-empt the prospect that the couple would be their Heads of State when the Queen dies.

Assuming there is no conquest by or surrender to an alien authoritarian empire of occupation by a foreign influence or power (such as the ex-USSR, an expansionist reunified Germany, America, China, Japan, Muslim peoples formerly under Soviet rule or Arab Islam) Western Europe is now waiting to surrender its sovereignty either voluntarily or by compulsion to a Western American-backed, German-funded conglomerate. This is set to be an internationalist expanded European Community, a United States of Europe in which Eastern-, Central- and Western-European nations will become a network of provinces within one politically united superpower looking towards the USA, with a constitutional structure similar to that of the USA (the unpopular new European constitution contained within a Reform Treaty which requires ratification), dominated by a reunited Germany (its main paymaster) and ruled from Brussels. It will initially include as states (in the US-style, such as California, Oregon and Nevada) the economically integrated nations whose common language is English, i.e. Britain and (eventually a united) Ireland (and perhaps a separate Scotland), France, Germany, Belgium, the Netherlands, Luxembourg, Italy, Spain, Portugal, Denmark, Greece and Turkey, 70% of whose legislation had passed from national parliaments to Brussels by 2005. It would stretch from the Baltic to the Aegean and would eventually include Switzerland, Austria, Norway and Sweden. Now Eastern Europe has broken away from the Soviet conglomerate and accepted American funding in a new Marshall Plan, many countries have applied to join the EU: Czechoslovakia, Hungary, Poland, Estonia, Lithuania, Latvia, Slovakia, Slovenia, Malta and Greek Cyprus (which joined the EEC in 2004), the former states of Yugoslavia, Romania, Bulgaria, Albania, and perhaps the USSR east of the Urals in a 48-member conglomerate (the idea behind Gorbachev's "common European home").

This expansionist secularizing cosmopolitan conglomerate which will for a while reunite all the European peoples including the European Russians and the Americans and Canadians, 90% of whom originated in Europe, will secularize each local religion (whether it is Church of England, Lutheran, Evangelical Protestant,

Catholic or Orthodox). It will embody the European Resurgence and will revive in one go the northern part of the Roman Empire, Charlemagne's Frankish Empire, the Holy Roman Empire, the Austro-Hungarian Empire and the northern part of the Ottoman Empire. With Syndicate help it is set to absorb the Arab, Israeli and North-African territories round the Mediterranean and Iran, so that it revives the entire Roman Empire and the entire Ottoman Empire.

The winner of the colonial conflict can (as in the case of Communism) be a section of the population (such as the Bolsheviks) that espouses a foreign ideology (Western Marxism), which conquers the civilization and has the effect of turning the civilization into provinces or satrapies (soviet republics).

The conglomerate of the USSR based on an internationalist foreign Marxian ideology, devised by a German Jew in European London and funded by American Illuminatist international financiers (see pp504-505), was imported by the Bolsheviks under Lenin, who was also funded by American and German international financiers. Imperial Russia surrendered her sovereignty to their repressive one party "dictatorship of the proletariat", and became a network of soviet republics or provinces. The new conglomerate, under a proletarian "dynasty" of atheist absolutists, persecuted and secularized the Orthodox Church from 1918 (despite re-establishing the patriarchate abolished by Peter the Great in 1917), executed millions (some estimates suggest 6 million) and set about expanding the Russian Empire, recovering all the European and Asian territories that had seceded. After an empire-building conflict with first Germany and then the USA it seized Eastern Europe and constructed a world-wide maritime empire of proxy bases in client-states, many of which were European colonies before the European decolonization of 1945-1988, and which reflected the USSR's status (achieved through anti-American espionage and the treachery of Fuchs) as a nuclear superpower.

The conglomerate has been expansive, and as the last of the European territorial empires was in decline in 1988 when Soviet troops withdrew from Afghanistan. This withdrawal was a result of Soviet economic stagnation, "openness" reforms, the introduction of limited capitalism and anti-absolutist restructuring (the introduction of an American Presidential system with more democracy and restrictions on the power of the Party) which have fueled demands for autonomy from the Baltic to Armenia, and which, as with Alexander II and the 19th-century Ottomans, failed to arrest the decline and further accelerated it. The 1990s saw the loss of the

East-European Empire (which began with the decommunization of Poland, Hungary, East Germany, Czechoslovakia and Romania), the maritime Empire and the beginning of the break-up of the conglomerate USSR with independence for Islamic and Asian territories. Gorbachev's moves towards federalism in 1990 led to the creation of the CIS (Commonwealth of Independent States) under Yeltsin and closed stage 43 (Communist Party rule) and brought in stage 46 (federal linkage of the different sovereign nationalities within the former Soviet Union).

The conglomerate can govern the declining civilization by invitation but its regime is generally imposed by or has the backing of force or legal pressure. There is a measure of political integration as the territory that forms the conglomerate is integrated within a new system, to which it surrenders its sovereignty. The nature of the conglomerate depends on whether it is accompanied by a renewal of the Light, which in turn depends on how young a civilization the winner of the colonial conflict comes from; the lower the number of the stage the winner's civilization is at (see table above), the more likely it will be to renew the Light. If the conglomerate is accompanied by a renewal of the Light, as in the Germanic-Scandinavian and Latin American conglomerates, then the conglomerate is less violent and less secularizing than if it is not, as in the case of the Russian and Chinese conglomerates. Fom the point of view of the civilization's Central Idea, the Light, the conglomerate is an internationalist, even alien, influence which is detached from the civilization's religion and further secularizes it.

In the following table c.2015? appears as a possible end-date of some conglomerates. This is the target date for a coming world government (see Hagger, *The Syndicate*), to which all conglomerates are supposed to surrender their sovereign control. I have concluded that China will be the last to surrender control over its conglomerate and have put the final date of the Chinese union as c.2020 rather than c.2015.

Civilization	Loss of sovereignty to conglomerate, which acts as secularizing foreign influence	Date
1. Indo-European Kurgan/	Unetice-Tumulus people's Empire in West with trade in Cornwall,	c.1550-1400 BC

Old European	Ireland, C. Europe & the Baltic	
2. Mesopotamian	Cyrus's Achaemenian Persian Empire which was united with Babylonia into a conglomerate	c.539-331 BC
3. Egyptian	Saite dynasty's Assyrian-backed conglomerate under the Assyrian vassal prince Psamtik I of Sais, who took the Assyrian name Nabu-shezibanni in 663 BC, became independent of Assyria & extended his rule over Egypt with Libyan soldiers & Greek mercenaries, subduing 11 Assyrian princes & vassals in the Delta c.658-651 BC & retaining the Kushite God's Wife of Amon & Votaress of Amon which blurred the traditional Egyptian Light & had a secularizing effect on Egyptian religion, but controlling them through his daughter; Egyptian sovereignty was under Assyrian control until Assyria's power declined from c.655 BC	c.664-525 BC
4. Aegean-Greek	Persian-backed Peloponnesian League controlled by the Persian Great King; Athens revived again from c.378 BC but was checked by the Persian Artaxerxes III Ochus & lost a Second Athenian Empire while the rest of Greece was a Persian-controlled conglomerate	c.404-337 BC
5. Roman	Empire of the German chieftan	c.476-540

Odoacer, who deposed the last Roman
Emperor in the West in 476 &
established a Kingdom of Italy;
Visigothic Kingdom in Spain &
France; Vandal Kingdom in N. Africa,
Sicily, Sardinia & Corsica; after
488, rule of the Ostrogoths who
invaded Italy, beseiged Ravenna &
overthrew Odoacer

6.	Anatolian	Cyrus's Achaemenian Persian Empire	c.546-334 BC
7.	Syrian	Cyrus's Achaemenian Persian Empire (language spoken, Imperial Aramaic)	c.538-333 BC
8.	Israelite	Cyrus's Achaemenian Persian Empire	c.538-333 BC
9.	Celtic	Secular internationalist Saxon rule spreading from E. Britain to W. Britain; (Saxon *foederati* were invited to Britain c.430, & their descendants conquered Britain & became fully Christianized, being converted by Roman Catholicism from 597 & Celtic Christians from 653, settling for Roman Catholicism after the Synod of Whitby in 664)	c.540-687
10.	Iranian	Arab Caliphate in Iran after the	c.642-821

Battle of Nahavand completed
the conquest of the Sasanians
(642-661), Arab Ummayad
Empire in Iran (661-750),
Abbasid Caliphate in Iran
(750-821)

11. European	European Union with new European constitution contained within a Reform Treaty is forming a United States of Europe eventually comprising 48 states (see p258)	From 1997/ c.2008: conglomerate created when an expanded, economically integrated European Community led to a USA-influenced politically unified United States of Western, Central & Eastern Europe
	This conglomerate has been unfolding since 1945 as follows:	
	(1) Eastern and Central Europe: already occupied by the authoritarian ex-Soviet Empire (one victor of 1945), and following decommunisation now turning to Western-European Community conglomerate,	1945-1991
	(2) Western Europe:	Foreign in-

occupied by American nuclear and military bases, established by the American victory of 1945 and the Marshall Plan when, to counter Communism, $12 billion of American economic aid was distributed to the Organization for European Economic Co-operation (OEEC), out of which grew the EEC; the Western-European Community conglomerate is ruled from Brussels but is within the sphere influence of the American civilization which divided the world with the Byzantine-Russian civilization at the Tehran Conference of 1943 and presides over a secular, internationalist world-wide Western civilization in the Free World.

fluence: 1945-c.2008; foreign conquest & occupation by: superstate after c.2008

12.	North-American	—	
13.	Byzantine-Russian	Conglomerate of USSR based on an internationalist foreign Marxian ideology and funded by the Syndicate (see pp502-503); Soviet Communism (see pp264-265)	c.1918-1991
14.	Germanic-Scandinavian	Reunification of the Franks under Mayors of the Palace, beginning with Pepin II & Charles Martel, who ruled of behalf of impotent Merovingian descendants of Clovis & who were known as Carolingians as they were all called Charles; the Carolingian Catholic (i.e. secular in relation to the Germanic Thor/Odin & Arian Christ)	c.687-843

conglomerate passed into stage 11 of
the growing European civilization;
occupation of Germanic territories
of Lombards, Frisians & Saxons
by Catholic Frankish Empire of
Charlemagne & his successors &
by Saxon Christianity in what is
now France, Germany, Italy &
Britain; (these were inter-connected
in the 8th C, Offa of Mercia being
closely associated on the Continent
with Pepin III the Short, the father of
Charlemagne whose kingdoms included
France, Germany & Italy; & Greensted
Church, Essex, the oldest wooden
church in the world, c.845, bears
witness to this phase of Saxon
Christianity in Britain); although the
Germanic tribes lived under the
Christian rule of what had just become
the European civilization & Saxony
became a part of the Kingdom of
Germany, Viking Normans entered
Frankish France in 911 & the religion
of Odin & Thor persisted at least until
c.1000

| 15. | Andean | Internationalist Spanish colonial Empire (while Portuguese Empire was established in Brazil) | c.1572-1810 |
| 16. | Meso-American | Internationalist Spanish colonial Empire | c.1542-1810 |

17. Arab	Arab world passed into internationalist European colonial Empires which secularized Islam in North Africa (the French in Tunisia from 1881 & Morocco from 1912, the British in Egypt from 1882 & the Sudan from 1899, the Italians in Ethiopia from 1889 & in Libya from 1912) & the Middle East (especially after 1st World War when Syria & Lebanon had French mandates, & Palestine & Iraq British mandates, and when Turkey became independent in 1920); independence was gradual: Ethiopia 1942, Jordan 1946, Libya 1951, the British Military Zone at Suez, the Sudan & Morocco 1956, Algeria 1962, Aden & Oman in the 1980s; US invasions of Afghanistan and Iraq, and occupation are semi-colonial	c.1881-1980 (Semi- colonial occupation 2001-6)
18. African	Internationalist European colonial Empires which secularized African religion following scramble for Africa; they lasted until independence after "wind of change" & decolonization by liberation movements from Portugal in 1970s	c.1914-1980
19. Indian	Internationalist British Empire (British Raj), unification of Indian states into one India under a conquering power which secularized Indian religion	c.1818-1947

20.	S.-E.-Asian	European colonization & Empires in S.-E. Asia (by British, French & Dutch in Burma, French Indo-china, Siam etc.), which secularized S.-E.-Asian religion	c.1876-1947
21.	Japanese	American occupation of Japan under Gen. MacArthur in 1945-51 resulted in constitutional reform along American lines which separated State & Shinto (the divine basis of the Emperor's authority), & secularized the State; demilitarization through pro-American democracy & control over Self-Defence Agency Forces; despite restrictions on national sovereignty, Japan is now a unified conglomerate of 47 prefectures or provinces (which since 1947 have been represented in the House of Representatives), a superpower looking towards America & managed via the Trilateral Commission (see p505 & Hagger, *The Syndicate*), but hampered by economic sluggishness	c.1945-c.2015/c.2020?
22.	Oceanian	Western (European and North-American) colonization & Empire in Oceania which secularized Oceanian religion; Australia's capture of islands from Germans during the First World War	c.1900-c.2015/c.2020? (Overlap as some islands have decolonised, some are still under Western rule)

23. Chinese   Conglomerate of People's Republic   c.1949-
                            of China based on an internationlist   c.2020?
                            foreign Marxian ideology, devised
                            by a German Jew in European London,
                            funded by American Illuminatist
                            international financiers (see pp502-503)
                            & imported from Russian in 1921 by
                            Chinese Communists – Chi'ang T'ang
                            (Sinkiang) was under Soviet influence
                            as early as 1928 – to whose repressive
                            one-party "dictatorship of the prolet-
                            ariat" under Mao China surrendered
                            her sovereignty in 1949 after the recovery
                            of Manchuria from Japan & the USSR,
                            becoming a network of Soviet-style
                            republics or provinces; the new
                            conglomerate, under a proletarian
                            "dynasty" of atheist absolutists,
                            persecuted the religious expression of
                            the Chinese Central Idea of *Ti*, &
                            secularized Chinese religion, expelling
                            the Christian missionaries between
                            1951 and 1956, & executed millions
                            (estimates vary between 3 & 20m, all
                            victims may total 70m); it set about
                            securing a world role for the Chinese
                            Empire, annexing Tibet in 1950-1 &
                            certain Indian territories, intervening in
                            N. Korea (1950) & N. Vietnam & even-
                            tually aiding the Khmers Rouges against
                            the Vietnamese (in the post-1979 Indo-
                            Chinese War between Communists)
                            & aiding some African liberation
                            movements while becoming an H-bomb

power (1967); the new expansionist conglomerate has passed through the extremism of the Cultural Revolution, & may already have begun to decline as by 1988 the realists & pragmatists were introducing limited capitalism & increasing democracy, & before the massacre in T'ienanmen Square of June 4, 1989 there were signs that American ideas had prevailed in the ideological conflict between Maoism & Americanisation & that China was becoming more pro-Western; in 2005 China had some 200 nuclear weapons pointing at the US, and bases at either end of the Panama Canal, and had held a rehearsal for the capture of Taiwan, raising the prospect of a US-China Cold War; the 21st C may see the loss of Tibet & the beginning of the break-up of the Chinese conglomerate with independence for some regions

24. Tibetan	European Internationalist Chinese occupation which has secularized Tibetan religion, reaffirmed by the massacre of 450 Tibetans in Lhasa on March 5, 1989 to stifle signs of Tibetan nationalism (If Tibet suddenly wins independence, this occupation should be seen as the end of stages 40-41, Tibet's imperial decline & colonial conflict; in which case the winner of the conflict, the	c.1951-c.2015/ c.2020?

inheriting conglomerate will soon

appear)

25. Central-Asian	Chinese Manchu occupation of	c.1644-1911
	Mongolia (conquest completed in	
	1759) which secularized C.-Asian	
	religion, ruled through a Tibetan "Urga	
	Living Buddha" (i.e. the Mongols were	
	ruled by a Manchu nominee)	

The conglomerate inherits the declining civilization's colonies. However, the inheritor is not always the decolonizer as we see from civilization 2 (which the Persians inherited from the Neo-Babylonians or Chaldeans).

Before we leave stage 43 we should return to civilization 11 and ask again: who has inherited the European empires and their colonies? At one stage it seemed that it was the Muscovite founder of a conglomerate governing all the republics of the USSR, the enemy of Western Europe in the 1950s and 1960s who created a maritime empire that had to be resisted, who encouraged puppets to take over European colonies. However the USSR withdrew from Afghanistan and collapsed. The states of the ex-USSR regrouped into a federal CIS (Commonwealth of Independent States), turned to market forces, applied for membership of the EU, and adopted a US-style Presidential system. It is now clear that the USSR has moved from stage 43 to stage 46.

Unless a new foreign power (such as Islam) conquers Europe and is seen to be the winner of Europe's 20th-century colonial conflict, the true inheritor of the European empires is the North-American civilization which, via the Syndicate (see pp508-509) is planning a globalist role. America is poised to inherit Europe from Soviet colonial conflict just as Persia inherited Mesopotamia from Neo-Babylonian colonial conflict. (Indeed, a new interest in Persian Achaemenian studies can be expected in America.) If we look at 20th-century history from the American point of view we can see that ever since its anti-European Declaration of Independence America has consistently acted with self-interest in her dealings with Europe, first by staying out of the First World War and profiting by Lend-Lease; by repeating this stance at the beginning of the Second World War; and then by Marshall Aid (which was seemingly altruistic but which increased American influence), by founding the EEC, by founding NATO, and by opposing Europe and Israel over Suez.

It is worth looking in greater detail at how America worked against the British and French Empires in the Middle East after 1945 in pursuit of her own interests. The American conquest of Hitler's Europe under Eisenhower sought to marginalize Britain's final position; hence the tension with Montgomery. From 1945 it was American policy to undermine the British Empire and the *Pax Britannica* in the Middle East. The US received the British oil interests in Saudi Arabia, which had been made over by Churchill in a deal to bring America into the war (see Hagger, *The Syndicate*). When in 1951 Mossadeq seized British oil installations at Abadan, Iran, America put pressure on Britain not to take them back by force, and when there was an Anglo-American overthrow of Mossadeq in 1953, America took half of British oil interests. In 1953 America pressed Eden (then British Foreign Secretary) to pull out of the British base in the Suez Canal Zone, and when in 1956 Nasser seized the Suez Canal through which came two-thirds of Europe's oil, giving Nasser in Prime Minister Eden's words "a thumb on our windpipe", and the Anglo-French operation to retake the Suez Canal was succeeding, President Eisenhower accused Britain and France of acting like imperialists, sided with Nasser, threatened to cut off British and French oil, and refused Britain and France credit when sterling was collapsing and a sixth of British foreign reserves had been spent. (Eisenhower, along with John Foster Dulles, then controlled the Republican party for the pro-world government Council on Foreign Relations, see pp505-506.)

The American torpedoing of the Suez operation undermined British influence in the Levant and French influence in North Africa for ever. This led to a pro-Nasserite *coup* in Iraq in 1958 and the closure of the British bases at Habanya and Basra, and to the eventual emergence of Saddam Hussein as a threat to Western oil interests. When in 1964 Nasser invaded the Yemen to support a puppet government against the Yemen monarchy, the US recognised the new government and supported Nasser. Britain and Saudi Arabia supported the royalists, and in the ensuing civil war the Americans supported Nasser's 30,000 troops, who only withdrew after his defeat in the 1967 Arab-Israeli war, itself another consequence of the failure of the Suez operation and of America's anti-British policy in the Middle East. Britain hung on to the Gulf States and the base at Aden. The Americans refused to join with

Britain in defending these last vestiges of Empire, and the British Labour government withdrew from Aden, handing the country over to Communists, and in 1970 the remaining British positions in the Gulf were abandoned.

With Britain gone, the Americans sought to control the Gulf through their ally the Shah of Iran, whom they armed. The Shah's pro-Western stance led to his downfall at the hands of Ayatollah Khomenei. The Iran-Iraq war gave the Americans another opportunity to police the Gulf, and they have had naval forces in the area ever since. Iraq's annexation of Kuwait, and Saddam Hussein's threat to Saudi Arabia and (as in 1956) two-thirds of the West's oil, have led to an increased American involvement in the Gulf area, to the committal of ground forces and an attempt to impose a *Pax Americana* in which Britain and (to a lesser extent) France are again involved. In 1990 America became engaged in an operation (the first Iraq war) very similar to the Suez operation which, out of American self-interest, America did so much to abort. And the second Iraq war continued the trend, ironically with British support. Eisenhower's vice-president Richard Nixon wrote, "In retrospect I believe that our actions (regarding Suez) were a serious mistake. Nasser became even more rash and aggressive.... The most tragic result was that Britain and France were so humiliated and discouraged by the Suez crisis that they lost the will to play a major role on the world scene." In fact, between 1945 and 2005 America has carried through a consistent policy of undermining the European empires to further the goal of American world domination, and the US tolerated Anglo-French involvement in the Middle East in 1990 first because an international camouflage was expedient, but mainly because America is now established as the inheritor of the European empires. The US was in conflict with France, Germany and Russia during the second Iraq war, a conflict based on a clash of interests.

Europe's imperial decline let in the USSR for a while, but it has been the Americans who have seen them off and won the Cold War. With hindsight the turning point in the American-Russian Cold War over Europe was 1984-5, when from the USSR the late Soviet Leader Brezhnev's KGB, now under his former aide Chernenko, attempted a revolution in Britain during the miners' strike (using Gaddafi, the NUM and the IRA) and had one last onslaught through international terrorism, both of which events the West found the will to resist. In quick succession two Russian leaders (Andropov and Chernenko) of the generation who remembered the Leninist rule of 1917 died, handing over to Gorbachev who, free from memories of the Tsarist days, compared Russia with the West and found Russia wanting. It seems that it will be the Americans who will grow through a coming imperial phase (stage 15).

America's present influence in Europe is largely through Germany. Despite the Anglo-American accord over Kuwait and overt US conflict with Germany during the second Iraq war there has been a US-German alliance in recent times that is just as strong as the US-German financial alliance during part of the First World War (see p502-503). American leadership of a coming European conglomerate was suggested by the NATO Summit of May 1989, when President Bush Sr united Britain and West Germany and received approval from all the European nations for his plan to cut conventional weapons by 20%. It was American pressure that achieved the reunification of Germany, and it was an American draft that led to NATO's leaders extending the hand of friendship towards Eastern Europe in July 1990, paving the way for a whole and free Europe "from the Atlantic to the Urals and the Baltic to the Adriatic" (President Bush Sr's words). The same London Declaration saw the Conference on Security and Co-operation in Europe (CSCE) as "bringing together the countries of Europe and North America".

America's role in the emerging European conglomerate will become clearer as the European civilization forms a United States of Europe in imitation of the United States of America, and adopts other aspects of the American Presidential system. (The new European constitution provides a United States of Europe in all but name; the words "United States of Europe" were deleted from a draft of the constitution to avoid offending British sensitivities.) The nature of America's protective involvement in a European conglomerate will become clearer when the first Islamic state manufactures an atomic bomb. This now threatens to be Iran. (At one time the threat came from Iraq, which the CIA – perhaps as a propagandist pretext for coming military action – estimated would threaten Southern Europe with nuclear weapons by 1993 unless it was stopped; Libya; or a southern state of the USSR.) For when Islam threatens Europe with nuclear weapons America will be welcomed by the Europeans even more greatly than American defence was welcomed when Iraq threatened Europe's oil interests in Saudi Arabia and the Gulf during the first Iraq war.

As to the nature of the conglomerate about to be entered by the European civilization (civilization 11), the movement in Brussels favouring political integration has gone farther and faster than many believed possible. The new constitution was set to be ratified by 2008. There were problems caused by No votes in the French and Dutch referenda and the constitution was replaced by a Reform Treaty of 2007 which was found by an independent group of 16 elder statesmen to be substantially the same as the constitution. The constitution had stated that if a four-fifths majority for ratification could be achieved from the 25 member states, Brussels would eventually control 48 nation-states in a US-style superstate.

44. SYNCRETISM & UNIVERSALISM AS RELIGIOUS SECTS DRAW TOGETHER WITH LIGHT AS COMMON SOURCE

There is now a general syncretism, as religious sects draw together in the shadow of the new conglomerate. This stage is a Universalist one; it is the stage the European civilization is entering now. Universalism has already surfaced in stages 15, 29 and 34. In this stage the Light is perceived to be the common source of all religions, and this book and its companion volume *The Light of Civilization* anticipate and are typical of works produced during this stage. In the European civilization, the Universalism emanating from the New-Age sects of the North-American civilization's stage 15 preserves the vision and knowledge of the Light for future generations. This Universalism emphasizes the common Light in all civilization's religions and sects and is essentially syncretistic, as we see from the following:

Civilization	Date & details of syncretism
1. Indo-European Kurgan/ Old European	From c.1500 BC, Unetice gods indentified with their predecessors, Ogma-Herakles as a result of Mycenaean Greek influence
2. Mesopotamian	From c.500 BC, Marduk was identified with Amon (& later Zeus)
3. Egyptian	From c.650 BC, Libyan Seth & Son of Amon (king's son as high priest of Thebes) became God's Wife of Amon under

Kushites after 730 BC, & under Saite dynasty, & Amon
under Persians; first identification of Isis, Serapis (or
Sarapis) & Anubis, & of Zeus-Serapis

4.	Aegean-Greek	From c.390 BC & certainly by c.300 BC, Zeus identified with local gods: Dionysus-Serapis in Alexandria
5.	Roman	From c.485, syncretism of Catholic (Roman), Arian (Ostrogothic) & pagan religion, especially as a consequence of Theodoric's rule
6.	Anatolian	From c.530 BC, Iranian, Greek & Anatolian gods blended (Mithra & Anahita, Zeus & Tarhun)
7.	Syrian	From c.530 BC, Syrian Baal was made the equivalent of Marduk & the Iranian gods
8.	Israelite	From c.530 BC, Jewish Yahweh as Elohim was made equivalent to Baal & Marduk by Persian rulers, but not by Torah-following Jews (who were too purist to allow the Samaritans to help with the rebuilding of the Second Temple c.520 BC)
9.	Celtic	From c.560, fusion of Saxon Thor & Christian Christ as the first Saxons were converted
10.	Iranian	From c.661, fusion of Zoroastrianism, Manichaeism & Islam
11.	European	From c.2008?, coming fusion of Christian sects & New-Age cults; since 1948, when America established & funded its World Council of Churches, there has been a drawing together of Christian sects (e.g. Roman Catholics, Church of England & Methodists) & a growing Ecumenical movement which may result in the reunification of

Christendom under the Pope during the expansionist European conglomerate; there has also been a drawing together of Christianity & other religions, as manifested in the New-Age cults

(The New-Age movement is in Christian terms heretical as it claims that the Christian age, the Age of Pisces, is ending)

12.	North-American	—
13.	Byzantine-Russian	From c.1960, drawing together of Christian/Freemasonic sects in Soviet Union, growing Ecumenism after the patriarchate of Moscow joined the World Council of Churches in 1961
14.	Germanic-Scandinavian	From c.711, syncretism of Christian crosses showing Germanic-Scandinavian (Saxon & later Danish) myths; syncretism of Muslim & Christian symbolism after Arab conquest of Spain in 711
15.	Andean	From c.1600, syncretism of Aztec Indian practices & Christian symbolism
16.	Meso-American	From c.1600, syncretism of Aztec Indian practices & Christian symbolism
17.	Arab	From c.1900, syncretism of Muslim religious practices & Christian symbolism
18.	African	From c.1930, syncretism of African tribal religious practices & Christian symbolism
19.	Indian	From c.1850, syncretism of Indian Hindu & Muslim religious practices & Christian symbolism

20.	S.-E.-Asian	From c.1890, syncretism of Hindu-Buddhist religious practices & Christian symbolism during European colonialism
21.	Japanese	From c.1960, syncretism of Shinto & Buddhist religious practices & Christian symbolism
22.	Oceanian	From c.1920, syncretism of Oceanian religious practices & Christian symbolism
23.	Chinese	From c.1960, religion in China became a tool of State policy, but Confucianism, Taoism & Chinese Buddhism survived both in Taiwan & in mainland China, & since the death of Mao have begun to draw together (a trend still in process)
24.	Tibetan	From c.1970, syncretism of Tibetan-Buddhist religious practices as Chinese Communism attempted to suppress them
25.	Central-Asian	From c.1675, syncretism of Central-Asian & Mongolian religious practices & Chinese Manchu religion

45. REJECTION OF PRESENT/YEARNING FOR LOST PAST OF CIVILIZATION: REVIVAL OF CULTURAL PURITY

The secularizing, internationalist foreign rule now has an effect on the "spirit of the Age", the *zeitgeist*. There is a discontent with the foreign rule of the present and with the syncretizing Universalism of stage 44. This expresses itself as a short-lived revival in which there is rejection of the present and a yearning for the cultural and religious purity of the lost past (notably, stage 28), before it was contaminated by foreign influences, and the revival places the civilization's stamp on its Universalism without reversing it. In fact, the Universalism of stage 44 and the revival of cultural purity of stage 45 eventually coexist. In the European civilization, the Universalism emanating from the New-Age sects in the North-American civilization's stage 15 can be expected to coexist with a revival of Christian mysticism drawing on the historical Classical/Baroque vision of stage 28. This mystical revival may well be led from Britain after the dismemberment of the United Kingdom when Ireland is reunited within the European conglomerate – and the blend of Universalism and Christian mysticism can be expected to create a new Baroque Age in which sense and spirit – social and metaphysical realities – are combined, and whose new vision produces an artistic renaissance. The revival of stage 45 emphasises the culture of an earlier phase of the civilization, as the following pattern shows:

Civilization	Movement which rejects present & yearns for lost past	Date
1. Indo-European Kurgan/ Old European	Renewal of old Bell-Beaker Battle-Axe culture?	c.1450 BC?
2. Mesopotamian	Revival of Old Babylonian religion at the temples of Babylon, which resulted in Xerxes destroying the places of Marduk in Babylon & executing priests	c.520-482 BC
3. Egyptian	Cultural revival of Old Kingdom under anti-expansionist Saite 26th dynasty as Psamtik I counteracted the legacy of foreign control of Kushites & Assyrians	c.650-595 BC
4. Aegean-Greek	Renewal of pre-Macedonian traditional way of Greek life	c.360-337 BC
5. Roman	Revival of Classical culture under	c.493-526

Theodoric, through the court writers
Boethius & Cassiodorus & through
classical buildings in Pavia, Verona
& Ravenna

6.	Anatolian	Revival of Greek culture in Caria, Lycia, Pamphylia & Cilicia, which were Hellenised while under Persian rule; there was a yearning for the pre-Lydian Greek culture	From c.500 BC
7.	Syrian	Revival of interest in Phoenician culture through Syrian temples, but there were no rebellions against the Persians until AD 346	From c.500 BC
8.	Israelite	Revival of the Torah-based Judaism of Hezekiah & Josiah under Ezra, to whom the Persian Artaxerxes I granted a charter making the Torah the law of the land in 444 BC	c.458-444 BC
9.	Celtic	Revival of old Celtic culture & art in Britain, & Celtic monastic revival in Ireland	c.630-687
10.	Iranian	Revival of old Iranian culture & art	c.700-750
11.	European	Has not happened yet; a coming return to & glorification of the Light-based medieval vision (as outlined in *The Light of Civilization*), & a new Classical/Baroque movement rooted in the Classical/Baroque art of stage 28?	From c.2008? (soon after stage 44)

12.	North- American	Has not happened yet	
13.	Byzantine- Russian	Began under Gorbachev with a yearning for pre-Leninist freedom of debate; subsequent return to traditional Russian Byzantine Light-based tradition, i.e. neo-Slavophile movement, within the context of coming federalism & a link with a United States of Europe?	From c.1987?
14.	Germanic- Scandinavian	Revival of old Germanic culture & art round the motif of Thor's hammer (brought by Vikings); this was a Germanic reaction to the Carolingian cultural revival which saw the Carolingian Empire as a revival of the Roman Empire in the west & which conquered & absorbed Saxony between 772 & 804	c.772-804
15.	Andean	Creole revival under Spanish occup- ation during Bourbon reforms	c.1750-1790
16.	Meso- American	Creole revival under Spanish occup- ation during Bourbon reforms	c.1750-1790
17.	Arab	Muslim revival of interest in funda- mentalist Islamic values at end of European colonial presence; (this began with Nasser & was continued by Gaddafi & Khomeini)	c.1956-1980
18.	African	African revival of interest in tribal	c.1956-1980

values after European colonial
administration, beginning with Suez
& "wind of change"

19. Indian	Indian cultural revival coinciding with the nationalist movement under British rule	c.1885-1947
20. S.-E.-Asian	S.-E.-Asian cultural revival as nationalist movements threw off European colonial rule	c.1910-1950
21. Japanese	Coming return to traditional Shinto Light-based culture which began at Emperor Showa's (Hirohito's) funeral & continued with the elevation into a State occasion in November 1990 of Emperor Akihito's Shinto *daijosai* (Great Food Offering Ritual), in which he lay down with the spirit of the Sun Goddess Amaterasu Omikami in the dead of night & became a "living god" like his father Hirohito (the basis of the Japanese over other nations)	From c.1989
22. Oceanian	A return (only partially completed) to the traditional Oceanian Light-based culture?	c.1945-2015? (Overlap as some islands have decolonized, some are still under Western rule)

23.	Chinese	Has not happened yet; coming return to traditional Chinese Confucian Light-based culture?	From c.2006 to c.2020?
24.	Tibetan	Return to traditional Tibetan Light-based culture?	From c.2006 to c.2020?
25.	Central-Asian	Return to traditional Mongolian Tibetan-Buddhist Light-based culture which was ruled after 1911 by "Urga Living Buddha"	c.1890-1911

46. FURTHER ATTEMPT AT COUNTER-THRUST UNDER FOREIGN FEDERALIST INFLUENCE AND FOREIGN GOD TO RESTORE PAST

Aware that it is failing to live up to past glories under the conglomerate, the conquered civilization now attempts to restore the past greatness with a further attempt at counter-thrust, this time through federalism. The hallmark of this federalism is that the different nationalities under the civilization's rule now recover their sovereignty and are now linked federally, forming an external linkage but becoming independent in internal affairs. At the beginning of stage 43 they were concerned at the impending loss of their sovereignty, and now, at the beginning of stage 46, it is glorious that they recover their sovereignty. For the beginning of the Chinese regional federalism, see p260. The different nationalities under the civilization's rule are linked more loosely than in a unified conglomerate, but under foreign influence, as the following pattern shows:

Civilization	Further expansion into empire to restore past	Date
1.	Indo-European Kurgan/	Late Wessex culture under Unetice or Mycenaean rule (?), traded with	c.1400-1200 BC

	Old European	Cornwall, Ireland, C. Europe, Baltic & Egypt (whose 14th C beads resemble 14th C British-made beads)	
2.	Mesopotamian	Seleucids' Empire in Babylonia; the Seleucid Macedonian kingdom (312-64 BC) was the result of military conquest & originally stretched from Thrace to India; the eastern Iranian part was runs as under the Achaemenian Persian Empire, & Babylonia & Anatolia were administered as federal satrapies under *strategoi*, who had independence in internal civil affairs	c.331-141 BC
3.	Egyptian	Achaemenian Persian Empire in which Egypt was one of six federal satrapies under Cambyses & a conquered province under Xerxes; Persian rule of Egypt was looser than Persian rule of Mesopotamia as Egypt was farther from Persia than Mesopotamia	c.525-332 BC
4.	Aegean-Greek	Philip's Macedonian hegemony over Greece & Alexander the Great's Macedonian Empire which reached as far as India; Panhellenic League of Greek city-states excluding Sparta	c.337-239 BC
5.	Roman	Byzantine (East Roman) reconquest of Italy under Justinian, whose general Belisarius wiped out the Ostrogoths; the Lombards overran N. Italy (568-572) & in the south formed the	c.535-605

Duchies of Spoleto & Benevento (572-
582), but were driven back in 590;
by 605 the Lombards occupied most
of Italy except for the Rome-Ravenna
corridor in the centre

6.	Anatolian	Seleucids' Empire in Anatolia (which continued alongside Attalids' independent state until 133 BC); the Seleucid Macedonian kingdom (312-64 BC) was the result of military conquest & originally stretched from Thrace to India; Babylonia & Anatolia were run as federal satrapies under *strategoi* who had independence in internal civil affairs	c.334-278 BC
7.	Syrian	Ptolemies' Empire in Syria in 320 BC	c.323-219 BC
8.	Israelite	Ptolemies' Empire in Palestine, ruled from Egypt until Palestine was conquered by the Syrian Seleucid Antiochus III in 198 BC	c.333-198 BC
9.	Celtic	Rise of Saxon Empire in Northumbria, Mercia & Wessex in Britain, under which Christian Celts lived or from which they withdrew to the British fringes	c.687-838
10.	Iranian	Iranian independence within Islamic context, Iranian renaissance & national revival under federal Islamic dynasties: the Tahirids (821-873), the Saffarids	c.821-1055

(867) & Samanids (875), & the
Ghaznavids (10th C) & Buyids
(or Buwayhids) (9th-10th C)

11.	European	Has not happened yet; a renewed surge under foreign influence, coming federation of independent European nation-states free from the European conglomerate of a 48-state politically united United States of Europe (including Russia and ex-Soviet republics)?	From 22nd C?
12.	North-American	Has not happened yet	
13.	Byzantine-Russian	A federalist post-Communist USSR/ CIS (Commonwealth of Independent States) in which foreign Moscow influences the different & varied nationalities of the ex-Soviet republics; this began with Gorbachev's moves towards federalism, & is being influenced by the EU/ the coming United States of Europe (i.e. expanded European Community), which it will enter, and by the North-American civilization?	From c.1991
14.	Germanic-Scandinavian	The Germanic Frankish Empire had now passed into the European civilization, & the Scandinavians took over as Saxons fled before Charlemagne from Saxony across	c.843-911

the border into Denmark; Germanic
counterthrust of Odin/Thor under
foreign Danish influence with Viking
Empire in Britain (Danelaw), Ireland,
Normandy (ceded by France in 911),
Varangian Russia, Canada, & Iceland

| 15. Andean | Independent Latin America under Creoles, descendants of former Spanish settlers, as opposed to indigenous Andean Indians, with Western (North-American-European) investment; regional federalist bloc under foreign US leadership, first through 9 Pan-American conferences (1889-1948) & then through the Organization of American States (OAS), which was set up in 1948 in Bogota, whose chief goal was to prevent the spread of Communism in the Americas, & whose 23 states expelled Cuba in 1962 (the Inter-American Conference meets every 5 years, & Foreign Ministers & ambassadors also meet); & then through the 34-state Free Trade Area of the Americas (FTAA) finally set up in 2005, later to become an American Union | c.1810-c.2015?/ c.2020? |

| 16. Meso-American | Independent Latin America under Creoles, descendants of former Spanish settlers as opposed to indigenous Meso-American Indians (who were excluded from power after | c.1810-c.2015?/ c.2020? |

helping to oust the Spanish) with
Western (North-American-European)
investment; regional federalist bloc
under foreign US leadership, first
through Pan-American conferences
& then through the anti-Communist
OAS and 34-state FTAA from 2005
(see 15 above)

17. Arab	Independent Islam in Middle East, Iran, southern states of ex-Soviet Union & North Africa (&Pakistan from 1947); with post-colonial oil revenues from the West (North America-Europe) & ex-Soviet arms; beginnings of federalism through the Arab League, which was founded in 1945 and was dedicated to the achievement of Arab unity; to the divided Arab states this meant unity under their own primacy in the Arab world, based on a feeling that nationalism does not work; coming federal linkage of Arab (& perhaps southern ex-Soviet states) within one regional Federation of Arab (& Islamic) states or United States of the Middle East/United Arab States (Gaddafi's dream in 1969), with Islamic nuclear weapons under a regional Arab superpower (now Iran, once Saddam Hussein's Iraq or Gaddafi's Libya)?	From c.1980/ c.2015?

18. African	Independent Africa of Western & ex-Soviet client-states with Western (North-American-European) or ex-Soviet investment; federal linkage of African states within one regional black Africa, the African Union or United States of Africa proposed by Gaddafi in 2000 & implemented in 2002? (This seems to have begun with the Organization of African Unity, which was established in 1963 and to which all independent African states except South Africa belong; Heads of State meet annually)	From c.1980/ c.2015?
19. Indian	Independent federal India/Pakistanc. with federally linked regions & Western (North-American-European) invest- ment; the Indian constitution is a quasi- federal document which provides for a unitary state with subsidiary federal features; this is linked to the 7-nation South Asian Free Trade Area (SAFTA) which India joined in 2004	1947-c.2015/ c.2020?
20. S.-E.-Asian	Independent states of S.-E. Asia with Western investment (e.g. Thailand)/ resisting American influence (e.g. N. Vietnam); coming federal linkage of S.-E. Asia into one regional bloc or S.-E.-Asian Federation? (This has grown out of SEATO, the anti-Communist S.-E.-Asian Treaty Organization which was signed in 1954, and ASEAN, the Association	c.1950-c.2015?/ c.2020?

of S.-E.-Asian Nations, whose 10
countries include Thailand, the
Philippines, Malaysia &Indonesia,
& which is to pass into an Asian
Economic Community in 2010; S.-E.
Asia may enter an expanded Pacific
Community in which China, Japan &
Oceania may also be provinces within
one superpower)

21.	Japanese	Has not happened yet; Japan is one of the 10 countries in ASEAN, which will pass into an Asian Economic Community in 2010 (see 20 above)	From c.2015?/ c.2020?
22.	Oceanian	Has not happened yet: coming independent Oceania with Western investment, coming federal linkage of Oceania in a Federation or Confederacy of Oceania or of the South Pacific which includes Australia & New Zealand, now within Asia and the Pacific within the Eastern Hemisphere (see Hagger, *The Syndicate*, p46)?	From c.2015?/ c.2020?
23.	Chinese	Has not happened yet; a federalist post-Communist China in which foreign Mandarin Chinese influence the different & varied nationalities of federally linked regions; China may enter a coming Federation of S.-E.-Asian states (eventually an expanded Pacific Community in which S.-E. Asia, Japan & Oceania are also provinces), which	From c.2020?

may grow out of ASEAN which China
has promised to join in 2010 (see 20
above)

24. Tibetan	Has not happened yet; coming	From c.2020?
	independence of Tibet with Western	
	investment & its possible merging	
	into a regional bloc (probably	
	Federation of S.-E.-Asian states/	
	Pacific Community)?	
25. Central-Asian	(Ex-)Soviet-Chinese federal control of	c.1911-c.2015?/
	Inner Mongolia & much of Central	c.2020?
	Asia (e.g. Soviet control of Uzbeks,	
	Tajiks or Tadzhiks who rioted in	
	February 1990 & set the central	
	committee building of the Communist	
	Party on fire, Turkmenians,	
	Kazakhs & Kirgizians); Soviet	
	federal control of Mongolian People's	
	Republic from 1961; eventual	
	federal control of Islamic C. Asia	
	by coming Federation of Arab &	
	Islamic states?	

47. ECONOMIC DECLINE AND INFLATION
LEAD TO FURTHER
CLASS CONFLICT AND PAVE WAY FOR FOREIGN
OCCUPATION

During the counter-thrust under foreign federalist influence the declining civilization fails to solve its economic problems. There is further economic decline and
inflation, which lead to class conflict as the gulf between rich and poor widens. The

malaise paves the way for foreign occupation (stage 49).

Civilization	Dates when economic decline & inflation led to class conflict
1. Indo-European Kurgan/ Old European	c.1300-1150 BC?, trade declined under Unetice or Mycenaean rule
2. Mesopotamian	c.160-120 BC, inflation & economic decline in Babylonia under Seleucid rule
3. Egyptian	c.373-332 BC, economic decline at end of Persian rule; the agrarian Egyptian economy could not bear the Persian attack on Egypt of 373 BC & Tachos's invasion of Palestine
4. Aegean-Greek	c.250-100 BC, free grain for the needy; slave uprisings in Attica 134-133 BC & 104-3 BC, class conflict in Dyme in AD 115; conflict between rich & poor more pronounced towards 3rd C AD
5. Roman	c.540-620, inflation had increased, economy was partly under State direction; in West, rural areas took over from cities, which were in decline; in 6th century, the State & taxation burdened productivity & living standards, & the poor resented the rich
6. Anatolian	c.300-150 BC, economy in decline under Seleucid rule
7. Syrian	c.300-150 BC, economy in decline under Ptolemaic rule
8. Israelite	c.250-180 BC, decline of economy under Egyptian Ptolemaic rule

9.	Celtic	c.796-851, decline of Saxon economy of Mercia during the rise of Wessex; Vikings put Mercian king to flight in 851
10.	Iranian	c.983-1071, decline of Buyid economy following the death of Adud ad-Dawlah, & of Ghaznavid economy following the Ghaznavids' expulsion by the Seljuqs c.1038-1040
11.	European	Has not happened yet
12.	North-American	Has not happened yet
13.	Byzantine-Russian	Has not happened yet
14.	Germanic-Scandinavian	c.843-950, increasing poverty of Viking Empire, whose domestic agriculture was not profitable, encouraging Vikings to raid abroad
15.	Andean	1980s, massive inflation in some Latin-American countries (e.g. Argentina), paving the way for coming foreign occupation by North Americans
16.	Meso-American	1980s, massive inflation in some Latin-American countries, paving the way for coming foreign occupation by North Americans
17.	Arab	Has not happened yet
18.	African	Has not happened yet
19.	Indian	Has not happened yet
20.	S.-E.-Asian	Has not happened yet

21.	Japanese	Has not happened yet
22.	Oceanian	Has not happened yet
23.	Chinese	Has not happened yet
24.	Tibetan	Has not happened yet
25.	Central-Asian	Has not happened yet

THE DECAY AND DEMISE OF CIVILIZATIONS

48. THE LIGHT CEASES TO BE PUBLICLY RECOGNISED BY RELIGION
49. FOREIGN INVADERS OCCUPY CIVILIZATION AND UNDERMINE LIGHTLESS RELIGION

Failure to renew the Light in successive generations coincides with a hastening of the decay of the civilization, and I have suggested that this decay may occur through lack of renewal or absence of the Light, albeit in combination with some of the alternatives.

We shall see that the peoples of a decaying civilization are attracted away to the Light of a foreign religion and culture. The attraction is partly due to the weakness of their own culture's Light, for which its increasingly secular organization may be responsible, and partly because of the strength of the foreign religion and culture; and we need to start with the context of decay, and consider what hold that foreign religion and culture have. The evidence shows that the foreign influence is invariably the result of a military threat or occupying power. The occupying power moves against, or suppresses, the religion of the decaying civilization, and paves the way for a successor civilization to take over. Foreign domination as a result of wars, invasions, occupations or alliances creates an influence which, in conjunction with a new political and economic power, offers a religion, Light and Central Idea that invites secession among the peoples of a decaying civilization.

Let us therefore relate the absence of the Light in a decaying civilization to the foreign military threat or occupying power whose religious influence attracts the peoples away from their civilization so that it passes into a successor civilization. The final decay of each civilization can be dated to the counter-thrust under foreign rule during decline (stage 46), when the Light ceased to be publicly recognised by the civilization's religion. I can list the date of the commencement of the final decay of each decaying civilization, and the date when foreign invaders occupied the civilization and undermined its religion, as follows:

Civilization	Final decay, dated from the counter-thrust against decline (stage 46), during which the Light ceased to be publicly recognised by the civilization's religion (stage 48)	Foreign invaders occupy civilization & undermine its religion (stage 49)
1. Indo-European Kurgan/ Old European	c.1400-1200 BC?	c.1200-1150 BC?,Celts of Bronze Age Urnfield culture
2. Mesopotamian	c.331-141 BC	c.141 BC-AD 165, Parthians
3. Egyptian	c.525-332 BC	c.332-168 BC, Alexander & the successors of the Greek general Ptolemy who ruled Egypt until the Seleucids took it over in 193 BC; they Macedonianized the Egyptian religion, Osiris-Apis becoming Serapis or Sarapis c.300 BC
4. Aegean-Greek	c.337-239 BC	c.239-146 BC, Romans (occupied Macedonia, Corinth)

5.	Roman	c.535-605	c.605-652, the Lombards, a Germanic tribe, clinched their occupation of N. Italy & Spoleto/ Benevento in S. Italy, leaving a corridor in the centre which became the East Roman/ Byzantine-controlled Exarchate (provincial governorship) of Ravenna, which included Rome
6.	Anatolian	c.334-278 BC	c.278-220 BC, Celts ravaged Anatolia & were settled in Galatia, where they were conquered by Attalus I
7.	Syrian	c.323-219 BC	c.219-198 BC, Seleucid Antiochus III captured much of Ptolemaic Syria
8.	Israelite	c.333-198 BC	c.198-141 BC, Antiochus IV of Seleucids conquered Jerusalem & attempted to Hellenise it, causing the revolt of Judas Maccabeus
9.	Celtic	c.687-838	c.838-896, Vikings
10.	Iranian	c.821-1055	c.1055-1157, a branch of Oğuz Turks (called Cumans or Ghuzz by the Byzantines) from the north, the Seljuq Turks, conquered Iran & ended Buyid power when Toghril Beg, the Seljuq Sultan, entered Baghdad

in 1055; the Seljuqs controlled an Empire stretching from the Mediterranean to the Indus & from the Oxus to the Persian Gulf until they eventually contracted into the Seljuq Sultanate of Hamadan, & in the 11th-13th C the "Assassins" of Alamut (so-called because they were religious fanatics who reached the Paradisal vision through hashesh) extended the ancient Iranian *haoma* cult

11.	European	—	—
12.	North-American	—	—
13.	Byzantine-Russian	—	—
14.	Germanic-Scandinavian	c.843-911	c.911-978, English reconquered Danelaw during the monastic revival; (961, German Saxons created the Holy Roman Empire in Germanic territory now within the European civilization)
15.	Andean	c.1810-present	—
16.	Meso-American	c.1810-present	—

17.	Arab	c.1980-present	—
18.	African	c.1980-present	—
19.	Indian	c.1947-present	—
20.	S.-E.-Asian	c.1950-present	—
21.	Japanese	—	—
22.	Oceanian	—	—
23.	Chinese	—	—
24.	Tibetan	—	—
25.	Central-Asian	c.1911-present	—

(— = has not happened yet)

The foreign threat undoubtedly contributed to the exhaustion and collapse of each civilization and to the alienation and disaffection of the heterogeneous peoples. As we examine the weakness of the Light in relation to the approaching end of each of the dead civilizations it is apparent that the weakness of the Light during the decay of each of the civilizations coincided with the foreign threat from an outside invader, marauder or occupying power which threatened to superimpose its culture and religion on the decaying civilization's culture and religion. Being on the receiving end of militarism or foreign occupation in a time of decay seems to have had a worse effect on a civilization's Light than when (as in the case of early Arab Islamic civilization) the civilization handed out militarism or foreign occupation, although secular military activity in the service of a metaphysical vision eventually seems to have had an exhausting effect on a civilization's Light.

My evidence suggests that it is reasonable to conclude that there is a connection between the decay of a civilization and the disappearance of the vision of the Light from its religion. This raises a cause-and-effect question, which we will leave open for the time being, as to whether a civilization decays because it loses its visions of the Light from its religion, or whether visions of the Light disappear from the religion as a result of the outer despair that is felt when a civilization is decaying.

50. FOREIGN INVADERS' DESTRUCTION OF THE STONES

Some foreign invaders made no attempt to suppress the culture of the civilization they took over. However, those foreign invaders that did move against, or suppress, the religion of a decaying civilization in the course of doing so destroyed many of the religion's stones, which were once revered, and thereby ruined the lapidary embodiments of the decaying civilization's Central Idea. The same destructive process is at work in the course of stage 49 (see asterisks below) and results in stage 50. For the sake of convenience the main instances of stone-destruction are listed in the following table:

Civilization	Foreign military threat or occupying power	Main stones destroyed by foreign power
1. Indo-European Kurgan/ Old European	Milesians ? Mesopotamians Funnel-Neck Beaker Folk Bell-Beaker Folk Battle-Axe culture Unetice-Tumulus culture Mycenaean Greeks Celts*	Monuments of Tuatha (?) Stonehenge IIIA?
2. Mesopotamian	Assyrians	Babylon, 689 BC, temple of Marduk Babylon, c.482 BC, temple of

		Marduk & Tower of Babel destroyed by Xerxes
	Iranians	Temples
	Syrian Romans &	
	Parthians*	Temples to Marduk
	Byzantine Arabs	Temples

3.	Egyptian	Mesopotamians	Jewish temple at Elephantine 410 BC
		Iranian Achaemenians	Temples to Ra/Isis
		Macedonians &	
		Ptolemies	Temples to Ra/Isis
		Seleucids*	Temples to Ra/Isis
		Romans*	Temples to Ra/Isis destroyed by Romans 145-30 BC, and by Christians
			Serapeum, Alexandria, destroyed AD 391 by Greek Orthodox

4.	Aegean-Greek		
	Minoan/	Mycenaeans	Knossos 1450 BC
	Mycenaean	Dorians	Mycenae c.1100 BC
	Greeks	Persians	Acropolis at Athens & temples sacked by Xerxes 480 BC, temples in Attica ravaged
		Romans*	Temples to Zeus destroyed 215-146 BC

5.	Roman	Etruscans	Temples destroyed
		Carthaginians	,,
		Christians	Pagan temples destroyed by Christians after 312
		Barbarians	Rome sacked in 410, 455

		(Germanic tribes)	& 476, temples destroyed, churches spared
		Lombards*	Temples to Jupiter destroyed
6.	Anatolian	Hittites	Mistress of animals temples destroyed 19th C BC
		Sea Peoples	Hittite temples destroyed c.1225 BC
		Celts*	Temples to Tarhun/Cybele destroyed c.278-220 BC
		Romans*	Temples destroyed 64 BC-AD 395
7.	Syrian	Assyrians	Temples destroyed
		Chaldeans	,,
		Iranian Achaemenians	,,
		Egyptians	,,
		Romans*	Temples destroyed, 64 BC-AD 614
8.	Israelite	Assyrians	Israel overrun 721 BC, Samaria wrecked, Ten Tribes dispersed
		Chaldeans or Neo-Babylonians	First Temple destroyed 587/6 BC Jerusalem torn down by Antiochus IV who dedicated the Temple to Zeus Olympius, 167 BC
		Iranians	Qumran destroyed AD 68
		Romans	Second Temple (down to Wailing Wall) destroyed AD 70 Masada AD 73
9.	Celtic	Romans	British Druid strongholds &

		temples destroyed by AD 61, probably including Stonehenge	
	Vikings*	Churches & monasteries destroyed by raiders c.838-1014	
10.	Iranian	Parthians	Fire-temples destroyed
		Romans	
		Turks	Fire-temples destroyed 540-
		Byzantines	633, especially after 560
		Arabs	Ctesiphon, the Sasanian capital, destroyed 637
		Mongols	
11.	European	Vikings	Churches destroyed
		Muslim Arabs	Jerusalem & Spanish churches damaged
		Nazi Germans/	Cathedrals & churches damaged
		Fascist Italians/	or destroyed in Europe in 2nd
		Japanese	World War; churches damaged
		Freedom-fighting colonials of British	
		Empire e.g. Indians	Churches damaged
12.	North-American	British	Churches damaged in Anglo-American wars
13.	Byzantine-Russian	Seljuqs/Muslim anti-Crusaders, Latins, Ottomans	Churches destroyed, Ottoman destruction 1355-1421; Hagia Sophia turned into a mosque 1453
		Bolsheviks & Nazi Germans	Orthodox churches destroyed
14.	Germanic-	Early Europeans	Temples to Odin & Thor

Scandinavian	(Christian Celts & Germanic Saxons)	destroyed from 4th-11th centuries
	Normans*	Temples destroyed 1016-1091
15. Andean & 16. Meso- American	Invaders/ Nahuans & Toltecs	Andean & Mayan sun-temples destroyed c.800
	Spanish Western Christians	Aztec & Inca sun-temples destroyed c.16th C
17. Arab (Islamic)	Europeans	Mosques destroyed in 1st & 2nd World Wars
	Israelis	Palestine lost to Israel with Jerusalem & mosques (e.g. the Dome of the Rock)
18. African	Europeans	Arab mosques, & Bantu stones (e.g. Great Zimbabwe) influenced from Egypt, destroyed by European invaders
19. Indian	Moghul Raj	Hindu temples destroyed by Muslim conquest
	British Raj	Hindu temples damaged during Western conquest of India & independence struggle
20. S.-E.-Asian (Buddhist)	Europeans & North Americans	Buddhist temples damaged during 2nd World War & independence struggles
21. Japanese	Europeans & North Americans	Buddhist temples & Shinto shrines destroyed in 2nd World War
22. Oceanian	Europeans & North	Civil wars/sacred stones (e.g.

	Americans	*moai*) destroyed
23. Chinese	Chinese	40,000 Buddhist stones & temples closed 843-5 by T'ang Taoists
	Europeans	Temples destroyed in Canton region 1839-60
	Japanese	Temples destroyed in Sino-Japanese wars, including 2nd World War
	Red Guards (civil war)	Temples destroyed during Cultural Revolution of 1966
24. Tibetan	Chinese	Temples & monasteries in Lhasa destroyed by Chinese Communists after 1966
25. Central-Asian	Russians/Chinese	Tibetan-Buddhist temples destroyed during 20th C occupation

By comparing the above table and the table for stage 54 we can see that the foreign military threat or occupying power that destroyed each civilization's stones during its time of decay also provided the foreign Light to which each decaying civilization's homegrown Light was attracted before it passed into its successor civilization.

51. The Loss of a Civilization's Central Idea through Secessions

When the heterogeneous peoples of a civilization are attracted away to a foreign culture, the decaying civilization loses its awareness of its own Central Idea. To put it another way, as a civilization declines, its Light dies down, the Light-based

Central Idea becomes less evident and is soon forgotten, and the heterogeneous peoples, who assented to the civilization's religion during its creation, become disaffected and secede. The civilization was unified by its religion, and now that the religion is not in evidence, the culture of the civilization disintegrates; it fragments into separate cultures. Let us now relate the disaffection and secession of the heterogeneous peoples who joined the civilization to this loss of the civilization's Light-based Central Idea:

Civilization	Heterogeneous peoples alienated from the civilization's religion & attracted to foreign cult	Date peoples seceded from religion/ to foreign cult in time of decline	Evidence for absence of civilization's Central Idea from secular outlook in time of decline
1. Indo-European Kurgan/ Old European	Europeans British (Pre-Iranians, Pre-Indians, Pre-Greeks,Pre-Celts, Pre-Germanic tribes)	c.1200-1150 BC?	Dyaeus Pitar gave way to Celtic gods & no longer affected crops & everyday life through the Light
2. Mesopotamian	Mesopotamian peoples, Kassites, Mitanni, Assyrians, Babylonians, Chaldeans	c.141 BC-AD 165	Marduk gave way to Parthian & Roman gods & no longer affected crops through Royal Sacred Marriage & the Light
3. Egyptian	Egyptian peoples	c.193-168 BC	Ra gave way to gods of Greek Seleucids' Zeus & no longer affected flooding of the Nile,

				growth of crops & everyday life through the Pharaoh & the Light
4.	Aegean-Greek	Kurgan Achaeans, Mycenaeans, Ionians, Aeolians, Dorians, Greeks & Greek colonies,	c.239-146 BC	Zeus gave way to Roman Jupiter & no longer affected everyday life through the Light
5.	Roman	Romans, Italian city-states & Roman colonies	c.605-652	Jupiter gave way to Germanic gods & no longer affected everyday life through the Light
6.	Anatolian	Phrygians, Lydians	c.278-220 BC	Tarhun/Cybele gave way to Celtic & Hellenistic gods & no longer affected crops & everyday life through the Light
7.	Syrian	Philistines, Aramaeans, Phoenicians, Seleucids	c.219-198 BC	Baal gave way to Seleucids' Zeus & no longer affected crops & everyday life through the Light
8.	Israelite	Twelve Tribes of of Canaan	c.198-141 BC	Yahweh/Elohim gave way to Seleucids' Zeus (& to Hellenistic, Roman & foreign

gods) & no longer covenanted with or defended the Israelites through the Light of the tabernacle

9.	Celtic	Britons & Gauls	c.838-896	Du-w's covenant with Celts (e.g. British) gave way to Viking Thor & Christian God & no longer affected crops through the Light of Taran;
		Irish peoples	c.850-12th C	In declining Ireland, the Culdee God the Father was weakened by the Viking gods & was eventually absorbed by the Roman Catholic God who affected the crops & everyday life through the Light
10.	Iranian	Iranian peoples Medes, Persians, Achaemenians Parthians, Sasanians attracted to Mithras & Ahura Mazda	c.1055-1157	Iranian pantheon gave way to Seljuq Allah & no longer affected crops & everyday life through Fire-temples
11.	European	European peoples	—	In secular, declining

	(Christian)		Europe the Light of God the Father has already given way to atheistic, sceptical, scientific materialism & paganism, e.g. astrology, & no longer affects crops & everyday life through the Light of Christ as widely as in the 19th C; can be expected to give way eventually to occupier's god
12.	North-American	— —	—
13.	Byzantine-Russian	Eastern peoples: Serbians, Greeks, Turks, Bulgarians, Russian peoples, Baltic peoples, East & Central Europeans, Ukrainians, Armenians, Georgians etc.	— In time of secular decline before Gorbachev, Orthodox God the Father has already officially given way to atheistic Communist ideology & no longer affects crops or everyday life through the Light of Christ but is unofficially still followed & is beginning to revive; can be expected to give way eventually to

occupier's god

14.	Germanic- Scandinavian	Germanic tribes: Visigoths, Vandals, Burgundians, Ostrogoths, Angles (English), Old or Frankish Saxons, Jutes, Frisians, Danes, Norwegians, Swedes, Icelanders	c.911-978	Tiwaz/Wodan/Odin/ Thor gave way to Catholic Christ & God & no longer affected crops & everyday life through the Light
15. 16.	Andean & Meso-American	Andean, Mayan, Aztec & other S.-American peoples	—	Sun-god has already given way to Christian God who no longer affected crops & everyday life through the Light; can be expected to give way eventually to occupier's god
17.	Arab (Islamic)	Muslim tribes & peoples from Spain & N. Africa to India, Iranian peoples	—	In secular, declining parts of Islam, the Light of Allah has already given way to foreign gods, e.g. Western God the Father, & no longer affects crops & everyday life through Mohammed; can be

			expected to give way eventually to occupier's god
18. African	Peoples of African continent	—	In secular, declining parts of Africa, the African gods (e.g. Mwari, Nzambi of Bakongo, Cghene of S. Nigerian Isoko, Ngai of Kikuyu, Leza of N. Rhodesian Ba-ila, Ndjambi Karunga of Herero, Raluvhimba of N. Transvaal Venda) have already given way to the Christian God, & no longer affect crops & everyday life through the shamanistic witch-doctor's Light; can be expected to give way eventually to occupier's god
19. Indian	Peoples of Indian subcontinent	—	In secular, declining parts of India, Hindu/ Buddhist Reality has already given way to foreign gods, & is no longer attained through the Light, Agni, Siva, Brahman or the

			Enlightenment of the Buddha; can be expected to give way eventually to occupier's god
20. S.-E.-Asian	Peoples of S.-E. Asia	—	In secular declining parts of S.-E. Asia, Theravada-Buddhist Reality has already given way to foreign gods, & is no longer attained through Enlightenment of the Buddha; can be expected to give way eventually to occupier's god
21. Japanese	Japanese peoples	—	In secular, declining circles of Shinto Japan, Kami/the Buddha have already given way to foreign gods, e.g. Western God the Father, & no longer affect crops & everyday life through the Light; can be expected to give way eventually to occupier's god
22. Oceanian	Polynesian & Melanesian	—	Sun-god's/Buddhist (?) Reality is already no

	peoples		longer attained through the Enlightenment of the Sun-god/Buddha; can be expected to give way eventually to occupier's god
23.	Chinese	Peoples of autonomous regions of China	—	In time of secular decline the Light of *Ti*/ Heaven has already given way to foreign gods, e.g.Christian God, & to atheistic, Communist ideology & no longer affects crops & everyday life through the Emperor; can be expected to give way eventually to occupier's god
24.	Tibetan	Tibetan peoples	—	In time of secular decline Tibetan-Buddhist Reality has already given way to atheistic Communist ideology; can be expected to give way eventually to occupier's god
25.	Central-Asian	C.-Asian peoples including Mongolians	—	In time of secular decline Tibetan-Buddhist Reality has

already given way to
atheistic Communist
ideology, can be
expected to give way
eventually to occupier's
god

Just as there are alternatives for the Central Idea in a time of growth, so there are alternatives for the absence of the Central Idea in a time of decay, and the absence of the Light must be seen within the context of these alternatives, all of which strengthen the hold of the civilization's secular organization (the State) over the metaphysical vision contained in its religion. Thus, while the heterogeneous peoples were seceding from their own Light over a period of time that has its roots in the imperial decline (stage 40), their civilization was also over a period of time that has its roots in stage 40:

1. losing its racial and militaristic dominance;
2. undergoing political de-centralization and devolution into regionalism at the expense of its unification;
3. failing to maintain its high living standards and superior technology;
4. losing its trading links and trade routes;
5. undergoing economic malaise and decline so that economic benefits and funding were no longer forthcoming;
6. experiencing imperial overstretch as its economic base weakened in relation to its military commitments;
7. having difficulty in maintaining its rule of law;
8. increasing its secularism and scientific materialism;
9. having problems with its fragmenting social organization;
10. proving itself incapable of surviving as one of "the fittest";
11. failing in planning and invention;
12. undergoing the proletarian overthrow of its priestly establishment;
13. having problems with its bureaucracy (civil service) and specialising of labour (trade unionism);

14. being influenced by other cultures;
15. unable to control and organize its cities;
16. showing symptoms of old age and exhaustion.

These alternatives are already at work in the European civilization, and can be expected to become more pronounced. However, fundamentally the absence of the Light accounts for the loss of the civilization's Light-based Central Idea and for the loss of its identity, drive and purpose during its time of decay, and the secession of the peoples is at heart a movement of disillusionment at the absence of the civilization's Light-based Central Idea.

52. FINAL INDEPENDENT PHASE OR NATIONALISTIC SWANSONG

The civilization attempts to reverse the secessions and now enters a nationalistic phase in which it briefly reasserts its traditional identity in freedom from foreign occupation. This, however, is the civilization's swansong, its last spell of independence. The pattern is as follows:

Civilization	Independent phase or nationalistic swansong	
1. Indo-European Kurgan/ Old European	c.1150-1100 BC	Independence from Urnfield Celts?
2. Mesopotamian	AD c.165-244	Brief independence from Romans
3. Egyptian	c.168-30 BC	Egyptian independence from Seleucids & from Rome from Cleopatra II to Cleopatra VII
4. Aegean-Greek	c.146-27 BC	Greek independence from Romans (& from Macedonia under Roman influence), reconstitution of a smaller Achaean

5.	Roman	c.652-728	The Exarchate of Ravenna resisted the Lombard occupation of much of N. & S. Italy; at first Byzantine (East Roman), it increasingly became a West Roman independent enclave & with the end of Byzantine rule in Italy turned into the Papal States at the same time that Venice became independent
6.	Anatolian	c.220-133 BC	Attilids' independence from Seleucids & Rome until Attalus III bequeathed Pergamum to Rome
7.	Syrian	c.198-163 BC	Syrian Seleucid Empire's independence from Ptolemaic Egypt, annexed Phoenicia, Trans-jordan & Palestine
8.	Israelite	c.141-64 BC	Hasmonean Empire after the Maccabees, in Palestine & Transjordan
9.	Celtic	c.896-1016	Independence of British, Franks & Saxons (Germans) from Norsemen who dominated Ireland (from 914 to 1014), pressed from Dublin (to York 919), conquered all England except Wessex, & took Normandy (911-933)
10.	Iranian	c.1157-1258	Independence from Seljuqs: the Shahdom of Khwarezm (or Khwarizm) which supplanted the Seljuqs in N.E. Iran & weathered the first Mongol invasion of 1220-1 under Genghis Khan before

succumbing to a grandson of Genghis's
c.1258 when the Mongols took Baghdad

11. European	—	
12. North-American	—	
13. Byzantine-Russian	—	
14. Germanic-Scandinavian	c.978-1042	Independence from Anglo-Saxons: Danish Empire which dissolved with Hardecanute's death in 1042, after which Denmark was ruled by a Norwegian king who was succeeded by Harald Hardraade
15. Andean	—	
16. Meso-American	—	
17. Arab	—	
18. African	—	
19. Indian	—	
20. S.-E.-Asian	—	
21. Japanese	—	
22. Oceanian	—	

23.	Chinese	—
24.	Tibetan	—
25.	Central-Asian	—

(— = has not happened yet)

53. FOREIGN POWER AGAIN OCCUPIES CIVILIZATION AND FURTHER SECULARIZES ITS LIGHTLESS RELIGION

A new foreign power now occupies the civilization and its decaying Lightless religion, which is further secularized by the foreign influence:

	Civilization	Date of foreign power's occupation	Occupying foreign power
1.	Indo-European Kurgan/ Old European	c.1100-1000 BC	New wave of Urnfield Celts in W. Europe (France and Spain) & British Isles as Urnfield culture expanded westwards
2.	Mesopotamian	c.244-395	Romans & Sasanians
3.	Egyptian	c.30 BC-AD 395	Romans
4.	Aegean-Greek	c.27 BC-AD 395	Romans, who made Macedonia a Roman province in 148 BC & conquered Greece in 146 BC, made Greece, S. Epirus & the Ionian & Cycladic Islands into the Roman province of Achaea in 27 BC

5.	Roman	c.728-756	The Lombards overran all Central Italy except for Venice & the area around Rome; Lombards under King Liudprand invaded Ravenna & took it from the Venetians c.750 (& the resulting intermingling of Lombards & Romans created the Italians); the Pope turned against the occupying Byzantine Emperor Leo III, excommunicating him for destroying icons from 727
6.	Anatolian	c.133 BC-AD 395	Romans
7.	Syrian	c.163-65 BC	Parthians & Armenians in E. & N. Syria, Nabataean Arabs in Transjordan & S. Syria (including Damascus); Huraean Arabs raided Phoenicia from Galilee & Lebanon
		c.64 BC-AD 395	Romans
8.	Israelite	c.64 BC-AD 395	Romans
9.	Celtic	c.1016-1066	Danes (Danish Empire of Canute) ruled Britain from 1016 & Normans conquered S. Italy, Sicily & Britain in 11th C
10.	Iranian	c.1258-1382	The Mongol Il-Khans (or "deputy Khans" to the Great Khan in China) took Baghdad, kicked to death the last Abbasid Caliph

			(thereby liberating Shi'ism from Sunni control), & conquered Iran; when their line became extinct in 1336 they were succeeded by the Jalayrids, a Mongol tribe which had supported the Il-Khan dynasty
11.	European	—	—
12.	North-American	—	—
13.	Byzantine-Russian	—	—
14.	Germanic-Scandinavian	c.1042-1106	Christianized ex-Scandinavian Normans (Viking Franks who had acquired Normandy in 911 & who were now regarded as a foreign power by the Scandinavians) conquered S. Italy & Sicily, & Saxon England from Normandy in 1066, with the support of the Catholic Church
15.	Andean	—	—
16.	Meso-American	—	—
17.	Arab	—	—
18.	African	—	—

19.	Indian	—	—
20.	S.-E.-Asian	—	—
21.	Japanese	—	—
22.	Oceanian	—	—
23.	Chinese	—	—
24.	Tibetan	—	—
25.	Central-Asian	—	—

54. CONTEMPLATIVE MYSTICS TURN FROM DECAYING RELIGION TO CULTS OF FOREIGN POWER

The occupying foreign power has brought its own cult or cults into which the civilization's Light now passes.

The Light is absent as the civilization's religion decays, and now contemplative mystics and some of the heterogeneous peoples are attracted to the Light of foreign cults. The evidence suggests that the Light began to be absent in the decaying religions largely as a result of military influences, and that the process continued largely because over a period of time (now accelerating) the seceding peoples were attracted to a Light elsewhere. It seems that just as the Light is taken to a new culture and civilization by migrants in a time of growth, so, in reverse procedure, in a time of decline the peoples are attracted away from the mature civilization to the Light of an occupying foreign culture and religion whose influence had risen. In other words, in times of early decay the Light is still present within the decaying civilization's geographical boundaries – in the companion volume, *The Light of Civilization*, my study of the Tradition has established that the Light has been present in every generation and culture – but it is no longer present in the institutions of its official religion. Rather, it is found in rival religions which have gained influence at its expense. Thus, the post-Macedonian Syrian contemplative mystics turned away from Syrian religion to the Zeus cults of the Hellenistic occupier. (The same process is at work whenever a civilization's Light weakens. In the Roman civilization, for example, the Light was present in 1st-3rd century AD Rome, but in the Asian cults of Asia Minor and in Christianity rather than in the Roman religion of Jupiter, whose end was consequently hastened.)

I can tabulate the background to the gradual passing of the Light from decaying religions into foreign cults as follows:

	Civilization	Date	Light passes from decaying home-grown religion of:	Civilization's Light passes into foreign cults
1.	Indo-European Kurgan/ Old European	c.1100-1000 BC	Dyaeus Pitar	Celtic cults, Greek religion of Zeus
2.	Mesopotamian	c.244-395	Utu, Shamash	Roman cults (Jupiter), Roman Christianity & Iranian Zoroastrianism & Manichaeism
3.	Egyptian	c.30 BC-AD 395	Ra, Isis, Serapis & Royal Mysteries (worshipped at the Ptolemaic capital of Alexandria)	Roman cults (Jupiter) & later Roman & then Byzantine Christianity
4.	Aegean-Greek	c.27 BC-AD 395	Zeus	Roman cults (Jupiter & the Imperial cult) & Christianity
5.	Roman	c.313-800	Jupiter	Roman, later Byzantine & still later Frankish

		568-652	"	Christianity Lombard Arianism (until the Lombards were converted to Christianity in 653)
		c.728-756	"	Western iconophile Christianity of Lombards; Eastern Christianity of Byzantine Empire
6.	Anatolian	c.133 BC- AD 395	Attis-Cybele (Magna Mater) of Roman Asia	Roman cults Christianity
7.	Syrian	c.163 BC- AD 395	Hellenized Judaism of Hasmoneans	Hellenized Greek & later Roman cults, Syrian Gnosticism, Christianity & Roman State Christianity after Constantine I
8.	Israelite	c.64 BC- AD 395	Romanized Judaism of Herod's successors	Christianity & Roman cults (Jerusalem was destroyed in 70 & the philhellene Hadrian rebuilt Jerusalem as a Roman colony with a shrine to Jupiter on the site of the Temple);
9.	Celtic	c.1016- 1066	Taran/Esus & Celtic Christ	Odin (Christianized in Denmark after 960 but still pagan in Britain

			in 1000) & Roman Catholic Christ
10. Iranian	c.1258-1382	Ahura Mazda of Sasanians	Islam (to which the Mongols were converted c.1300 when the Il-Khan Ghazan abandoned his Mongol Buddhism for Islam)
11. European	—	—	—
12. North-American	—	—	—
13. Byzantine-Russian	—	—	—
14. Germanic-Scandinavian	c.1042-1106	Odin & Thor of Danes & Iceland	Norman Christianity
15. Andean	—	—	—
16. Meso-American	—	—	—
17. Arab	—	—	—
18. African	—	—	—
19. Indian	—	—	—
20. S.-E.-Asian	—	—	—

21. Japanese	—	—	—
22. Oceanian	—	—	—
23. Chinese	—	—	—
24. Tibetan	—	—	—
25. Central-Asian	—	—	—

55. CIVILIZATION RESISTS THE FOREIGN OCCUPIER

The civilization now resists the foreign occupier, into whose cult or cults the Light has passed:

Civilization	Date of resistance	Resistance to foreign occupier
1. Indo-European Kurgan/ Old European	c.1100-1000 BC?	Indo-European Battle-Axe Kurgans' descendants' resistance to Celts
2. Mesopotamian	c 244-395	Many instances of resistance to Romans
3. Egyptian	c.30 BC-AD 395 (especially 22 BC)	Resistance to Romans; especially when Candace of Nubia challenged advancement of Roman frontier beyond First Cataract
4. Aegean-Greek	c.27 BC-AD 395	Resistance to Romans, especially in Nero's time
5. Roman	c.728-756	Resistance to Lombards under iconophile Pope Gregory II who sought the support of

			the dukes ("*duces*") of Spoleto & Benevento
6.	Anatolian	c.133 BC-AD 395 (especially c.96-66 BC)	Resistance to Romans, especially by Mithradates VI, King of Pontus
7.	Syrian	c.163 BC-AD 395 (especially 4 BC)	Resistance to Romans, especially to Herod the Great, Roman client ruler (named by the Romans "King of the Jews"), which led to massacre of the first-born
8.	Israelite	c.64 BC-AD 395 (especially AD c.26, 66-77, 115-116 & 135)	Jewish resistance to the Romans, including Masada (AD 73)
9.	Celtic	c.1016-1066	Saxons resisted Danes & Normans, finally under Harold of Wessex who resisted Harald Hardraade & William the Conqueror & was killed in 1066
10.	Iranian	c.1258-1382	Iranians resisted Mongol Il-Khan Sultan Mohammed's setting up an anti-caliph, which alienated the subject people
11.	European	—	—
12.	North-American	—	—
13.	Byzantine-Russian	—	—

14. Germanic-Scandinavian	c.1042-1106	Scandinavians resisted the Anglo-Norman take-over of England, & the Norwegian Harald Hardraade was killed attempting to reconquer England in 1066
15. Andean	—	—
16. Meso-American	—	—
17. Arab	—	—
18. African	—	—
19. Indian	—	—
20. S.-E.-Asian	—	—
21. Japanese	—	—
22. Oceanian	—	—
23. Chinese	—	—
24. Tibetan	—	—
25. Central-Asian	—	—

56. CONTEMPLATIVE MYSTICS DEFECT FROM OCCUPIERS' RELIGION AND ARE PERSECUTED

The resistance to the foreign occupier leads to a new generation of contemplative mystics withdrawing their support for the occupying foreign power's religion. As a result the occupying foreign power persecutes the illumined men who have defected from the foreign occupier's cult or cults, as the following pattern shows:

Civilization	Date & details of persecution	
1. Indo-European Kurgan/ Old European	c.1100-1000 BC?	Urnfield Celtic persecution of defectors: defection of illumined men from Urnfield Celtic cults & consequent persecution?
2. Mesopotamian	c.244-395	Roman & Sasanian persecution of defectors: illumined Mesopotamians became Roman & later Byzantine Christians or Iranian Manichaeans, & were persecuted (especially under the Sasanians)
3. Egyptian	c.30 BC-AD 395	Roman persecution of defectors to Gnosticism & Christianity: illumined Egyptians became Gnostics & Christians, & later on Greek Neoplatonists, & were persecuted under Nero & Decius; the Desert Fathers fled from these persecutors into the Egyptian desert
4. Aegean-Greek	c.27 BC-AD 395 (especially AD c.40-60)	Roman persecution of defectors to Christianity: Athenians became Christians after St Paul's address to the Athenians; persecution under Nero, who toured Greece & renamed the Peloponnese the Neronese
5. Roman	c.728-756	Lombard persecution of Byzantine iconoclasm
6. Anatolian	c.133 BC-AD 395	Roman persecution of defectors to Gnosticism & Christianity: Attis/Cybele

devotees persecuted for joining Christians
& Gnostics

7.	Syrian	c.167 BC-AD 395 (especially 1st C AD)	Roman persecution: Syrian Christians & Gnostics persecuted
8.	Israelite	c.64 BC-AD 395 (especially AD c.26)	Roman persecution of defectors to Christianity: Christ & followers persecuted by Jewish State & Romans
9.	Celtic	c.1016-1066	Danish & Norman persecution of defectors to Saxon Christianity; (some illumined Saxon Christians defected to paganism & were denounced by Bishop Wulfstan)
10.	Iranian	c.1258-1382	Islamic Mongol persecution of defectors to Timurid Sufism
11.	European	—	—
12.	North-American	—	—
13.	Byzantine-Russian	—	—
14.	Germanic-Scandinavian	c.1042-1106	Scandinavian persecution of defectors to Christianity: illumined men defected to Norman Christianity & were persecuted in pagan parts of Scandinavia
15.	Andean	—	—

16. Meso-American	—	—
17. Arab	—	—
18. African	—	—
19. Indian	—	—
20. S.-E.-Asian	—	—
21. Japanese	—	—
22. Oceanian	—	—
23. Chinese	—	—
24. Tibetan	—	—
25. Central-Asian	—	—

57. COTERIES CONTINUE LIGHT FROM DYING/DEAD RELIGION AND CENTRAL IDEA IN MYSTERIES

As the religion of the civilization approaches death, followers detach themselves from it and form a coterie or coteries. These coteries consist of groups of followers, tiny minorities who seem to have known of the Light and who continue the religion and the civilization's Central Idea in isolation and exile. This process has started earlier during the decay of the civilization, and seems to prepare for the coming demise. These coteries are still in existence after their religion dies, and they survive the death of their civilization as mystery cults. We can list these coteries now:

Dead or decaying civilization	Coteries/followers who continued Light of dead or dying religion of Central Idea in isolation or exile
1. Indo-European Kurgan/ Old European	Fire-temple mysteries, e.g. Stonehenge?
2. Mesopotamian	Chaldean mystery schools of Median/Persian Magi
3. Egyptian	Isis mysteries, Hermeticism, Alchemy
4. Aegean-Greek Minoan } Mycenaean } Greek	Dionysian bull-mysteries survived Eleusinian, Dionysian, Orphic & Pythagorean mysteries, Neoplatonism
5. Roman	Pagan mysteries e.g. of Jupiter, Mithras
6. Anatolian	Attis/Cybele mysteries, Neo-Hittite mysteries of Adonis
7. Syrian	Baal mysteries in Diabolism (Baalzebub)
8. Israelite	Judaism, Kabbalistic coteries in Chaldea (Babylon), Spain & France after Diaspora
9. Celtic Irish-Celtic	Druid mysteries, Celtic legends
10. Iranian	Mysteries of Magi, Parsi
11. European	— (New-Age mystery cults of Cosmic Christ?)

12.	North- American	— (Christianity still surviving)
13.	Byzantine- Russian	— (Hesychast icon-worshippers)
14.	Germanic- Scandinavian	Icelandic sagas or *Eddas*, mysteries of Odin cult (revived in Nazi Germany)
15.	Andean	— (Sun-cults after Christianization)
16.	Meso- American	"
17.	Arab	— (Sufis? Islam still surviving)
18.	African	—
19.	Indian Hindu Muslim	— (Advaita groups? Hinduism still surviving) (Sufis?)
20.	S.-E.-Asian	—
21.	Japanese	(Zen temples & arts)
22.	Oceanian	—
23.	Chinese	— (Taoists in Taiwan, Buddhists in exile)
24.	Tibetan	—

(Dalai Lama in exile)

---

25. Central-Asian   —

(Buddhist coteries in exile)

It is very clear that shortly before the demise of each of the dead civilizations their religion, and therefore their Light, ended. This appears to support the logic of my evidence, that the absence of the Light first hastens the end of their religion and then hastens the decay of their civilization.

58. FURTHER OCCUPATION BY FOREIGN OCCUPIER

There is now a further occupation of the civilization by a foreign occupier, as the following pattern shows:

Civilization	Date of further occupation	Details of foreign occupier's further occupation
1. Indo-European Kurgan/ Old European	c.1000-900 BC	Urnfield Celts' occupation of W. Europe & British Isles
2. Mesopotamian	c.395-602	Byzantine (East Roman)/Sasanian occupation of Mesopotamia after Alaric ravaged Greece in 395
3. Egyptian	c.395-616	Byzantine (East Roman) occupation of Egypt, which Justinian reorganized into four parts, administering it from Constantinople
4. Aegean-Greek	c.395-602	Byzantine occupation of Greece while

Byzantine civilization was still East
Roman

5.	Roman	c.756-774	Frankish occupation of Papal States, a Frankish dependency, which Pepin enlarged to the size of the former Byzantine province at the Pope's request
6.	Anatolian	c.395-602	Byzantine occupation of Anatolia while Byzantine civilization was still East Roman
7.	Syrian	c.395-634	Byzantine occupation of Syria, during which Iranians attacked Syria from 540, capturing Damascus c.614, until the Byzantine liberation of Syria (c.620-634)
8.	Israelite	c.395-634	Byzantine occupation of Palestine, during which Iranians attacked Palestine from 540, capturing Jerusalem c.614, until the Byzantine liberation of Jerusalem (c.620-634)
9.	Celtic	c.1066-1166	Norman occupation of Britain (and after 1106, under Henry I Anglo-Norman occupation of France including Frankish Normandy); Ireland (independent from Norsemen under High Kings after 1014) affected by Norman church reform
10.	Iranian	c.1382-1501	Timurid occupation of Iran: Timur entered Iran in 1380 & set up the Timurid Emirate (c.1383), captured Baghdad in 1393 & set up the "Timurid Renaissance" whose Central

Asian Samarkand styles included blue tiles with geometrical patterns & reflected Iranian miniature painting & Persian carpets; after his death the first Timurids established the Emirate of the Black Sheep Turks (c.1406)

11.	European	—	—
12.	North-American	—	—
13.	Byzantine-Russian	—	—
14.	Germanic-Scandinavian	c.1106-1187	English occupation of Normandy: England conquered Normandy under Henry I in 1106, & the Norman line died out in both England & Normandy in 1135; the English survived in Normandy until 1187; occupation of parts of Scandinavia by the Norwegian empire, which included unions with Greenland & Iceland (1261-2), the Faeroes & the Scottish Isles, Sweden & Finland (1362), reflect a Christianized European approach which led to the Kalmar Union
15.	Andean	—	—
16.	Meso-American	—	—
17.	Arab	—	—

18.	African	—	—	
19.	Indian	—	—	
20.	S.-E.-Asian	—	—	
21.	Japanese	—	—	
22.	Oceanian	—	—	
23.	Chinese	—	—	
24.	Tibetan	—	—	
25.	Central-Asian	—	—	

59. THE DECAYING LIGHTLESS RELIGION IS SUPPRESSED AND DIES

The renewed spell of foreign occupation results in the foreign occupier's religion suppressing the decaying Lightless religion, which now finally dies, as the following pattern shows:

Civilization	Now Lightless religion	Date religion (& Light) ended	Lightless religion suppressed by	Absence of religion's Light
1. Indo-European Kurgan/ Old European	Dyaeus Pitar	c.1000 BC	Urnfield Celts	c.1000-800 BC
2. Mesopotamian	Utu/ Shamash	c.395 (suppressal	Roman & then Byzantine	c.4th C-642

| | | pantheon | began 313) | Christianity/ | |
| | | | | Iranian Sasanians | |

3.	Egyptian	Ra pantheon	c.395 (suppressal began 313) (378 edict of Theodosius I banned the worship of Osiris & Isis. Last hieroglyphic inscription at Philae dated August 24, 394. Faces of Hathor/old gods on reliefs defaced by Christian Copts at Dendera in 5th C.)	Roman & then Byzantine Christianity/ Christian Copts	4th C-642
4.	Aegean-Greek	Zeus	from 395 (suppressal began 313)	Roman & then Byzantine Christianity	313-629
5.	Roman	Jupiter	from 756 (suppressal began 313/ 535)	Frankish Christianity (Roman & then Byzantine Christianity)	4th C-787
6.	Anatolian	Attis/ Cybele	from 395 Christianity	Byzantine	c.395-626
7.	Syrian	Baal pantheon	c.395 (suppressal began 313)	Roman & then Byzantine Christianity	4th C-636
8.	Israelite	Elohim	c.395 (suppressal	Roman & Byzantine	c.135-636

			began c.135, Judaism ended in Jerusalem/ Jewish home-land survived in exile)	Christianity, when Rabbinic Judaism became a Diaspora religion, pro-ducing the *Mishna & Talmuds* without access to Jerusalem or the Temple	
9.	Celtic	Du-w/ Taran & Celtic Christ	c.1066 (suppressal began 664, Synod of Whitby)	Roman Catholics, then Normans	c.1066-1171
10.	Iranian	Ahura Mazda	c.1382 (suppressal began 7th C when Zoroastrians or Gabars became outcasts in Kerman or Yazd after Arab-Muslim conquest)	Timurid Sufism	c.1382-1511
11.	European	God as Light	—	—	—

#					
12.	North-American	God as Light	—	—	—
13.	Byzantine-Russian	God as Light	—	—	—
14.	Germanic-Scandinavian	Odin/Thor	c.1106 when English conquered Normandy & eliminated last traces of Scandinavian religion, following conversions to Christianity: 4th C (Visigoths) 5th C (Vandals, Burgundians, Ostrogoths) 6th-7th C (English) 8th C (Old Saxons or Frankish Saxons) 10th C (Danes) 10th-11th C (Norwegians, Swedes, Icelanders)	English Christianity	After c.500 (Germanic)/ after c.800 (Scandinavian) -1214

15. Andean	Sun-god	—	—	—
16. Meso-American	Sun-god	—	—	—
17. Arab	Allah/ Mohammed	—	—	—
18. African	African gods (e.g. Mwari)	—	—	—
19. Indian	Reality	—	—	—
20. S.-E.-Asian	Buddha	—	—	—
21. Japanese	Kami/ Buddha	—	—	—
22. Oceanian	Buddha?/ Sun-god?	—	—	—
23. Chinese	*Ti*	—	—	—
24. Tibetan	Buddha	—	—	—
25. Central-Asian	Shamans/ Buddha	—	—	—

60. Sudden Final Conquest of Religionless Civilization

A consequence of the attraction of visionaries away from a Light to foreign cults, of the eventual crushing of its embers by persecution, and of the resulting end of a religion, is the lingering demise of a civilization. The demise of my civilizations should therefore be seen in relation to the death of their religions. The final conquest of the exhausted religionless civilization is delayed, but takes place relatively suddenly, as the following pattern shows:

Civilization		Date & details of civilization's final conquest
1. Indo-European Kurgan/ Old European	c.900 BC	Hallstatt culture's conquest of Urnfield Celts; (the dating of the Hallstatt period is disputed, but early Hallstatt finds can be dated to c.1100-1000 BC, & the later Hallstatt period had triumphed by c.800-700 BC, giving our dating for the conquest of Urnfield)
2. Mesopotamian	c.602-642	Iran captured Mesopotamia under Khosrow II but the Byzantine Heraclius invaded Iran (622-8); the Arabs conquered Mesopotamia AD 636-642
3. Egyptian	c.616-642	Persian conquest of Egypt, which reverted back to Byzantium under Heraclius I in 628. In 639 the Arabs invaded Egypt, & the Byzantines evacuated Egypt in 642.
4. Aegean-Greek	c.602-629	Conquest of Greece (& Balkans) by the Avar Khanate, & reconquest by Byzantine Heraclius, after which the East Roman Empire was transformed into the medieval Byzantine Empire

5.	Roman	c.774-787	Conquest of Italy, in which Charlemagne defeated the Lombards & the Franks occupied Spoleto, leading to coronation of Charlemagne as Roman Emperor (Pirenne was the first to hold that the Roman Empire ended much later than 476 – in the 8th C after the Muslim expansion, he thought; c.800 is a better date as secular Roman civilization ceased to exist then, passing into the clerical Frankish Empire, &, following the division of this Empire c.843 between Charlemagne's three grand-sons, who ruled most of what is now France, Germany & Italy, there were three successor kingdoms from 888; Italy was conquered by Germany 951-961 & was incorporated in the Holy Roman Empire which lasted from 962 to 1806)
6.	Anatolian	c.602-626	Conquest of Anatolia by the Avar Khanate & Persians, & reconquest by Byzantine Heraclius, after which the East-Roman Empire was transformed into the medieval Byzantine Empire
7.	Syrian	c.634-636	Arab conquest, following the battle of the Yarmuk river, of a Syria weakened by Iranian & Byzantine domination
8.	Israelite	c.634-636	Arab conquest of a Palestine weakened by Iranian & Byzantine domination
9.	Celtic	c.1166-1171	Anglo-Norman invasion of Celtic Ireland, culminating in Henry II's arrival in Ireland

in October 1171 & the triumph of Roman Catholicism over Celtic Christianity there.

10.	Iranian	c.1501-1511	Islamic Safavids, who claimed descent from the Shi'ite imams, conquered Iran under Esma'il, head of the Sufis of Ardabil who sought to purify Iran from Mongol contamination & annexed Baghdad & Mosul; & Iran passed into Islam, remaining Muslim throughout the Safavid time (until 1736) & under later dynasties: Nader Shah, Zand, Qajars, Pahlavi & Khomeiniists; Iran is now of Shi'ite Islam & has always been militantly anti-Sunni (anti-Ottoman & recently anti-Iraq)
11.	European	—	—
12.	North-American	—	—
13.	Byzantine-Russian	—	—
14.	Germanic-Scandinavian	c.1187-1214	French conquest of English domains in France, including Normandy
15.	Andean	—	—
16.	Meso-American	—	—
17.	Arab	—	—

18. African	—	—
19. India	—	—
20. S.-E.-Asian	—	—
21. Japanese	—	—
22. Oceanian	—	—
23. Chinese	—	—
24. Tibetan	—	—
25. Central-Asian	—	—

61. THE DEAD CIVILIZATION PASSES INTO A SUCCESSOR CIVILIZATION

The dead civilization now passes into a successor civilization which has its own religion and its own Light. People still live in the territory that used to belong to the dead civilization, but now they are citizens of the successor civilization.

I have argued that the demise of a civilization is a consequence of the demise of its religion. It follows that in determining the time of death of a decaying civilization, I should look for a date after the death of its traditional religion (and Light), and settle on the date when its traditional religion (including its Light) is replaced by another religion and Light. Thus under the Achaemenian occupations of Mesopotamia and Egypt, the Mesopotamian and Egyptian religions and Lights continued, so a later date has to be sought for the demise of these two civilizations. The following pattern is clear:

	Civilization	Successor civilization into which dead civilization passed	Date civilization died
1.	Indo-European Kurgan/ Old European	Celtic	c.800 BC
2.	Mesopotamian	Arab	642
3.	Egyptian	Arab	642
4.	Aegean-Greek	Byzantine-Russian	c.629
5.	Roman	European	c.787 (formalized in 800)
6.	Anatolian	Byzantine-Russian	c.626
7.	Syrian	Arab	636
8.	Israelite	Arab (Judaism now within an Arab context in Palestine, Babylon & Spain)	c.636
9.	Celtic	European (through Normans)	1171
10.	Iranian	Arab (absorbed by Shi'ite Iranian Safavids)	1511
11.	European	—	—
12.	North-	—	—

American

13. Byzantine-Russian	—	—
14. Germanic-Scandinavian	European	800 (Germanic) 1214 (Scandinavian)
15. Andean	—	—
16. Meso-American	—	—
17. Arab	—	—
18. African	—	—
19. Indian	—	—
20. S.-E.-Asian	—	—
21. Japanese	—	—
22. Oceanian	—	—
23. Chinese	—	—
24. Tibetan	—	—
25. Central-Asian	—	—

How Light-based Religion/16 Alternatives Contributed to Demise/Survival of Each Civilization

As the successor civilization's religion replaces the dead civilization's religion, I need to give a brief account of how the demise of each civilization's Light-based religion contributed to the demise of each dead civilization within the context of the 16 alternatives of stage 51.

We have seen that a failure to renew the Light and a civilization's Central Idea results in its illumined men and then its peoples being attracted to the Light and Central Idea of a foreign invader, with the result that in due course its religion is taken over by a foreign religion. I have asked whether a civilization dies because it loses its visions of the Light from its religion, or whether visions of the Light disappear from the religion as a result of the outer anxiety and despair that is felt when a civilization is decaying. I now need to summarize the process of decay and demise in each of the 25 civilizations and their religions, and relate it to the 16 alternatives of stage 51, paying attention to the role of the foreign threat or occupying power which created unsettled conditions for the decaying civilization and generated an outward anxiety which undoubtedly made it harder for the vision of the Light to be sought and received. We need to see how each dead civilization decayed because, under foreign influence, its Light-based religion ended, and therefore ceased to attract and unify its peoples, who switched to the occupier's religion; or alternatively, how each surviving civilization has survived because, despite foreign occupation, its Light-based religion has continued to attract and unify its peoples:

1.   The Indo-European Kurgan Light seems to have flourished c.4000-2600 BC when the religion of Dyaeus Pitar spread. We know that after c.2600 BC some of the Kurgan peoples experienced foreign threats from the Mesopotamian megalith-builders and the Spanish Beaker culture, and that having invaded the territory of the North Pontians and Trans-Caucasians, some of them were driven out by the Semitic Akkadians. About 2200 BC Battle-Axe Kurgans drove out the Pelasgian Greeks and c.2000 BC more attacked the Scandinavians. The Kurgans were mobile and comprised many peoples, and over a period of time they fragmented into many groups which passed into the

Sumerian, Mycenaean/Greek, Iranian, Indian, Celtic and Germanic civilizations, in all of which Dyaeus was superseded by another god (for example, the Greek Zeus). This happened c.3000 BC (in the case of Sumeria), c.2250/2000 BC (in the case of Greece and Iran), before c.1500 BC (in the case of India), and before c.800-500 BC (in the case of the Celts and Germans). There was a new wave of Unetice conquerors c.1500 BC, and eventually W. Europe was settled by the Urnfield culture. We have given c.900 BC as the date when the Kurgan religion was effectively ended by the Hallstatt Celts, but before then there were signs of decay: loss of military dominance, increase in regionalism, fragmentation, and economic decline. Coteries must have kept the Indo-European Light alive in fire-temples after Dyaeus was superseded. The later Stonehenge probably served as a Fire-temple. In short, the Kurgan civilization decayed because, under foreign influence, its Light-based religion of Dyaeus ended and therefore ceased to attract and unify its peoples, who switched to Zeus and Du-w, the god of the Hallstatt Celts who came from W. Europe.

2. The Mesopotamian Light seems to have been weak during the militaristic Assyrian occupation (910-538 BC). The Assyrians lost their military dominance to the Medes, and during the aggressively militaristic Chaldean time (when Nebuchadrezzar took Jerusalem and deported the southern tribes of Israel to Babylon, 586-538 BC) the Mesopotamian religious tradition revived and the Chaldean mystery schools taught the Light. Mesopotamia passed into the Persian Achaemenian, Seleucid, Parthian and Sasanian Empires and was a Roman battleground, but during this time Marduk and Anu were recognised alongside Zeus, and the Mesopotamian Light still flourished in Sasanian times. The Mesopotamian Light-based religion died in the 4th century AD when the East Romans (Byzantines) occupied part of Mesopotamia and it was overshadowed by Byzantine and Nestorian Christianity. By then Mesopotamia had long since lost its military dominance and in the rise of regionalism, Mesopotamia was economically weak. It was finally absorbed by the Islamic Arab Empire in AD 642. The Mesopotamian Light was kept alive in the Chaldean mystery schools which had been influenced by the Persian Magi, some of which survived into Islam. In short, the Mesopotamian civilization decayed because, under foreign influence, its Light-based religion of Utu/Shamash ended and therefore ceased to attract and unify its peoples, who switched to Byzantine and

Nestorian Christianity and then Islam.

3.   The Egyptian Light seems to have been weak during the foreign occupation of the Libyan dynasty (c.935-730 BC) and during the Ethiopian-Assyrian militaristic contest for Egypt (c.730-664 BC), when central control weakened and the emphasis on Seth weakened the Central Idea of Ra. From 525 BC Egypt passed into the Achaemenian, Ptolemaic and Roman Empires but the traditional religious cults survived. The Egyptian Light began to be Christianized possibly in the 1st century AD but certainly after Gnosticism by the 3rd and 4th centuries AD. The traditional religion co-existed for a while. The Egyptian religion can be said to have died with the Christian East Roman (Byzantine) rule from Constantinople (from AD 395) when it was finally Christianized, and Egypt eventually passed into Islam in 642. Arabization was at first largely voluntary and was not completed until the 8th century, and the Egyptian Light was kept alive in the Isis mysteries, and in coterie Alchemy and Hermeticist schools which survived into the Middle Ages (and, indeed to this day). In short the Egyptian civilization decayed because, under foreign influence, its Light-based religion of Ra ended, and therefore ceased to attract and unify its peoples, who switched to Byzantine Christianity and later Islam.

4.   In the Aegean-Greek civilization, the Minoan Light of the sun-bull seems to have weakened after c.1450 BC when, following the eruption of Thera, conquerors from the mainland arrived in Crete and destroyed the Minoan Palace culture that had flourished since c.2200 BC. As a result the open-air Cretan sanctuaries were no longer used, and under the invader the Light probably ceased to be seen until the final destruction of Minoan culture by more mainland invaders c.1100 BC. Coterie groups may have carried the Minoan Light into the mainland Dionysian bull-mysteries.

The Mycenaean Light which began with the Achaean Mycenaeans (originally Battle-Axe Kurgans) before the Dorian invasions c.1100 BC and grew during the intensely religious classical Archaic period (1100-c.700 BC), weakened during the 5th century BC as a result of the Persian invasion and civil war. Greece was occupied by the Macedonians and then the Romans, and in AD 395 it was ruled from Constantinople by the East Romans (Byzantines), when the Greek Light was Christianized. Coterie groups preserved the Greek Light in the Eleusinian, Dionysian, Orphic and Pythagorean mysteries, and in

Neoplatonism, and the Greek civilization ended c.629. In short, the Greek civilization decayed because, under foreign influence, its Light-based religion of Zeus ended, and therefore ceased to attract and unify its people, who switched to Christianity.

5. The Roman Light of pre-Etruscan times was weakened during the Punic wars of the later Roman Republic when foreign cults were imported to co-exist with Jupiter-Apollo of the State religion. It broke down during the last century of the Republic. During the growing materialism of the imperial epoch, the State religion left a void which was filled by pagan philosophy (for example Stoicism and Neoplatonism), and the author of *Sublimity in Style* (1st or 3rd century AD) laments "the low spiritual tension in which all but a few chosen spirits among us pass our days. In our work and in our recreation alike our only objective is popularity and enjoyment. We feel no concern to win the true spiritual treasure." By the 3rd century AD there were campaigns against the Christians (AD 250) and the Light was further weakened by the raids of the barbarians (Germanic tribes). There was loss of central control and economic decline. Living standards collapsed, and lacking military dominance, the Romans were unable to impose the rule of law on the barbarians. Rome was Christianized (312-395) and, its religion dying, eventually fell to the barbarians (410). Roman civilization in the West collapsed in 476. Coterie groups preserved the Roman Light in pagan mysteries of Jupiter and Mithras, while the Desert Fathers preserved the Christian Light for the coming West Roman (i.e. pre-European) Christian and East Roman Byzantine civilizations. There was a further Germanic occupation under the Lombards until the Franks incorporated Italy into the new European civilization c.787. In short the Roman civilization decayed because, under foreign influence, its Light-based religion of Jupiter ended, and therefore ceased to attract and unify its peoples, who switched to Christianity.

6. The Anatolian civilization is very ancient, and painted bulls at Çatalhüyük date from c.6500 BC. The Hittites borrowed their Light along with their gods from Anatolia, and unlike the Mesopotamian and Egyptian rulers, the Hittite monarch was a secular being; he was not divine until his death. The Hittite Light seems to have weakened after the militaristic campaigns that captured Babylon c.1590 BC, and although the Hittites defeated the Mitanni and

fought the battle of Kadesh against Ramesses II of Egypt in 1288 BC, there seems to have been loss of central control and the Hittite Storm and Weather god weakened. The Hittites were expelled to Syria by the Sea Peoples. There they are known as the Neo-Hittites. It is probable that a coterie Neo-Hittite group carried their Syrian Light into the mysteries of Adonis. The Phrygians flourished in the 7th century BC before they were defeated by the Cimmerians. Cybele and Attis were weakened, but Attic rites were kept going by coteries. Anatolia was occupied by the Romans and was then ruled by the East Romans (or Byzantines). In short, the Anatolian civilization decayed because, under foreign influence, its Light-based religion of first Tarhun-Teshub and then Cybele-Attis (Magna Mater) ended, and therefore ceased to attract and unify its peoples, who switched to Byzantine Greek Christianity.

7.   The Syrian civilization goes back to c.9000 BC when there was a settlement in Jericho. The Syrian/Phoenician Light dimmed after it passed into the Achaemenian Empire (539-332 BC), which was conquered by Alexander the Great. It was then ruled by Ptolemaic Egypt and the Seleucids. The Carthaginian Phoenicians were involved in militaristic campaigns with Rome, and were incorporated into Rome in 146 BC. Syria was Romanized and, after Gnosticism, its religion was Christianized in the 4th century AD. It passed into the Byzantine Empire, and the civilization ended when it passed into the Islamic civilization in AD 636. In short, the Syrian civilization decayed because, under foreign influence, its Light-based religion of Baal ended, continuing among coteries as Diabolism, and therefore ceased to attract and unify its peoples, who switched to Christianity and then Islam.

8.   The Israelite Light had been weakened by the division of David's kingdom in 922 BC and by the fall of Israel to the Assyrians in 721 BC, and it was entering materialistic times when the prophets warned of the impending Fall of Jerusalem, which happened in 586 BC. After the Neo-Babylonian (Chaldean) occupation of the southern kingdom, Palestine passed into the Achaemenian Empire, which was conquered by Alexander the Great. It was then ruled by Ptolemaic Egypt, and passed under the Syrian Seleucid dynasty and was Hellenised, especially under Herod I of Judaea. The Judaistic Light was further weakened by doctrinal conflict between the Pharisees and the Sadducees – Christ was in conflict with the Pharisees – and during the Roman time it was

kept alive by the Essenes and of course coterie Christians. The Romans destroyed the Temple in AD 70, and the Jews were scattered under Roman and then East Roman (or Byzantine) rule, and the Arabs conquered Palestine in 633-641. The Jewish religion survived these blows in exile but in Palestine the Israelite civilization had come to an end. During the Diaspora Kabbalistic coteries kept the Judaistic Light alive. The survival and growth of the Jewish faith among coteries abroad has seen Zionism return to Israel in our own time in the form of a Western pseudo-colony. However, in the Roman times the Israelite civilization decayed because, despite foreign influences, its Light-based religion of Yahweh or Elohim ceased to attract and unify many of its peoples who were Romanized and then Arabized AD c.636.

The Israelite civilization seems to have reached stages 54, 55 and 56 in the 1st century AD but its religion did not end, and renewals kept the civilization alive until the 7th century AD. The modern state of Israel is very much that of a coterie culture which has briefly restored its former glory. At first sight the new Israel has the appearance of a new civilization. Its Light originated in the ancient Israelite civilization and there was a migration to a new culture (stages 1 and 2). However there the similarity ends, for no new religion has been created; it is the religion of Jews throughout the world that unifies the heterogeneous Jewish peoples in modern Israel.

Let us remind ourselves of the facts. The Central Idea of Zionism is God's promise of the land of Israel (the promised land of Palestine, one of the hills of ancient Jerusalem being called Zion) to the people of Israel. Zionism had been kept alive by coteries ever since the Diaspora which followed the capture of Masada by the Romans in AD 70, and in the 16th and 17th centuries "messiahs" advocated the return of the Jews to Palestine. In the 18th century the Haskala (Enlightenment) urged that Jews should assimilate into Western secular culture, and the Hoveve Zion ("Lovers of Zion") movement was a reaction and led to Herzl convening the first Zionist Congress at Basel in 1897. By 1914 there were 13,000 Jewish settlers in Palestine (mainly Russian, Austrian and German Jews, many supported by the French Baron Edmond de Rothschild), and in World War I the Zionist leadership passed to Russian Jews living in England, most notably Chaim Weizmann who secured the 1917 Balfour Declaration promising British support for a Jewish national home in Palestine. The Declaration was in

Britain's League of Nations mandate over Palestine, and from 1922 to 1933 there were new settlements until by the rise of Hitler there were 238,000 Jews in Palestine. Hitler's anti-Semitic policies, and the Nazi extermination of allegedly 6, certainly 5 million Jews during the Second World War increased the feeling of Zionism, and in spite of Arab opposition (there were Arab revolts in 1929 and 1936-9), following a Jewish campaign of terror against Britain in 1947 the UN proposed an Arab-Jewish partition of Palestine and an internationalised Jerusalem. Israel was created in 1948 with Hebrew as its official language, and increased its territory following the Arab-Israeli wars of 1948-9, 1956 and 1967 when the surrounding Arab states sought to obliterate Israel.

The pre-1948 settlement pattern, spanning 50 years, may recall the settlement of the USA in the 17th century and has led to claims that Zionism, a cultural synthesis of Ashkenazi (Central and Eastern Europe), Sefardi and Oriental (Mediterranean and Middle and Far East) rite Jews, is a new and growing civilization in its own right, but the lack of a religious motive in the territorial colonization suggests otherwise.

The new Israel should be seen as a colonizing reaction to the Nazi holocaust, a determination to end the homelessness that resulted in the Nazi persecution; and Israel of course has a desire to defend herself, to secure her frontiers, using conquered parts of Syria, Jordan and Egypt as buffer zones. The new Israel should thus be seen as a new colony of Western Jewry which was established with the connivance of Western governments rather than as a new spiral of Israelite civilization; it is an armed refuge for the persecuted descendants of coterie exiles rather than a new expansionist, militaristic force.

9. The Celtic Light seems to have been strong in the 8th century BC, and *The Light of Civilization* shows that it was linked with the Levitical Samarians. It was probably weakened during the spread of the Druid universities and the struggle to repel the militaristic Roman invader and occupying power. When Druidism was Christianized in AD 156, the original Druid Light was kept alive by coteries, which have survived to this day. The first Palestinian-British Light was kept alive on islands like Iona by coterie groups of Culdees who rejected Roman centralism. Some of these seem to have founded the Irish branch of the Celtic civilization.

The Irish-Celtic Light seems to have originated as the Culdee Light, which found its way to Ireland from Wales and Iona in the 1st-2nd centuries AD. (St Columba's visit to Iona c.563 was probably a return visit.) There are many stories of missions to England by early Irish saints, but officially Ireland was converted by St Patrick in the 5th century. St Piran arrived in Cornwall from Ireland in the 6th century. Monastic cities were founded in Ireland during the 6th century, the foremost being Clonmacnoise which became a centre of learning by the 9th century, and Clonard. The Irish escaped the Saxon raids but were conquered by the Vikings, who settled half Ireland in the 9th century. The Irish-Celtic Light dimmed during this military occupation, and after further Viking raids in the 11th century, the Irish-Celtic Light was Romanized in the 12th century. Coterie groups preserved the Celtic Light until the Protestant Reformation. In short, the Irish branch of the Celtic civilization decayed because under foreign influence its Light-based religion of Du-w and Taran and then of Celtic God through Christ weakened, and ceased to attract and unify its peoples who switched to Roman Catholicism. In short, the Celtic civilization decayed because, under foreign influence, its Light-based religion of Du-w and Taran ended and therefore ceased to attract and unify its peoples who switched to Christianity.

10. The Iranian Light which had been renewed by the Medes and the Persians passed into the Parthian Empire (3rd century BC-AD 226) but re-emerged in the Sasanian period in the heretical Zoroastrian Light of Ahura Mazda as the first Sasanian king, Ardashir I (224-241), had ancestors who conducted the rites of the fire-temple at Istakhr which was known as "the Anahid Fire". Zoroastrianism made a come-back, and Zoroastrian Magi condemned Mani in 274. Mazdaism (the worship of Ahura Mazda) flourished as well as Manichaeism and Gnosticism. However, from the 4th century on there were military conflicts with Rome, the Turks and Byzantium, and despite Mazdak's Mazdakism in the 5th century the Sasanian Light was exhausted by the time the Arabs conquered it in 651 and absorbed the Iranian religion into the Islamic civilization. The Iranian Light was kept alive by coterie Magi and turned Sufi, breaking with the past. From 821 there was an Iranian renaissance through Iranian Islamic dynasties, and Iran was eventually conquered by the Seljuq Turks and the Mongols (who became Muslim in 1300), and was fully absorbed into Islam by the Shi'ite Safavids c.1511. In short, the Iranian civilization decayed because, under foreign influence, its Light-based religion of Ahura

Mazda ended within its borders, and therefore ceased to attract and unify its peoples who switched to Islam.

11.   Western civilization is an amalgam of the European and American civilizations just as the Graeco-Roman civilization after c.180 BC was an amalgam of the Aegean-Greek and Roman civilizations, and just as the Roman civilization after AD 330 was an amalgam of the West Roman and East Roman/Byzantine civilizations.

The European civilization has its roots in the Christianized Germanic tribes of the 5th century, and it took shape as the Goths and Ostrogoths settled in Italy, the Franks in France, the Angles and Saxons in Britain, leaving the Old Saxons in Germany. It grew through its Frankish conquest of Italy c.800, and Alfred's unification of Britain. Following the Viking invasions and the establishment of a Viking Norman kingdom in Normandy and the Norman invasion of Britain, European civilization grew through the Crusades, the Reformation, Puritanism (which created its colonial offshoot, American civilization) and the time of Romanticism and the Evangelical Revival. The European Light was strong from the 5th century to the 17th century. During the revolution and wars of the 18th, 19th and 20th centuries, missionaries spread Christianity round the world, and with it Western culture, while the Industrial Revolution spread a scientific and materialistic outlook (machines and railways) which came to dominate. To the First British Empire in America, which collapsed, was added a Second British Empire in the non-American parts of the world, and all the European countries had empires in Africa or Asia.

By c.1880, the vision of the Light weakened and seemed almost to have become lost. Europe went into imperial decline in 1910, a decline that has its origins c.1880, and since 1914 Europe has no longer ruled the world. The late 19th century and 20th-century militaristic colonial conflicts (the Boer War, the First and Second World Wars and the colonial wars of decolonization) have all further weakened the Christian Light and Central Idea, and Europe's division has deepened. The Second World War saw much of Europe occupied by the Nazis' attempt to revive the Germanic-Scandinavian civilization, including Scandinavia, France, and Eastern Europe, and later by the Americans, and finally by the USSR which occupied Eastern Europe from 1945 to c.1991.

The European Light of Christianity has been weakened by foreign influence and occupation, and Europe seems about to become a series of provinces in a conglomerate. It would be pessimistic to anticipate the end of Christianity and the obliteration of European civilization by a nuclear Islam, and European Christianity is continuing, as is demonstrated by the millions who flocked to see the Polish Pope John Paul II. It may be that in stage 43 Europe will experience a new unity through a politically integrated European Union that will include Eastern Europe and indeed eventually part of the ex-USSR west of the Urals. In short, European civilization has survived because, despite foreign occupation, its Light-based religion of God through Christ has (albeit only just) continued to attract and unify its peoples (including the Christian peoples of the Commonwealth for whom the British monarch is Head of the Anglican Communion).

12.   North America, on the other hand, is a young nation. It did not exist in the European consciousness until Columbus discovered it in 1493/4. It is therefore post-medieval. From 1607 colonies were settled for profit on territories sold by the crown, and they attracted religious exiles including Catholics (Maryland), Puritan Separatists from the Church of England (Plymouth, Massachusetts), those who sought to reform the Church from within, and Quakers (Pennsylvania). The *Mayflower* Puritan exiles of 1620, the Pilgrim Fathers, were typical of the new spirit that colonized America, and the Great Awakening that swept America in the 1730s and 1740s found receptive hearts. America won free from Britain in the War of Independence (1775-83) and unified the growing civilization and fought off the British in 1814. America created the basis of the United States before the arrest in her growth with the invasion from the Confederacy during the so-called civil war from 1861 to 1865. It renewed its Central Idea through the growth of many diverse religions, and rose to world power in stage 15 from 1913 when Europe went into decline. America stayed out of the First and Second World Wars long enough to profit from extensive arms sales – in 1966 the Europeans owed America $21 billion for World War I alone[2] – and after 1945 led the Free World with the Truman Doctrine. Having invented computers and reached the moon with unparalleled scientific technology (a Second Industrial or Technological Revolution that has been American-led), America (at stage 15) gives the impression of having plenty of vitality and growth, along with its national vulgarity, with 38% attending church

services as against 1.7% in Britain.[3] America regards itself as having inherited the leadership of Western civilization just as the Byzantine Empire regarded itself as being the true Roman empire. In short, American civilization has survived because, free from foreign occupation, its Light-based religion of God through Christ has continued to attract and unify the peoples of the various states, all of whom can say with the Declaration of Independence "In God we Trust".

Western civilization is now like "West Rome" and "East Rome" before 476, when there were two emperors. Half occupied until 1989-1990, Europe, like West Rome, is spent and secular, and Muslim terrorists and until recently Communist "barbarians" have threatened its internal security. America, like Byzantium, however, is growing, and has never been occupied (except, like Byzantium, when it was a colony). The tension between America and Europe is like that between Byzantium and Rome: a simplistic, almost naive growing faith contrasted with a complex, disillusioned, secular decay. (It is a tension Henry James is close to catching in his American-European novels.) If our association of stage 43 with the European Union is incorrect and European Christianity ends and European civilization is threatened in stage 43 by a new occupation from Russia or Islam (perhaps as a result of nuclear weapons), then one can be confident that Western civilization, and the Central Idea of God as Light, will continue in and through America. On the other hand, it is more likely that if America, which oscillates between isolationist neutrality and interventionism, retains an international role, then an American-backed European Union or United States of Europe may expand to absorb and include the ex-Soviet colonies, and parts of the ex-USSR herself, in which case not only would Europe's decline be reversed by a new European renewal of the Light; it is possible that just as Justinian used East Roman forces to reconquer Italy c.550, so American-European influence would revive and create a world cultural hegemony.

13.   The Byzantine Light was still strong in the time of St Symeon the New Theologian (died 1022) as *The Light of Civilization* shows; it had converted Russia in 988. It was weakened by the militaristic activity of the Crusades (1098-1291) at the start of which it was threatened by the Seljuq Turks, and it finally broke down before the Ottomans, who eventually captured

Constantinople in 1453. The Byzantine religion and Light passed into the Russian Light in haloed icons which are still used in Greek and Russian Orthodox churches.

The Russian Light originated when Greek missionaries from Byzantium introduced Christianity in 988. After the fall of Byzantium the Russian Orthodox Church received its own ecclesiastically independent patriarch, an office which was suppressed in 1721 by Peter the Great, who abandoned Russia's identity (dear to the Slavophiles) as successor to the Byzantines for the identity (dear to the "Westernizers") of a Protestant Reformation state, and sought to Westernize Russia by letting in secularized Western culture. By his Spiritual Regulation he placed the Church under the State, and State secularism facilitated Russian rule over the Islamic provinces. It also had the effect of enclosing the Church, which inadvertently brought about a monastic revival, and as a result, the Russian Light was strong until the 19th century. Communism likewise dimmed the Light but inadvertently led to its revival.

The "Westernizers" had always been atheists, and their reformism following the abolition of serfdom in the 1860s turned revolutionary, linking with American international financiers and Western-European Marxism, which saw history as being propelled by class struggle, and they brought in the American-German backed Bolshevik revolution of 1917 which ended the Russian Empire, plunged Russia into civil war, State terror and decline, and put an end to the scholarly and spiritual Russian Orthodox tradition by introducing stage 43. Although the Patriarchate was restored six days after the Bolshevik takeover in the first flush of change, the Bolsheviks regarded religion as "the opium of the people" and they persecuted the Orthodox faith in the course of enforcing their slogan of "peace, land and bread" (i.e. stopping the First World War, abolishing private property and feeding the starving). They deprived the Church of the right to own private property in 1918 and confiscated its treasures in 1922, (officially in order to feed the starving), and under Stalin thousands of Orthodox Christians were killed. During a protracted civil war that lasted throughout the 1930s and whose outcome unified the USSR, Stalin built up a centralized, tyrannical and ruthlessly repressive system designed to prevent the transfer of power from the Party, and by 1939 the Church had virtually been suppressed as there were only four functioning bishops and 100 functioning churches.

Communism (i.e. egalitarianism, the proletariat's equal right to land, bread and wealth through class struggle and civil war) was confined to the USSR at first but Lenin had always envisaged a world revolution, and following the Second World War Stalin used the Soviet armies in Eastern Europe to achieve a defensive ring of allies, and by stages acquired a Soviet-dominated bloc of Eastern-European states in which all opposition was suppressed. The West was unwilling to intervene, and when Soviet spies stole American nuclear secrets and gave the USSR nuclear weapons the danger of nuclear war froze the situation for over 40 years. Soviet spies stole Western technological and space secrets and improved Soviet military might, and the USSR became a great power that threatened Europe and later acquired a maritime empire. After 1939 churches had been allowed to spring up in the USSR, and by 1959 there were some 25,000. Between 1959 and 1964 the persecution of the Orthodox Church was renewed and Krushchev reduced the number to 10,000. Persecutions caused an Orthodox diaspora, and the Orthodox Church is found in the Balkans, the Middle East, and the USA.

Following the end of Communism the Orthodox religion returned to the ex-USSR, and there are now between 25 and 50 million Russian Orthodox Christians. The Byzantine-Russian Light has survived and is undergoing a revival as coterie groups were reported to have renewed it in exile and in the Siberian prison camps, where the Orthodox religion was strong. The Metropolitan Anthony was a key figure among the exiles, and Solzhenitsyn's religious outlook was typical of the Gulag.

Since Communism, the Byzantine-Russian civilization has been divided. On the one hand, Byzantine-Russian civilization has survived because, free from foreign occupation since the Nazi invasion, its Light-based Neo-Byzantine Orthodox religion of God through Christ has survived despite official attitudes, and its religious Central Idea has continued to attract and unify the Slavophile, pro-Orthodox peoples, although not, of course, the atheistic revolutionary "Westernizers". On the other hand, the Byzantine-Russian civilization was in stage 43 from 1917 to 1991 because, reacting to foreign threats from the Germans and then the West during the Cold War (for that is how Soviet citizens saw it), the "Westernizers" Party replaced the Byzantine-Russian Central Idea based on the Byzantine vision of God as Light with the centralized, proletarianized terroristic "dictatorship of the proletariat". With its use of State terror and force and long suppression of free thought it has therefore ceased to attract and unify the crushed Slavophiles who, when the Party lost control and the Soviet bloc crumbled, renewed the Byzantine-Russian civilization by renewing their Light-based Neo-Byzantine Orthodox religion. Whether the new openness of *glasnost* will permit complete religious freedom remains to be seen.

Our pattern shows that after a period of imperial decline the post-USSR Byzantine-Russian civilization has entered stage 46 and passed into a federation of independent states which may join up with and pass into an expanding European Union, perhaps after shedding some Asian republics. The Byzantine-Russian civilization has survived because, despite Communism, its Light-based religion and Central Idea have continued to attract and unify the Russian peoples who dominate the Russian-Muslim USSR.

Civilizations that have denied their own Central Idea for a while have generally returned to it (as did the European civilization after the English and French revolutions), and even though the former Soviet Union exploited one period of *detente* to expand into a maritime empire, following *glasnost* the ex-USSR could move close to the West and the Orthodox hierarchy could ecumenically join forces with Western Christianity, as recently espoused by a Polish Pope, and take part in a reunification of Christendom which might also one day see Western Russia (the USSR west of the Urals) joining the European Union.

14.   The Germanic-Scandinavian culture began in South Sweden c.500 BC and was first recorded by Tacitus. The Germanic-Scandinavian gods were Romanized and identified with Jupiter and Apollo; they had therefore presumably embodied the Indo-European Light. Not a great deal is known about the essentially shamanistic Germanic-Scandinavian Light, but it can be presumed to have accompanied the many Germanic "barbarian" tribes (such as the Goths and Vandals) during their migrations throughout Europe and North Africa after they were displaced by the Huns in the 4th and 5th centuries AD, and it can be presumed to have dimmed during the militaristic Saxon-Viking raids on Britain and elsewhere during the 6th-11th centuries. The Saxons were Christianized during the 7th century and their branch of the civilization thus died soon after their religion died. The Danes were Christianized by 960; coterie groups preserved the Germanic-Scandinavian Light after the Dark Ages in Odin mysteries

and in Icelandic sagas or *Eddas* (12th-14th century). The Christian ex-Viking Normans continued the civilization, but once the French had reconquered the Norman lands c.1214, the civilization entered the European civilization, from which the Norwegian Empire ruled the Scottish Isles and elsewhere. Hitler made an attempt to revive the Germanic-Scandinavian civilization in our own time, returning to the pre-Western Germanic origins and glorifying Nordic man and Wagner's Valhalla. In short, the Germanic-Scandinavian civilization decayed because, under foreign influence, its Light-based religion of Odin and Thor ended, and ceased to attract and unify its peoples, who switched to Christianity and European civilization.

15/16.   The Andean and Meso-American Lights began at different times, and they were both Christianized and passed into the European civilization in the early 16th century. The Andean Light dimmed when Huari and Tiahuanaco were abandoned for unknown reasons c.800, but it revived and saw the growth of the Chimu and Inca Empires which fought each other in the 15th century. There was civil war when the Spanish arrived, and militaristic activity clearly weakened the Andean Light. The Classic Mayan culture also collapsed c.800 for unknown reasons; there is no evidence of a foreign invader or of a peasant revolt, and the sites were simply abandoned; possibly there was a threat of a foreign invader or civil war. A foreign successor occupied the Mayan sites until the arrival of the Spanish, and the Mayan Light would have been dimmed as a result, being unable to find social expression. The Aztec Light replaced the Mayan Light in Mexico after c.950. The Aztecs were warriors who conquered nearly 500 states, and their militaristic activity and enormous economic organization probably dimmed their Aztec Light before the 16th century. The American Mississippian and South-Western Indian Lights are not recorded. New World coterie groups preserved their sun-cults after Christianization.

The Andean and Meso-American civilizations have been under Spanish occupation and are now ruled by the descendants of the foreign settlers, but there is evidence that the old pre-Inca and pre-Aztec sun-cults have survived among the Latin-American Indians. The Andean and Meso-American civilizations are now in stage 46, within the regional Organization of American States and Free Trade Area of the Americas under US leadership. In short, the Andean and Meso-American civilizations have survived because, despite foreign influence, their Light-based religions of the sun-god survived despite the predominance of Christianity and continued to attract and unify their peoples despite their switch to Christianity.

17.   The Arab (Islamic) Light was strong from c.620 and absorbed many other Lights until its expansion was checked by the Christian Light during the 200 years of the Crusades. It weakened when it passed into the Ottoman, Safawi and Moghul Empires (16th-17th centuries). Following the collapse of the Ottoman Empire after the First World War, the Arab countries which became Western protectorates after the First World War formed themselves into small independent and often warring states. Palestine, the Golan Heights and the Gaza strip have been occupied by an American-financed foreign colonial invader (Israel), and throughout the period of loss of Arab sovereignty to the Western conglomerate the Arab civilization has been in disunited decline. The Arab world is now an independent network of client-states under foreign superpower (either Western or ex-Soviet) influence and with foreign (either Western or ex-Soviet) funding where Arab oil revenues do not accrue. In 1956 the Arab civilization passed into stage 45 (revival of cultural purity). It is in the process of forming itself into a pan-Arabian union. Gaddafi's dream of reuniting the Arab peoples would renew Arab civilization, but until that happens and despite the renewal of Iranian Islam, the Islamic Light has to compete with the outlook of barbarian war bands (Arab-Israeli wars, the Iraq-Iran war), heroic martyrdom (Palestinian suicide bombers and Arab terrorists) and anti-US Sunni-Shi'ite insurgency in Iraq. Coterie groups have preserved the Sufi Light, which can still be contacted. In short, despite the fragmented nature of "the Arab nation", the Arab civilization has survived because, despite foreign occupation, its Light-based religion of Allah through Mohammed has continued to attract and unify its peoples who have not switched to any other religion.

18.   The African Light was strong under Egyptian influence from c.2000 to c.400 BC, and after Africa was occupied by the Arabs it weakened with the European occupation which began in the 16th century. Africa has just finished its loss of sovereignty to a secularizing conglomerate (the European Empires) and it is currently an independent network of client-states under foreign superpower (either Western or ex-Soviet) influence and with foreign (either Western or ex-Soviet) funding. In 1956 the African civilization passed into stage 45

(revival of cultural purity). It is about to form itself into a pan-African union, the African Union implemented in 2002. The African civilization has survived because, despite foreign occupation, its Light-based religion of shamanistic African gods has continued to attract and unify its peoples despite the advent of Christianity.

19.   The Indian Light was strong from c.1500 BC and it was still strong in the 5th century BC after which, as *The Light of Civilization* shows, there were various periods of decline and renewal. The Light seems to have weakened when it passed into the Moghul Raj (1572-1707) and, following military activity, the British Raj (1818-1947), when there was loss of Indian sovereignty to a British secularizing conglomerate. In c.1885 the Indian civilization passed into stage 45 (revival of cultural purity). India is now a pan-Indian federal republic (stage 46). Its constitution is a quasi-federal document which provides for a unitary state with subsidiary federal features, and India is an independent state under foreign superpower (either Western or ex-Soviet) influence and with foreign funding. Many pre-coterie groups have kept the Vedanta Light of the Upanisads alive, for example Advaita groups, and it seems that the Light is still present in Hinduism, and that Tantrism is still a living force. In short, Indian civilization has survived because, despite foreign occupation, its central Light-based Hindu religion of Reality has continued to attract and unify its peoples, as have its minority religions of Islam, Buddhism, Jainism and Sikhism.

20.   The South-East-Asian Mahayana-Buddhist Light was strong from c.1st century AD. It can still be found throughout South-East Asia. There was loss of South-East-Asian sovereignty to a Western conglomerate (c.1840-1950), and South-East Asia is now an independent network of client-states under foreign superpower (either Western or ex-Soviet) influence and with foreign funding (stage 46). It is about to form itself into a South-East-Asian regional bloc, which would be an extension of SEATO and ASEAN (see stage 46). The South-East-Asian Buddhist Light was briefly eroded by Communism in Southern China and in Vietnam, but there are signs that it has survived. Pre-coterie groups have preserved the Buddhist Light, which can still be contacted. In short, the South-East-Asian Buddhist civilization has survived because despite foreign occupation, its Light-based Buddhist religion continues to attract and unify its peoples.

21.   The Japanese Light was strong from the 4th-15th centuries. Although it was less strong during the rule of Hideyoshi and the Tokugawa Shogunate (1603-1844), Japan was then enclosed and therefore not subject to foreign influence, and the Light therefore continued. Japan was of course expansionist during the Second World War, and following her defeat suffered American occupation until 1951. Japan has been Americanized and Westernized, and has entered stage 43 as a conglomerate of 47 prefectures or provinces. It has since grown into a major world power, and Japanese religion is very evident. There are many Shinto shrines and Buddhist temples, and the Mahayana Light is kept alive in coterie Zen temples, and can be contacted. The Japanese civilization is now passing into stage 45 (revival of cultural purity). Japan is primarily a Buddhist nation – in 1969 there were 75 million Buddhists against 68 million Shinto adherents, some people being both Buddhist and Shinto – and Japanese civilization has survived because its Light-based Shinto and Buddhist religions have continued to attract and unify its peoples.

22.   The Oceanian Light is of unknown age, but may go back to the 1st century AD or to the 5th-century Huns or *Hunas*. Easter Island was invaded c.1100. The Oceanian Light weakened after c.1680 and the detailed knowledge surrounding the Easter Island giant stone Buddha-like "heroes" became partially lost. There is a similar story in Melanesia. Coterie groups have kept aspects of the Oceanian Light alive in Huna. The Oceanian civilization lost its sovereignty to the European secularizing conglomerate from c.1870, and many Pacific islands are still European-owned. The Oceanian civilization entered stage 45 (revival of cultural purity) from 1945. It is awaiting independence, and it may form itself into a regional bloc, perhaps within a Confederacy of the South Pacific. The Oceanian civilization has survived because despite foreign occupation and the advent of Christianity, its Light-based religion has continued to attract and unify its peoples.

23.   The Chinese Light emerged from the early shamanistic religion and the development of *T'ien* (Heaven). It strengthened with the evolution of the *Tao* and of 6th-century-BC Confucianism. It was strong in the 6th-3rd centuries BC. Mahayana Buddhism spread as it did throughout South-East Asia and became linked with Taoism, as *The Light of Civilization* shows, and this revived 8th-century Light was eventually suppressed in 845 when 200,000 Chinese

monks went back to lay life. China was occupied by the Mongols and invaded by Japan. Foreign religions came to China, and the West brought the Christian missionary Light (c.1600). As *The Light of Civilization* shows, despite Western influence Taoism was still alive in 1794. The Taoist Light dimmed during China's imperial decline and colonial conflict (c.1840-1949), when it was suppressed by the materialist philosophy of Communist absolutism (stage 43). The Communist Mao organized the expulsion of 20,000 Christian missionaries between 1951 and 1956 in an attempt to eradicate Christianity. Coterie groups have preserved the Taoist Light in Taiwan.

Since Communism, the Chinese civilization has been divided as has the Byzantine-Russian civilization because of the division Communism created between the regime and the people. On the one hand Chinese civilization has survived because, free from foreign occupation since the departure of the Japanese in 1945, its Light-based religion of *T'ien*/*Tao*/the Buddha has survived among the people despite official attitudes: in 1959 there was a debate as to how materialistic or idealistic Lao-Tze's *Tao* was, and from 1960 to 1962 there were 13 discussions on Confucius's view of the Heavenly mandate, and although it was resolved that both Lao-Tze and Confucius should be interpreted materialistically, both *T'ien* and the *Tao* were nevertheless studied and discussed, while Buddhism was sufficiently strong to be attacked by the Red Guards from 1966 to 1969 in a Cultural Revolution that is now branded a mistake. China's religious Central Idea has continued to attract and unify the traditionally-minded or bourgeois Chinese peoples. On the other hand, the Chinese civilization has been in decay since the end of the civil war because, after fighting the Nationalists for the territory surrendered by the Japanese, the Communist regime replaced the Confucian Central Idea of an idealistic Heavenly mandate and centralized control with a proletarianized, materialistic interpretation that permitted a "dictatorship of the proletariat" (i.e. Mao's tyranny) if it gave the starving food and equality of property (i.e. abolition of all private ownership and religion for food-producing communes), and it has therefore ceased to attract and unify the crushed traditionally-minded "bourgeois reactionaries" among the Chinese peoples who, if the Party regime lost control or liberalised, would renew Chinese civilization by renewing their Light-based religion. Whether the new openness will permit a new religious freedom remains to be seen.

Civilizations that have denied their own Central Idea for a while have generally returned to it, and under the Chinese openness before the massacre of the students on June 4, 1989 (which saw calls for Western-style democracy and a replica of the Statue of Liberty in T'ienanmen Square) China indicated that it may move towards the West and allow a new religious pluralism, and with Hong Kong becoming Chinese in 1997, the regime permitted the return of Christian missionaries; in short, despite its hard-line Communism of June 1989 the regime has allowed China to embrace capitalism and assume a semi-Western identity. If China's abandonment of her Central Idea were to continue in hard-line self-interest, China may again move against the West and fulfil the Western nightmare of a Yellow Peril, a new Mongol-like Golden Horde that may one day invade Europe.

It seems that despite the events of June 1989, China is in a period of Americanization backed by American investment, with a greater desire for Westernization than when it lost its sovereignty to a secularizing Westernized Communist conglomerate. The Chinese civilization has survived because despite foreign occupation during the colonial conflict and despite the iconoclastic Cultural Revolution of 1966, China's Light-based religion of Confucianist Taoism and Buddhism has survived and has continued to attract and unify its people.

24. The Tibetan Light was strong from c.200 BC and weakened under Chinese occupation from c.1850. After a period of colonial conflict which ended in 1951 Tibet has lost its sovereignty to a secularizing conglomerate (the Chinese People's Republic) and has suffered occupation by Chinese troops and great damage to the Lhasa monasteries during the Cultural Revolution of 1966, which attempted to wipe out the Tibetan-Buddhist tradition. The Dalai Lama in exile has formed coterie groups which have kept the Tibetan Light alive and there have been calls within Tibet for the return of the Dalai Lama. In due course Tibet can be expected to enter stage 45 (revival of cultural purity) and recover its independence under foreign federalist influence. The Tibetan civilization has survived because despite foreign (Chinese) occupation, its Light-based religion has continued to attract and unify its peoples.

25. The Central-Asian Light was strong from c.500 BC. Central Asia including Mongolia was a Buddhist kingdom by the 9th century AD, and

reached its height under the Mongolians from 1206 to 1370. The Mongol Empire stretched as far as Eastern Europe. After a period of colonial conflict which ended in 1644 Central Asia was occupied by the Chinese until 1911, during which period Buddhist Enlightenment and the Central-Asian Light weakened. Central Asia is now in counterthrust (stage 46) under federal ex-Soviet and Chinese influence, and the Mongolian People's Republic is an ex-Soviet-controlled client-state. In due course Central Asia can be expected to recover its independence, and it may form a regional bloc that is independent of the ex-USSR and China. The shamanistic Central-Asian civilization has survived because despite foreign occupation, its Light-based religion has continued to attract and unify its peoples.

REVOLUTIONS

A word on revolutions, which bring about a sudden change in a civilization and move it from its existing stage to the next stage more rapidly than would otherwise be the case.

Looked at in terms of the 61 stages, the main revolutions destroy a previous stage and bring in a new stage. The American Revolution was actually a destruction of British colonial rule and a bringing in of the North-American civilization's political unification (stage 11) as the Founding Fathers gathered round the American Light – a combination of the traditional Puritan Light of the planting Pilgrim Fathers, the Protestant non-Puritan Light of many of the early settlers and the Founding Fathers' own Freemasonic rational Deism – and created a new world paradise. Within the European civilization, the Reformation Revolution brought in a heretical sect, Protestantism (stage 17) and later triggered the resistance to their heresy that led to civil war (stage 25); while the British Puritan Revolution brought in a secession from the Humanist new people (stage 30). The Glorious Revolution of William III brought in the prevailing of the Protestant religion of the new people, the Protestants (stage 31), in part of the European civilization. Still within the European civilization, the French Revolution brought in the new peoples' heirs' further expansion into empire through Napoleon (stage 34); and the Imperialist Revolution brought in the later European expansion into empire (stage 34). The Russian Revolution speeded up the Byzantine-Russian civilization's loss of sovereignty to a conglomerate (stage 43). The Chinese Revolution did likewise (stage 43).

Revolutions occur in a number of different stages. They are not found in one stage alone. They speed up change. As my study *The Secret History of the West* shows, revolutions are inspired by Freemasonic occultists rather than by followers of the Christian Light, and effect material changes in the social structure of their civilizations, as a result of which a new development becomes possible. Revolutions are secularizing forces which weaken the Light and contribute to the destructive-creative tension between an old stage and a new stage, and therefore to the rise-and-fall pattern of civilizations. They blow away a stage's dead leaves like a winter wind and prepare for the budding of new leaves in a new stage. Their role in the rise-and-fall of civilizations is not unlike the reputed role of the Devil in God's creation; the Devil, too, is reputed to destroy the old so that the new can come into being. Revolutions help move civilizations from a stage that is finished to the next stage, and must be understood as facilitators of historical stages rather than as enduring achievements in themselves.

A Universalist Pattern

My summaries of the decaying process of my 25 civilizations and their distinctive religions do show a clear Universalist pattern. The same process of decay, involving an interaction between religion and civilization, seems to be at work in each civilization. The Light dims when foreign or Western-style Communist rule stifles religious expression or when prolonged military or militaristic activity leads to exhaustion and make for a secular and materialistic outlook. In such unenlightened times of decline, coteries preserve the vision of the Light for better days: the Light seems to go out but it keeps rekindling even in the deepest decline. So long as the Light is given public expression and renewed, the religion and therefore the civilization survive. But if the renewers change to another religion which belongs to another civilization then the civilization's Light is not renewed, its religion ends and the civilization dies. Civilizations die when their religion ends and is superseded by a successor civilization's religion. As a healthy religion enshrines a sense of purpose in its visions of God as Light, the disappearance of visions of God from a religion causes its further atrophy and decay, a sense of aimlessness and despair, and therefore its civilization's demise.

The pattern suggests that, as we shall see more fully in the next section, there is a two-way causal connection between visions of the Light and a civilization. The disappearance of visions of the Light is ominous for a civilization, for our summary and earlier evidence show that civilizations keep going so long as their Light is strong, and that those that have died have done so after their visions of the Light disappeared. The disappearance of the vision of the Light suggests that a civilization lacks the spiritual energy and vitality that express themselves in creative work and a high culture. Of course the 16 alternatives we listed in stage 51 are all involved as a civilization's Central Idea goes out, but conscious materialistic incentives such as tax reductions are no substitute for this Central Idea and its fundamental reservoir of unconscious energy. Conversely, once a civilization goes into decline, it seems to be extremely difficult for the collective sense of exhaustion to be reversed, and for the energy involved in contacting the Light to be released except among coteries, which often choose to separate themselves from their civilization rather than put their Light back into them.

Throughout these 61 stages the Light of the civilization's religion is like a structural pattern down the full length of a Persian carpet or a Tibetan *thanka*, a flaming fire holding together all the triumphant wars and empires until it cools into stones and fades from view among menacing foreign invasions and occupations. To an observer, this fire may not seem important to the whole, but in fact it holds all together, so that when it is removed, in Yeats's words:

> "Things fall apart, the centre cannot hold;
> Mere anarchy is loosed upon the world."

The pattern of the complex parabola of (3) on pp 4-5 includes five related pairs of opposites ((a)/(k), (b)/(j), (c)/(i), (d)/(h), (f)/(g)), each pair symmetrically balancing growth and decay, and there is balance between (e) and (l). I can sharpen (3) by stating it more precisely and incisively in terms of a rainbow-like diagram with 61 stages (see chart 1, pp528-529). My restatement of the universality will then look as follows:

(3)   the universality with which past civilizations reveal the following 61 stages in the pattern of their life cycle:

The Genesis of Civilizations

1. The Light originates in an earlier civilization;
2. the Light migrates to the new culture;
3. the new civilization's Light conquers or absorbs the new culture and its religion;
4. the Light creates a new religion through a religious unification;
5. the Light/new religion precede the genesis of a new civilization;
6. the Light of the new religion creates the Central Idea that unifies and sustains a growing civilization;
7. the Light attracts and converts heterogeneous peoples to the new civilization's Central Idea and unifies their cultures;

The Growth and Arrested Growth of Civilizations

8. the metaphysical vision of the Light is strong during a civilization's growth;
9. the Light inspires the erection of the growing civilization's stones;
10. the Light is interpreted in conflicting ways, and there is doctrinal controversy in the growing civilization's religion;
11. the new civilization undergoes a political unification that formalizes its religious unification, which was based on the Light;
12. the new civilization's religion undergoes a schism and there is allegiance to conflicting gods, creeds or beliefs;
13. an occupying or confining foreign threat deals the civilization a military blow;
14. this reverse contributes to an arrest in the growth of the new civilization lasting some 50 years, and as a result the new civilization becomes more secularized, its State controlling its religion (a first decline);
15. there is a counter-thrust by the State of the new civilization, a secularized territorial expansion and some renewal of growth;
16. this growth inspires an oral heroic epic literature which reflects it (even though it is sometimes written down in later times of breakdown);

The Breakdown of Civilizations

17. secularization, or State control of religion, weakens the religion and encourages heretical sects, and in particular one heretical sect which has originat-

ed in the doctrinal controversy and which has spiritual energy;

18. such heresies are persecuted;

19. the religion and church decline (a second decline);

20. mystics renew the Light and resist the decline;

21. a new foreign threat menaces and deals a further military blow;

22. the civilization undergoes breakdown during a period of some 100 years when the Central Idea of the Light is modified in the course of a modification to its religion;

23. the State, paralysed by the military blow, increases its powers in the interests of the defence of the realm and controls and secularizes religion;

24. during this time there is a revival or Renaissance of another civilization's culture;

25. in the course of renewing their resistance to the civilization's heresy, the broken down leaders fight a civil war, which they lose;

26. a new people come to power and now hold the limelight;

27. there is a fundamental change in the civilization's religion as the heresy is grafted on to the Central Idea, the original religion giving way to a new modified phase which is an extension of the main heresy, to which many of the peoples secede, making yesterday's heresy today's orthodoxy;

28. the new people renew the Light as they graft their heresy onto the civilization's Central Idea;

The New People's Renewal of Civilizations

29. there is a geographical expansion into empire by the new people, an expansion which is a substitute for growth, a renewal which replaces growth;

30. another fragmentation creates another sect which secedes from the new modified religious phase;

31. the seceders are persecuted by the new people of the new modified religious phase, whose vision triumphs and is confirmed as the new orthodoxy;

32. a bout of scientific materialism derived from another civilization weakens the religion and prepares for further expansion;

33. there is an artistic reaction against scientific materialism and this emphasises Vitalism against Mechanism;

34. the heirs of the new people of the new modified religious phase now

undergo a further expansion into empire which overextends the civilization, but they fail to renew the Central Idea;

The Decline of Civilizations

35. the metaphysical vision of the Light is weak during decline as the civilization's energy is dispersed abroad;

36. as a consequence of external cosmopolitanizing military influences, the Light generally disappears from the official religion;

37. as a result in the next generation there is a breakdown of certainties following a military event;

38. the civilization's Central Idea and religion weaken and the arts become restless and secular;

39. there is a prevailing scientific materialism, philosophical rationalism and scepticism as a result of the weakening religious outlook;

40. there is an imperial decline in which an undefeated power either conquers or inherits territory from the civilization;

41. the civilization has overextended itself, and there is a colonial conflict which is a result of the imperial decline and which is won by a challenger for the empire's colonies (i.e. by the undefeated power);

42. by the end of the imperial decline and colonial conflict the civilization undergoes an authoritarian proletarianization and egalitarianization;

43. the foreign, internationalist power now forms a conglomerate in which the civilization becomes a province or series of provinces or satrapies, with loss of national sovereignty, either by conquest or by pressured invitation, and it has a further secularizing effect on religion;

44. there is a syncretism as foreign influence brings a Universalist vision that perceives the oneness of the world, and religious sects draw together with the Light as their common source;

45. the secularizing conglomerate causes a rejection of the present and a yearning for the lost past, which is really the revival of an earlier phase in the civilization's history;

46. there is an attempt at a counter-thrust under a foreign Federalist influence and foreign god as the conglomerate fragments into federally linked sovereign states and further expands into empire, seeking to restore the civiliza-

tion's glorious past but failing to renew the civilization's Central Idea, of which it has lost sight;

47. economic decline and inflation lead to further class conflict and proletarianization and pave the way for foreign occupation (stage 49);

The Decay and Demise of Civilizations

48. there is a final decay when the metaphysical vision of the Light ceases to be publicly recognised by the decaying civilization's religion, which is Lightless, and is absent during the civilization's decay;

49. foreign invaders occupy the civilization and undermine its largely Lightless religion;

50. foreign invaders have destroyed the civilization's stones, and do so again in the course of undermining its religion;

51. there is a loss of the civilization's Central Idea as the heterogeneous peoples secede to the foreign invader's culture, causing cultural disintegration, and the civilization fails to recover its awareness of its Central Idea;

52. the civilization tries to reverse the secessions and there is a final independent phase, a nationalistic swansong;

53. a foreign power again occupies the civilization and further secularizes its decaying Lightless religion;

54. Such traces of the Light that remain pass from the decaying religion into the cults of the foreign power;

55. the civilization resists this occupying foreign power;

56. the occupying foreign power persecutes the illumined men who have defected from its cults;

57. followers of the decaying religion detach themselves from it and form coteries, which continue the decaying religion's Light and Central Idea in mysteries, and which will survive the religion's demise;

58. there is a further occupation of the civilization by a foreign occupier;

59. the decaying Lightless religion is now suppressed by the foreign occupier's religion, and dies;

60. the final conquest of the religionless civilization, though delayed, happens relatively suddenly, and its demise is abrupt;

61. the dead civilization passes into a successor civilization which has its own

religion/Light.

I have now completed my survey of the 61 stages in the rise and fall of civilizations. I have tried to be exact with my dating; it may be that a stage can be deemed
as continuing a decade or two shorter or longer than I have stated, but by and large
the principles hold good, and the broad areas of geographical expansion, imperial
decline, colonial conflict and foreign occupation can be widely agreed.

It is worth summarizing the principles behind the dating of the 61 stages in my
pattern. They are as follows:

1 is earlier than 2;

2 is approximately the same as 3 and 5;

2, 3 and 4 take place within 100 years;

6 starts with 4 and ends with 11; and is the same as 7;

9 generally starts later than 8;

13 is the same as the first date of 14;

15 starts with the last date of 14 and ends with the first date of 19;

17 is within the dates of 15 and is largely responsible for 19;

18 is earlier than 19 but there may be some overlap;

19 & 20 start with the last date of 15 and end with the first date of 21;

22, 23 & 24 start with the last date of 21 and end with the first date of 28;

25 comprises the last few years of 22;

27 = 28;

28 & 29 are the same and start with the last date of 22, 23 & 24 and end with
the first date of 34;

30 & 31 are within 28/29 and precede 32/33;

32 lasts approximately 100 years, 33 is towards the end of this period and a
decade or two before 34, for which it prepares;

34 is the same as 35;

36 is shortly before the end of 35;

37 starts with the last date of 34/35 and ends with the first date of 40;

38 & 39 begin a decade or so before 36 and last around 60 years;

40 is the same as 41;

42 is the last date of 41;

43 starts with the last date of 40/41 and ends with the first date of 46;

44 begins shortly after 43;

45 is near the beginning of 43 and soon after 44, and coexists with 44;

46 starts with the last date of 43 and ends with the first date of 49;

47 starts within 46 and paves the way for 49;

48 is the same as 46;

49 starts with the last date of 46/48 and ends with the first date of 52;

51 is the same as 49;

52 starts with the last date of 49/51 and ends with the first date of 53;

53 starts with the last date of 52 and ends with the first date of 58;

54 is the same as 53;

55 is the same as 53/54;

56 is the same as 53/54/55;

58 starts with the last date of 53/54 and ends with the first date of 60;

59 is the first date of 58;

60 starts with the last date of 58 and ends with the first date of 61;

61 is the last date of 60.

The Law of History

In these 61 stages I have identified the workings of the main law of history. Like a physicist observing physical phenomena and stating the law of thermodynamics I have observed historical phenomena and I have scientifically stated the main law of history, that civilizations "endlessly" rise and fall in accordance with the energy they derive or fail to derive from the Light in their social religion which is their Central Idea. The law, a Grand Unified Theory of world history, shows that religion is as important to a decaying civilization as it is to a growing one, and reveals that in any conflict between two civilizations, the younger defeats the older (see pp244, 255) – growth always conquers decay. To put it another way, a decaying civilization is always conquered by one that is less decayed.

The law suggests that the present life cycle of living civilizations mirrors the life cycle of the dead civilizations. It is a law of great symmetrical beauty that gives meaning to history.

PART TWO

LESSONS AND PREDICTIONS

3. Civilizations as Light-Bearers: The Process of Growth, Breakdown and Decay

The Presence/Absence of Light in Growing/Decaying Civilizations

The logic of my evidence regarding the parabola pattern has led me to consider the conclusion that the growth, breakdown or decay of civilizations is related to the presence, weakening or absence of the vision of God as Light, and that civilizations should therefore be seen as Light-bearers – see (4) on p5. The complexity of the process must be emphasised. Just as a ray of light bears a spectrum of colours, and the rainbow also; so, it must be reiterated, each Light-bearing civilization contains seven bands which are present simultaneously and have to be seen both in relation to each other and as a whole. Each of the 61 stages is a cross-section of a rainbow (see chart 1) with some bands brighter and some more faded than others, depending on the stage, and some more visible in growth than in decay, and vice versa. The cross-section, we can remind ourselves (see p9), is as follows:

Central Idea/absence of Central Idea;
alternatives;
religion-heresy-coteries;
stones inspired by Light/stones destroyed;
peoples and cultural unity/seceders and cultural disintegration;
foreign military threat/foreign cults
secularizing State/expansion into empire.

As I write these words, a heart-shaped crystal hangs in my window. The sun pours in and fills my room with tiny rainbows. They are everywhere: on the wall, on the carpet, on my desk, on my hands. A poetic image for the fundamental oneness of history in terms of the Light or Sun is: a crystal and 25 rainbows.

It is now time to draw my evidence together, to summarize the process of the growth and decay of civilizations, to show more fully how all civilizations obey the same law and, though economic and environmental factors clearly play a part, how the rise and fall of civilizations is fundamentally related to the amount of Light they contain.

We have seen that the vision of the Light within a civilization is strong when that civilization is growing, and weak when it is in disintegration. We have seen that there is widespread acceptance of the Light through a civilization's metaphysical vision and religion when it is growing, and that small coteries keep the Light alive when the civilization is disintegrating. These coteries are often outside, or at any rate apart from, that civilization, having seceded from it in mental outlook.

It seems, then, that the vision of the Light is the force which explains the genesis, growth, renewal, breakdown and disintegration of civilizations, the "positive factor" Toynbee never found (see p2). This idea, for which I have accumulated a considerable amount of evidence, is one of enormous importance to cultural history for it explains the shift from metaphysical to secular cultures during the last five thousand years. The evidence suggests that all history is a tussle between the metaphysical phase of a culture which channels the Light, awareness of whose spiritual energy makes a civilization grow, and an eventual secular phase which shuts out, indeed blocks out, the vision of the Light and brings about a civilization's hardening and decline. (During the secular phase there are of course revivals of the metaphysical vision which keep the civilization alive.)

Here I must be quite clear on one point. It could be argued by teleologists that man has been "shaken" by the Light of God itself, but whether the Light as God is actually providentially and teleologically – purposively – involved in the making of history for a people that, like the Israelites, regards itself as God's "chosen people", lies outside our phenomenological and scientific method which regards the notion that history has a goal as a matter of faith. It may be that it is so involved. We cannot finally know without entering the terrain of faith. The point is, the vision of the Light – the vision of God – stirs the soul, spurs a people into action, and motivates a people, has an effect on their actions, has a social effect. When the vision is withdrawn, the civilization loses its Central Idea and eventually goes under to a successor civilization which has a stronger Light, a stronger vision of its Central Idea, and therefore a clearer idea of its purpose.

The genesis of a civilization begins with a metaphysical vision of the Light that gives meaning and purpose. The energizing vision is well known to all existing religions: my evidence has shown that the Light of each religion can be traced back via a migration to the Light of a previous religion (stages 1 and 2), and that the traces stop at the beginning of recorded history with the Indo-European Kurgans who came out of Central Asia; for the knowledge about the shamanistic religion of Central Asia between c.50,000 BC and 500 BC, is lost. The vision is taken to a new place during a migration and enters the religion there (stage 3) – our evidence has shown that religions precede the growth of their civilization (stage 4) – and it is then reinforced by renewing visions, like the Arab Mohammed's vision in his cave or (long after the vision of the Light of the World) the European St Benedict's vision in his cave which Pope Gregory took over. The vision becomes the metaphysical standard for several cultures and heterogeneous peoples, and unites them into a civilization (stage 6). The vision is in the religion that unites the peoples, and is followed, as were the teachings of Mohammed and the Benedictine Rule. It becomes the centre of a religion, and is transmitted to the age as a whole, whose masses are in contact with it. The art and culture of the roused people seek to catch and reflect this vision of meaning and purpose, and in striving to rise to its heights, the people see a purpose which provides the *élan* that is required to create a civilization. (This purpose is continued in the Central Idea of the civilization, which has surfaced in stage 5.) A great number of the leaders and masses are therefore subordinated to the truth of the creative vision which has transformed them. The genesis of civilizations is closely tied to religions, whose organizations trap the metaphysical vision, and my study has shown that religions are Light-bearers. As my evidence has shown (in stages 3 and 4), religions teach infant civilizations the transforming power of the Light (which is the vision of God), and religions, rather than the political leaders, energize souls at this early stage of a civilization's life. Religions supply the metaphysical Light to growing civilizations, and consequently civilizations grow as Light-bearers.

A civilization grows with an *élan* precisely because there has been a widespread acceptance of the Light by its members, whose souls have in consequence been transformed and dynamized by its creative vision of meaning and purpose (stages 7 and 8). As my evidence has shown (in stage 9) the members of a growing civilization have a vision of meaning, based on the Light, which they express, through self-denial and self-sacrifice, in the stones of fine architecture. More and more individuals become illumined by the Light of God and add to the civilization's metaphysical vision in stone. The civilization rises because the vision is renewed first through a doctrinal controversy (stage 10) and later a schism (stage 12) and through its religious unification it achieves a political unification (stage 11) and a high cultural level.

Spiritual growth happens when the contemplative perception of the "intellect" (the *intellectus*) creates a metaphysical yardstick by which the civilization can measure itself. Each generation, contemplative men reinterpret and find new meaning in the metaphysical vision and (as my evidence shows in stage 8) they pass the meaning on to their civilization, which has a purpose, direction and goal: for example, the European Light's recovery of Jerusalem through the Crusades. This common purpose provides a common culture in the sense that all respect the contemplative power behind the culture (as can be seen in the poetry of the Grail legend). Every generation has its illumined men, and when a civilization's culture is growing and healthy, the illumined put the Light back into it, and thus reinforce the civilization's Central Idea, as St Bernard did by creating the Templars and organizing the Second Crusade.

When a growing civilization allows its secular organization to dominate its metaphysical vision (as stages 14 and 17 of my evidence suggested), there is a breakdown and an immediate loss of Light and therefore of the civilization's Central Idea, which the Light enshrines, and the immediacy of the vision fades. This temporary secularization is caused by a military blow (stage 14) which paralyses the civilization for some 50 years and arrests its growth, causing it to become obsessed with defence and to expand (stage 15) to the accompaniment of heroic epic poetry (stage 16). Growth is then resumed, but the civilization's Light is weakened. The growing civilization enshrines the founder's vision and when it turns militaristic and expansionist, like early Islam which sought to spread the vision by Holy War, and to some extent like the later Christian Crusaders, it loses some of the founder's vision and encourages a heretical sect (stage 17), which is persecuted (stage 18). It is axiomatic throughout the life cycle of a civilization that the more a civilization expands geographically, the less Light it has in the public domain. This was the case with Islam, for the Light passed from the warrior Muslims to the Sufis who had no part in the worldly expansion of Islam. The Crusades dispersed Christendom's Light in military activity, and the ensuing worldliness of the crusading Popes hastened the Reformation.

So long as a religion goes on supplying Light-transformed men to a civilization, then that civilization is renewed (see pp394-412), and it lasts like the Hindu Indian civilization and the Christian Western civilization. Of course there are good generations and bad, there are ups and downs, the ups (in terms of a civilization's renewal of itself) being periods when the metaphysical vision is strong and the Central Idea is renewed, and the downs periods of materialistic affluence when the vision of the Light is in decline. There can be a long process of alternating periods of renewal and decline (see pp412-428). War sometimes constitutes an up, sometimes a down; the criterion is the effect it has on the soul, whether the Light is still seen. *A civilization lasts as long as the Light lasts within it*, and for so long will its dynamic, transformed energies perpetuate the visions of meaning and purpose which created them. The Egyptian civilization lasted some 3,000 years, and it crumbled when the Egyptian metaphysical vision and therefore its religion crumbled and the Egyptian Light passed into Christianity, Gnosticism and Hermeticism and eventually into Islam. So long as the metaphysical vision has followers and the illumined supply a civilization with Light, that civilization has the vision of meaning and purpose through its renewed Central Idea to continue in existence.

A civilization has broken down when it ceases to reflect the Light which is its Central Idea and which gave it birth. There is a new military blow (stage 21) which paralyses the civilization for some 100 years, in the course of which the Central Idea of the Light is modified (stage 22). Again the civilization's obsession with defence acts as a secularizing force (stage 23), and there is a revival of another civilization's culture (stage 24). In the case of the European civilization, the breakdown coincided with the Reformation, when the Catholic Light was modified by Protestantism, and the revival was the Renaissance of Greek and Roman culture. By the end of a civilization's breakdown, in the vast majority of the leaders and the masses the secular organization has escaped from the control of the metaphysical vision of its religion and the State rules supreme, as it did in the Russia of Ivan III. The process is gradual. Disgusted at the material affluence and spiritual decay in an increasingly secularized culture, and attracted away to the Light of a foreign cult, the illumined withdraw their vision of the Light (their vision of God) from their civilization, which no longer receives its life-giving energy. The heresy is renewed, often attracting the defectors, and official resistance to it results in a civil war (stage 25), as a result of which a new people come to power (stage 26) who adopt the heresy as the main religion (stage 27) and graft it onto the civilization's Central Idea (stage 28).

The civilization is now renewed. The new people expand into empire (stage 29), an expansion which is a substitute for growth, and a new sect senses this and secedes (stage 30) and is persecuted (stage 31), as were the Puritans by the official Protestants in the European civilization. There is now a bout of scientific materialism (stage 32) which weakens the Light. In Europe, as E. W. F. Tomlin pointed out[1], in the 17th century the advent of the scientific revolution caused the intellect – the intuitive *intellectus*, Latin for "perception", which perceives universals, glimpses metaphysical meaning, and creates a society with a metaphysical vision – to collapse into reason, the logical faculty which analyses everyday particulars, which is hostile to metaphysics, which perceives aimlessness, futility and meaninglessness, and which creates a secularized, Humanist society. There was an artistic reaction to scientific materialism (stage 33), which in the European civilization's case was Romanticism. There is then a further expansion into empire (stage 34) which overextends the civilization. Secularization leads to nationalism and subsequently militarism. European civilization passed into a nationalist phase when its colonial nationalism led to militaristic conflicts with other European powers and caused wars. Geographical expansion always involves a loss of Light, which may be exported abroad by missionaries and not replaced at home, and this was true of the British expansion into empire after c.1880 (in the course of stage 34) – the approximate date when European nationalism began – and of the repressive Russian empire in stage 34, many of whose Orthodox priests are now in exile; for the attitudes of repressive empires are not missionary attitudes, and they preclude the Light.

Militaristic nationalism is an expression of the active side of a secular State. Sometimes it leads to exhaustion. In such a time of material affluence, the Light appears to go out, the metaphysical vision is forgotten, religion dwindles, scepticism increases. The vision of meaning and purpose which was based on the Light darkens even more. Pampering becomes the *zeitgeist*, and occasional appeals to return to self-sacrifice fall on deaf ears. In the European civilization, Humanism first established secularism after the metaphysical Middle Ages, and religion became increasingly Humanistic and secularized while encounters with the Light became increasingly infrequent except in times of metaphysical revival. In such conditions, soon the Light virtually disappears.

The civilization is now in decline. The Light is weak (stage 35), and following further military hostilities the Light disappears from the official religion (stage 36), as it did in the European civilization in c.1880. (It is interesting that Europe's loss of the Light in c.1880 coincided with the 19th century expansion of Europe into Empires.) In the next generation there is a breakdown of certainties (stage 37) as the old absolutes based on the Light collapse and are replaced by new relatives. Everything is now relative, as it was in Europe by 1920, and the civilization's Central Idea further weakens and the arts become secular (stage 38), as they did during European Modernism, and scientific materialism, rationalism and scepticism prevail (stage 39). The overextended empire goes into decline (stage 40) and, following a colonial conflict (stage 41) during which there is an end-of-empire authoritarian proletarianism and egalitarianism (stage 42) and during which the secular State opts for its passive side and pampers itself with a Welfare State, with lavish benefits, luxuries and pay settlements, a process to which all political parties contribute in varying degrees, loses territory and colonies to a great power, which now occupies the civilization (stage 43). The civilization is now a province or satrapy (or a number of provinces or satrapies) in a conglomerate, and it has lost its national sovereignty.

Culturally, the occupying conglomerate creates a Universalist syncretistic vision which perceives oneness and unity (stage 44). There is now a revival of an earlier phase of the civilization's history, a revival of cultural purity (stage 45). There is an attempt to restore the civilization by a further Federalist expansion under foreign influence, but it fails to renew the civilization's Central Idea (stage 46). There is class conflict and further proletarianization (stage 47).

We should note in passing that the same empire can stimulate different stages in two civilizations. Thus the Persian conquest stimulated stage 43 in the Mesopotamian civilization in 539 BC but stage 46 in the Egyptian civilization in 525 BC. The reason for the difference is to be found in the local conditions: Persia and Mesopotamia were neighbours and actually united under Cyrus; whereas Egypt, being farther away, had a looser, more federal association, and was the sixth Persian satrapy.

The civilization is now in decay. The Light ceases to be publicly recognised by its religion and is absent (stage 48), and foreign invaders occupy the civilization (stage 49), undermine its religion and destroy many of its stones (stage 50).

The heterogeneous peoples withdraw their support and secede from the foreign invader (stage 51), and there is now a final independent phase, the civilization's swansong (stage 52) until a foreign power again occupies the civilization (stage 53). The Light now passes into the foreign cults of the foreign power (stage 54), and when these are resisted (stage 55) the illumined who have defected from the civilization are persecuted by the foreign occupier (stage 56).

When the civilization and culture have broken down and are decaying, the contemplative mystics or illumined men are persecuted, or cold-shouldered for attaching themselves to the Light of a foreign religion or cult, and a new generation of contemplative mystics or illumined men withdraw their Light from the occupier's religion, as did the Christian Desert Fathers from the decaying Roman civilization. Or, to put it the other way round, their dissatisfaction with the intolerant material affluence of the civilization causes the beginning of their secession during which they withdraw their Light, and so the civilization and culture go into spiritual decay. A civilization collapses when the Light ceases to be reflected in it because the illumined have seceded. There are still contemplative mystics or illumined men, but their secession means their energy goes elsewhere rather than into their own civilization. They form coteries which keep alive the civilization's Light (stage 57) until the civilization dies and is replaced by its successor civilization.

The demise of the civilization is swift. A foreign occupier again occupies the civilization (stage 58) and suppresses the civilization's Lightless religion (stage 59), which dies. The final conquest of the civilization happens suddenly (stage 60) and the dead civilization passes into a successor civilization which has its own Light (stage 61).

A civilization collapses, then, because its religion fails to continue providing it with the Light and dynamized energy it needs to sustain its vision of meaning and purpose, its Central Idea. Decline is swift when the religion loses contact with its own metaphysical vision of the Light and therefore with its own vision of God. A temporary failure to renew the vision of the Light and its resulting disappearance from a religion weakens a civilization's identity in terms of its Central Idea, spiritual exhaustion sets in and the civilization goes into decline. If the disappearance becomes permanent, it eventually decays. In a time of unarrested decay, disintegration follows rapidly for the underlying malaise is deeper than the policies and economic statistics of its rulers, just as a civilization's Central Idea is deeper than the balance of trade and prosperity which govern its economics. In a time of unarrested decay the rulers and masses live exclusively in the external world, the heterogeneous peoples are no longer unified by a common vision; and religion, the basis of the civilization's culture, has lost its metaphysical common ground. Reason, which replaced the perceptive intellect during the civilization's opening to scientific materialism, now collapses into irrational prejudice and fanaticism, there is now a persecution of the decaying religion from outside, an attempt at suppressal by a foreign or ideological enemy. Progressive change is preached; there is class strife.

The more a civilization loses its unifying power and disintegrates into separate cultures, the more secular it becomes, and the more likely it is to attempt to expand even though it is now under foreign influence. After a civilization's early stages, expansion is a substitute for growth, that response to a vision of meaning and purpose which gives the masses the energy and power to grow a civilization. The Light is only to be found in an isolated few within civilizations whose disintegration has reached an advanced stage. The few embody the traditional culture that has degenerated into decay, but many who have seceded from the dying civilization into coteries preserve the vision outside (initially in the sense of "apart from" and later in the sense of "in another civilization than") the civilization. Thus during the Greek disintegration the Greek vision of meaning contained in the Mystery religions passed into the secularized Roman Empire – it is no accident that Greek sculptures have "unseeing" eyes without eyeballs, whereas Roman sculptures look out at the world – and the Light was not to be found among the Roman administrators although it was very much present in Rome, as *The Light of Civilization* shows.

My evidence has put us in a position to give definitive confirmations on the two "universalities" (see (3) and (4) on pp4-5).

My evidence suggests that there is a two-way connection between the growth of a civilization and the continued appearance of visions of the Light. My evidence suggests that a post-migrational civilization grows because of the energy created by continued visions of the Light, which pass into its religion, and that conversely further visions of the Light find their way into the religion because the civilization is growing and spiritual energy is in abundance.

Similarly, my evidence suggests that there is a two-way connection between the decay of a civilization and the disappearance of the vision of the Light. It seems that a civilization decays because the energy created by visions of the Light disappears from its religion, leaving it uninspired, weary and unable to resist the challenge of a foreign threat, and that conversely further visions of the Light are hard to achieve because the civilization is already in decline. To put it another way, once a civilization has begun a downward slide into ease, enjoyment and materialistic self-indulgence, leaving its deeper energies anaesthetised, it is less likely that a living tradition of the Light will be handed on to the next generation than if the civilization had retained its spiritual vitality. My evidence suggests that a civilization disintegrates because it has lost the vision of the Light and that its spreading secularization and materialism are terminal symptoms, cancerous effects which then themselves become causative as they hinder the recovery of the Light and contribute to the death of the civilization.

VARYING TIME-SCALE WITHIN CIVILIZATIONS

Chart 2 (see pp530-531) lists the nodal (i.e. most significant) points in the growth and decline of our civilizations. Below and to the right of each date is given the number of years since the last nodal point. As we look at the pattern of growing and decaying civilizations with a scientific eye, analysing the past directions taken during each stage of each civilization with a view to arriving at the underlying law, it is clear that the time-scale varies. Some civilizations (the Indian and Chinese for example) span 4,000 years, whereas others (the Greek, Roman, Anatolian, Israelite and Celtic for instance) do not last three quarters of that time. Of course, local conditions vary, and where the terrain is inhospitable jungle or inaccessible desert and there are few outside influences, the time-scale of a stage will lengthen.

More crucially, however the differences are chiefly accounted for by the civilizations' religions. Quite simply, if their main religion or religions survive and are renewed, i.e. if the Light is renewed, then there is no reason why the civilizations should not last indefinitely. If on the other hand the religion changes (as it did when Mesopotamia, Iran and the Byzantine Empire were Islamized) then the affected peoples find themselves living in a different civilization. If the religion does survive and if the peoples remain unified round the religion, then their cultures survive, and therefore so does the civilization and it is therefore theoretically possible for a civilization to be frozen at a particular stage for 1,000 years or more provided the Light in its religion is renewed each generation.

The same variable principle explains the varying lengths of time it takes for civilizations to undergo arrest of growth and breakdown. Some break down relatively quickly because the State is given control over the Church swiftly. Others break down relatively slowly because State control over the Church is delayed, or, as in the case of India, is attempted and then abandoned because the conditions of growth still prevail and stages 5, 6, 7 and 8 still apply.

The arrest in the growth of a civilization usually follows relatively quickly after the unification (around 100 years in the case of the European and Roman civilizations, and within 100 years in the case of the Byzantine-Russian and North-American civilizations) as neighbours tend to check the new civilization's rapid growth by delivering a military blow. On the other hand, geographical position is a factor and where there are no mighty neighbours growth can proceed unchecked, as is the case with the isolated Egyptian civilization whose unification lasted 526 years and whose religion was not subjected to the surrounding foreign influences that contaminated the Israelite religion in the 11th century BC. The variation can be attributed to differing impacts of military powers, for example the differing impact of the Arab civilization on different civilizations. The timing of Arab impacts can be related to the unification (stage 11) of different civilizations. Thus in the case of the European civilization, the Muslim challenge surfaced from Spain 100 years after Charlemagne's unification; the Seljuqs threatened 200 years later, whereas the main challenge of the Ottomans followed over 500 years later. On the other hand, in the case of the Byzantine-Russian civilization the Muslim challenge surfaced earlier, within 100 years of Justinian's unification, whereas the Seljuqs threatened 400 years later and the Ottoman challenge surfaced 650 years later.

The expansion that follows an arrest of growth can last between 200 and 500 years. (Some expansions have lasted 700 or even 900 years, and in one case 1,080 years.) Differing local conditions of expansion and growth bring about different forces which affect the civilization's religion. The European expansion took place round the European Light's conflict with the Turkish Muslim Light, whereas the Byzantine-Russian expansion took place earlier; it weathered the Arab onslaught of the 7th century and took place round the Byzantine conflict with the successors of the barbarians who had occupied Italy, and the Ottoman Turks, who delivered two military blows, did not appear until much later, thus adding 150 years to the time-span pattern.

The time between breakdown and the end of the new people's imperial decline varies from as little as 300 years (Israelite civilization) to as much as 1,050 or 1,150 years (Mesopotamian and Egyptian civilizations), while in between there are civilizations with 550 years (European and Byzantine-Russian civilizations) and some with nearly 700 years (Anatolian and Syrian civilizations). The variations can in large part be attributed to the purity of the new people's religion. Thus the Mesopotamian new people, the Assyrians, preserved their religion from foreign contamination whereas the Israelite new people's religion was contaminated by Syrian and Assyrian gods and their geographical area kept contracting, with the result that they succumbed far earlier than did the Mesopotamian new people.

Similarly the time between the loss of national sovereignty and demise of civilizations varies from 325 years (Roman civilization) to 1,100 years (Mesopotamian, Egyptian, Anatolian, Syrian and Israelite civilizations).

Such variations (we cannot call them discrepancies) are a feature of Light-based history and must be accepted as part and parcel of local conditions without recourse to the notion of a strictly uniform pattern. This having been said, there is an average uniform period of 100 years between unification and arrest of growth; a widely varying 370 years between arrest of growth and breakdown (a standard or average 50 years for the arrest, 170 years for the expansion and 150 years for the religion's decline); an average 700 years between breakdown and loss of national sovereignty; and a widely varying average of 700 years between loss of national sovereignty and demise.

As a general rule the continuation of a religion in its pure form, free from foreign influences, perpetuates the civilization, whereas syncretism weakens a religion as it did in the Israelite civilization. On the other hand, the Universalist view which incorporates all religions and sees the whole and expresses the truth, inevitably and somewhat paradoxically tends to syncretism. It seems to be axiomatic that a civilization needs to preserve the integrity of its religion and retain it free from foreign contamination in order to survive, whereas some blending with other religions is inevitable if it adopts a world role. The differences in the lengths of civilizations can in a large part be attributed to the degree to which their religions have preserved their integrity and resisted contamination from foreign influences. (The shining example again is the Egyptian civilization which flourished apart from any neighbour and lasted 1,200 years longer than the Israelite civilization, which was contaminated from Phoenicia.)

Because the criterion of a civilization's survival is the state of its religion (i.e. Light), it appears to make no difference that materialistic conditions and technologically advanced communications in the surviving civilizations are different from those in the dead civilizations. Today supersonic flight and computerized missiles have replaced firearms and galleys as instruments of war, and air power is more significant than sea power, but like the dead civilizations the surviving ones began round the Light, and are declining in the absence of the Light, and the materialistic conditions of civilizations – whether this one has bronze, that one iron, or the other one nuclear power and computers – do not appear to affect the basic pattern. The evolution of the 61 stages does not appear to have been affected by the modern discovery of nuclear weapons any more than by the ancient discovery of iron or bronze weaponry.

If the variable principle is as I have said, then we can reasonably conclude that each generation has the freedom to renew the stage of the civilization at which it finds itself. There seems to be nothing deterministic in our pattern. Although all civilizations obey my law of growth and decay, they pass through the 61 stages because human freewill (i.e. the choices of their leaders) takes them from stage to stage. A civilization could theoretically last for 50,000 years if each generation renewed the Light and kept its vision of meaning and purpose alive, and civilizations decay because they are failed by the leaders of a few successive generations. I therefore do not hold with Spengler that civilizations age like people, nor do I hold with Toynbee that there are cyclic periods of approximately 400 years within civilizations. Such views are too rigidly deterministic and do not take account of the existential freedom of the contemplative mystics' will to renew and therefore preserve, perpetuate or even save their civilization each generation. When the empirical philosopher Karl Popper claimed (as he did at the World Congress of Philosophy in August 1988) that the future is not the result of an unfolding drive from the past (as Descartes and Marx believed) but the result of the lure or attraction of future propensities or possibilities, he was saying no more than that it is the lure or pull of *the next stage* rather than the push of *the last stage* that creates a development in a civilization, a view that fits in with my own historical outlook.

I hold that there is no determinism in history or religion; there is freewill, the freedom to bring Providential potentialities or possibilities into manifestation, or not to do so. The existential responsibility for bringing these Providential possibilities into being lies with the leaders of a civilization's religion, who in the growth phase are contemplative mystics.

4. ILLUMINED MYSTICS AND THE RENEWAL AND DECLINE OF CIVILIZATIONS

THE ROLE OF CONTEMPLATIVE MYSTICS IN CREATING AND RENEWING THEIR RELIGIONS/CIVILIZATIONS

From what has been said above it should be clear that, contrary to popular secular perception or awareness, the contemplative mystics are the true heroes of civilizations as they are in touch with the Light that keeps the civilizations going and which renews civilizations. So long as the civilization remains in touch with its Central Idea, its *raison d'être*, it prospers; and it is the mystics who perpetuate the Light who perpetuate its Central Idea.

To put it another way, in each civilization the contemplative mystics had glimpses of the Light and presented them in terms of a distinctive god. They created the religions that contributed the Central Idea of their civilizations. At first the divinely inspired Sacred Rulers embodied the god of the religion – how they differed from the undivine rulers of late, secular periods of a civilization – and later more contemplative mystics renewed their religions, as the following summary shows:[1]

Civilization	Main gods to which contemplative mystics related their glimpses of the Light	Mystic Sacred Rulers who embodied newly created god/priests & known contemplative mystics whose Light renewed religion which became Central Idea of civilization
1. Indo-European Kurgan/	Dyaeus Pitar	Indo-European king as Sky Father; shaman priests to

Old European		Sky Father & Sun-god
2. Mesopotamian	Anu/Ogma/Utu Shamash/Tammuz/ Marduk/Ashur	"Great Shining Ones, great Sons of Anu"; King as Tammuz/Marduk; priests of Anu, Utu & Shamash etc. & Sacred King, Magi
3. Egyptian	Ra/Amon/Aton Horus/Osiris/Apis	Egyptian Pharaoh as Sun-god; writers of texts in Book of the Dead; priests of Ra & Amon etc. & of Sun-god Akhenaton
4. Aegean-Greek	Zeus/Apollo	Cretan king Minos as Sky-god Zeus in the form of a bull; Mycenaean king (*wanax*) of sacred rites; priests to Zeus & Apollo, Dionysiac, Eleusinian & Orphic initiates; Pythagoras, Plato, Plotinus
5. Roman	Jupiter/Apollo	Roman king of sacred rites of Jupiter (*rex sacrorum*); priests of Jupiter & Apollo, Astarte, Cybele, Mithras & Isis; Christ, early Christians, St Paul, St Augustine
6. Anatolian	Storm-and-Weather god Tarhun	Hittite king as Storm and Weather god; priests to Storm and Weather god
7. Syrian	El/Dagon/Baal	Syrian/Phoenician king as

		Storm-god Baal; priests to Baal
8.	Israelite	Yahweh	Davidic king of Psalms, chosen & inspired by Yahweh; high priests to Yahweh; Moses, Prophets e.g. Amos & Hosea (8th C), Jesus Christ
9.	Celtic	Du-w/Taran	Celtic king as Druid of Truth; Druid priests to Du-w & Taran
10.	Iranian	Mithras/Ahura Mazda	Iranian king as Mithras/ Ahura Mazda; Zoroastrian priests of Fire-altars; Zoroaster, Mani, Mazdak
11.	European	God as Light/ Transfigured Christ	European king as God's Chosen; priests to God; Jesus Christ, Cassian, St Benedict, Pope Gregory the Great, St Bernard & European mystics to T. S. Eliot, who attempted to renew the Light/ religion's Central Idea of 20th C. Europe
12.	North-American	God as Light/ Transfigured Christ	American President as God's Chosen; priests to God; early Puritan mystics
13.	Byzantine-Russian	God as Light/ Transfigured Christ	Byzantine Emperor & Russian Tsar as God's Chosen; priests

			to Orthodox God & Christ; Dionysus the Areopagite, Symeon the New Theologian, Byzantine mystics & Hesychasts
14.	Germanic-Scandinavian	Odin/Thor	Chieftan embodied Odin/Thor in wooden or stone temples
15.	Andean	Smiling god/ Quetzlcoatl	King as Sun-god; priests of Sun-king
16.	Meso-American	Kinich Ahau (or Itzamna)/ Huitzilopochtli	King as Sun-god; priests of Sun-king
17.	Arab	Allah	Mohammed as Allah's Chosen; priests to Allah; Sufi mystics
18.	African	African gods	African king as Sun-god (from Egypt); priests to Light
19.	Indian	Agni/Brahman/Atman Siva/Sakti/Visnu	Indian king as Fire- /Light-god; Hindu & Buddhist priests; Patanjali, the Buddha, Mahavira, Sankara, Bhakti mystics, Guru Nanak
20.	S.-E.-Asian	The Buddha	S.-E.-Asian king as the Buddha, priests to the Buddha
21.	Japanese	Kami/Amaterasu/ the Buddha	Emperor as Sun-goddess Amaterasu; priests to Shinto Kami; Buddhist sages, Eisai,

22. Oceanian	Andean Smiling god?/ Inti?/the Buddha?	Oceanian king as Sky Father/ Sun-god/Buddha (?); priests of *moai*
23. Chinese	*Shang Ti/Ti'en Ti/* the *Tao*	Chinese king as Supreme Ruler (*Shang Ti*, or *Ti*); priests to *T'ien Ti*; Lao-Tze, Hui-neng
24. Tibetan	The Buddha	Tibetan king as Enlightened Buddha; priests to Buddha; Padmasambhava, Naropa, Marpa, Milarepa, Sa-skya lamas & Dalai Lamas
25. Central-Asian	The Buddha	C.-Asian king as shamanic Sky Father/Enlightened Buddha; priests to the Buddha

As we look back on the creative efforts of the contemplative mystics over five thousand years, we see that in each generation there is a centre of civilization to which contemplative souls gravitate, which contemplative souls must be near. Egypt, Mesopotamia, Persia, Greece, Rome, Europe – these centres of civilization play a vital part in transmitting civilised values and the gains of the past, to which contemplative souls relate themselves. If our contemplative souls only live this one life these centres of civilization connect our souls to the civilised past and make contact with the divine Light. If each spirit lives many lives, discarding the body when it is old and taking another body in physical renewal, then these centres of civilization nourish our souls in successive lives, and, having contributed to a centre of civilization in one life, we can return and renew the spirit's contact with the Light through it in another life. Such is the vision of the world's Buddhists and Hindus, and of many Christians before pre-existence was declared a heresy in AD 543. In either event, the world's centres of civilization (of which, despite the decline in British Christianity, Britain is currently one) pass on the Light to the contemplative mystics who can renew their civilization's Central Idea.

What lessons can be drawn about the renewal or failure to renew civilizations? As the Light is at the heart of each civilization's Central Idea it will be helpful to survey all known periods when the Light/Central Idea is renewed and all known periods when the Light/Central Idea is in decline. We have seen that during a civilization's growth the Light of the Central Idea is strong, and that it is renewed every generation during growth. Conversely, we have seen that during a civilization's decline the Light of the Central Idea is weak, and that it is not renewed for several generations. Just as all renewals of the Light have renewed their civilization's Central Idea, so all failures to renew the Light have contributed to the decline of their civilization by weakening its Central Idea.

THE LIGHT'S RENEWAL OF RELIGIONS AND CIVILIZATIONS

To show that renewals of the Light which have renewed religions have renewed their civilizations' Central Idea, I will list the main known renewals of the Light in each civilization and state their presumed effect on their civilization's Central Idea, showing how they gave their civilization a new lease of life. The data which I can extract from *The Light of Civilization*, and which, reflecting religious revivals rather than historical expansions, sometimes only partly coincides with the dating of our historical stages, looks like this:

Civilization and dates Light strong	Main known period when Light was renewed	Date	Presumed effect on civilization's Central Idea
1. Indo-European Kurgan/ Old European	Battle-Axe culture's building of	c.1900 BC	Linked Heaven and Earth so crops could grow, strengthen- ed belief in civilization as

	(c.3700- 1750 BC)	megaliths such as Stonehenge III (Fire- temple)		guardian of the sacred Light, strengthened assent of peoples to civilization
2.	Mesopotamian (c.3500- 11th C BC)	Akkadians	c.2400 BC affected	Shamash and Akkadian pantheon everyday life through Light & strengthened assent of peoples to civilization
		Old Babylonians	c.1894-mid 18th C BC	The Amorite Hammurabi renewed Central Idea
		Assyrians	from c.1490 BC	Religion renewed as Assyrians had same gods and Central Idea as Babylonia
		Chaldeans (Neo- Babylonians)	c.626- 539 BC	Religion renewed
		Hellenism	from 331 BC	Under Alexander Marduk temples restored
3.	Egyptian (c.3100- 11th C BC)	Old Kingdom	c.2686- c.2160 BC	New sun-based ideas brought in Pyramid Age
		Middle Kingdom	after c.2040- 1786 BC	Reunification & renewed emphasis on Amon
		New Kingdom	c.1567- 1085 BC	Expulsion of foreign (Indo- European) Hyksos & renewed emphasis on divine kingship & on high priests during Ramesside period
		Akhenaton	c.1379 BC	Failed attempt at renewal through Aton
		Saite	c.664-525 BC	Cultural & religious revival of Old Kingdom & therefore

			of Egyptian Central Idea, especially under Ahmose II (Greek Amasis) (570-526 BC)
	Romans	4th C BC- 3rd C AD	Renewal of Light through Isis, later under foreign rule
	Egyptian Gnosticism	1st- 2nd C AD	Renewal of Light

---

4. Aegean-Greek (c.2200-8th C BC)

Minoan	Minoans	c.2200- 18th C BC	Bull rites in Crete contained Central Idea
		17th C- 1450 BC	Renewal of Cretan Central Idea
Mycenaean	Mycenaeans	c.1600- 1450 BC	Mycenaean gods had no temples, shared King's palace & by their centrality renewed Aegean Idea
Greek	Archaic Dorians: Dionysian & Eleusinian mysteries, Orphism	c.1100-750 BC	Renewed Mycenaean Light in growing Dorian-Greek civilization by giving importance to temple area in growing city-states; Archaic architecture dominated by temples, altars & sanctuaries
	Pythagoras	6th C BC	Renewal of Central Idea
	Athenians	5th C BC	Rebuilt temples destroyed in Persian attack of 480 BC: rise of Athens
	Plato's "Fire" (i.e. Light)	4th C BC	Renewal of Central Idea
	Macedonians	from c.330 BC	Alexander took the Greek Light of the Mysteries

				throughout the Hellenistic world

5.	Roman (c.800-50 BC)	Monarchy	8th-7th C BC	King had religious authority & presided over intense religious life, priests admini-stered divine law (*ius divinum*); Temple of Jupiter Capitolinus dedicated as symbol of Rome, expansion of Roman Light throughout Italy,spread of Roman piety after Etruscans
		Early Republic	c.509-264 BC	Renewal of Central Idea
		Roman hegemony	c.205-133 BC	Light from cults of Asia Minor
		Early Roman Empire	c.30 BC-AD 270	Renewal of Roman Central Idea under Empire Augustus, religion flourished
		Christians	AD c.26-193	Renewed Roman Light
			c.270-395	Cults; Constantine renewed Light & turned Rome Christian; St Augu strengthened interpretation of the Light & widened appeal of Christianity among peoples; Roman Light passed into Christian Light which was adopted by barbarians (e.g. Franks) in growing European civilization

6.	Anatolian (c.2000-700 BC)	Ugarit (Ras Shamra)	from c.6000 BC	Embryonic Central Idea
	Hittite	Old Kingdom	c.1700-1500 BC	Light renewed Central Idea
		New Kingdom	c.1400-1190 BC	Treaty of Suppiluliumas with king of Mitannians c.1380 BC refers to Mitra, Varuna & Indra
	Phrygian		c.1180-8th C BC	Renewal through Cybele
7.	Syrian (c.3000-700 BC)			
	Canaanite	Ugarit	14th-13th C BC	Renewal through Baal
		Phoenicians	11th C BC	Canaanite survivors renewed Central Idea
		Neo-Hittites	c.1125-9th C BC	Renewal through Melqart/ Astarte
	Lydian	Lydians	7th C BC	Renewal of Central Idea
	Syrian	Gnosticism	1st C AD	Renewal under Simon Magus
8.	Israelite (c.1800-600 BC)	Moses	13th C	Central Idea of Light
		Solomon/ David	10th C BC	Renewal through Temple, which commanded assent of tribes & made unification possible (based on tripartite sanctuaries of Hazor & Alalakh in Levant)
		Prophets (Isaiah, Ezekiel,	8th-6th C BC	Pointed to danger to Jerusalem of neglecting Light of Elohim, prepared the way

	Jeremiah etc.)		for Second Temple after exile
		c.538-486 BC	Rebuilding of Second Temple by Zerubbabel, Yahweh worshipped again in Jerusalem after fall of Jerusalem to Chaldean Neo-Babylonians
		c.135-76 BC	Independence from Iranians, Hasmonean Empire in Palestine & Transjordan until Pompey imposed Roman hegemony in 64 BC;
	Essenes	2nd C BC-1st C AD	Semi-monastic renewal that probably produced Christ
	Christians	1st C AD	Renewal by Jewish sect whose vision would pass into European civilization
	Merkava	7th C AD	Renewal of Jewish Light
	Kabbalism	12th-13th C AD	Renewed Central Idea of Judaism at a difficult time & handed it on

9.	Celtic (in France as Gauls, in Britain, Ireland, Balkans, Anatolia) (c.1200 BC-2nd C AD)	Druid universities in Britain	1st C BC -1st C AD	Renewed Druid Light during Roman invasions, contributed to national belief & identity
			AD c.52-313	Renewal through Esus/Jesus
		Arthur	5th C AD	Christianized Celts renewed Celtic Central Idea during Saxon invasions
	Irish-Celtic (6th-7th C AD)	Monasticism	6th C-AD 795	Irish monasticism and illuminated manuscripts, Irish works on lives of saints renewed Central Idea
			AD c.968-	Decline of Viking power &

		1014	renewal of Light until Catholic European influence of diocesan reform

10. Iranian (c.2250-4th C BC)	Old Elamites (in Khuzistan)	c.2700-1520 BC	Dominated by Akkadians c.2334-c.2154 BC & Ur III & acquired Mesopotamian Light;
		c.1700 BC	renewed in religion of Mithras
	Middle Elamites	c.1285-c.1100 BC	"
	Neo-Elamites	c.742-639 BC	"
	Iranians	c.1500-c.850 BC	"
	Medes	c.728-6th C BC	Renewed Light through Zurvan, produced Zoroaster who renewed Light & strengthened Light's influence over peoples, strengthened civilization
	Persians	6th C-330 BC	Renewed Light through Ahura Mazda, adopted Zoroastrianism
	Magi in post-Chaldean Babylon	after 539 BC	Renewed Light
	Parthians	c.247 BC-AD 2	Magi spread cult of Mithras & Anahita in Asia Minor
	Iranian Gnosticism	1st-2nd C AD	Renewed Light
	Sasanians	c.226-364	Restored Zoroastrianism as Mazdaism
	Mani	3rd C AD	Renewed Light

11.	European	Pope	6th C	Renewed the Central Idea of
	(5th-17th C)	Gregory the		Western (Christian) civiliza-
		Great		tion after Justinian's recon-
				quest of Italy & widened its
				appeal
		Charlemagne	800	Unified all lands in a
				Frankish-Papal Christian
				Europe into precursor of Holy
				Roman Empire embodying
				the Central Idea of the
				civilization
		Otto II	962	Established an embryonic ver-
				sion of German-Papal Holy
				Roman Empire (term used
				1254)
		Crusades	11th-13th C	Triumph of Christian Light,
				renewed by St Bernard, over
				Islam in Crusades; & in Latin
				conquest of Byzantium 1204
		Reformation	c.1494-1600	Reformation, prepared for by
				European mysticism of 14th-15th C, & Counter-
				Reformation (St Teresa & St
				John of the Cross) renewed
				Central Idea (individual &
				Light) even though
				Renaissance had secularizing
				effect; through discoveries,
				Europe set for world
				hegemony
		Puritanism	c.1648-1700	Puritan and Protestant
				mystics & Anglican
				Metaphysicists &
				Evangelicals renewed Light &

			Central Idea of civilization even though Holy Roman Empire fragmented following Thirty Years War & despite the Scientific Revolution
	Romanticism/ Evangelical Revival/ Missionaries	c.1790-c.1880	Romantic Neoplatonists renewed the Light through Industrial Revolution; missionaries exported Christianity round world in 19th C despite scientific materialism associated with Industrial Revolution
		by 1970	Renewal of a secular version of Holy Roman Empire in European Community – will the Light now be renewed throughout Europe as a result of a Metaphysical Revolution?
12. North-American (c.1620-present)	Settlers	from c.1607-1854	Colonies settled by religious exiles from Europe, mainly Puritan Separatists & Reformists, & Quakers (e.g. Penn); Great Awakening of 1730s & 1740s renewed Light; War of Independence from Britain created nationhood, unification of United States
	Americans	c.1896-present	Rose to world domination through imperialism (wars against Spain), wars of liberation (against Germany) &

religious diversity, leadership
of Western civilization after
1945 with 38% attending
church & the Light still present in American evangelical
Christianity

13. Byzantine- (360-1000)	c.491-565	Renewal of Light during growth of Byzantium & Justinian's reconquest of Italy; independence of Byzantine Central Idea from Rome
	c.610-717	Heraclius saved Byzantine empire from Islam, recaptured the True Cross from the Persians in 630 & renewed Light
	c.867-1025	Macedonian dynasty gave Church new unity and vitality, missionaries spread Orthodox Light, St Symeon renewed Central Idea of Byzantine civilization
	1261- 1421	Cultural revival under the Palaeologi, new flowering of Byzantine mystical tradition & Central Idea in Hesychasm under Gregory Palamas
Russian (c.1000-1900)	c.900- c.1100	Rise of Rus through Scandinavian Viking Varangians & the rise of Kiev, where the patriarch of Constantinople brought the Byzantine Light in 988

c.1340-1606	Theological & monastic revival of Russian Hesychasm renewed its Byzantine Light; rise of Muscovy, Ivan the Great expanded under Rurikids & built national churches in the Italianate style with icon murals which renewed the Russian Orthodox Light & Central Idea
c.1689-1855	Peter the Great isolated the Church in the course of his secular Westernising expansionist policy, & inadvertently produced a revival of monasticism & Hesychasm which renewed the Russian Light (Dostoevsky visited the monastic elders or *startsy* of Optino & based Zossima on them in *The Brothers Karamazov*)
c.1944-present	Since 1987 *glasnost*, there has been a further renewal of the Russian Orthodox Light which has inadvertently been encouraged by the isolation of the Church under the decline of atheistic Communism, & part of a federal ex-USSR is voluntarily westernizing & joining an expanded Europe that stretches from the Atlantic to the Urals; while

			Stalin & his successors consolidated the Eastern-European empire (inherited from the Nazis), founded a maritime empire, & became a nuclear & space power, they isolated & persecuted the Church & inadvertently pro-duced a revival of the Russian Light among Orthodox exiles (e.g. the Metropolitan Anthony) & in the Siberian Gulag, where to be Orthodox Christian (or Catholic & with the Polish Pope) is to declare for the Russian Central Idea against the Communism that, for all its military might, weakened it
14. Germanic- (c.500 BC- 5th C AD)	Germanic tribes	c.300 BC- AD 300	Indo-European barbarians took Odin's Light to many Roman territories until federated with-in Roman Empire & converted to Christianity
		c.375-476	Renewal through Arian Christ
Scandinavian (7th C)	Vikings	8th-9th C	Brought Odin to Russia, Ireland, England, France, Italy, Iceland, & Greenland before converted to Christianity
15. Andean (c.1200 BC- AD 1525)		c.2000 BC	Sun-cult appeared c.2000 BC, periods of renewal of Light in different regions

	Early Horizon: Chavin	c.1000-200 BC	Renewal of Light
	Middle Horizon: Huari	c.600-800	Renewal through Doorway god
	Late Intermediate:	c.1000-1470	Renewal of Central Idea
	Chimu	c.1370-1460	Renewal of Central Idea
	Inca	c.1320-1525	Renewed Central Idea of Andean civilization which had appeared c.2000 BC

16.	Meso-American (c.1150 BC-AD 1519)	Olmec	c.1150-900 BC	At San Lorenzo
		”	c.800-400 BC	At La Venta
		Mayan:		
		Early Classic	c.100-600	Renewal of Light
		Late Classic	c.600-900	Renewal through Kinich Ahau (or Itzamna)
		Post Classic	c.1300-1519	Renewal of Light
		Aztec	c.950-1519	Light strong after 1325

17.	Arab (Islamic) (5th-17th C)			Arab Light goes back to Israelite exiles after 721 BC
		Caliphate Empire & Seljuq Turks	c.622-1092	Renewal of Arab Light by Mohammed & his Ummayad, Abbasid & Fatimid successors, & under Seljuq Turks (flourished 1055-1092) before Crusades; widened appeal of civilization among peoples
		Persian	c.1092-	Renewal of Light by Persian

Sufism	c.1300	Sufis, including Suhrawardi during time of Crusades
Ottoman Empire	c.1300-1566	Renewal of Light in Middle East & in India, e.g. Sufism/ Kabir (AD 1500) & Sikhism, (inspired by Sufism & Hindu Vaisnavism, 16th C AD)

(After 1920 Ottoman Empire disintegrated into many Middle-Eastern & North-African states, but in 1989 there were signs of a coming revival of Islamic strength & belief, & perhaps renewal of the Light, in Iran, Libya, Iraq & other post-colonial Arab nations opposed to Western secularism; this asserted itself in the extremist attacks, inspired by bin Laden, on New York on September 11, 2001 and in the defiant nuclear ambitions of Saddam Hussein)

18. African (c.2000 BC-16th C AD)		c.656 BC-400 c.740-1500	Renewal through Meroe Renewal through African Allah

19. Indian Hindu (c.1500 BC-16th C AD)			
	Indus Valley	c.2500-1750 BC	Embryonic Central Idea
	Hindus	c.1000-500 BC	Hindu Light arrived c.1500 BC
	Buddhism	6th C BC	Renewed Light & appealed to many peoples
	Jainism	6th C BC	"
	Mauryan	c.325-150 BC	Promoted Buddhism & Jainism
	Gupta Empire	c.320-450	Saivist Light 2nd-4th C, Tantric Hinduism 5th C, coincided with invasion of Huns

		or Hunas
Pallavas	6th-7th C	Built temples in Southern India
Tantric Hinduism	5th-8th C	Building of temples & monasteries
Tantric/ Tibetan Buddhism	6th- 11th C	Promoted Saivism in 8th C & Vaisnavism in 9th C, Bhakti from 11th C
Medieval Hindu	c.750-1200	Renewal of Light
Indian Muslims	c.1236- 1526	"
Bhakti	11th- 19th C	Kept alive Hindu Light during Islamic influence in India
Sikhism	16th C	Blended Light of Bhakti & Islamic Sufism
Maratha	c.1627- 1740	Renewed Indian Light
Vedanta revival	c.1872- present	Hindu tradition affirmed, co- inciding with independence movement & rise of Hindu- influenced Theosophy

20. S.-E.-Asian (1st-16th C)		Mahayana-Buddhist Light from 1st C AD, many stone images of Buddha & Hindu gods renewed Light
Burma	c.500- 13th C	1056 Burma declared Theravada Buddhist & streng- thened Light
Thailand	6th- 11th C	Dvaravati Mon kingdom, strengthened Light
	13th- 17th C	Thai kingdom, originally Mahayana, turned Sinhalese

			Theravada 12th/13th C & strengthened Light: Emerald Buddha national palladium 15th C
	Cambodia	1st-9th C	Kingdoms of Funan & Chenla
		9th- 13th C	Khmers renewed Light
	Vietnam	2nd- 14th C	Kingdom of Champa, streng- thened Light
	Indonesia	7th- 13th C	Central Java
		c.927- 16th C	East Java
	(Philippines		Spanish & therefore Christian after 1571)

21.	Japanese (c.250 BC- 19th C AD)		Japan borrowed religions from China & then Japanized them
		1st- 15th C	Taoist Light & *Yin-Yang* in- troduced from China, Shamanism from Korea; all combined to form Shinto
		6th C-1192	Buddhism introduced 538 or 552 from China & Korea, became family religion with many temples built in Nara period; Shinto spread through- out Japan by 7th C ; Tendai & Shingon in 8th-9th C
		c.1391- 1573	Zen Buddhism
		c.1580- 1867	Tokugawa Shogunate closed Japan, suppressed Christianity on pain of death from 1616 to

			1873, controlled Buddhist priests & adopted Neo-Confucianism as a philosophy & a pure form of Shinto; 280 years of peace in which culture flourished, Japanese Central Idea was renewed, & Light expressed itself in Japanized religions, e.g. Zen
		c.1951-present	Japan has become a major world power, Light renewed through many new religious sects, including Soka Gakkai (a Nichiren sect), & through Zen
22. Oceanian (c.380-1680)	Easter Island	c.380-1100	Central Idea through Sun-god/ Buddha(?)
		c.1200-1500	Sun-god
23. Chinese (c.2000 BC-17th C AD)			The Light of *Ti* & *T'ien* goes back to at least c.1766 BC
	Chou	c.1122-481 BC (c.1143 BC?)	Renewal of *Ti* that led to unification, renewed Light through *I Ching*, Lao-Tze & the *Tao*
	{ Ch'in Han	c.221 BC-AD c.100	Renewed Light through cult of Heaven (which replaced Supreme Unity cult in 31 BC), & through import of Buddhism along silk route
	Sui & T'ang	c.581-753	Supported Taoism & adapted Buddhism to Chinese thought

			in new schools, including Ch'an Zen & Pure Land
Sung	c.960-1189		Light renewed by Neo-Confucian metaphysics which drew on Buddhism & Taoism & opposed low moral standards
Ming	c.1368-1550		Light renewed by new blends of Confucianism, Taoism & Buddhism, e.g. Wang Shou-jen (or Wang Yang-Ming, died 1529) who sought "the unity of know-ledge & action"; Ming ("Brightness") renewed the Light
Ch'ing	c.1646-1796		Renewed the Light through syncretistic religious group that were mainly Buddhist with some Confucian & Taoist teachings, & through the *Book of Consciousness & Life*

24. Tibetan
    (c.200 BC-
    18th C AD)

	6th-9th C		Light known through Bon Buddhism established throughout kingdom, renewed Light
	1358-c.1720		Yellow Hat Dalai Lama estab-lished independence with Mongol help in 1578, Tibetan-Buddhist Light renewed
	1911-1951		Independence, Tibetan-Buddhist Light renewed

25.	Central-Asian (c.500 BC- AD 1700)	Mongol Empire & successor states	c.1200- 1650	Mongol Empire c.1200-1368, revival of Buddhism c.1540- 1600 when Dalai Lama (a Mongol title) was invited to Mongolia to establish Tibetan- Buddhist influence, Genghis Khan's lineage found to be "Living Buddha"

If we ponder each entry in the above table we shall see that each renewal of the Light had the effect of renewing the civilization's Central Idea (see table for stage 7 in *Part One*), and therefore made a contribution to giving the civilization a new lease of life. It must be stressed again that all the alternatives to the Light co-exist- ed at different times of a civilization's life and no doubt in some cases also made a contribution. But the renewal of the civilization's Central Idea was of paramount importance. The renewers of the Light thus had a heroic role in relation to their civ- ilization; hence they felt their lives had meaning, and hence their sense of destiny.

Because there is a spread of Light between civilizations, a renewal of the Light in one civilization could have a creative effect on another and a destructive effect on a third civilization. This is what happened in the case of the Essene-Christian renewal within the Israelite civilization, which prepared the way for the European civilization and in so doing weakened the Roman civilization to which the early Christians were opposed. (*The Light of Civilization* shows how the Christian Light eventually captured the Roman Light which had persecuted it.)

THE WEAKNESS OF THE LIGHT DURING RELIGIONS'/CIVILIZATIONS' TIMES OF DECLINE

Just as there are periods when the Light is renewed after each civilization's first growth, so there are times of decline when the Light is weak before the civiliza- tion's final decay. During such periods of decline the Light-based Central Idea of the civilization tends to be forgotten, the Light is ignored, and both the religion and the civilization weaken and die a little. Times of decline coincide with relatively early periods of foreign rule, and I should therefore list the foreign element here. The main known times of decline are as follows:

Civilization	Date after which Light permanently weak	Main known periods when Light was in decline under foreign rule or foreign threat	Date	Presumed effect on civilization's Central Idea
1. Indo-European Kurgan/ Old European	after c.1750 BC	Milesians?/ Funnel-Neck Beaker Folk	c.2600- 2550 BC	Weakened Indo-European link between Heaven &
		Mesopotamians/ Akkadians	c.2400- 2100 BC	Earth which made crops grow
		Battle-Axe Kurgans	c.2000- 1900 BC	"
		Mycenaean Greeks	c.1750- 1625 BC/ c.1500- 1200 BC	"
		Celts	from c.1200 BC	"
2. Mesopotamian	after c.1000 BC {	Elamites Amorites	c.2050- 2000 BC	Destroyed Ur III, weakened Akkadian pantheon & Shamash
		Kassites	mid-18th C-1490 BC	Caused decline of Babylonia
		Hurrians/ Mitannians	c.1500- 1350 BC	Weakened Shamash "
		Egyptians	c.1000- 626 BC	"

	Medes	c.640-612 BC	Hastened decline of Assyria, which had same gods & Central Idea as Babylonia	
	Iranian Achaemenians	c.538-330 BC	Ruled in New Babylonian Empire & Iranized the Mesopotamian Light	
3. Egyptian	after c.1085 BC	First Intermediate Period	c.2160-2040 BC	Decentralization & growth of Osiris-worship at expense of Ra-worship in which Pharaoh was central
		Hyksos in Second Inter-mediate Period	c.1786-1567 BC	Collapse of central control before Hyksos, weakened Ra
		Akhenaton	c.1379-1363 BC	Aimed to renew Light but attacked Amon & Central Idea of Amon-Ra, weakened Egyptian Central idea
		Libyans/ Kushites (Ethiopian)	c.1085-667 BC	Emphasis on Seth at expense of Ra, weakened Central Idea
		Iranian Achaemenians	c.525-404 & c.343-332 BC	Weakened Ra
4. Aegean-Greek	after	Invaders?	18th-	Destruction of

Minoan	c.1450 BC		17th C BC	palaces, weakened Minoan religion
		Mycenaeans?	c.1500-c.1100 BC,	After eruption of Thera conquest of Crete c.1450 BC, after which hilltop sanctuaries not used
Mycenaean	after c.1450 BC	Dorians	c.1450-1100 BC	Dorian invasions temporarily ended Greek Central Idea
Greek	after 8th C BC	Persians	c.750-480 BC	Sacked Acropolis & temples
		Spartans	c.404-323 BC	Sparta's victory & end of Athenian empire weakened spread of Greek Central Idea (as did the 5th C Sophists' scepticism about religion)
5. Roman	after 3rd C AD	Etruscans	c.616-509 BC	Weakened Roman Light
		Celts	c.390-341 BC	"
		Carthaginians	c.264	"
		Numidians, Germanic tribes	c.133-30 BC	Decline of republic, Gracchi, Jugurtha & civil wars
		Germanic tribes	c.193-AD 270	Importation of eastern cults which weakened Roman Light
		Germanic tribes	c.395-	Migrations, inva-

			AD 500		sions & hegemony, Rome sacked by Visigoths 410, end of Roman Empire at hands of Odoacer in 476

#					
6.	Anatolian Hittites	after c.1400 BC	Akkadians Amorites Hurrians Hanigalbat Mitannians Egyptians Phrygians Sea Peoples	c.2300 BC c.2100 BC c.1500- 1400 BC c.1240 BC c.1225- 1125 BC	Weakened Anatolian Storm and weather god " " " " "
	Phrygians	after c.900 BC after 7th C	Aramaeans Assyrians Cimmerians	c.900- 715 BC c.715- 696/5 BC	Conquered Neo-Hittites Weakened Attis
7.	Syrian	after c.980 BC	Hittites Hebrews Sea Peoples (Luwians/ Philistines) Neo-Hittites Aramaeans Assyrians Iranian Achaemenians Macedonians	c.1400 BC 14th C BC c.1225- 1125 BC c.1200 BC 10th C BC 10th C BC c.980- 710 BC c.546- 330 BC c.330-	Weakened Baal pantheon & Central Idea " " " " " " "

		Hellenism	300 BC from AD c.300	"	
		Celts	c.288-5 BC	"	
		Romans	from c.133 BC	"	
8.	Israelite	after c.640 BC	Sea Peoples (Philistines)	c.1190-1140 BC	Division of David's kingdom into
			Egyptians	c.922 BC	Judah & Israel after Egyptian invasion
			Assyrians	c.841-721 BC	Fall of Israel, loss of Ten Tribes
			Chaldeans Neo-Babylonians	c.587-538 BC	Fall of Jerusalem, exile of Jews to Babylon
			Macedonians	c.333-136 BC	Hellenistic weakening of Light
			Romans	c.65 BC-AD 70	Roman occupation of Palestine weakened the Jewish Central Idea
9.	Celtic	c.313 BC	Romans & Germanic tribes	mid 1st C -2nd C AD	Squeezed between Romans & Germanic tribes (e.g. Taran & Du-w Franks), weakened
			Saxons	c.313-446	Central Idea weakened
	Irish-Celtic	after c.850	Vikings	c.795-920	Viking conquest of Ireland led to decline
			W. Europe	c.1014-	W.-European

			1171	Catholic reform movement weakened Celtic idea ending with Henry II's invasion of 1171 which made Ireland Catholic
10. Iranian	3rd C BC/ 3rd C AD, after 4th C	Invaders	16th C- c.1285 BC	End of Old Elamite period
		Babylonians	c.1100- 750 BC	End of Middle Elamite period
		Assyrians	c.692- 639 BC	End of Neo-Elamite period
		Persians	5th C BC	Decline of Medes
		Macedonians	c.330- 280 BC	Destroyed Persian capital, weakened Central Idea
		Seleucids	3rd C BC	Revolt of Parthia
		Romans	c.51- 226	Decline of Parthia, fusion of Greek & Iranian cults
		Romans	c.276- 651	Prolonged & exhausting wars of Sasanians although purity of Zoroastrianism renewed
		Hephthalites	c.364- 572	
		Byzantines	"	
		Turks	"	
11. European	after 17th C (& especially after 1880)	Islam	7th-11th C	European Idea weakened by loss of Holy Land, North Africa, Spain, Sicily, Italy
		Vikings	8th-9th C	European Idea weak-

		ened by loss of Russia, Ireland, England, Gaul, Italy, Iceland, Greenland, Normandy
Spanish Muslims/ Magyars	c.900-951	Weakened European Idea
Viking Normans	11th C	European Idea weakened in Italy by Norman-Papal alliance
Mongols & Turks		Central Idea weakened
Avars, Huns		
Arabs	c.1250-1453	Defeat of Crusaders by Islam, decline of Popes, decline in Light until mystics renewed it
Ottomans	c.1453-1555	Ottomans weakened European idea
Turks	c.1680-1750	Scientific Revolution and its consequence, the - rationalistic Enlightenment, weakened Christian Light
Germans Russians	c.1880 present	European Idea weakened as Europe no longer commanded world & world mar-

			kets & could no longer export Christianity so universally; breakdown of certainties; no Light after 1880; Fascist dictatorships, two World Wars & end of European empires weakened European Idea; Eastern Europe occupied by Russians; churchgoing down to 1.7% in Britain; European law supreme over national laws, i.e. loss of legal independence to Brussels
12. North-American	Southern Confederacy	c.1854-1896	National disunity over slavery; secession of southern states & civil war weakened Light
13. Byzantine-	Monophysites	5th C	Doctrinal controversy weakened Central Idea in Alexandria
	Lombards	c.565-610	Central Idea weakened

		Persians, Avars, Arabs	c.626	"
		Iconoclasm	c.717-867	Doctrinal conflict weakened Central Idea
		Muslims	c.1025-1260	Decline during Crusades under Western influence & Muslim pressure
		Venetian Latins	c.1204-1261	Capture of Constantinople
		Ottomans	c.1354-1462	Decline before final Ottoman Turkish assault
Russian	after c.1689	Mongol Tatars	c.1100-1340	Decline of Kiev & disintegration of Rus at hands of Golden Horde
		Poland Sweden	c.1606-1681	Time of Troubles under Romanovs
		European French	1689-1812	Peter the Great secularized Central Idea before Napoleon
		Great Britain, France, Turkey, Japan, Germany	c.1855-c.1944	After Crimean War defeat, revolutionary outlook & defeat by Japan before 1st World War weakened Russian Central Idea, as did the civil war started by atheistic Communism

14.	Germanic-	after c.476 (Germanic)	Romans	c.12 BC-AD 38	Germanic tribes federated in
			Romans	c.270-375	Roman Empire & converted to
			East Roman Empire	c.476-596	Christianity, slowly lost their Central
			British Celts	"	Idea of Odin
			Avars	"	
	Scandinavian	after 800	English	11th C	Destroyed Danish Empire, weakened Central Idea
15.	Andean	after c.1200	Invaders		New World idea weakened as sites were mysteriously deserted
			Nazca/Moche	c.400-350 BC	Central Idea weakened
			Middle Horizon invaders	c.500-600	Early Intermediate period
				c.800-1300	Late Intermediate period Huari & pre-Inca
			Itza	1519	Itza invaded c.1000
			Incas	c.1200-1460	
			Spanish	c.1500-1530	Collapse of New World civilization before Christianity
16.	Meso-American	after c.1200	Post-Olmecs	c.400-350 BC	Weakened Central Idea
			Mayan invaders	c.200-300	"
			Nahua invaders	c.850	"

		Aztecs	c.1200-1428	"

17. Arab (Islamic)	after c.1683	Byzantines, Crusaders, Mongols	c.740-790 c.1092-1258	Implementation of Islamic Central Idea temporarily weakened by decline of Abbasids & Seljuq Turks during Crusades, but renewed by Sufis & Ottomans
		Habsburgs Iran, Venice Russia, Austria, Great Britain	c.1566-1920	Islamic idea weakened by decline of Ottomans

18. African	after c.1500	Aksum Empire Arabs European colonizers	c.320-370 c.640-740 c.1500-1980	Weakened Central Idea "

19. Indian	after c.1526	Bactrians Scythians	c.70-120 or c.240-290	Weakened Central Idea
		Huns or Hunas	c.450-750	Huns weakened Central Idea by destroying many Buddhist monasteries
		Arabs	7th-8th C	Islam weakened Indian Hindu
		Turkish Muslims (North)	c.1200-1526	Central Idea

	Moghuls (South)	c.1350-1680	"	
	Moghul Empire	c.1526-1627	"	
	British	c.1740-1946	Decline of Maratha, British Raj weakened Central Idea	

20.	South-East-Asian	after c.1550			Invasions weakened Central Idea & beliefs that inspired Hindu/Buddhist stones
	Burma		Nanchao	c.800-850	Central Idea weakened
			Chams	c.1177-1287	"
			Mongols	after 1287	Doctrinal dispute lasting 300 years weakened Light
	Thailand		Khmers	after 11th C	Central Idea weakened
			Burmese	18th C	"
	Cambodia		Thai	13th C	"
	Vietnam		Khmers	after	Khmer attack AD 1145
			Chinese	14th C	Chinese persecuted Buddhism 1414-1428
	Indonesia		Islam	after 16th C	Central Idea weakened
	Philippines		Spanish	after 1571	Christianity weakened Central Idea

21.	Japanese	after c.1573	Chinese & Koreans	c.663-710	Decline of old patri-cian culture & rise
			Mongols & Koreans	c.1274-1391	of new *samurai* war-rior class weakened Central Idea; cor-ruption among clergy dealt with by importing Zen Buddhism (Rinzai & Soto), Pure Land & Nichiren sects from China, early 13th C, which kept Light alive;
			Portuguese	c.1546-1573	civil war & advent of Christianity
			Americans	c.1863	Japan opened up to
			British, French	c.1868-1951	the world, Catholic & Protestant
			Russians		Christianity weak-
			Chinese		ened Japanese Central Idea, expan-sionist wars with China & British Empire in Second World War resulted in defeat & American occupa-tion; Light kept go-ing through Buddhism rather than militarily cor-rupted Shinto

22. Oceanian	after c.1500	Settlers from S.-E. Asia	c.800-850	Central Idea weakened
		S. Americans	c.1100-1200	"
			c.1500-present	Polynesian idea of *manas* weakened

23. Chinese	after c.1644	Huns or *Hsiung-nu*	c.481-222 BC	"Warring States" period; Great Wall of China begun in 4th C BC as defence against the Huns; end of
		16 barbarian kingdoms	c.100-590	Han, six dynasties, division & barbarian invasions; suppressal of Taoism in AD 184 led to debased alchemical Neo-Taoism
		Nanchao kingdom	c.755-960	End of T'ang, five dynasties & internal rebellions, Buddhism suppressed 843-5 with 40,000 temples & shrines closed; Light kept alive in *The Secret of the Golden Flower*.
		Juchen-Chin	c.1086-1126	Manchurian Juchen at war
		Mongols	c.1211-	Genghis Khan &

			1368	Kublai Khan weakened Chinese Light
		Japan Manchus	c.1571-1645	Late Ming, decline of Taoism & Buddhism into badly organized popular religions.
		Westerners, Muslims, Japan	c.1796-present	End of Ch'ing, uprisings & Muslim rebellions, & Christianity weakened Chinese Central Idea; Japan in China 1937-45, civil war 1945-9; proletarian Communism & Cultural Revolution weakened the Chinese Light
24. Tibetan	after c.1720	Mongols	9th C-1358	Mongol conquest of Tibet in 1247
		Tumed Mongols	c.1565-1642	Central Idea weakened
		Manchu Chinese	c.1720-1913	Under Manchu Chinese rule from 1720
		Chinese	c.1951-present	Under Chinese rule again, many monasteries & Tibetan-Buddhist temples destroyed in the Chinese Cultural

				Revolution of 1966, Light suppressed.
25. Central-Asian	after c.1370	Chinese	c.51 BC-AD 1	Central Idea weakened
		Juchen-Chin	c.1125-1206	"
		Uzbek Black Sheep & White Sheep	c.1370-1543	"
		Chinese Manchus	c.1650-1923	Conquest of Mongolia by Chinese after 1644
		Soviet Union	c.1924-present	Under Soviet or Chinese rule

By comparing contemporary periods of renewal and decline we can see that they dovetail (occasionally overlapping where periods of renewal and decline co-exist, as they do during the European Reformation and Puritanism), and that the history of my civilizations contains a constant play of two opposing forces, the renewal of the Light/Central Idea by the leadership of contemplative mystics and the failure to renew it in Lightless, sceptical times.

Mystics' Defections to Foreign Cults, and Decline

I can go further and probe behind why renewal may fail to take place. We have seen (pp389-394) that contemplative mystics or illumined men renew their civilization's Central Idea when they channel their Light into their civilization's religion. Conversely, they fail to renew their civilization's Central Idea when they fail to channel their Light into their civilization's religion. The main reason for this failure is that they channel their Light into the cults of other civilizations, thus accelerating the decaying civilization's decline, for which the decaying civilization's religion persecutes them.

I can sharpen our awareness of the connection between defection and decline, and between persecution and renewal, by listing some of the known defections from the faded Light of a decaying religion into foreign cults, which prove attractive to contemplative mystics as they seem to contain more Light, and by listing some of the known persecutions of contemplative mystics who have attached themselves to foreign cults. As a result of these persecutions the decaying religion renews itself for a while. We can then see that a religion renews itself and continues to attract its contemplative mystics so long as it has spiritual energy (i.e. contains the Light), and that it ceases to renew itself and goes into decline when it loses its contemplative mystics to cults with greater Light.

We shall see that there is a cumulative process of defections during periods of decline long before stage 54, when an occupying foreign power imposes its religion on the homegrown Light of the civilization's decaying religion, and then persecutes the contemplative mystics who have defected to other cults. This tradition of defection from the civilization's own religion makes it all the more certain that there will be a defection from the foreign occupier's religion in stage 54. Asterisks denote proximity to stage 54.

Civilization	Declining religion in terms of Light of:	Foreign religion/ Light to which contemplative mystics defected from civilization's Light	Date contemplative mystics known to have defected from civilization's Light into foreign religion during period of decline
1. Indo-European Kurgan/ Old European	Dyaeus Pitar	Greek religion of Zeus	c.2200-1500 BC
		Mesopotamian-Akkadian (influence of Utu/Shamash)	after c.2400 BC
		Ogma	c.1850 BC?
		Celtic*	c.1100 BC

2.	Mesopotamian	Utu/Shamash	Mitannian Mitra	c.1875 BC
			N. Jews' Judaism	8th C BC
			S. Jews' Judaism	6th C BC
			Iranian	after 539 BC (Achaemenian occupation)
			Syrian	after 312 BC (Seleucid occupation)
			Greek	after 331 BC/after AD 165 (Macedonian conquest)
			Parthian	c.141 BC-165 BC
			Roman/Sasanian*	c.165-7th C AD
			Nestorian Christianity	3rd C
			Byzantine	6th-7th C
			Islam	c.637-642
3.	Egyptian	Ra pantheon	Mesopotamian	c.671/667 BC (Assyrian occupation)
			Iranian	c.525-404 BC/616-AD 628 (Achaemenian occupation)
			Greek	332-168 BC (Hellenism)
			Roman*	c.30 BC-AD 395
			Byzantine	c.395-616
4.	Aegean-Greek	Zeus	Ionian	Ionian gods c.950 BC
			Macedonian	c.330-30 BC (Hellenism)
			Roman*	c.27 BC-AD 395
5.	Roman	Jupiter	Astarte }	Cults of Asia Minor

		Cybele	}	3rd C BC
		Mithras		
		Isis		1st C BC
		Early Christian		1st C AD
		Christianity		c.313-800
		Lombard		c.568-652
		Arianism		
		Lombard		c.728-756
		Christianity*		
6.	Anatolian	Tarhun/Teshub/	Ionian/Lydian	c.1225-8th C BC
		Cybele	Greek religion	"
			of Zeus	
		Neo-Hittite	Mesopotamian	7th C BC
			Roman*	c.133 BC-AD 395
7.	Syrian	Baal-worship	Assyrian	after 8th C BC
			Chaldean	after 605 BC
			Iranian	after 538 BC
				(Achaemenian
				occupation)
			Greek	c.333 BC (Macedonian
				occupation)
			Egyptian	after c.300 BC
				(Ptolemaic rule)
			Roman*	c.163 BC-AD 395
			Christianity	3rd-4th C
			Islam	c.633
8.	Israelite	Judaism	Chaldean,	after 586 BC
			Iranian (both	"
			during exile at	
			Persian Babylon)	
			Christianity	1st C AD

		Roman*	c.163 BC-AD 395
9. Celtic	Druidism	Roman (Mithras)	1st C BC
		Christianity	"
Irish-Celtic		Viking Odin*	after 8th C AD
		Roman Catholic Christ*	c.1016-1066
10. Iranian	Zoroastrian	Roman	after AD c.121 (several Roman invasions)
		Christianity	3rd C
		Turkish	c.560
		Byzantine Christianity	after c.572
		Islam	642
		Non-Sunni, non-Shi'ite Islam*	c.1258-1382
11. European	God as Light/Christ	Indian (Theosophy from British Indian Empire & Indian sects)	after 1880
		New-Age cults	20th C
12. North-American	Puritan-Evangelical God as Light/Christ	New-Age cults	20th C
13. Byzantine-	Orthodox God as Light/Christ	Latin Christianity	after 1204
		Islam	"

Russian		Protestant Christianity (e.g. Baptists)	after 1919
14. Germanic-Scandinavian (Vikings)	Odin	Christianity Norman Christianity*	4th-11th C c.1042-1106
15. Andean & 16. Meso-American	} Sun-gods	Christianity	16th C
17. Arab	Allah	Christianity (under Ottomans & present regimes)	17th-20th C
18. African	Bantu gods	Islamic religion Christianity	after 8th C after 16th C
19. Indian	Reality	Islam Christianity	16th-19th C 19th-20th C
20. S.-E.-Asian	Buddha	Christianity	18th-20th C
21. Japanese	Buddha/Shinto	Christianity	16th-20th C
22. Oceanian	Sun-god	Buddhism? Andean Sun-god? Christianity	from c.800 " after 18th C
23. Chinese	*Tao*	Christianity	18th-20th C
24. Tibetan	Tibetan Buddha	Chinese	after 18th C

	Confucianist		
	Taoism	20th C	
	Christianity	"	

25. Central-Asian	Chinese	after 18th C
	Confucianist	
	Taoism	
	Islam	after 18th C

PERSECUTIONS OF CONTEMPLATIVE MYSTICS/ILLUMINED MEN, AND RENEWAL

The civilizations persecuted the defectors to foreign cults, and in so doing re-established the authority of their homegrown religions and renewed their own Lights. By the time the civilizations reached stage 54 they had lost the will to persecute defectors and so failed to re-establish their authority. The main persecutions are as follows:

Declining civilizations	Declining home religion	Foreign cults to which contemplative mystics attached themselves during decline of home religion and as a result were persecuted	Date and details of persecutors
1. Indo-European Kurgan/Old European	Dyaeus Pitar	Akkadians? Beaker Fire- / Light-cults? Greeks? Egyptians?	Kurgans between 2400-1500 BC?

2.	Mesopotamian	Utu/Shamash/ Marduk	Mitannian Mitra	Ashurites c.1875 BC
			N. Jews' Judaism	Assyrians 721 BC
			S. Jews' Judaism	Neo-Babylonian Chaldeans 587/586 BC
3.	Egyptian	Ra	Atonites	Amonites c.1358 BC
			Roman Paganism	Alexandrian patriarchs
			Pre-Byzantine	4th C AD Egyptian
			Heterodox	Church c.391, e.g.
			Christian (e.g.	Theophilus
			Arians &	
			Monophysites)	
4.	Aegean-Greek			
	Minoan	Zeus	Mycenaeans	Minoans before 1450 BC?
	Mycenaean	"	Minoan Cretans	Mycenaeans before 1100 BC?
			East Greeks (Anatolians)	"
			West Greeks (Dorians)	"
			Ionian gods	Dorian Apollonians c.900 BC
	Greek	Zeus	Rationalist philosophers of 5th C AD	Ideological conflict rather than persecution
			Hellenistic mysteries (e.g. Cabeiri of Samothrace, Isis &Serapis)	Tension between Greek religion & cults
5.	Roman	Jupiter	Druids	AD c.60

			Early Christians	Tiberius & Nero 1st C, Decius c.250, Diocletian c.303-312
			Early Desert Fathers	
6.	Anatolian	Tarhun/ Teshub/ Cybele	Pagan cults	Theodosius AD c.395
7.	Syrian	Baal	Worship of Yahweh	8th C BC, Phoenicians
8.	Israelite	Yahweh	Asherah Hellenistic Seleucids' worship of Zeus Olympius in the Temple	Hezekiah, c.715 BC Judas Maccabeus' rebellion of the Hasmonean Jews which wrested the Temple from the Greek Seleucids in 164 BC following Antiochus IV's banning of Judaism (Judas's action is possibly reflected in the Dead Sea Scroll, *The War of the Sons of Light Against the Sons of Darkness*, & the recovery of the Temple is celebrated in the Hanakah, the Jewish Festival of Lights)

		Essenes	Pharisaic Judaism
		Jewish	,,
		Christians	(under Saul before AD c.35)
9. Celtic Irish-Celtic	Du-w Celtic Christianity	Romans Roman Catholics through diocesan reform movement	Celts 1st-2nd C AD? Gaelic Irish in 11th-12th C who resisted Norman church reform
10. Iranian	Ahura Mazda	Manichaeans Christians	Sasanians Zoroastrians executed Mani in 274/7, & persecuted Christians after 339 (in the reign of Shapur II), & when Khosrow I (reigned 531-579) was crown
		Zurvanites Mazdakites	prince pronounced the Zurvanites heretical c.528
11. European	Catholic	Albigensian Cathars & Waldenses Templars	Simon de Montfort's crusade & siege of Montségur in 1244 & medieval Inquisition's suppressal of Templars in 1312
		Heretics, e.g. Illuminists (Alumbrados) Protestants &	Spanish Inquisition under Torquemada; Roman Inquisition under Paul IV (1555-

		Huguenots	9), all States that created Protestant martyrs c.1540-1640 e.g. Dutch state militia's persecution of Mennonite Anabaptists;
	Protestant	Unitarians	Calvinist Protestants burned Michael Servetis, a Neo-platonic Unitarian in 1553, Protestants who drove Puritan, Reformist & Separatist *emigrés* from Britain & Holland to settle in America c.1620-c.1700 & imprisoned Bunyan
		Catholics	Shaftesbury's persecution in 1680s
		Quakers	Restoration persecution in 1662-1686, 500 Quakers died in prison
	Puritan	Quakers	Cromwell's persecution of Quakers
	Catholic	Lefebvrists	Catholic excommunication in 1988
12. North-American	Puritan Christianity	Quakers	Boston magistrates executed 4 Quakers 1659-1661

		New-Age cults	Legal moves against cults, e.g. Scientologists, Moonies, in 20th C
13. Byzantine-	Orthodox Christianity	Western Latins	Persecution of Latin Christianity in 13th C after the fall of Constantinople in 1204 & recovery under the Palaeologi c.1261
Russian	Russian Orthodox Slavophile Christianity	Westernizers/ revolutionary socialists	Ideological conflict rather than persecution in 19th C
14. Germanic-Scandinavian	Odin	Catholic Christians	Arian persecutions of Germanic defectors 4th C
15. Andean	Inca Sun-god	Rival tribal gods	Religious authorities included defectors in human sacrifices
16. Meso-American	Sun-gods of Mayan	Rival tribal gods	Religious authorities included defectors in human sacrifices
17. Arab	Allah	Sufis	Abbasids who executed Bayazid (874); al-Hallaj (922); & Suhrawardi (1191)
		Christians	Mamluks (1250-1517)

			who closed all churches in Egypt, 1301
	Safavids		Ottomans c.1502-1544

18. African	Bantu gods	Islamic religion	African persecutions of African Muslims after 8th C
		Christianity	African persecutions of African Christians after 16th C

19. Indian			
Hindu (not decaying)	Hindu Reality	Muslims ⎫	20th C massacres preceding
Muslim	Allah	Hindus ⎭	Indian independence

20. S.-E.-Asian	Hindu Reality	Vaisnavism	Persecutions during
	Saivism	Mahayana	changes e.g. at Angkor
	Hindu Reality	Buddhism	Wat
	Vaisnavism	Theravada	
	Mahayana	Buddhism	
	Buddhism		

21. Japanese	Shinto/ Buddhism	Christians	Tokugawas executed Christians 1616-1873

22. Oceanian	Cult of long-eared statues which seems to have migrated from S.-E. Asia &	Short Ears	Long Ears' persecution of Short Ears ended when Short Ears massacred the Long Ears c.1680

	influenced		
	Peru		
23. Chinese	Confucianism/ *Tao*	Buddhists	Wu Tsung, Taoist, suppressed Buddhism as a social institution in 843-50; Mao Tse-Tung's Cultural Revolution attacked Buddhism in 1966
		Christians	Mao Tse-tung indirectly expelled 20,000 missionaries in 1951-6 & persecuted many pro-Christian Chinese
24. Tibetan	Tibetan Buddhism	Pro-Chinese Dalai Lama	Pro-Chinese Dalai Lama imposed by Chinese c.1705; persecutions by Tibetans during Tibetan civil war 1727-8
25. Central-Asian	Buddhism	Chinese Confucianism	Mongol nobles persecuted pro-Chinese Mongols, e.g. Chingunjav's revolt against Manchu c.1750

So the main lesson to be learned from the past as regards a civilization's renewal is that contemplative mystics have to pour their Light into their civilization's religion, and that there is a strong link between their defection from their religion and the decline of their religion and civilization. And this brings us back to perhaps the fundamental question about my law of growth and decay. We have been conditioned to think economically and administratively, and sceptically. Can we really believe that it is renewed or declining religions rather than renewed or declining economies ("successes or failures of economic growth") or governments that embody the Central Idea of a civilization and affect the outcome of Light-bearing civilizations, especially in a sceptical, complex, secular Europe which has marginalized churches and religious broadcasting?

The dispassionate answer to such a sceptical question is that modern European economies and governments are run by Lightless (rather than by Light-bearing) people who do not see their civilization's Central Idea or consider a people's self-belief, and that scepticism is typical of stages 40 and 41 of a civilization's decline and assumes that economies and governments are always run by Lightless people who have lost sight of the Central Idea of their civilization and therefore of the whole question of a civilization's self-belief. In short, the question is part of the problem, and the answer involves questioning, probing and rebutting conditioned attitudes. There is very extensive evidence both in my 61 stages and in my treatment of periods and renewal and decline (above), which relates past renewals of civilizations' Central Idea to renewals of the Light, that renewals of the Light inspire renewals of civilizations, and that religions, which are central to cultures, are vital to their civilizations.

It may seem that the concept of civilizations being renewed through visions of the Light is very far removed from a starving human being in an Eastern-African famine, and the image of a thin, emaciated, dying man who is hungry makes the Light seem a luxury beside a crust of bread. However, we must not forget that the man is starving because the civilization has got into a mess, and that the mess it is in is related to one of our stages. When the context is properly viewed, that thin man's plight is seen to be directly connected with his civilization's decline, which I have related to its loss of belief in the Light (to find which the Desert Fathers voluntarily became emaciated, starving men).

Now I have completed my review of the evidence for a Light-based Universalist approach, I submit that the evidence overwhelmingly supports the view that civilizations grow and decay in proportion to the amount of Light their religions channel to their peoples.

My survey shows that all these civilizations went through the same stages and the evidence is that the length of each stage varies in accordance with local conditions, and with the amount of Light – and therefore belief in the Central Idea, or self-belief – within each civilization.

5. PREDICTIONS

I am now in a position to relate the surviving civilizations to the 61 stages of a civilization's growth and decay.

History is the science of the past, and historians do not make predictions as so far no historian has discovered a reliable method of interpreting the past which allows for predictions about the future. I claim to have discovered a method of projecting, and therefore of predicting, future stages; if I list the surviving civilizations and the stage which each has now reached, I can then predict the coming stages from our pattern. By studying the past scientifically we can predict the future with a degree of precision and accuracy. Or as Eliot put it, "Time present and time past/Are both perhaps present in time future/And time future contained in time past."

Owners of businesses and their accountants are accustomed to making five-year projections for their bank manager. They analyse the past and the present, and project figures for the coming five years, allowing for inflation and market trends. Using round figures, skilful projectors can anticipate profits with a degree of accuracy that with hindsight seems staggering, and yet the profit was always there in the patterns and round figures on the bottom line of the spreadsheet. My historical predictions are in the spirit of a business spreadsheet that is submitted for the scrutiny of a bank manager who broadly accepts the patterns of the past (in my case, the 61 stages and dates in the life cycle of dead civilizations) and remains to be convinced about the patterns of the future. As with bank projections, the acid test of all extrapolations of the future from the past is performance, i.e. do the future patterns happen?

Such an enterprise, when applied to history, has nothing deterministic about it as in each of our 61 stages we have abstracted past patterns of freewill in which Providential possibilities or tendencies are brought into being at different stages of each civilization's rise and fall. It is future patterns of freewill that we can predict as these seem to follow the existential or psychological law that can be extracted by analysing the past *patterns of freewill*. To put it another way, leaders and contemplative mystics of different civilizations react in similar ways to similar situations involving the Light, occupying enemies and the absence of the Light, even though the pressures they face are all different and occur in different times.

LIVING CIVILIZATIONS' COMING STAGES

I am now in a position to make the following predictions:

Living civilizations	Stage they are now at	Prediction of next stages
11. European	42/43	End of colonial conflict (stage 42); loss of national sovereignty to secularizing conglomerate (expanded & fully integrated European Union from 2008) (stage 43); syncretism of the Universalist vision (stage 44); revival of cultural purity & glorification of the medieval mystical vision in a new Classical/Baroque movement (stage 45); federalism of independent European nation-states free from the European conglomerate under N.-American influence (stage 46); economic decline (stage 47); absence of the Light (stage 48); occupation by foreign invader (stage 49)
12. North-American	15	Continuation of global expansion into empire (stage 15); epic poetry (stage 16); creation of Light-based heretical sect (stage 17); resistance to it (stage 18); decline of religion (stage 19); attempted renewal by mystics (stage 20); military blow (stage 21); breakdown of civilization (stage 22)

13. Byzantine-Russian	43-45/46	Ending of loss of national sovereignty to secularizing Soviet conglomerate (stage 43); continued syncretism of the Universalist vision (stage 44); continued revival of cultural purity of Russian past & glorification of the Russian Byzantine medieval mystical/ Hesychast vision (stage 45); continuing independent federalist ex-Soviet republics free from the Soviet conglomerate within the CIS (Commonwealth of Independent States) with western republics being associated with the EU and eastern republics forming a federal association, with independence for much of Central Asia and associate membership of the EU in which the republics will be provinces under European influence (stage 46); economic decline (stage 47); absence of the Light (stage 48); occupation by foreign invader (stage 49)
15. Andean & 16. Meso-American	46	Continued federalism within the Organization of American States and Free Trade Area of the Americas under N.-American influence (stage 46); economic decline of Latin America (stage 47); absence of the Light (stage 48); occupation of Latin America by foreign invader (stage 49); destruction of Latin America's stones, i.e. churches (stage 50); secession of Latin-American peoples from the foreign occupier & from the civilization, causing cultural disintegration (stage 51)
17. Arab	46	Independent Arab nation-states' expansion into empire through federalism (e.g. pan-Arab union) funded by oil wealth & embracing the

Middle East, Iran, perhaps the southern states of the ex-Soviet Union & N. Africa, under N.-American influence (stage 46); economic decline of Arab world (stage 47); absence of the Light from Islamic religion (stage 48); occupation of Arab world by foreign invader (stage 49); destruction of Arab stones, i.e. mosques (stage 50); secession of Arab peoples from the foreign occupier and from the Arab civilization, causing cultural disintegration (stage 51)

18. African	46	Independent African nation-states' expansion into empire through federalism (e.g. pan-African union – the African Union of 2002) after the end of white rule in South Africa, under N.-American influence (stage 46); economic decline of Africa (stage 47); absence of the Light from African religion following the receding of Christianity (stage 48); occupation of Africa by foreign invader (stage 49); destruction of African stones, i.e. churches & mosques (stage 50); secession of African peoples from the foreign occupier & from the African civilization, causing cultural disintegration (stage 51)
19. Indian	46	Continued independent federal India's expansion into empire with federally linked regions, under N.-American influence (stage 46); economic decline of India (stage 47); absence of the Light from Hindu religion (stage 48); occupation of India by foreign invader (stage 49); destruction of Indian stones, i.e. temples (stage 50); secession of Indian peoples from the foreign

occupier & from Indian civilization, causing
cultural disintegration (stage 51)

20. S.-E.-Asian	46	Independent S.-E.-Asian nation-states' expansion into empire through federalism (e.g. S.-E.-Asian union or membership of an expanded Pacific Community or regional bloc following ASEAN), under N.-American influence (stage 46); economic decline of S.-E. Asia (stage 47); absence of the Light from S.-E.-Asian Buddhism (stage 48); occupation of S.-E. Asia by foreign invader (stage 49); destruction of S.-E.-Asian stones, i.e. temples (stage 50); secession of S.-E.-Asian peoples from the foreign occupier & from S.-E.-Asian civilization, causing cultural disintegration (stage 51)
21. Japanese	43-45	Continued loss of national sovereignty to secularizing US-influenced conglomerate, cf present deprival of offensive role for Self-Defence Forces (stage 43); continued syncretism of its Universalist vision (stage 44); revival of cultural purity & continued glorification of the traditional Shinto, Buddhist & Zen-Buddhist vision (stage 45); federation of independent Japanese regions free from a US-influenced conglomerate with a link to an expanded Pacific Community in which Japanese regions are provinces, under N.-American influence (stage 46); economic decline (stage 47); absence of the Japanese Light (stage 48); occupation by a foreign invader (stage 49)

22. Oceanian   43   Imminent end of loss of Oceanian islands'
national sovereignty to secularizing con-
glomerate (Western colonization) (stage 43);
syncretism of the Universalist vision (stage
44); revival of cultural purity & glorification of
the traditional Oceanian shamanistic religion
(stage 45); independent Oceanian nation-states
free from the Western conglomerate's
sovereignty & creating a unified Oceania or
Confederacy of the South Pacific, including
Australia & New Zealand, under N.-American
influence (stage 46); economic decline (stage
47); absence of the Oceanian Light (stage 48);
occupation by a foreign invader (stage 49)

---

23. Chinese   43   Continued loss of sovereignty of Chinese
nationalities to a secularizing Communist
conglomerate (stage 43); syncretism of the
Universalist vision (stage 44); revival of
cultural purity & coming glorification of the
traditional Confucianist, Taoist & Buddhist
mystical vision (stage 45); an independent
federalist China with federally linked regions
free from the conglomerate & perhaps linked to
an expanded Pacific Community in which S.-E.
Asian & Oceanian regions are provinces, along
with Japanese regions, under N.-American
influence (stage 46); economic decline (stage
47); absence of the Light (stage 48); occupation
by a foreign invader (stage 49)

24. Tibetan   43   Continued loss of national Tibetan sovereignty to the
Chinese conglomerate (stage 43); syncretism of
the Universalist vision (stage 44); revival of

cultural purity & glorification of the traditional Tibetan-Buddhist mystical vision (stage 45); an independent Tibetan nation-state free from the Pacific conglomerate but linked federally to expanded Pacific Community, under N.-American influence (stage 46); economic decline (stage 47); absence of the Light (stage 48); occupation by a foreign invader (stage 49)

---

25. Central-Asian   46   A Central Asia under federal ex-Soviet & Chinese influence; (stage 46); economic decline (stage 47); absence of the Light (stage 48); occupation by a foreign invader (stage 49)

That is the overall pattern of freewill. But can I go further and offer a more specific interpretation of these generalised projections or predictions, seek to clarify future foreign invaders? An immediate word of caution is necessary. Projecting or predicting the future, even on a scientific basis like ours, is inevitably very hazardous. In offering practical answers we can go wrong. In suggesting time-scales when freewill applies, we can go wrong. Although I am confident that all my 14 living civilizations will pass through the stages in the predictions, so far I have conducted a strictly scientific analysis of the past and the present, whereas now that I seek to sharpen my future predictions, a certain amount of intelligent guesswork must inevitably creep in. Nevertheless as this is a phase of the argument which will eventually attract intense interest and provoke debate, and as this is the section that will interest the politicians, let me certainly attempt to do the impossible, and project, and therefore predict, the future of the next 200 years, or indeed the broad sweep of the next 600 years assuming that no nuclear holocaust or a sudden acceleration of the greenhouse effect will put an abrupt end to our extant civilizations.

Let me therefore apply the growth-decay process to our Christian Western civilization, i.e. to the European and North-American civilizations; relate the Light to the stages these two civilizations have now reached in our post-Cold-War time; and consider what foreign invaders lie ahead.

DECLINING EUROPE'S CONGLOMERATE

We have already seen in my summary of the decaying process of civilizations and in my consideration of the previous stages, that Europe (now approaching stage 43) seems to be to America (now advancing into stage 15) as Greece (in stage 43 c.404-337 BC) was to Rome (in stage 15 c.341-218 BC) in c.341 BC or as Rome was to Byzantium in the 4th century AD (although Rome was then still approaching stage 43 and Byzantium had not yet reached stage 15). What can we glean about Europe from the stages of the decline and decay of civilizations?

We have seen that breakdown, and therefore secularization, took place between 1453 and 1555. Indeed Holbein caught the troubled look of breakdown on a crucial day, Good Friday 1533, in his portrait of "two Ambassadors", for that day (the day caught in the painting) Henry VIII's ultimatum to the Pope expired, thus widening Luther's Reformation and heralding a new age in which State controlled Church. We have seen that the scientific materialism of the 17th century accelerated the process of decline, and this acceleration coincided with the Industrial Revolution. On the other hand, both the Reformation and the Puritan Revolution had the effect of renewing the Light by making it more accessible to individuals in the new climate of individualism. There was a weakening in the European Light from 1690 to 1750, and there was a further decline in the prevalence of the Light from c.1880. This coincided with Europe's expansion into the European empires, and led to the breakdown of certainties in Europe c.1910 when everything suddenly changed at the time of the Liberal Reforms in Britain (when the relationship between master and servant, employer and employee and man and woman was different, and religious ideas were questioned). We have seen that decline deepened from 1914, when as a result of her colonial conflict Europe's place in the world began to be diminished, and with hindsight we can see that since this time Europe has been engaged in self-wounding and self-destructive civil wars which weakened the European empires, making decolonization inevitable, and from which the Byzantine-Russian civilization, itself more advanced towards decay than Europe, has temporarily profited.

Since c.1880 (as we have seen) the Light has been missing from European religion (certainly Western-European religion), and the Central Idea of the European civilization has begun to be forgotten. The great majority of Europeans no longer believe that God as Light makes the crops grow, as a result of which Harvest

Festival has traditionally been celebrated, and that it affects everyday life in response to prayer. Many European stones were destroyed in the two world wars, and from 1947 to c.1975 the colonial peoples have seceded from the decolonizing European Empires. There has been foreign dominance; the eastern half of Europe was occupied by a foreign power for over forty years.

It is important to have a true understanding of Europe's role in the Western victory in the Cold War. Europe is traditionally defined as the western part of the Eurasian landmass; its westward limits run from the Norwegian Svalbard islands, the British Isles, the Danish Faeroes, Iceland, the Portuguese Madeira Islands and the Spanish Canary Islands, while its eastward limits extend south along the eastern foothills of the Ural Mountains, the Mugodzhar Hills, along the Emba River, the northern shore of the Caspian Sea, the Kumo-Manych Depression and the Kerch Strait to the Black Sea. Europe has always therefore included the Christian countries of Eastern Europe, many of which were Catholic (like Hungary and Poland). Eastern Europe was sandwiched between the Holy Roman Empire/Germany (the backbone of the European civilization which included Italy) and an expanding ex-USSR (of the Byzantine-Russian civilization), and was constantly squeezed between the two. It was the Western-European nations that built empires and which were on the receiving end of decolonization (stage 41); whereas for much of the 20th century the Eastern-European nations were in effect colonies, either of Austria (Hungary)/Germany (Poland, Czechoslovakia) within the European civilization, or of the ex-USSR within the Byzantine-Russian civilization, and their concern was freedom from colonization rather than the maintenance of any empires that were being decolonized. The second 20th-century civil war in Europe (1939-1945) accelerated this decolonizing stage, and it was initially fought to decide whether West-European Germany should colonize and absorb Poland and Czechoslovakia, which in 1938-9 Germany in effect regarded as little more than German colonies in Eastern Europe. (In the Great Power politics within the nation-state Europe of the late 1930s, Britain could not permit Hitler's racist Germany to expand into Eastern Europe, nor could the USSR.) The outcome was that the USSR (of the Byzantine-Russian civilization) moved in on Eastern Europe, including Poland and Czechoslovakia, and imposed the Communist system and economic stagnation, thereby colonizing Eastern Europe. The American and (Western) European civilizations counterposed their free market and democratic system, which they defended with NATO. They obstructed Soviet attempts to colonize, or extend influence in, Africa, Asia and Latin America.

In November 1990 the Cold War was officially declared at an end when the Heads of State of 22 NATO and six Warsaw Pact countries – including of course the American and Soviet Presidents – signed the first treaty for the reduction of conventional arms in Europe.

The Western victory in the Cold War cannot be regarded as a NATO triumph over the Warsaw Pact. It was a result of the ex-Soviet Union's poor economic performance under Communism in relation to America's and Western Europe's, which led to Gorbachev's political reforms; and of Eastern Europe's consequent decolonizing rejection of Communism and move towards West-European democracy near the end of stage 41. In other words, the victory was not so much a result of what the West had done, of any American or Western-European renewal; it was rather a result of what Eastern Europe had done, i.e. it was a consequence of an Eastern-European renewal. Western Europe cannot be said to have renewed its Central Idea/Light during this time – NATO merely held a line – whereas Eastern Europe can be said to have renewed *its* Central Idea through Christianity during its struggle against Soviet colonialism. In all the Eastern-European countries, but particularly in Hungary and Poland, Catholic Christianity has been strong and has played an important role in opposing Communism (especially under a Polish Pope), and it may well be that we now learn from Eastern-European sources that the Light was widely present in Eastern Europe in the 1980s, when television pictures showed huge congregations at churches in Eastern Europe. If so, then the European civilization has begun to renew itself by renewing its Central Idea of the Light in the decolonizing east, and by throwing off the Soviet occupation; and the next stage is for Eastern Europe to transmit its Light to Western Europe, which in turn may now renew its Central Idea of the Light during the gathering European Resurgence (or widening of the Western-European Community).

Meanwhile, Western Europe is still in decline, and Western Europe is only a missile's trajectory from a nuclear attack and from submitting to a foreign threat. The homegrown Christian Light has weakened before Communism and is found not in established Christianity, but in foreign cults (thought of as "New-Age", drawn from Hinduism, Buddhism and Sufism), whose influence in Europe is therefore a sign of European decline. There has been persecution of Christians by USSR

Communists, as we have seen, and there have been secessions to Communism and the foreign cults, and some of the New-Age groups are embryonic, potential coteries which can preserve the Christian religion. So far the Christian religion has not disappeared in Europe, and the Catholic Church seems to be holding its own following more than 25 years under a Polish Pope.

The symptoms of decline are to be found throughout Europe, but they are not far advanced. (Europe is after all only just entering stage 43.)

Europe is waiting to enter the conglomerate of stage 43. As we saw on p274, the Reform Treaty of 2007 replaced a constitution that would have involved Europe's member nations in loss of sovereignty to a superstate. A group of 16 elder statesmen (the Amato group) have found that the Treaty is substantially the same as the constitution but leaves aside the symbols of union (anthem, flag and the title of constitution). It seems that the member states *have* surrendered their sovereignty to a superstate. The conglomerate will take place at the instigation of the winner of Europe's colonial conflict.

It used to be thought that the coming European conglomerate would comprise an *economically* integrated, expanded American-backed European Union of nation-states linked as "a grand alliance of democracy" that would "stretch from the Atlantic to the Urals and beyond" (Margaret Thatcher, ex-Prime Minister of Britain, speaking in the presence of the West German Chancellor Helmut Kohl in March 1990), with the European Union, the USA and Canada forming a NATO-based free trade area and (possibly euro-based) currency regime that would include European Free Trade Area (EFTA) members and Hungary (as proposed by Margaret Thatcher and her adviser Sir Alan Walters in June 1990), with no loss of economic or political sovereignty for the nations concerned, and with states' nationalism discouraging political integration (i.e. not a true conglomerate).

An economically integrated European Community with a common currency would not by itself achieve a conglomerate of provinces or satrapies, such as we find in stage 43. An economic association is in fact a resistance to the coming stage 43, and merely delays its arrival. Britain's ex-Prime Minister Mrs Thatcher in her Aspen speech in the USA in August 1990 called for the European Community to include the emerging democracies of Eastern Europe. (She claimed that the Eastern-European nations have not escaped Communist centralization to pass into a centralized European Community, but it could be argued that only a Union with enhanced central control of financial resources would have sufficient power and flexibility to help the emerging East-European democracies). Mrs. Thatcher also called for the 35 nations of the Conference on Security and Co-operation in Europe to endorse a Magna Carta which would extend the principles of free trade, democracy and the rule of law into the former Communist bloc; and for the ex-Soviet Union to be included in the Group of Seven leading industrial nations, who would then become a Group of Eight (which has happened). These arguments stated a negotiating position in a British campaign to resist European economic and political union along the lines of the Delors plan. Despite its ill-fated decision to join the European Exchange Rate Mechanism (ERM), the attitude of the British Government under Margaret Thatcher towards Europe resembled an economic resistance to the coming stage 43.

There are several scenarios for the conquest of Europe by another power, e.g. by the ex-USSR or Islam (neither of which were the winner of the European colonial conflict); or America.

CONQUEST BY THE EX-USSR?

We need to see where the Byzantine-Russian civilization fits in. For as Eastern Europe was occupied by the Soviet Union, the future survival of Christianity in Eastern Europe is linked to the putting off of the Communist yoke, which happened following the fall of the Berlin Wall. If the Communist yoke on the Christians had lasted indefinitely, Eastern-European Christianity would have been in danger of disappearing. *Glasnost* and *perestroika* (i.e. freedom of speech and restructuring on the model of democracy) suggested that Christianity will survive within the ex-USSR but there is a sense in which until recently the future of European civilization hinged on the future attitude towards it of the ex-Soviet Union. The ex-Soviet Union can hold one of four positions, depending on whether hard-line conservatives or moderate reformers hold power:

1. The Cold War option: the ex-USSR will invade and absorb Western Europe, a possibility that has long been a Western (and NATO) nightmare.
2. The liberalising option: the USSR relaxed its grip on Eastern Europe, reduced the Cold War tensions by disarmament treaties and by accepting a reunified

Germany within NATO, but has preserved Party rule, struggling to retain its Muslim peoples within the ex-Soviet Republics and moving towards federalism while allowing more Orthodox expression and more human rights.

3. The Slavophile option: the ex-USSR will turn isolationist and restore her Orthodox, Byzantine, Russian identity, shedding all except the Slav republics and part of Kazakhstan, to achieve which there would have to be an anti-Communist challenge to the Party.

4. The pro-Western option: a part of the ex-USSR will allow itself to be absorbed – as has Eastern Europe – into a fully united Europe, or American-backed United States of Europe, in which Russia west of the Urals participates. This option carries the policy of Peter the Great to its extreme, and has been achieved by *glasnost* diplomacy and by Putin's pro-Western take-over of the Party leadership (which followed from the commitment to multi-party democracy of February 1990), and the Muslim republics in the south are set to join Europe – although some would prefer to join an Arab Union.

The world believes that, although his approach may have begun as a Communist exercise in deception whose liberalizing got out of control, Gorbachev excitingly chose option 2, the Chernobyl accident having changed his view of nuclear weapons, and that he moved away from the Communist conglomerate and union (stage 43) towards federalism for the Moscow-ruled nationalities.

Putin has sent out signals that he would like Russia to return to superpowerdom. He has opposed the US's siting of its missile defence system in Eastern Europe and has threatened to target Western cities with Russian missiles. He has planted the Russian flag under the ice in the waters of the North Pole to claim Arctic seabed oil. He had refused Britain's request to extradite a murder suspect. All these measures hint at a coming return of the Cold War.

If there were to be a return to the Cold War (option 1) and if under Putin's leadership some of the ex-USSR's republics were to invade and occupy a disarmed Europe, then the ex-Soviet Union would be the winner of the European civilization's colonial conflict, Europe's stage 43 would be a violent Communist occupation, Christianity in Europe would be suppressed by Communism, and there would be no renewal of the Light.

Despite Putin's blustering, it seems that option 2 and 4 have been pursued, and that the ending of the Soviet occupation of Eastern Europe opened the way for a renewal of Eastern Europe's Central Idea/the Light, which through Christianity and the visits to Poland of a Polish Pope addressing mass meetings in code, may well have already contributed to the Eastern-European countries' rejection of Communism, and thereafter a renewal of Western Europe's Central Idea/the Light. What is certain is that the European civilization can now be renewed and saved from total occupation by an outside foreign power.

The Slavophile option (option 3) was called for in September 1990 by Solzhenitsyn, who urged the dismantling of the USSR and the creation of a new state comprising the Slav republics and part of Kazakhstan. An Orthodox revival within the ex-USSR (option 3) has already happened, and, together with Putin's moves towards Europe at G8 meetings (option 4), has paved the way for the reunification of Christendom, with Catholic, Orthodox and Protestant Christians reunited in one fold. The public funeral of Pope John Paul II was an ecumenical service in which Orthodox ritual played a part.

Which option is the most likely in terms of the ex-USSR's position in the process of decay? The ex-USSR was 74 years in stage 43 (c.1917-1991), which could have been expected to last another 50-70 years if we go by other civilizations. The move by Gorbachev and then Yeltsin towards CIS/Russian Federation federalism for Russia's different nationalities brought about the end of stage 43 and the beginning of a federal stage 46, in which the different Moscow-ruled nationalities are now linked federally and are free from Communism.

The move towards federalism was accelerated by the election in May 1990 of Boris Yeltsin as the first President of the Russian Federation (the pre-1917 Russia), which comprised more than half the ex-Soviet Union's 280m people. This gave Yeltsin a power base from which to undermine Gorbachev's USSR authority (although by August 1990 Gorbachev had reached agreement with Yeltsin to establish a 30-man committee to draw up a new plan for Soviet economic reform). Yeltsin enacted laws that would strengthen Russian sovereignty and would take the heart of the Soviet Union out of Gorbachev's control; Yeltsin allied Russia with the Ukraine, the second largest republic in the Soviet Union which had also voted to become a neutral sovereign state with its own army and currency, and with Moldavia and Byelorussia, which did likewise; and challenged the implementation of Gorbachev's painful economic free market reforms and his resistance to secessions from the USSR, thereby accelerating the break-up of the stage 43 USSR into Russia and 14 smaller republics, which could be expected to be linked federally (stage 46). Some of Gorbachev's aides remarked that Yeltsin's appointment helped Gorbachev to "elaborate a new kind of Soviet Federation to replace the old style centralized Union" (the London *Times*, May 31, 1990, p8), i.e. to move from stage 43 to stage 46.

In June 1990 Gorbachev met Yeltsin and offered a new federal or confederal Soviet Union of decentralized sovereign republics which choose to delegate certain powers to the Union's central government instead of being cemented to the Union by the rule of Stalinist terror. *Pravda* commented, "The idea of confederation (i.e. a move to stage 46), totally unacceptable in previous years, is now being put forward by the President of the USSR." In November 1990 Gorbachev proposed, without success, that the USSR should become the Union of *Sovereign* (not Socialist) Soviet Republics, with the central government retaining many powers, a Federalist arrangement that would create a United States of Eurasia. The Baltic republics and Georgia said they would not agree to this arrangement. The new ex-USSR became less of a union than the stage 43 Communist conglomerate and more of a loose, federally linked network of independent states.

As the Byzantine-Russian civilization is more decayed than the European civilization by some 90 years (having passed into stage 43 in 1917 as opposed to Europe's 2008 – interestingly, the unification of the Byzantine-Russian civilization took place AD c.540, 260 years before Europe's), the ex-USSR republics are unlikely to invade and absorb Western Europe (option 1). Comparisons between the atheistic ex-USSR and the barbarian Germanic tribes, which had already begun to put aside Odin when they invaded and absorbed mighty Rome, do not hold as the Germanic tribes were at the time in stage 29 and younger than the Roman civilization, whereas the Byzantine-Russian civilization is now in stage 46 and older than European civilization. Liberalizing *glasnost* and *perestroika* (option 2) make the prospect of a Russian invasion of Europe look unlikely, although the spectre of starvation which the ex-USSR experienced in the winter of 1990 may tempt the post-Soviet leadership to solve its problems by reinvading Eastern Europe for its food and by seizing Middle Eastern oil. Europe, with the co-operation of the Russian Federation's leadership, has absorbed Eastern Europe and is absorbing Putin's Russian Federation (option 4) into a full USE (United States of Europe). In early

2004 the following ex-Soviet republics joined the EU: Poland, the Czech Republic, Hungary, Slovakia, Slovenia, Lithuania, Latvia and Estonia; and Romania and Bulgaria were expected to join by 2007. In 2003, in Yalta, Putin called for a common market that links the EU with Russia, the Ukraine, Kazakhstan and Belarus. In view of the growing federalism of the Russian republics (stage 46 of the Byzantine-Russian civilization) the largest sovereign Russian republics may remain separate from a United States of Europe while being economically associated with it. They may retain more internal autonomy (the norm for stage 46) than the Western-European nation-states (which are now entering stage 43). Such an autonomous federalism may sit easily with the Slavophile option (option 3), which may preserve Russia's independent destiny rather than give in to complete and overwhelming union with Europeanization and Westernization (which are more a feature of stage 43).

On balance, then, and using my parabolic analysis of Europe and the USSR to predict the coming pattern, it seems that the ex-USSR has chosen option 2, that the western ex-Soviet republics – especially those round the Caspian that export oil – have inclined to Europe (Gorbachev's "common European home") and a Western identity; and that autonomous federalism (stage 46) and greater freedom for formerly-Soviet Christians may result in a reunification of Orthodox Christianity with Catholic (and perhaps Protestant) Christianity. This would mean a renewal of the Light among Orthodox, Catholic and perhaps Protestant Christians, because such a European renewal could not happen without a renewal of the Light, according to our parabolic vision.

If I am right, the European West is not about to be swallowed up by a dominating ex-Communism (which was anyway not the winner of the colonial conflict), but has joined with Eastern Europe (which has for most of its history been under Byzantine, Ottoman, Habsburg or Russian rule, particularly the Balkans) and eventually some sovereign federalist Russian republics may form an association to link with an expanded Europe (in which Ireland is reunited) which includes both NATO and the Warsaw Pact countries, both Western and Eastern Europe: a United States of Western and Eastern Europe (perhaps USWEE for short). An ex-Soviet conquest of Europe is unlikely.

Conquest by Islam?

Despite 9/11 and the second American invasion of Iraq, and retaliatory al-Qaeda bombings in Madrid and London, conquest from Islam looks unlikely at present, although the break-up of the USSR and an American oil grab in the Caspian could set in motion the beginnings of a migration of Muslim peoples westward (such as the formerly Khanate Azerbaijanis who burned down their border with Iran and made war on Armenia in January 1990). Israel is a permanently festering issue. Arab countries may follow Libya's lead in demanding reparations from Europe for the period of colonial rule. It is interesting in this connection that Gaddafi sent boat-loads of Libyans to Italy to demand reparations from Italy for Italian colonial rule in Libya, which, he claimed, resulted in the death of 750,000 Libyans. (European historians put the figure at 175,000.) Gaddafi's action may anticipate future aggressive Arab demands against Europe.

The prospect of an Islamic threat to Europe has been brought closer by the Wahhabist Saudi extremism of Osama bin Laden following his attack on America on September 11, 2001. In 2005 bin Laden was (if not dead) apparently still at large, threatening *jihad* (Holy War). Although he presided over a secular State, similar rhetoric was heard from Saddam Hussein of Iraq, who in August 1990, after annexing Kuwait, called for a Holy War against the Western forces (the Americans and British) sent to protect Saudi Arabia, and against the "emirs of oil" in Saudi Arabia. He called for Mecca to be freed from foreign control and from what many in the Middle East saw as an anti-Islamic "Western crusade", language echoed by bin Laden. Saddam was known to want to re-establish Harun ar-Rashid's empire which extended from Morocco to the borders of India (786-809), and his appeal to Arab nationalism and Islamic Fundamentalism sent a shudder through the Arab leaders at the Cairo Summit of August 1990, 12 out of 20 of whom agreed to join a 10,000 strong pan-Arab force to defend Saudi Arabia against Iraq. One of Saddam's objectives was the conquest of Israel (something the Babylon-based Nebuchadrezzar, or Nebuchadnezzar, achieved three times, finally destroying Jerusalem and its temple in the 6th century BC), and after the annexation of Kuwait statements on Baghdad radio ended, "Here's to the day we all meet in Jerusalem." Statues of him showed an arm outstretched, pointing towards Jerusalem. As a result many people in the Arab world looked to Saddam as a new Saladin who would take Jordan and then liberate Palestine and Jerusalem just as Saladin expelled the Crusaders from the Holy Land. Saddam Hussein helped spread the myth that he would acquire nuclear weapons capable of threatening Southern Europe between 1993 and 1995, and therefore shared the responsibility for having his bogus nuclear/wmd programme stopped by force.

The chief threat to the European and North-American civilizations, then, is Islam, from a revivified, fanatical, nuclear-armed Arab civilization which is determined to eliminate Israel. (To capture Jerusalem has always been Gaddafi's aim, which is why he codenamed his 1969 Revolution "Palestine". It was also Saddam Hussein's aim.) Now it seems inconceivable, as Europe and North America are so much more technologically advanced than Islam, that Europe should fall to an Islamic occupier, to a westward push by the southern ex-Soviet Islamic hordes and to the coming Federation of Arab States, and that there would be a new Dark Age in the European civilization, whose conglomerate (stage 43) would be Islamic; and that Islam would turn out to be the winner of the European civilization's colonial conflict. Should Paris and London fall, it is likely that Western civilization would continue within the North-American civilization in America just as Roman civilization continued in Byzantium after the fall of Rome – provided America retains its Puritan vision of the Light; although if (as I do not believe) we are wrong in seeing the arrest of America's growth as taking place in 1861 at the hands of the "foreign" Confederacy, America herself may then suffer a military blow that will paralyse her growth for some 50 years (stages 13 and 14). It is worth pointing out – although of course the date does not fit our pattern – that 9/11 was not that blow as, far from paralyzing America, it stimulated America into victories in Afghanistan and Iraq.

The Arab Central Idea has weakened in some parts of the Arab world, but not in the countries where the *Koran* still has absolute sway, and not in Fundamentalist Iran or Libya. Although Islam is further along the road to decay than is younger Europe (stage 46 against stage 43), and although wars and fanatical martyrdom have distracted Islam from its Light and much of Islam is very secularized, Islam's religion is still a strength, especially since its revival of cultural purity (stage 45), and it can justifiably look down on the West as being more decadent than itself, a view Ayatollah Khomeini had. (Stage 46 involves a counter-thrust to restore an eroded past, and as in the Roman civilization c.540, the counter-thrust is accompanied by a religious revival which makes a stage-43 civilization under a secular conglomerate appear decadent.)

Despite his support for international terrorism, Col Gaddafi's Revolution, which prohibited Western alcohol and scrubbed all Western lettering off the streets of Tripoli, had a policy of forcing the West to decolonize that made sense from the point of view of resisting decay and the influence of Western decadence and restoring the Arab civilization's Central Idea. With nuclear weapons to neutralise Israel's nuclear weapons, Arab Islam could soon menace Europe in a way that has not happened since the Ottoman Turks moved against Vienna in 1683. In 1986 Col Gaddafi was attempting to manufacture nuclear weapons at a missile base near Sebha before the American bombing of Libya according to D. J. McForan's *The World Held Hostage*. In June 1990 Gaddafi made a speech on Libyan State Radio in which he urged Libya to become the first Arab power to acquire nuclear weapons. He exhorted Libyans to "work day and night to shorten time and intensify efforts to reach space and manufacture the atom bomb in defiance of America". Until the Gulf War, which began on January 16, 1991, Iraq was the most likely nation to be the next to acquire nuclear weapons according to the American CIA director. In 1990 Saddam had three sites for missile development, testing and production near Baghdad, a uranium mine in the north of Iraq and was building a uranium production plant, according to reports at the time; and an Iraqi businessman unsuccessfully attempted to smuggle 40 nuclear trigger devices from the US in March 1990. Unless Iraq had been stopped by the first Iraq war, between 1993 and 1995 Iraq could have expected to have intermediate range ballistic missiles capable of delivering 500 kilogram nuclear war heads that would menace much of Southern Europe. According to America's Defence Intelligence Agency Saddam Hussein planned to develop a nuclear bomb in early 1991 and to use the oil wealth of Iraq-Kuwait to develop intercontinental ballistic missiles that would threaten the U.K. and all Europe. We are sceptical about claims that nations have wmds now, but now that Libya has renounced nuclear ambitions and Iraq has been prevented from continuing to hold them attention has turned to Iran, which has defied UN resolutions and the IAEA to press on with its nuclear programme in Natanz and many other sites.

Stage 46 Islamic Fundamentalism looks to have as vital a Light as the stage 46 Orthodox peoples repressed under atheistic Lightless Communism, and it could be that America and Russia are reaching nuclear agreement and making nuclear treaties too late to prevent the Arab civilization from becoming widely nuclear. If the barbarian Goths could sack mighty Rome (in stage 29 of the Germanic-Scandinavian civilization), could not a neo-barbarian dictator (in Christian terms) threaten Europe with nuclear weapons? Could not such an Arab dictator eventually threaten to drop a nuclear missile on key Western capitals, including America's, unless Israel is dissolved and Jerusalem is returned to the Arabs?

Stage 43 which Europe is about to enter is full of violent occupiers who have obliterated or sacked cities. Islam (in stage 46, having been through occupation by the European powers) now looks poised to enter a Federation. Such an Arab confederation would begin with the creation of four blocs in the Arab world. They would consist of: the Gulf states, Iran, Iraq and the Kurds; Jordan, Syria and Palestine; Egypt, Libya and the Sudan; and Tunisia, Algeria and Morocco (the Mahgreb). The Arab Federation would eventually be a pan-Arab Federation of Arabia and the southern ex-USSR (Gaddafi's dream). During this stage, extremist Fundamentalist/Wahhabist Islam will be dangerous to Europe's stage 43 and to America.

Europe's stage 43 could be one of violent occupation – by Islam; in which case the Arab civilization would be the winner of Europe's colonial conflict. However, a stage-46 civilization has never swallowed a stage-43 one according to the law of my parabolic system – the younger always swallows the older in my law of history. In short, the occupation of Europe by Islam is unlikely as a stage-46 civilization does not occupy a stage-43 civilization (although nuclear weapons still make it a possibility).

GROWING AMERICA AND A UNITED STATES OF EUROPE

America has been largely free from the processes that have eroded Europe, being younger (at stage 15) and unoccupied. We have seen that America's unification was in 1787, and that it led to American expansion into the United States. We have seen that the American Light seems to have been renewed in the 20th century; Billy Graham has given missionary expression to the renewal in our time. American stones have not been destroyed; the American Central Idea is still strong with 38% attending American churches each week in 2001. America's inexhaustible religious vitality is evidenced by the fact that 68 new sects were founded in the 1950s and

184 in the 1960s. (By contrast, in Britain just 1.7% of the total population, 1m out of 58.8m, attended Church of England services every Sunday in 2003, and in France just 2% attended Mass on a Sunday during the 1990s.)[1] America is certainly more shallow than Europe and lacks Europe's intellectual complexity; young civilizations always seem shallow and unintellectual when contrasted with older civilizations. (The Greeks looked down on young Rome, as the Romans later looked down on young Byzantium.)

Nevertheless, we have seen that unless a new foreign power such as Islam conquers Europe and announces itself as the winner of Europe's 20th-century colonial conflict, globalist America (or its world-government masters) will inherit Europe's empires, and from the point of view of my parabola, the North-American civilization, more than any other living civilization, has much growth ahead and is poised for world leadership. The United States remains the world's dominant military power and has the world's most productive economy and the world's most creative culture (with GDP purchasing power parity of $11.75 trillion in 2004 against Japan's $3.745 trillion and West Germany's $2.362 trillion).[2] America has won the Cold War in the sense that as a result of the ex-Soviet Union's poor economic performance in relation to America's and Western Europe's, and of Eastern Europe's consequent rejection of Communism, the ex-Soviet Union made political changes which have given the appearance of democratizing the Communist system. As a result the Cold War's ideological conflict between Communism and the Western democratic, free market technological system has been settled, and as a result the world's model will be the American system. As we see from the American Roman-style punitive raid on Libya and invasions of Grenada and Panama, and, of course, the invasion of Afghanistan and two invasions of Iraq, America is now perceived as the world's leading power.

Saddam Hussein's invasion and annexation of Kuwait in August 1990 gave the US an issue and a theatre through which to continue her global role and protect Europe's interests. America signalled her willingness to give world leadership, when with ex-Soviet approval she acted as the sole remaining superpower and organized a world trade and arms embargo against Iraq and sent American ground troops and warplanes to defend Saudi Arabia (and US and European oil interests) against Iraqi attack. According to Pentagon officials the involvement reached 400,000 American troops, the highest such commitment since Vietnam, and the aim was ostensibly to force Saddam to leave Kuwait but in reality to overthrow him before he acquired nuclear weapons in 1992. It was a sign of America's global role that, like the Roman expeditions against Mithradates VI of Pontus (who launched two unsuccessful wars against the Romans from what is now the Ukraine), President Bush Sr should attempt to topple Saddam as a threat to vital long-term US interests (i.e. because he was a potential intimidating force from within OPEC who was on the verge of obtaining nuclear weapons and who would drive up oil prices, precipitating recession and worsening the American trade balance). At the same time America was able to take advantage of Europe's initially isolationist response to the crisis; for Britain aside, lacking a common foreign and defence policy Europe (notably Germany and to some extent France) ignored the threat to the oil on which Europe's economic strength depends, and was ready to shelter behind America's defensive umbrella, thus emphasising America's dominance in relation to Europe. Following 9/11 the US invasion of Afghanistan and the second Iraq war which finally overthrew Saddam in 2003 proved to be a re-run of US interventionism and European isolationism.

America has at different times been both isolationist and interventionist in the 20th century, and if America continues her world role and does not withdraw from Europe and NATO (assuming NATO still has a future), this world leadership can develop. In fact a Pentagon "defence planning guidance" document, still unpublished in February 1990, moved the focus from Europe to a more global setting emphasising long-range cruise missiles, B-2 bombers and aircraft carriers so that US forces can respond quickly anywhere in the world without depending on foreign bases. Bush Jr's expanding military budgets, his neo-con PNAC (Project for a New American Century) and his missile defence shield have all advanced US globalism (see *The Syndicate*). America has the rest of stage 15 – the stage of the first beginnings of the Roman Empire – ahead of her during which time a number of civilizations (the two Latin-American, Arab, Indian and African civilizations) can be expected to reach stage 49, when they will be occupied.

By a process of elimination I am left with a European conglomerate that is established at the instigation of the winner of Europe's colonial conflict, which in mid-2007 seems to be the US; in other words, an American-backed *politically* integrated German-dominated European Union stretching from the Atlantic to the Urals and from the Baltic to the Aegean, a European Resurgence or United States of

Europe (a concept first urged by Churchill in Zurich immediately after the Second World War). It will have a single currency, a European central bank, a common and foreign security policy and the principle of a constitution, and include much of the territories of five Empires (the Roman Empire, Charlemagne's Empire, the Holy Roman Empire, the Austro-Hungarian Empire and the Ottoman Empire). A federal system is one in which states form a unity but remain independent in internal affairs, whereas political integration assumes loss of internal independence and full-scale political union in Europe. A Reform Treaty containing most of the new European constitution, if ratified, would deliver the political union of twenty-five European nation-states. (Under the rules of the earlier constitution – see the constitution document, 'Declarations', no. 30 – if four-fifths of the members, i.e. 20 out of 25, ratified, then the Council of Ministers could decide to adopt the constitution even though up to five members – France and the Netherlands being two – had voted against.)

The movement towards European political integration has been strengthened by Europe's lack of a common foreign and defence policy, which initially paralysed the European response to the Kuwait crisis in August 1990. A common European defence policy would put an end to nationalistic ventures. To those who believe that Britain (along with the USA) used the Kuwait crisis and the alleged threat of Saddam as an excuse to return to the Gulf and appropriate Arab oil with a resurrected show of foolish imperialism, the coming European integration into a United States of Europe will end British (but not American) imperialism for ever, causing the two Iraq wars to be seen as the last gasp of British imperialism before the Arabs achieve federalism.

Under American guidance Europe took practical steps towards integration. In July 1990 at American instigation a historic 16-nation summit of NATO leaders extended friendship to the countries of Eastern Europe, "our adversaries in the Cold War", and reduced NATO's reliance on nuclear weapons – which will now be purely defensive "weapons of last resort" – in a transformation of the alliance that paved the way for a whole and free Europe "from the Atlantic to the Urals, and the Baltic to the Adriatic" (President Bush Sr's words). It was as a result of American diplomacy that soon afterwards Chancellor Kohl of Germany secured ex-Soviet agreement to a united Germany within NATO, in return for German financial aid for the ex-Soviet economy. European political integration would lead to a conglomerate of provinces or satrapies in keeping with stage 43, and it is not impossible that this would fall within a growing American Empire. (The American leadership of Europe was reaffirmed by the image of President Bush Sr uniting the Europeans, notably Britain and West Germany who were at loggerheads, at the NATO Summit of May 1989, and by the United States' vigorous support in early 1990 for German reunification. Bush was then determined to maintain a substantial American force in Europe even if the Warsaw Pact is completely dissolved, and the American-German alliance of 1989/90 may accelerate the constitutional framework for a United States of Europe. A new American Marshall-style Plan for the emerging democracies of Poland, Hungary, East Germany, Czechoslovakia and Romania, funded from savings in the nuclear arms budget, highlighted the American leadership of the new Europe.) In June 1990 European Community judges ruled in Luxembourg that British courts have the right to grant injunctions against the British Parliament's laws if they conflict with Community law, thus mounting a direct European challenge to national Parliamentary sovereignty. By 2005, over 70% of European legislation had passed from national parliaments to Brussels' centralized control.

Political union is the option the process of growth-decay suggests is the most likely but with associate status for the Russian Confederation which is in stage 46. This is the option seen by the British pro-Europeans like Edward Heath, who in effect looked forward to and welcomed stage 43; and the fall of Margaret Thatcher in November 1990 and the election of first Major and then Blair as British Prime Minister all opened up the prospect of greater European integration. However, as many civilizations that have entered stage 43 have been violently occupied, the option we have considered more likely is clearly – in terms of my parabolic process of growth and decay – linked to an American-inspired renewal of the Light which will renew the European civilization's Central Idea, and therefore its vitality and purposiveness, for a time, while further secularizing and therefore weakening Europe's religion of Christianity. (The conglomerate secularizes because it is set up through a foreign influence that is outside the civilization. However in this case the secularizing effect will be reduced because the American religion, Protestant Christianity, is close to the European religion, which is a mixture of Protestantism and Catholicism; although American Universalism will have a secularizing effect on European Christianity.)

Europe has passed stage 36, the stage when the Light ceases to be officially expressed by a decaying religion, but it has not yet reached stage 48, the stage by which the Light ceases to be publicly recognised by the religion – there are still fleeting references to it in Christianity – and it has certainly not reached stage 59, the end of the religion which precedes the end of the civilization. I see the Americans as establishers of a European conglomerate and conclude that unless the Light of the European civilization's Central Idea is renewed soon by the winner of the colonial conflict during this transitional period between stages 41 and 43, European religion will begin to wither, and European civilization may be occupied rather than – at the instigation of the winner of the colonial conflict – create a Resurgence, for the nature of the conglomerate (how violent or peaceful it is, how occupied or free) seems to depend on whether it is accompanied by a renewal of the Light.

I have identified the North-American civilization as the winner of Europe's colonial conflict and seen Europe's stage 43 as the triumph of the European Resurgence through an American-backed renewal of Europe's Light-based Christian Central Idea. If the invasion of the North by the Southern Confederacy in 1861 was not the arrest in American growth I believe it was, it may well be that the military blow which will arrest America's growth (stages 13 and 14) – assuming that this was not delivered by the North Vietnamese defeat of America in Vietnam in 1973, a few months after five men were arrested at the Democratic headquarters at the Watergate building in Washington – will come from Islam. I have said that 9/11 was not that blow as it did not arrest the US's expansion but had the opposite effect of goading the US on to military intervention in Afghanistan and Iraq. Islam looks like the deliverer of a military blow against Europe rather than an occupying power in Europe, but it remains to be seen whether the possession of nuclear weapons can reverse the historical pattern and enable a stage-46 civilization to conquer (by nuclear obliteration) a stage 43 one. Otherwise, the Arab civilization looks as though it could be occupied by the European conglomerate in the 21st century. The Arab civilization can be expected to reach stage 49 c.2100, and it could then be occupied by the North-American civilization.

A violent conquest of Europe by America seemed inconceivable in mid-2007; given America's relatively benevolent attitude towards Europe. We can discount a violent conquest of Western Europe by her American ally at present, although this may well happen in two centuries' time. A conquest of Europe by Germany is similarly inconceivable at present, given the Europeanism of the German outlook (although there are fears that Prussian militarism may again rear its head);[3] and both America and the ex-USSR favour limiting German military strength within NATO as the price of reunification. Conquest by China or Japan seems unlikely, even fanciful, in view of the distances involved and the current postures of China and Japan.

According to a study by the Pentagon discussed in March 1990 (a paper written by Peter Petersen, a Soviet expert on the staff of the American Defence Secretary), the ex-Soviet Union had then already resigned itself to a new map of Europe which in some measure reflected political union. It saw a "West European Confederation" comprising a united Germany, France, Spain and the Benelux countries, and two other power blocs which would be associated members of the European Community, a "Nordic Council" of the Baltic republics and Scandinavian countries, and a "Middle Europe Group" of the former Yugoslavia, Austria, Hungary and Czechoslovakia. Britain, Italy and Portugal would retain American bases and remain outside these groupings according to the study, which looked towards the year 2000 and not towards ultimate political integration into a stage-43 conglomerate or a revitalisation of Europe's Central Idea (the Light) that would strengthen links between the power blocs despite the secularizing nature of conglomerates. According to the study a Russian Confederation would become an associate member of the European Community, and this view was in keeping with the Byzantine-Russian civilization's being about to enter a federalist stage 46 in which some of the ex-USSR republics may be federally linked to Russia.

Russia attempted to pre-empt European political union by promoting its own version of a united Europe. In May 1990 the ex-Soviet Foreign Minister Edward Shevardnadze published an article in NATO's Sixteen Nations calling for the profound involvement of the US and Canada in a Greater Europe including a United Germany and both NATO and the Warsaw Pact. This statement amounted to a formal policy statement by the ex-Soviet Union, and proposed the transformation into a structured organization of the 35-member Conference on Security and Co-operation in Europe, which was set up in Helsinki in 1975 for all the European states except Albania and which included the US and Canada. The proposal ran somewhat counter to the European Community's drive for political union with increased powers for a European Parliament, but the NATO summit of July 1990 agreed to the widening of the Conference on Security and Co-operation in Europe into a forum for political dialogue and saw the CSCE as becoming "more prominent in Europe's future, bringing together the countries of Europe and North America".

China has replaced Japan as the economic superpower of our time. China is now expanding economically at an unprecedented rate. Both China and Japan entered stage 43 around the same time (Japan in 1945, China in 1949). During the 1960s and 1970s Japan became richer than the USA in assets and controlled South-East Asia economically. Japan (now in stage 43) has a revived Shinto Central Idea strong enough to dominate the funeral of Emperor Hirohito in 1989 and make his son a "living god". In November 1990 the Emperor Akihito communed with the gods of Heaven and Earth in the shamanistic Shinto rite of *daijosai* (Great Food Offering), in the course of which he walked between Heaven and Earth under a white sedge canopy and on rush matting, like a shaman. He then met his ancestress Amaterasu, the sun goddess, on a "god bed" of pressed straw mats. (Historically the Emperor made symbolic love to the sun goddess to become one with the divine.)

There is already an inkling of what I have detected in the East. A view is already abroad that the future is in the East. The European peoples are reuniting, including the deeply religious peoples who have broken away from the ex-Soviet Empire, and press articles suggest that the process is being covertly resisted by the American and British governments on the grounds of materialistic self-interest. The view has been spread abroad that America is declining from a global power into a regional power, that America's huge budget deficits will make others the paymasters of Europe. I have already disagreed with this view. The North-American civilization wants a United States of Europe, which it has funded, as an important bloc in its coming world rule; and emerging nationalism, with "terrorist" nationalists threatening to seize nuclear weapons, will create dangerous situations ahead that will give the US good reason to remain a global power. Nevertheless, regardless of the life that is left in the West – and the future is American as the North-American civilization is poised for world rule in its global phase – the day of the East is undoubtedly coming, and the souls of spiritually powerful Eastern Europeans, Chinese and Japanese, who have been tempered by suffering, are far closer to mysticism than are the vast majority of souls that have been anaesthetised in the comfort and luxury of the materialistic West. (Indeed, it can be maintained that the West has been kept alive by the few active souls of contemplative mystics who have resisted the passive, hedonistic climate in which, to their discomfort, they have been obliged to spend their days.)

MORE DETAILED PREDICTIONS FOR SURVIVING CIVILIZATIONS

The above general reflections and observations enable us to project the future from the present with greater precision.

On the basis of a practical view of the present as absorbed through the media, I expect:

11. Europe to continue her decline (as manifested by the 1930s depression, decolonization, the Cold War, the 1971-3 oil crisis between two nuclear superpowers), and, now that there is only one superpower, to form an extended European Union by 2008 that will be a full United States of Europe in all but name, with a common political authority;

12. America to continue running a world trading empire based on the free market economy and extending throughout the world by virtue of her sea-power and her dominance of the Pacific – since 1980 American trade with the Pacific zone has exceeded American trade with Western Europe – and to continue the creation of regional blocs (the Free Trade Area of the Americas, the European Union, the African Union, the Middle East, Asia and the Pacific) which may become federated into a world federation under America, although her world hegemony has resulted in a budget deficit;

13. Byzantine-Russia to continue running a federated ex-Soviet empire of western republics associated with the EU, retaining strong links with ex-Soviet territories in Eastern Europe and the Balkans, and a looser federation of eastern republics, all of which will be associated with the European Union;

15/16. South America to continue within the Free Trade Area of the Americas but in mounting economic crisis with huge debts, until it eventually passes into a world federation;

17. Arab Islam to continue her upsurge of anti-modernizing (i.e. anti-Westernizing) Fundamentalism (Gaddafi, Khomeini, the Muslim Brotherhood) which was the response to decolonization by traditional societies in the shadow

of the two nuclear superpowers, and to continue to agitate against (albeit a de-settling) Israel, until it passes into a regional bloc, a United States of the Middle East, and eventually a world federation;

18. Africa to remain under the domination of the US superpower, which seeks African oil, while passing into the African Union of 2002 and eventually into a world federation, while continuing to struggle against starvation (e.g. in Ethiopia and the Sudan);

19. India to continue running a federated ex-union – her stage-43 union which broke up, shedding Pakistan on independence – and to remain underdeveloped although free from famine until it eventually passes into a world federation;

20. South-East Asia to continue its federated bloc under the domination of the US superpower, through ASEAN and later through an Asian Economic Community or Pacific Union, until it eventually passes into a world federation;

21. Japan to continue as a federated bloc following her economic growth of the 1960s and 8% annual growth between 1973 and 1981 under the domination of the US superpower, through ASEAN and later through an Asian Economic Community or Pacific Union, until it eventually passes into a world federation;

22. Oceania, i.e. the S. Pacific, to continue the federated economic progress of Australia and New Zealand in a Federation or Confederacy of Oceania, until it eventually passes into a world federation;

23. China to continue to control her territory and, subject to the new policy of June 1989, to change cautiously towards more realistic and pragmatic policies and, after challenging the North-American civilization, to break up into a con-federation (stage 46) and through ASEAN take part in an Asian Economic Community or Pacific Union until it eventually passes into a world federation;

24. Tibet to continue as part of China (which it essentially is not) until China's union breaks up, and to form part of a new Chinese confederation until it even-tually passes into a world federation;

25. Central Asia to continue as part of China and the USSR (which it essential-ly is not) until China's union breaks up, and to form part of a new Chinese con-federation until it eventually passes into a world federation.

My analysis of the process of growth and decay suggests that in the 21st centu-ry (the short term) the following specific trends are likely:

11. Europe will expand into a politically integrated European Union that revives the Roman, Carolingian, Holy Roman, Austro-Hungarian and Ottoman Empires, at first partially and later possibly fully, and may absorb part of Western Russia (which would leave the ex-Soviet federalist structure);

12. Assuming that America suffered an arrest of growth in 1861, America will found a world empire like the Roman Empire (which also grew in stage 15) after the world's regions have been divided into two blocs, a Western American-led bloc and an Eastern Chinese-led bloc, and out of the dialectic between these two blocs will emerge an American-led world government as China passes from stage 43 (conglomerate) to stage 46 (federal linkage);

13. Russia's ex-Soviet empire has turned federalist (stage 46) and lost Eastern Europe, its maritime Empire and the Asian territories, but it will retain its links with the Eurasian ex-USSR republics and will be linked with Europe;

15/16. South America will continue its economic decline and federation to the Free Trade Area of the Americas, and will be absorbed and occupied by America within an American Union;

17. The Arabs will form a pan-Arab Federation of Arabia (and perhaps of the southern ex-Soviet Islamic states) or Arab Union before going into economic decline and passing into a world federation;

18. Africa will form a pan-African Federation of Africa or African Union before going into economic decline, being occupied and passing into a world federation;

19. India will continue its pan-Indian Federation of India before going into economic decline and passing into a world federation;

20. South-East Asia will form a pan-South-East-Asian Federation of South-East Asia, and enter a Far-Eastern or Pacific Community or Asian-Pacific Union under American influence;

21. Japan will continue to expand into Empire and enter a Far-Eastern or Asian Economic Community, and a Pacific Community or Asian-Pacific Union, an Eastern civilization (in its present stage 43);

22. Oceania will form a Federation of Oceania or of the South Pacific and enter a Pacific Community or Asian-Pacific Union;

23. China will continue to run the Communist conglomerate (in stage 43) until it turns federalist (stage 46) and eventually enters a Far-Eastern or Pacific

Community or Asian-Pacific Union under America's influence (stage 46);

24. Tibet will escape from the Chinese Communist conglomerate and join a regional bloc (a Far-Eastern or Pacific Community, or Asian-Pacific Union);

25. Central Asia will escape from the influence of the Communist conglomerates (stage 46) and part will join a Federation of Central-Asian states which may be a Federation of Arab and Islamic states and will enter a Far-Eastern or Pacific Community or Asian-Pacific Union under America's influence; some Central-Asian peoples will move westwards as invading Turkic hordes, will be checked by Europe and will be occupied (perhaps by Americans).

On the basis of my summary I can predict that the following specific developments are likely in the 22nd century (the long term):

1. The Federation of Arabia (and perhaps the southern ex-Soviet Islamic states) (stage 46 of the Arab civilization, Gaddafi's dream) will be occupied by an expanded European Union/Israel with American help after a westward invasion of Europe;

2. The American-influenced politically integrated European Union or United States of Europe (stage 43 of the European civilization) will recover its vision of the Light and will be strong enough in its Central Idea to repel the Islamic invasion; it will occupy the Arab/Islamic civilization (in stage 49 of the Arab civilization) in conjunction with Israel, and Europe will then cover all the territory once possessed by the Roman Empire;

3. America will continue to expand into a world empire (in stage 15) that includes a federally-linked Europe (when in stage 46), Arabia (when in stage 49) and Western Russia (when further advanced in stage 46), which will have broken away from the confederation of ex-Soviet republics and joined an expanded European Union, and which will be controlled by the USA; America's empire will also include South America (when in stage 49), India (when in stage 49), Africa (when in stage 49) and all other blocs which will form part of a world federation;

4. The Chinese and Japanese civilizations, having formed a Far-Eastern or Pacific Community or Asian-Pacific Union that will include South-East Asia, Oceania, Tibet and Central Asia, an "Eastern civilization", will be occupied by

America and form part of a world federation.

In the past the average length of stage 43 was 150 years, of stage 46 was 100 years, of stage 49 and stage 52 were each 75 years, and of stage 53 was 150 years. However, global communications may have shortened – perhaps halved – the length of these stages as the Soviet conglomerate lasted 74 years (stage 43). If we stick to the pattern of the past bearing in mind this *caveat*, then we can put an approximate time-scale (accurate to within 50 years) on the immediate prospects of each civilization as follows:

Civilization	c.2000-c.2050	c.2050-c.2100	c.2100-c.2150	c.2150-c.2200	c.2200-c.2250	c.2250-c.2300
11. European	European Resurgence (political integration) under American inspiration (stage 43)	→	→	federally linked under America (stage 46)	→	occupied by (probably non-American) foreign invader (stage 49)
12. North-American	American world expansion (stage 15) – Europe & other blocs	American world expansion (stage 15) – blocs including Latin America	→	American world government – Europe & Russia, Arabia	→	decline of religion (stage 19)?
13. Byzantine-Russian	post-Communist federalism	federally linked with	→	occupied by American	independent phase	→

	(stage 46)	Europe (stage 46)		world government (stage 49)	(stage 52)	
15. 16.	Andean & Meso-American	continuation of stage 46	occupied by American Union within American world rule (stage 49)	independent phase (stage 52)	→	occupation by foreign power (stage 53)	→
17.	Arab	Federation of Arabia (stage 46)	→	occupied by Europe with American help (stage 49)	occupied by America	independent phase (stage 52)	occupation by foreign power (stage 53)
18.	African	Federation of Africa (stage 46)	→	occupied by America? (stage 49)	independent phase (stage 52)	→	occupation by foreign power (stage 53)
19.	Indian	independent federal India/ Pakistan (stage 46)	occupied by Asian-Pacific Union within American world rule	independent phase (stage 52)	→	occupation by foreign power (stage 53)	→

(stage 49)

| 20. | S.-E.-Asian | Federation of S.-E. Asia (stage 46) | occupied by Far-Eastern or Asian-Pacific Union within American world rule (stage 49) | indepen-dent phase (stage 52) | → | | occupation by foreign power (stage 53) | → |

| 21. | Japanese | Union of Japanese provinces or prefectures (political integration) (stage 43) | Japanese provinces federally linked to American world Empire via Asian-Pacific Union (stage 46) | → | occupied by American world govern-ment (stage 49) | indepen-dent phase (stage 52) | → |

| 22. | Oceanian | Federation of Oceania or South Pacific (stage 46) | → | occupied by American world govern-ment (stage 49) | indepen-dent phase (stage 52) | → | occupa-tion by foreign power (stage 53) |

| 23. | Chinese | Commun- | federally | → | occupied | indepen- | → |

		ism (stage 43) turns federalist (stage 46)	linked to Far-Eastern or Pacific Community or Asian-Pacific Union with Japan (stage 46)		by world govern-ment (stage 49)		dent American (stage 52)		phase
24.	Tibetan	Chinese Commun-ism (stage 43)	federally → linked to Far-Eastern or Pacific Community or Asian-Pacific Union with China (stage 46)		occupied by American world govern-ment (stage 49)		indepen- → dent phase (stage 52)		
25.	Central-Asian	federally linked to Comm-unist con-glomerate & perhaps Feder-ation of Arab & Islamic states (stage 46)	occupied by Europeans, later Americans while federally linked to Asian-Pacific Union (stage 49)		indepen- → dent phase (stage 52)		occupation → by foreign power (stage 53)		

I am now in a position to restate my "predictions of next stages" with a sharpened view of the occupiers, and with more precise dates:

Living civilizations	Stage they are now at	Prediction of next stages
11. European	42/43	End of colonial conflict (stage 42); loss of national sovereignty to secularizing conglomerate c.2008-2150 (expanded & fully politically integrated European Union from c.2008) (stage 43); syncretism of the Universalist vision from c.2000 (stage 44); revival of cultural purity & glorification of the medieval mystical vision in a new Classical/ Baroque movement (stage 45); federation of independent European nation-states free from the European conglomerate but federally linked to American global power, c.2150-2250 (stage 46); economic decline (stage 47); absence of the Light (stage 48); occupation by (probably non-American) foreign invader c.2250-2325 (stage 49)
12. North-American	15	Continuing counter-thrust, a global expansion into empire with a possibility of world government c.2000-2250 (stage 15); epic poetry (stage 16); creation of a Light-based heretical New-Age sect (stage 17); resistance to it (stage 18); decline of religion c.2250 (stage 19); attempted renewal by mystics (stage 20); military blow c.2400 (stage 21); breakdown of civilization c.2400-2500 (stage 22)

13.	Byzantine-Russian	46	Movement away from loss of national sovereignty to secularizing conglomerate of Communism and loss of E.-European Empire & maritime Empire of client-states, & with independence for much of Central Asia c.1991-2050 (stage 43); continued syncretism of the Universalist vision (stage 44); continued revival of cultural purity of pre-Leninist past which began c.1988 & coming glorification of the Russian Byzantine medieval mystical Hesychast vision (stage 45); independent federalist Russian republics free from the Communist conglomerate & linked to or partly linked to a politically integrated European Community c.1991-2150 (stage 46); economic decline (stage 47); absence of the Light (stage 48); occupation by American world government c.2150-2225 (stage 49); destruction of Russian stones, i.e. churches (stage 50); secession of Russian peoples from the American occupier & from Russian civilization, causing cultural disintegration (stage51); independent phase c.2225-2300 (stage 52); occupation by foreign power, from c.2300 (stage 53)
15.	Andean &	46	Continued federalism within the Organization of American States/Free Trade Area of the Americas and American Union under N.-American influence (stage 46); economic decline of Latin America (stage 47); absence of the Light (stage 48); occupation of Latin America by American invader c.2050-2125 (stage 49);
16.	Meso-American		

destruction of Latin America's stones, i.e. churches (stage 50); secession of Latin-American peoples from the North-American occupier & from the Andean/Meso-American civilizations, causing cultural disintegration (stage 1); final independent phase c.2125-2200 (stage 52); occupation by foreign power c.2200-2350 (stage 53)

| 17. Arab | 46 | Independent Arab nation-states' expansion into empire through federalism (e.g. pan-Arab union) funded by oil wealth & embracing the Middle East, Iran, the southern states of the ex-Soviet Union & N. Africa c.1980-c.2100 (stage 46); economic decline of Arab world (stage 47); absence of the Light from Islamic religion (stage 48); occupation of Arab world by European invader c.2100-2175 & by America from c.2125 (stage 49); destruction of Arab stones, i.e. mosques (stage 50); secession of Arab peoples from the American occupier & from the Arab civilization, causing cultural disintegration (stage 51); final independent phase c.2175-2250 (stage 52); occupation by foreign power c.2250-2400 (stage 53) |

| 18. African | 46 | Independent African nation-states' expansion into empire through federalism (e.g. pan-African union, i.e. African Union of 2002) after the end of white rule in South Africa c.1980-2100 (stage 46); economic decline of Africa (stage 47); absence of the Light from African religion following the |

receding of Christianity (stage 48); occupation of Africa by American invader c.2100-2175 (stage 49); destruction of African stones, i.e. churches & mosques (stage 50); secession of African peoples from the American occupier & from the African civilization, causing cultural disintegration (stage 51); final independent phase c.2175-2250 (stage 52); occupation by foreign power c.2250-2400

19. Indian	46	Continued independent federal India/Pakistan's expansion into empire with federally linked regions c.1947-2050 (stage 46); economic decline of India (stage 47); absence of the Light from Hindu religion (stage 48); occupation of India by foreign invader (America via China/ Japan of Asian-Pacific Union) c.2050-2125 (stage 49); destruction of Indian stones, i.e. temples (stage 50); secession of Indian peoples from the foreign occupier & from Indian civilization, causing cultural disintegration (stage 51); final independent phase c.2125-2200 (stage 52);occupation by foreign power c.2200-2350
20. S.-E.-Asian	46	Independent S.-E.-Asian nation-states' expansion into empire through federalism (e.g. S.-E.-Asian union or membership of an expanded Pacific Community or regional bloc, an Asian-Pacific Union) c.1950-2050 (stage 46);economic decline of S.-E. Asia (stage 47); absence of the Light from S.-E.-Asian Buddhism (stage 48); occupation of S.-E. Asia by foreign invader (American world rule via

Far-Eastern or Pacific Community, Asian-
Pacific Union) c.2050-2125 (stage 49);
destruction of S.-E.-Asian stones, i.e. temples
(stage 50); secession of S.-E.-Asian peoples
from the foreign occupier & from S.-E.-Asian
civilization, causing cultural disintegration
(stage 51); final independent phase c.2125-
2200 (stage 52); occupation by foreign
power c.2200-2350 (stage 53)

| 21. Japanese | 43-45 | Continued loss of national sovereignty to secularizing American-influenced conglomerate with possible creation of an expanded Pacific Community or Asian-Pacific Union, a regional bloc ahead c.1945-2050 (stage 43); continued syncretism of the Universalist vision (stage 44); revival of cultural purity & continued glorification of the traditional Shinto, Buddhist & Zen-Buddhist vision (stage 45); independent federally linked Japanese regions free from the Pacific conglomerate federally linked to American world Empire c.2050-2150 (stage 46); economic decline (stage 47); absence of the Japanese Light (stage 48); occupation by American world government c.2150-2225 (stage 49); destruction of Japanese stones, i.e. temples (stage 50); secession of Japanese peoples from the American occupier & from Japanese civilization (stage 51); final independent phase c.2225-2300 (stage 52); occupation by foreign power c.2300-2450 (stage 53) |

| 22. Oceanian | 43 | Imminent end of loss of Oceanian islands' |

national sovereignty to secularizing
conglomerate (Western colonization, e.g.
Australia and New Zealand with Queen as Head
of State) (stage 43); syncretism of the
Universalist vision (stage 44); revival of
cultural purity & glorification of the traditional
Oceanian shamanistic religion (& of Aborigines
& Maoris) (stage 45); independent Oceanian
nation-states free from the Western
conglomerate's sovereignty & creating a
unified Federation of Oceania or Federation
or Confederacy of the South Pacific, including
Australia & New Zealand c.2006-2100
(stage 46); economic decline (stage 47);
absence of the Oceanian Light (stage 48);
occupation by a foreign invader (American
world rule via Far-Eastern or Pacific
Community or Asian-Pacific Union) c.2100-
2175 (stage 49); destruction of Oceanian
stones, i.e. temples & churches (stage 50);
secession of Oceanian peoples from the foreign
occupier & from Oceanian civilization (stage
51); final independent phase c.2175-2250 (stage
52); occupation by foreign power c.2250-2400
(stage 53)

23. Chinese	43	Continued loss of sovereignty of Chinese

nationalities to the secularizing conglomerate
of Communism c.1949-2020/2050 (stage
43); syncretism of the Universalist vision
(stage 44); revival of cultural purity & coming
glorification of the traditional Confucianist-
Taoist & Buddhist mystical vision (stage 45);
an independent federalist China with federally

linked regions & nationalities free from the Communist conglomerate & perhaps eventually linked to an expanded Pacific Community in which S.-E. Asia & Oceania are provinces, along with the super-power Japan c.2020/2050-2150 (stage 46); economic decline (stage 47); absence of the Light (stage 48); occupation by American world government c.2150-2225 (stage 49); destruction of Chinese stones, i.e. temples (stage 50); secession of Chinese peoples from the American occupier & Chinese civilization (stage 51); final independent phase c.2225-2300 (stage 52); occupation by foreign power c.2300-2450 (stage 53)

| 24. Tibetan | 43 | Continued loss of national Tibetan sovereignty to the Chinese Communist conglomerate c.1951-2020/2050 (stage 43); syncretism of the Universalist vision (stage 44); revival of cultural purity & glorification of the traditional Tibetan-Buddhist mystical vision (stage 45); an independent Tibetan nation-state free from the Communist conglomerate but in a regional bloc (Pacific Community dominated by Japan?) c.2020/2050-2150 (stage 46); economic decline (stage 47); absence of the Light (stage 48); occupation by American world government c.2150-2225 (stage 49); destruction of Tibetan stones, i.e. temples (stage 50); secession of Tibetan peoples from the American occupier & Tibetan civilization (stage 51); final independent phase c.2225- |

		2300 (stage 52); occupation by foreign power c.2300-2450 (stage 53)

25.	Central-Asian	46	A Central Asia under Russian & Chinese influence & later linked to a Federation of Arab & Islamic states c.1911-2050 (stage 46); economic decline (stage 47); absence of the Light (stage 48); occupation by Europeans, & later Americans (or Far-Eastern or Pacific Community or Asian-Pacific Union) c.2050-2125 (stage 49); destruction of C.-Asian stones (stage 50); secession of C.-Asian peoples from the foreign occupier & from C.-Asian civilization, causing cultural disintegration (stage 51); final independent phase c.2125-2200 (stage 52); occupation by foreign power c.2200-2350 (stage 53)

From the above we can see that if my premises are correct, America will dominate the history of the next 300 years, and that her chief rival will be China. It seems that c.2250 will be a turning point in world fortunes as America's religion declines and Europe is occupied by a new power which may eventually deliver the military blow that causes American breakdown.

Looking further ahead, on chart 3 (the 61 stages – see p532) I have averaged future stages in the round figures of a bank manager's projections (e.g. 150 years for stages 43, 53 and 58, 100 years for stage 46, and 75 years for stages 49 and 52) and I have projected the living civilizations forward to their demise. This exercise shows that I would expect the European civilization to continue until c.2725, the date our round figure averaging projects it will reach stage 61.

6. THE FUTURE OF WESTERN CIVILIZATION

A superficial experience of the European and North-American civilizations does not give the feeling that the West is in decline. The material benefits of the North-

American and European civilizations are enjoyed all round the world; is that not a sign of vitality? The young North-American civilization (now at stage 15) does not show any of the signs of exhaustion and lack of spiritual energy which augurs a civilization's collapse. Christian meditation groups are springing up in both America and Europe, and there are numerous other groups and religious sects within the West which are potentially capable of supplying the Light (the vision of God) which Western civilization needs to survive, even if they are not supplying it to the European civilization at present, preferring (mainly in Europe) existence within a secessionist coterie "alternative culture" (the New-Age movement) to putting their Light back into the Christian civilization.

However, *a civilization begins to disintegrate*, we have seen, *when its vision of the Light disappears*, leaving a secular Age of the Body. It is obviously serious that in Europe the Christian religion is not communicating and interpreting the experience of the Light as it used to – this is tantamount to saying that the European civilization's religion has ceased to communicate the vision and experience of God, its Central Idea – and that it has therefore lost its original *raison d'être*. Since the Second World War, the European Christian West has clearly lost its metaphysical vision and turned secular.

THE WEAKENED METAPHYSICAL VISION OF EUROPE

The European metaphysical vision was first weakened by the post-Humanist philosophy, and the Tradition of the Light has been ignored by virtually the whole of post-Renaissance philosophy, but not by the poets.

Ever since the outset of the Scientific Revolution the poets have warned against the folly of allowing scepticism to erode the metaphysical vision. The Christian poet John Donne (later Dean of St. Paul's) wrote in 1611, "And new Philosophy (i.e. scepticism) calls all in doubt,/The Element of fire is quite put out." Blake echoed this in 1803: "If the Sun and Moon should doubt/They'd immediately go out." In 1802 Blake referred to the single vision of scepticism, materialism and Humanism, which had been strengthened by the Scientific Revolution, as "Newton's sleep". (Ironically, Newton spent the last thirty years of his life seeking an expanding, creative force in the universe which balances gravity, and he ended his life very much on the side of metaphysics.) It is now apparent that the Era of

Humanism can be seen as a secularization of European civilization's Central Idea, the Light, which, like fire and the sun, has not been "put out" by doubting philosophers, and T. S. Eliot has borne contemporary witness to the poet's metaphysical role.

Today there are many symptoms of secularization and cultural disintegration in Europe. The weakening of unifying Christianity in parts of Europe (for example, in Britain), as opposed to the United States, has had loosening effects. Classes and groups have separated and fragmented. The metaphysical, philosophical, religious and artistic sensibilities have generally been divorced, except in a few luminaries like Eliot. The arts and the sciences have largely separated, a process C. P. Snow protested at in his *Two Cultures* (which was a scientist's attack on artists' ignorance of scientific developments). Knowledge has become specialised, and few have the panoramic vision to attempt its reunification. Today, all Western people share a popular, materialistic-consumeristic "television culture". While this claims to reflect the culture of each class, it inevitably inclines towards proletarian culture in the interests of mass communication. At its worst, the result is a kind of secularized LCM that appeals to all, trivializing and vulgarizing to retain viewers' attention and, as F. R. Leavis saw, encouraging passivity, apathy and sloth.

THE LIGHT AS THE SAVIOUR OF EUROPEAN CIVILIZATION

We have seen that Europe is poised to enter stage 43, and that the Light, which generally disappeared from Christianity in stage 36, is set to be completely absent from the civilization, whose Central Idea it provides, by stage 48. We have seen that European civilization's Central Idea is not democratic freedom and the entrepreneurial spirit; these are rather consequences of a once vigorous Central Idea which emphasised the freedom to approach God. I have concluded that Europe can either be violently occupied (most possibly by Islamic hordes who would then be the winner of Europe's colonial conflict), like many other civilizations that have entered stage 43, or else (our preferred view) renew her Christian Central Idea through a renewal of the Light by the stage-15 American winner of Europe's colonial conflict, and, her vitality and sense of purpose renewed for a while, bring about the European Resurgence, the revival of five Empires which I have seen ahead. We have seen that although conglomerates secularize because the winner of the colonial conflict generally has a different religion or religious approach from that of the stage 43 civilization, the secularizing effect of an American-backed conglomerate will be reduced as the North-American and European civilizations both share forms of Christianity; although the growing American heresy of Universalism, which will become the orthodoxy in stage 27 of the North-American civilization, *will* have a secularizing effect on European Christianity.

Observing the process of approaching decay, we may feel that as Lightlessness is going to happen anyway, the demise of European civilization is ultimately inevitable (possibly around 2725 according to my projections), and that consequently a certain detachment (i.e. studied indifference) is required. With the prospect ahead of Europe's declining from stage to stage, it may seem meaningless to think of "saving" our civilization as in one sense no civilization can be "saved" from reaching stage 61 (when it will pass under the Light of a new, growing civilization).

A civilization can, however, be protracted, and certain stages within it can be prolonged. The Byzantines, for example, prolonged their stage 15 for nearly 400 years, during which time they continued to receive the Light, whereas another civilization might have passed on from stage 15 within 150 years. The European civilization can be expected to last 700 years more, but not in its present form at its present stage, with its present values and freedoms. As the disappearance of the Light of its Central Idea will promote the decay of European civilization as we know it, it is vital that the Light of the European civilization's Central Idea should be prevented from becoming completely absent for as long as possible. Stage 48, in other words, should be resisted in good time, and not ushered in. (It is worth noting that an extreme political conservatism resists the change that brings in the next stage and attempts to put the clock back to the previous stage, reversing what has happened in the meantime, while a less extreme form – liberalism – welcomes the next stage in.)

More immediately, as Europe faces violent conquest by a foreign occupier such as the Arab civilization, which may turn aggressive towards Europe, and by related Islamic hordes seceding from the federation of southern ex-USSR republics, or a more peaceful passage to its stage 43 conglomerate through the European Resurgence as a result of the youthful stage 15 North-American civilization's

Christian and Universalist Light and potentiality to bring about a renewal of Europe's Central Idea (an alternative scenario for stage 43), I can meaningfully say that Europe can be saved from being violently occupied by Islam (so that she can pass into a politically integrated American-backed Resurgence) if she opens herself to American vitality and a Universalist, New-Age vision of the Light, and strengthens her metaphysical vision and therefore *recovers her belief in her civilization's Christian Central Idea*, i.e. all that is valuable and needs defending, because then the European resolve will be firmer and affect the outcome. In other words, *a civilization's survival is largely a question of self-belief*, and a weakened metaphysical vision, no matter how much it bristles with secular armies and weapons, lacks belief in its civilization's Central Idea and will eventually attract foreign conquest (as will the still officially beliefless Byzantine-Russian civilization unless it fully recovers its belief in Christianity), whereas a strengthened Light, also reinforced with armies and the missiles and trappings of defence, has belief in its civilization's Central Idea and destiny and will resist conquest by a foreign civilization during the conglomerate stage (stage 43). A European civilization confident in its own metaphysical Christian Central Idea and spirit will have the determination to resist a culturally pure Arab/Islamic civilization which has a fanatical devotion to Islam in a way that it would not if it merely looked to its democratic and entrepreneurial freedom, which is essentially materialistic.

Today, European civilization needs to recover the common metaphysical vision of its religion if it is to find the resolve and belief in its own value that will achieve the American-backed European Resurgence in stage 43 rather than be violently occupied. Implicit support for such a view, and for the general principle of our parabolic vision, comes from T. S. Eliot, who agrees with the historian Arnold Toynbee that if the metaphysical vision goes, the civilization which includes the culture will perish: "Scepticism is a highly civilised trait, though when it declines into pyrrhonism, it is one of which civilisation can die," Eliot writes, and "I do not believe that the culture of Europe could survive the complete disappearance of the Christian faith".[1] (I would say that a civilization dies because it loses belief in, i.e. becomes sceptical about, its Central Idea, and that the complete disappearance of Christian faith, although impossible before stage 59, when the end of our civilization's stage 61 would be very near, is the end of a process in which belief in the Central Idea of the Light has been lost.) It is important to save European civilization from occupation as civilization only advances through individual civilizations which trap the Light and become Light-bearers, and the occupation of European civilization by a dictator and the onset of a new Dark Age would almost certainly deprive Westerners of free access to libraries and to the long, civilised, written Tradition of the Light. The European civilization's Central Idea, which is now forgotten, would then become irretrievably lost. A reawakening of the vision of the Light in our time is vital for the future of Europe, and, economic considerations like the future of oil aside, *the European West can be saved from occupation and can achieve the coming Resurgence in stage 43, by a renewal of its vision of the Light*, which can temporarily at least, restore its belief in its Central Idea and destiny, its sense of meaning and purpose. Europe can renew its purpose within its declining state and survive the coming challenge of a Fundamentalist Islam in our neo-Crusading time when once again Jerusalem is under attack.

We have said that it is extremely serious for Europe that the Christian religion, its traditional metaphysical supplier of the vision of the Light, and therefore of belief in Europe's Central Idea, has ceased to be widespread in Europe since the Second World War. A medieval churchgoer who returned from the dead today would immediately see what is wrong; he would think that something had gone wrong with the attitude in our churches. John Cassian in his *Conferences* saw the practice of prayer and worship in ordered stages – confession, praise, thanksgiving, reading of Scripture and intercession – during which the worshipper is lifted out of himself and sees God. In *Ancrene Riwle* ("the Anchoress's Rule") the medieval communicant was enjoined: "After the kiss of peace in the Mass, when the priest communicates, forget the world, be completely out of the body, and with burning love embrace your Beloved who has come down from heaven to your heart's bower, and hold Him fast until he has granted you all that you ask." But with the Renaissance and the Reformation, the attitude to prayer changed radically, and for the worse. Bishop Kirk in *The Vision of God* sees the 1570-1580 decade (shortly after the European breakdown and secularization of 1453-1555) as the offending turning-point in both Catholic and Protestant church attitudes towards mysticism. An anti-mystical hierarchy, suspicious of St Teresa and St John of the Cross, stifled the traditional view of worship as adoring homage, mystical prayer, contemplation (which Kirk defines as "looking towards God") and the vision of God; these were all allowed to lapse in a "reversal of tradition", and petition and intercession regarding matters in the outer world took their place.[2]

Consequently at no secularized services today is scope given for contemplative abandon to the divine. To the medieval mind, the attainment of such a state was the very reason for going to church, and the *raison d'être* of the Church. The act of worship is still very much a part of our public life, but it has lost the meaning it had for Cassian and St John of the Cross. For them it meant the worship of the Light in the vision of God which illuminated all prayer. And that is what a new Movement will have to regain.

The restoration of a Light-based Christianity will mean a widespread turning away from scepticism back to the transforming, dynamising Light. If Christianity is to achieve such a mass transformation, it must return to its pre-Humanistic message. There will have to be a new mystical Reformation, a de-secularization. This should be the objective of the Christian Reawakening. In short, in stage 45 (the revival of cultural purity which occurs in the course of the existence of the conglomerate of stage 43) Christianity will have to return the West to the traditional culture of its past.

How can this be done? For a start, our civilization needs to change its attitude to itself. Our Christian European civilization did not perish with the Renaissance. We should not be encouraged to think of our civilization as an irrevocably secular and scientific one that changed irreversibly during the Renaissance. As we have seen, it has always been an essentially Christian civilization that has shed its Renaissance secularism at different times of its subsequent history (for example, during the Puritan time of the Quakers c.1650). T. S. Eliot recognised this; it is the assumption behind *The Idea of a Christian Society.*

Secondly, there will have to be a conscious revolt against Western secular culture which has questioned the traditional culture of the post-Renaissance nation-states. After two democratising world wars, and new technology, ideas of liberty, equality, social responsibility, humaneness and brotherhood have prevailed, and through the mass media (radio, television, magazines and newspapers) European art, literature and music have all been popularised. Many artists who now contribute to Western secular culture have turned against traditional culture on the grounds that it was aristocratic and *élitist* and that it has made the West heartless, and some have sought to liberate themselves from the conventions of Western civilization by rebelliously obscene language, disposable art, and debased manners. There is talk of smashing "oppressive" Western culture to bring in peace, brotherhood and equal rights. Many artists, writers and musicians who are contributors to Western culture have become deliberately self-destructive, and the metaphysical vision is now over-laid by secular attitudes which dismiss it. Western culture urgently needs a return of the Light which can create a new art, science, philosophy, social and moral rela-tions, political state, and religion that will uphold the traditional values of European civilization; a new cultural phase based on gnosis rather than scepticism, contem-plative mysticism rather than materialism, and personal growth rather than arid and despairing rationalism.

The spadework for a widespread European return to the Light has already taken place in science, of all disciplines. The new biology and physics, which have orig-inated in growing America, share a world-view which is close to that of mysticism, and these are already challenging European Humanism with a new anti-materialis-tic outlook. The new American biology and physics have moved away from a European world-view that is based on the senses, and are seeking a Grand Unified Theory akin to metaphysics. They have already begun a massive reinterpretation of our cultural heritage which would fit in with my reinterpretation of our contempla-tive heritage here. They have in particular begun to revalue the European Scientific Revolution and European Humanism, which are both based on the senses. In time the new, predominantly American view will be reflected in art and education, but the point is it is now but a relatively small step for this anti-Humanist movement to concern itself with the Light, and to link up with Christianity. What is needed is for a new cross-disciplinary T. S. Eliot to dominate modern thought, remould attitudes and launch a new Metaphysical Revival, a new Metaphysical Movement.

Those wishing to save the traditional Christian European civilization (in the sense of preserving its traditional Light-based values from foreign – possibly Islamic or less possibly Communist – occupation) need to get the message across loud and clear that the Light opposes the materialistic world-view of Communism from which many Islamic states have pulled away and in which a human being is material that can be remoulded to suit the Party. On the contrary, a human being is capable of rising to the vision of God as Light, as prisoners in the atrocious mate-rial conditions of the ex-Soviet Gulag know. A Russian dissident poetess, Irina Ratushinskaya, has said that Russian prisoners think of God all the time to encour-age themselves and others, and that by contrast God is hardly mentioned in the comfortable material conditions of Europe (although God is still in the midst of some as Light). The Light can transform a Communist inquisitor's mind as swiftly as it transformed the mind of the persecutor Saul of Tarsus, and it has always had the capacity to enable Europe's secular ideology to resist the secular materialism of Communism which, as *The Secret History of the West* shows, began as a Western secular ideology that rivalled capitalism in London before it was adopted by a menacing Byzantine-Russian civilization. For ideological reasons no Communist can acknowledge the truth of the Tradition of the Light – and therein lay the fundamental weakness of Communism in relation to both its Islamic southern states and in relation to our civilization, if our civilization could only have recovered the belief, or rather gnosis (knowledge of the Light), to exploit it.

A decommunized Russia will increasingly become the European and North-American civilization's ally against Islam, which all three, out of mutual self-interest, will contrive to cut down to size, whether in the ex-USSR, the Middle East or North Africa (notably Libya). A decommunized Russia will increasingly rediscover the Byzantine-Russian civilization's Central Idea of the Orthodox Light, which is the same Christian Light that comprises the European and North-American Central Ideas. We have seen that Communism has now ceased to be the main threat to the West, and has been replaced by a fanatical Fundamentalist Islam, whose southern ex-USSR hordes may attempt to seize ex-Soviet thermonuclear weapons. Now is the time for the European and North-American civilizations to rediscover belief in their own Central Ideas.

In *Civilisation* Kenneth Clark (who was unaware that European civilization is only two-thirds through, at stage 43 out of 61 stages) writes: "It is lack of self-confidence, more than anything else, that kills a civilization. We can destroy ourselves by cynicism and disillusion.... The moral and intellectual failure of Marxism has left us with no alternative to heroic materialism, and that isn't enough."[3] There is another alternative to materialism: heroic contemplation, the recovery of the sense of the metaphysical and of belief in our civilization's Central Idea of the Light – which is enough.

WORLD-WIDE STAGE OF THE NORTH-AMERICAN CIVILIZATION IN THE 21ST-22ND CENTURY

The way forward for Western culture and Western civilization, i.e. for the European and North-American civilizations, is a global expansion. We have seen that European civilization may expand round the Mediterranean (stage 43) and that, far from declining and becoming a merely regional power, as Paul Kennedy suggests in *The Rise and Fall of the Great Powers* (which fails to relate the European and North-American empires to stages in their underlying civilizations, and therefore gets it wrong), the North-American civilization looks set to retain its superpower status in 21st century, as Joseph S. Nye argues in *Bound to Lead*, and eventually to take over the European conglomerate in a global expansion (stage 15) in which Western civilization – our Christian civilization – may pass into a world-wide stage of the North-American civilization.

Western technology conquered every country in the 20th century. As a result of the Second Industrial Revolution, planes, cars, TVs, radios, computers and Western dress have been adopted in China, Asia and Africa as well as in Europe and the Americas. The revolution in communications has made the world a smaller place, and live link-ups bring opposite sides of the world to the television screen via satellites in space. The earth increasingly looks like the one united ball that can be seen from the moon, the American conquest of which has been another materialistic Western triumph over Nature. Western culture and habits have become a world-wide standard which everywhere co-exists with local, regional variations. As John Roberts says in *The Triumph of the West*, "Western civilization has not lost its world dominance, whatever the political story, because political power was only one part of it."[4]

A coming world-wide civilization on earth was predicted by Arnold Toynbee in his great if flawed work, *A Study of History*. He predicted that the West – we would say Europe rather than America – would continue to disintegrate until it entered a world-wide, ecumenical "Universal State", which would be a Western-based civilization with a Western (we would say American) framework, drawing on non-Western contributions from the non-Western countries of the world. (The chart of civilizations in the last volume of *A Study of History* shows all civilizations flowing into a "future oecumenical civilization, starting in a Western framework and on a Western basis, but progressively drawing (sic) contributions from the living non-Western civilizations embraced in it".)[5] A more optimistic statement of the same view is to be found in Karl Jaspers' *The Origin and Goal of History* (1953), which concludes that a new world civilization will evolve from Western civilization, a new world political confederation in which man's soul and spirit, his aspirations and institutions will be changed. In such a unity, all the world's divisions will be healed: the divisions between East and West Germany (which are now reunified), Northern and Southern Ireland, the Arabs and Jews, Pakistan and India, North and South Korea.

My evidence has suggested that Western civilization is an amalgam of two separate civilizations, the European and American civilizations, just as following the two Punic Wars the so-called Graeco-Roman civilization of c.180 BC proved to be an amalgam of the declining Aegean-Greek and rising Roman civilizations, and just as the Roman civilization of the 4th century AD turned out with hindsight to be an amalgam of the declining Western Roman and the rising Eastern Roman/Byzantine civilizations. We have seen that European civilization can therefore be expected to continue for several hundred years and decline as it advances towards the last stage of the growth-decay process, when a successor civilization will replace it, while the young American civilization can still expand into a world-wide phase; and this could coincide with the transition of European civilization from stage 43 to stage 46.

It is of this coming American stage that Francis Fukuyama, the US State Department's policy planner, wrote when he described a "perfect equilibrium" following America's victory as a result of the collapse of Communism in the Cold War. He wrongly regards it as Hegel's synthesis, "the end of history", failing to see that civilizations pass through many stages without reaching a synthesis. The crisis caused by Iraq's annexation of Kuwait heralded in a more dangerous phase of history than the Cold War, one in which Europe and extremist Islam will confront each other, and are already doing so, and made nonsense of the claim that the end of the Cold War was "the end of history". When a civilization reaches its end it passes into another civilization, and so the rise and fall of civilizations is endless.

There are therefore two possibilities regarding a new world-wide civilization:

1. When she reaches a certain point in her current stage 15 America will become

the dominant force in a world-wide civilization that will for a while absorb European civilization, and perhaps the Byzantine-Russian civilization and most or all of the other living civilizations we have explored (including the Chinese and Japanese civilizations);

2. There will be a complete break with precedent, and contrary to the experience of our 25 civilizations during the last five thousand years there will be a world political union – a new global civilization with a world government – which may grow out of the United Nations' recovery in 1990 of the world role it was intended to have when it was first set up, which will be created by the North-American civilization as in possibility 1 but into which the North-American civilization will die, and this world political union will be the successor civilization that will absorb all our civilizations for a while (for such a millenarian world regime cannot be expected to last for ever).

Possibility 2 is without precedent and can only be suggested as a very theoretical possibility. The likelihood is that possibility 1 will be the result of the North-American civilization's stage 15, and there is no precedent for any civilization's having conquered the whole world.

I can restate these two possibilities in terms of Western religion, Christianity. Either Western civilization, in this case America, can become the dominant force in a world-wide civilization which will include the European civilization, in which case its metaphysic of Christianity will be renewed and will be central to a world-wide cultural hegemony which the West (i.e. America) will impose, Roman-style, on all the world's regional cultures and religions, which can be expected to blend syncretistically with Christianity. Or (and it only seems a theoretical possibility) both the European and North-American civilizations will be absorbed into a world political union and die into a new world-wide civilization, in which case Christianity may blend with other religions and be absorbed into a world-wide, syncretistic religion (and we have already seen that a contamination of Christianity by foreign influences – a Universalist blend that is philosophically desirable and perceived to be progressive, an idea whose time has come – can only hasten the eventual end of the North-American civilization).

I can put these possibilities the other way round. Either Christianity will renew itself, in which case the American-led West may achieve a world-wide cultural hegemony, the basis for which would be a strong and appealing Christianity. Or Christianity will decline still further into secularism, in which case eventually, during the European civilization's stage 59, it may die into a syncretistic mixture of other religions, out of which may grow a new world-wide religion that would assist the growth of a new world-wide civilization into which the North-American civilization may eventually die.

AMERICAN-LED WORLD RULE

An American-created world-wide civilization in the 21st and 22nd centuries would not be founded on 20th-century American secular capitalist attitudes. It would be Light-led, like all stage-15 expansions. It would be a civilization in which there would inevitably be a multiplicity of existing religions. America would preside (as did Rome) over the merging of all religions; just as Isis, Mithras, Cybele, Apollo and Jupiter merged in the Light, so might Christ, Mohammed, Siva, Visnu, the Buddha and Confucius. The existing religions would thus merge syncretistically, for a time, on their common Light, and the Light of each past civilization would be available to each region throughout the world. The syncretism would take place within stage 15 of the North-American civilization, and it would only last while stage 15 of the North-American civilization lasted.

Through American influence Christianity would have a special position among the religions, despite being dangerously contaminated by foreign influences (although no doubt it would in due course be purified) just as it did in the 4th-century-AD Roman Empire.

A blend between Christianity and the New-Age Eastern outlook in the 21st century, within a world-wide perspective, could eventually lead to a strengthening of Christianity as a preparation for American hegemony, just as Clement of Alexandria's reconciliation of Christianity and Gnosticism at the end of 2nd century AD similarly strengthened Christianity in preparation for the late Roman hegemony; in which case, Christianity would become a truly dominating world-wide religion, and in a sense the millennium would have arrived.

I must stress again that there is no precedent for an American-led fully world-wide civilization of this kind (possibility 1) for no civilization has ever succeeded in imposing a world hegemony. The Roman hegemony covered only part of the world. However, we can see how it might happen if the world were to draw together into large regional blocs which would consent to American hegemony at a certain point in stage 15 of the North-American civilization. An American world hegemony could happen if a politically integrated European Union absorbed or became affiliated to the Eastern-European states (the Warsaw Pact nations) and to a Westernized Russia, and at the same time to a newly created United States of Eurasia (which Gorbachev proposed), United States of South America (an extension of the current Free Trade Area of the Americas), United States of Africa, United Arab or Islamic States, United Indian States, and eventually an Asian-Pacific Union that became a United States of the Far East. We have seen that all these regional blocs can be expected in stage 46 of their respective living civilizations, which they are all expected to achieve in the 21st or 22nd centuries. It is at present hard to imagine the divided territories concerned forming themselves into unified blocs, and still harder to conceive that some of them would place themselves voluntarily under American hegemony, let alone consent to such a hegemony, but the logic of the American parabola does suggest a global role.

A coming American world-wide civilization must be seen in relation to space exploration. We know the Americans are the most powerful nation on earth when we see the American Voyager 2 speed past the moons of Jupiter, the rings of Saturn and the corkscrew (i.e. spiral) magnetic field of Uranus, and (in late August 1989, at a time when seething unrest in the Baltic signalled weakness in Russia, America's great rival) send back stunning pictures of Neptune's rings and huge storm from nearly 2,800 million miles away, opening up the outer planets to the earth in a way that has never happened before and making possible a new Universalism in which our earth is regarded as one unified ball. Voyager 2's twelve-year-long exploration, made possible when Gary Flandro applied the theory of gravitational slingshot to spacecraft, has proved a triumph of American technology and spirit of adventure for the whole world to admire. The same admiration for American technology is felt when we see America's Magellan spacecraft go into orbit round Venus (in August 1990) after a 15-month journey and begin mapping the entire planet's surface in thin strips by using radar to penetrate the dense clouds (Venus's atmosphere is 90 times heavier than the Earth's), a mission that may determine whether the furnace-like temperatures of 480C on Venus are a result of global warming like that on the Earth.

Now it is likely that there will be a permanent settlement on the moon, a manned expedition to Mars and a scientific station on one of Jupiter's moons. In short the new worlds will be colonized by their discoverers from the North-American civilization just as the New World was colonized by its discoverers from the European civilization, and it is likely that people will set out for the new worlds without intending to come back. A long colonization of the inhospitable stars will help to preserve life when our sun expands in 5 billion years' time and burns the earth to a cinder. The coming American world-wide civilization must be seen not just in a global context but within the context of the solar system; and the shift of emphasis of its new Universalism will not regard the earth merely as a unified ball but also as an inseparable part of our solar system and the wider universe. In our time man is ceasing to be earth-bound and will begin to settle the planets, and this will happen in the course of the expansion of the North-American civilization in stage 15.

It is not widely recognised that there has been a largely unpublicised attempt, which I described in *The Syndicate*, to create an American-influenced world government over all civilizations on earth ever since 1776. The idea can be traced back to the Enlightenment, and to the Illuminati, the Freemasonic secret society we have already mentioned which was founded in Bavaria in 1776 by the now execrated (and perhaps misunderstood) Adam Weishaupt, a Professor of canon law at the University of Ingolstadt who had been educated at a Jesuit school and who was affiliated to Freemasons as existing documents prove. In fact the organization of the order was based on Freemasonry; it was a mystic closed sect and its members were to be the "creative minority" in establishing a new world order.

To understand the Illuminati's world aspirations we need to go back to the old Germanic *Vehmgericht*, which seems to have been associated with the *Baeume Gericht* (Tree Law) under which individuals were hanged on trees like Odin; and to the "*Geheimgericht*" or "Secret Tribunal" which Charlemagne established in 772 after conquering Germanic Saxony.[6] Anyone who transgressed against Charlemagne's law against crime, paganism, witchcraft or dissent was condemned by this *Vehm* or Secret Tribunal, and hanged, in his or her own house, barn or street. This *Vehm* was revived in 1404 by King Robert, probably to suppress the Knights Templar, whose German refugees worshipped the Baphomet, which was by then the severed head of John the Baptist. These refugees from Templarism were known as the *Johannes Brüder*, the Brethren of St John the Baptist. The associates of King

Robert's *Vehm* were described as "illuminated" (*Die Wissenden*). A pun was intended as the word *Witze* is the old Teutonic word for punishment. These 15th-century Illuminati hanged their victims on lime trees at sacred geomantic sites, generally with a rope made of willow twigs. In 1767 a new Masonic cult group, the Order of the Architects of Africa, was established by King Frederick the Great of Prussia. This group was descended from the *Johannes Brüder*, and the group's inner order was the Knights of Light, who, like the *Vehm*, were called *Die Wissenden*, "The Illuminati". Frederick the Great's librarian Dom Antoine Joseph Pernetty left Germany and founded the *Illuminés d'Avignon*. And it was in 1776 that a group bearing the name *Die Wissenden* was founded by Adam Weishaupt.

Weishaupt's secret society, then, was in the tradition of the Charlemagne's universal rule, and it has influenced the American Central Idea more than people realise. It sought to replace Christianity with a religion of reason that could merge syncretistically with other religions (compare America's 18th-century, secular, disestablished Christianity), and it promoted democratic republicanism and world government until it was banned by the Catholic, monarchist Bavarian government in 1785. (It is to be distinguished from the Spanish Illuminati or Alumbrados of the 16th and 17th centuries.) Its aim was to destroy existing states by revolutions, which, as in America and France, and later in Russia, would be internationalist. Thomas Jefferson was an Illuminatist and so was Benjamin Franklin, and there are traces of Illuminatism in the American Declaration of Independence of July 4, 1776 (which was announced two months after the foundation of the Illuminati on May 1, 1776). George Washington denounced the Illuminatist aims in two letters written in 1798. According to contemporary sources[7] the Illuminati went underground and were behind the Reign of Terror in France (through the Illuminati Danton, Mirabeau and Robespierre), ran Cagliostro's French campaign for world government, and through their offshoot the League of Just Men, or the League of the Just (a secret society of German *emigrés* in London), perhaps financed Karl Marx while he wrote the *Communist Manifesto*. This drew on Hegel's dialectic, Feuerbach's materialism, Rousseau's absolutist General Will and Voltaire's hostility towards Christianity, and sought world domination. (The League sent a representative to Marx in 1847 and asked him to write their pamphlet and when Marx and Engels agreed and produced the *Communist Manifesto*, writing it in the building in Brussels' Grand'Place now occupied by the Swan restaurant, it changed its name to the Communist League.)

There have been claims (for example in Elizabeth van Buren's *The Secret of the Illuminati*) that the Illuminati has remained a Brotherhood of Enlightened Ones, working for a world united in a religion of One Truth in the manner of many sects encountered in *The Light of Civilization*; that their two Masonic-style symbols, the Eye and the number 333, go back to the Eye of Horus and Solomon's signet ring which Mme Blavatsky shows in *Isis Unveiled* (the figure 33 standing for the number of years Solomon's Temple stood before it was pillaged by Shishak, for the number of years David reigned in Jerusalem, and for the age of Jesus Christ when he died); and that the Illuminati have had nothing to do with political or materialistically-orientated plots to dominate the world and become Masters of an enslaved mankind. My own research contradicts this; I have dealt very fully with the Freemasonic Illuminati's influence on the American and French revolutions in *The Secret History of the West*, and on 20th-century history in *The Syndicate*. Be that as it may, the Freemasonic Illuminati were apparently taken over and run by billionaires in the 19th century, notably the Rothschild family, who backed any power capable of bringing about a world unity which the financiers could dominate, starting with the world governmental programme of the Illuminati.

The Rothschilds are the most famous of the European banking families. Their House was founded in 1744 in Frankfurt, and the family profited from the French Revolution and the Napoleonic wars, making loans to warring princes, smuggling and trading in wheat, cotton and arms, and transferring international payments between Britain and the Continent, which Napoleon tried to close to British trade. There are reports that the Rothschilds funded Adam Weishaupt from 1770 to 1776, when Weishaupt founded the Order of the Illuminati. Metternich took notice of them in 1815, when Nathan Mayer Rothschild had become the most powerful banker the world had ever known, and was popularly known as the "Ruler of England" (see *The Secret History of the West* and *The Syndicate* for full details); and it was in the 1820s, over 40 years after the founding of the Illuminati, that the House of Rothschild emerged as a power. After France's defeat by Prussia, the Rothschilds made two "liberation" loans in 1871 and 1872 which kept the French government in power, while in London in 1875 they loaned Disraeli the £4 million that enabled the British government to become the main stockholder in the Suez Canal Company. Having begun in Frankfurt, the Rothschilds spread into Vienna (where they became Barons of the Austrian Empire), France and Britain, where the head of the British Rothschilds has always been considered the head of British Jewry.

The descendants of the financiers who backed the American Revolution and the French Revolution also backed the Kaiser by giving him $300m to finance the First World War and build the Berlin-to-Baghdad railway (see Hagger, *The Syndicate*) – and the Soviet Revolution. To put it starkly, the German Max Warburg of the Rothschild-allied Warburg family bank in Frankfurt, and his brother's father-in-law Jacob Schiff, between them gave certainly $20m, and perhaps as much as $26m, to Lenin and Trotsky around the time of Communist Revolution (see *The Syndicate*), and the Rothschild-backed secret Round Table group headed by Lord Milner gave 21 million roubles to the Bolsheviks to further the world government ideas of a syndicate of international financiers that included Morgan and Rockefeller interests. It is worth looking in greater detail at the American-German basis of the Communist drive for world government. Max Warburg, who ran the Rothschild-allied Warburg bank at Frankfurt, was responsible for financing Lenin, the Bolshevik leader who in 1915 proposed a "United States of the World" (in No. 40 of the Russian organ, *The Socialist Democrat*). Through his go-between Alexander Helphand (alias "Parvus"), he sent Lenin into Russia with $5 to $6 million in gold. Lenin took this gold with him to Petrograd on the "sealed train". (The official reason for the sealing of the carriage was so that the Russians could not talk to the German guards and be accused of treason.) The German high command was behind Max Warburg as it hoped Lenin would take power in Russia and sue for peace with Germany, allowing Germany to transfer troops from the eastern front to the western front. The idea worked in so far as the Bolshevik Revolution initially took place in Petrograd; it was only later that it spread throughout the rest of Russia.

The international dimension to the arrangement becomes apparent when it is realised that the German high command did not inform the Kaiser of the plan to foment a Communist revolution in Russia, and that while Max Warburg was running the German finances his brother Paul Warburg was financing the American war effort, having been a prime mover in establishing the American central banking system, the Federal Reserve System, in 1913 and having become a member of the Federal Reserve Board. Paul Warburg resigned from his American Federal Reserve post as soon as news of his brother's involvement in the German war effort leaked out. Another prime mover in establishing the Federal Reserve System was

"Colonel" House (the military rank was honorary), confidential adviser to Woodrow Wilson from 1913 to 1921 and described by Woodrow Wilson as his "*alter ego*" and by some historians as the real President of the USA during the Wilson years. It was House who pressed the Canadians to release Trotsky in 1917 and who sent him to join Lenin with an American passport. The Federal Reserve System has increased the American national debt from $1 billion in 1913 to $455 billion in 1971, and American indebtedness to European banks, including Rothschilds. It was the father-in-law of Max Warburg's other brother, Felix, the banker Jacob Schiff, senior partner in Kuhn Loeb & Co., America's most powerful international banking firm where Paul and Felix Warburg were also partners, who financed Trotsky and established the Bolsheviks in Russia. Lenin later said that the establishment of a central bank was 90% of communizing a country. According to a report on file with the US State Department, Kuhn Loeb & Co. bankrolled Stalin's first Five-Year Plan. The Soviet Union was at its outset a financial satellite of American-German capitalism, and notably of Kuhn Loeb & Co.; and between 1918 and 1922 the victorious Bolsheviks transferred 600 million roubles in gold to Kuhn Loeb & Co., Jacob Schiff's firm. It is worth noting that Schiff was linked to the Rothschilds: in the 18th century the Schiffs and Rothschilds shared a double house in Frankfurt, and Schiff reportedly bought his partnership in Kuhn Loeb & Co. with Rothschild money. It is also interesting that Lord Milner, Paul, Felix and Max Warburg all represented their respective countries at the Paris Peace Conference at the conclusion of World War I.

After Stalin's Communism was established, American-German financiers linked to the American Round Table (a branch of Lord Milner's secret society) backed the rise of Hitler, who also dreamed of world hegemony. The most notable of these financiers were the Warburgs, who were still part of the Rothschild empire, through their Mendelsohn Bank of Amsterdam, and the J. Henry Schroeder Bank. In the United States, the Illuminati eye on top of a Pyramid appeared on the reverse side of the Great Seal of the United States, and in 1933 (the year of Roosevelt's New Deal) the Illuminati insignia, with a triangle and Latin inscription *novus ordo seculorum* ("a new order of the ages"), appeared on the reverse side of the American dollar bill.

The descendants of the Illuminati are still very active today, and Winston Churchill wrote in 1919, "From the days of Spartacus Weishaupt" (Adam

Weishaupt took the Roman name Spartacus) "to those of Karl Marx (Moses Mordecai Levi) and down to Trotsky (Russia), Bela Kuhn (Hungary), Rosa Luxembourg (Germany), and Emma Goldman (United States), this world conspiracy for the overthrow of civilization and for the reconstitution of society on the basis of arrested development, of envious malevolence and impossible equality, has been steadily growing." (There is evidence that Churchill, like Stalin, collaborated with the world government financiers for the rest of his life.) The world government ideals of the Illuminati are apparently now enshrined in the mysterious Council on Foreign Relations (CFR) in 68th Street, New York whose admitted goal is to establish a world government. The chief agent in the founding of the CFR in 1919 was "Colonel" House (according to the CFR's Joseph Kraft in *Harper's* of July 1958), "supported by" Walter Lippmann, John Foster Dulles, Allen Dulles and Christian Herter. House hosted the Round Table Group meeting in Paris on May 19, 1919 which committed the latter-day Illuminati to the creation of the CFR. Kuhn Loeb & Co. were represented, and Paul Warburg was one of the incorporators of the CFR, together with Jacob Schiff, John D. Rockefeller, Averell Harriman and others.

After the American Round Table (a branch of Milner's secret society) funded the rise of Hitler through the Warburg-controlled Mendelsohn Bank of Amsterdam, the CFR engineered a take-over of the US State Department and set up a Committee on Post-War Foreign Policies which was completely staffed by the CFR. This group designed the United Nations as a step towards a world superstate, and there were at least 47 CFR members among the American delegates to the founding of the UN in San Francisco in 1945. The membership of the CFR is interlocked with that of the United World Federalists (UWF), one of the most important groups promoting world union which advocates turning the UN into a world government which would include the Communist nations. Soon the formal membership of the CFR included 1,500 of the most *élite* names from American government, labour, business, finance, communications, the Foundations (including the Rockefeller, Ford and Carnegie Foundations) and academic life.

The CFR is now both very anonymous and very influential; it has controlled most post-war American Presidents. Richard Nixon (who was not overtly connected with the CFR after 1962) appointed at least 110 CFR members to high positions in his administration, including Dr Kissinger, who was a paid staff member of the CFR immediately prior to joining the Nixon administration, an appointment arranged by Nelson Rockefeller (according to the *Salt Lake City Desert News* of March 27, 1970). The CFR-related publication of the UWF, *World Government News*, announced in October 1948: "Richard Nixon: Introduced world government resolution (HCR 68) 1947, and ABC (World Government) resolution 1948." This is interesting in view of the Nixon-Kissinger dentente with Russia and China, and the aims of the CFR are undoubtedly being furthered by the US-Soviet accord of 1987 reached between Reagan and Gorbachev.

Prince Bernhard of the Netherlands, the late head of the secret, one-world Bilderberger movement, worked with the Rothschilds through Royal Dutch Petroleum (Shell Oil) and held meetings with US officials, bankers and industrialists of the CFR to explore the merging of the US and the (then) Soviet Union into a world government (the aim of the Bilderberg Group, founded in 1954, and the Trilateral Commission, founded in 1972).[8] There are rumours that an Illuminatist Third Force, or Force X, has controlled Moscow's foreign policy through SMERSH and has kept the Soviet leaders in line – sources raise the mind-boggling possibility that Philby was a Third Force or "Trust" agent – and it is claimed that the Illuminatist Third Force was Ian Fleming's "Spectre" and "the Brotherhood" of Orwell's *1984*, both of which were universal dictatorships. (Both Fleming and Orwell were of course politically very well informed.) To advance the cause of world government this Third Force apparently intervenes to bring down a Western government, as, according to one expert who made a study of the event, to whom I have spoken (a member of the British aristocracy), it apparently did through the Profumo affair in 1963. It is interesting that the ex-British Prime Minister Edward Heath, who stood for a united Europe, had a latter-day Rothschild, Lord Victor Rothschild, as Head of his Think-Tank in the early 1970s; and that Rothschilds have been linked to the privatization flotations of Mrs Thatcher's British government during the 1980s. (Mrs Thatcher has publicly denied that Lord Victor Rothschild who died in 1990 was the fifth man who ordered Philby to defect to Russia, and it is most unlikely that Lord Victor Rothschild was a Soviet agent; as *The Secret History of the West* shows, the early Soviet Union immediately after the Kerensky Soviet Revolution was virtually a financial satellite of the Rothschild empire.)

It has been alleged that the descendants of the Illuminati have also sought to control the Vatican, and have won control over our recent Popes; and that they have apparently been responsible for Paul VI's introducing the bent or broken cross which has been carried by the Popes since the 1950s. (The bent cross has been a Satanic symbol since the 5th century AD and to some it reflects the corruption of the Illuminati ideal and recalls one of the Fatima prophecies: "Satan will reign even in the highest places. He will enter the highest position in the Church." To others the bent cross may symbolize the bending of Christianity to accommodate other religions.)

These details may seem unbelievable, but there is much evidence, which I have drawn together in *The Syndicate*, that the global vision of the Illuminati is still a reality. In so far as the successors of the Illuminati seek the financial domination of the world, the destabilizing and communizing of Western governments and the Satanizing of Christianity, and use the terror techniques of Charlemagne's *Vehm*, they are to be deplored and resisted. They claim to bring in universal peace and justice through a new American-led democratic world order and one universal religion, but have been corrupted by the occult.

Every revolution is preceded by a revolution in communications, and so it is with the global perspective of world government. Increasingly satellite technology is capable of reaching all the regions of the world simultaneously. In what was at the time the largest live link-up enabled Pope John Paul II to address 1.5 billion people. With the rapid advance of the internet and other sophisticated technology and its wholesale adoption by such countries as Finland and Indonesia, it is only a matter of time before the whole world is linked by one communications network. The time is coming when an American-organized world government will have the capability of communicating with every corner of its world empire simultaneously.

As I have shown in *The Syndicate*, the world government internationalists appear to be winning. However, they may be a pressure group for the North-American civilization as was the Round Table for the British branch of the European civilization; and we can discount the possibility that there will be a world-wide civilization that is not tied to America or to any of our 25 civilizations (possibility 2). This would be a new 26th civilization that would include the whole world and with it the North-American and all other civilizations. Such a new civilization would presumably begin like any other. After a migration of an energizing vision of the Light, a new religion would attract peoples away from, and therefore appeal to, all existing religions. It would have to emphasise the one common Light. It would draw on Christianity without allowing Christianity to dominate, and its civilization would then presumably emerge into the early stages of growth.

There is no precedent for any sort of a world-civilization in its own right, and the very idea of it goes against our understanding of the process of the growth and decay of our 25 civilizations. Without tying it to an existing civilization (i.e. stage 15 of the North-American civilization, possibility 1) we are in totally new and untried territory. It seems that such a civilization would be based in New York, which is where the world's capital would be. Such a world government would be a glorified UN. The very idea that such a body could actually agree about anything may seem inconceivable, but while discounting it, if we are to understand how such a theoretical possibility could happen, then we must imagine the same process that created the American world hegemony: the drawing together of large regional blocs which freely choose, in stage 46 or 49 of their civilizations, to be federally linked to or to be occupied by a new world government and its civilization; just as in the 2nd century BC the Greek states chose to die into the Confederation of Roman States. The North-American civilization's dying into such a new world government's civilization would thus be a voluntary rather than an involuntary act, and although at the time it may seem to represent a final ending of the North-American Christian civilization, and as such would be hailed as a great achievement, it is extremely unlikely that it would last for more than one stage of the lifespan of the North-American civilization, which would then pick up the pieces and enter a new stage of its growth.

Nevertheless, I have to concede that a possibility-2 World-Wide Movement could come into being if world citizens clamour for an internationalist brotherhood that has nothing to do with materialistic Communism or the secular Western ideology, and demand world government on human grounds; and European fund-raising during the many Ethiopian and Sudanese famines may be a forerunner of such a Movement. Such a Movement seems very far-fetched and remote from our consideration of the growth and decay of civilizations, and I find it most unlikely that some great power in the future can do what all civilizations have dreamed of doing at some time or another: break out of the cycle of rising and falling civilizations, bring in a political world government and a new world-wide civilization and then voluntarily die into it. It is a dream that a great power such as America could persuade the ex-Soviet Union, China and Africa as well as Asia, South America and Europe's former colonial territories to group themselves into one world-wide organization and attempt an untried world rule that may be superior to everything that has gone before – and die into it. A world government may be forced on the world leaders one day by the need to pool and conserve oil and energy resources, but it is extremely unlikely that it will not be tied to a particular civilization. For the dream to come into being the world leaders would, like Dag Hammarskjöld, need to express the illumined's sense of unity in an administration in which all citizens live at peace and there is a new secular non-totalitarian world order.

Further reflection suggests that the world order of possibility 2 may seem a dangerous thing: what if a Hitler, Stalin or Mao emerged as world dictator? What could be done if Big Brother controlled the world? On the other hand, a democratic world government would have the power to abolish war and local starvation and arrange for universal social justice, and are such prizes not worth the risk of a world dictatorship? And does not the logic of civilizations lead to such an attempt?

I have seen that all our dead civilizations have died into larger groupings (most notably into the European and Arab civilizations); can it be that those larger groupings will themselves die into one overall larger grouping, one world-wide (albeit American-created) civilization? The chart on pp532-533 of *The Light of Civilization* shows all the various cultures and civilizations springing from one source and flowing into one civilization, perhaps in our time: from one to one. Is this the end of the vision of the Light – the vision of God – in history: to unify all the world's civilizations into one?

I have said that there is "an underlying metaphysical unity beneath the cultures and history of the world", and there is therefore an underlying unity beneath the civilizations of world history in terms of the Light. We have seen that there is a sameness in the rise and fall pattern of each civilization. Since all is one, all civilizations are fundamentally one and it would therefore be fitting, and aesthetically very satisfying, if the impossible dream which we discount finally came to pass and they finally evolved into one civilization.

THE LIGHT AND AN AMERICAN-LED WORLD-WIDE UNIVERSALIST RELIGION

If an American-led world-wide civilization (possibility 1) takes place in the 21st-22nd centuries, like all stage-15 renewals of growth its renewal of growth will be

Light-led. In other words, its growth will be created, unified and sustained by one world-wide Light (its Central Idea) which will be transmitted to the world's masses through one religion. This Light would draw on the sum total of the regional Lights we have been examining. In other words, the Lights of all 25 civilizations would combine to form the world-wide religion's Light just as they do in the chart on pp532-533 of *The Light of Civilization*. The religion would include all the existing Lights and coteries. It would use the revolution in satellite technology and world communications to promulgate its message, for a TV programme on the Light can now be broadcast and received everywhere in the world simultaneously.

Every civilization is founded on a "new" idea of man, which is in fact an ancient idea that seems new at each particular time. The European civilization was founded on the worth of the individual soul in the Light, as expressed first through the monastic ideal and then through the individual will and moral choice. The North-American civilization will develop a seemingly new idea of man that will in fact be the ancient Puritan or Revivalist metaphysical view, for as we have seen civilizations grow through renewing their metaphysical vision. The new view of man would condemn the egotism and the imperfections which separate man from his brothers in the One Light, and would advocate man's openness to the Eternal Light and his potential for enlightenment. Instead of being a body and mind (Humanist man), the new man will also be a soul, spirit and divine spark (the Illumined man). The new man will break with Humanist man. He has already appeared: he is the New-Age restatement of the ancient and medieval contemplative mystic or Christian man who is open to the Light. He is the man of the Tradition of the Light we find in *The Light of Civilization*.

The Light would have a crucial role to play in such a world-wide civilization as it already provides the common ground for growing world unity. Without the inspirational common Light, the world's classes and groups, races and creeds would be forced to find their common ground in a shallow secular-materialistic Western popular (in the sense of proletarianized) "television culture" which lacks a truly metaphysical vision. The many traditional civilizations and cultures that have retained their metaphysical visions – notably, all the oriental societies and cultures that like the Indian culture have not degenerated into totalitarianism or secularism – would find such a world-wide secular culture very unappealing, for they would not be able to relate their regional visions to it. Unless the world-wide culture is centred on a vision of Reality which unifies all cultures and civilizations, it will not last very long as many traditional souls will secede from it.

An American-led world-wide civilization would be unified by the Light and can therefore be expected to draw its metaphysic from the East and blend it with what metaphysical vision has survived in the West and it would spread the "new" knowledge among the masses through its religion. It would thus embody an internationalist brotherhood in the Light, a pan-Light-ism that is drawn from the East as well as from the West.

An American-led world-wide civilization could only satisfy illumined Easterners who come from regions which retain a traditional, metaphysical culture based on the Light if it is aware that they reject the technological "paradise" of the West, holding that the North-American conditions of material affluence are not the conditions in which traditional mysticism thrives, as they can encourage spiritual laziness. The author of *Sublimity in Style* could have been expressing an Eastern view of the West today when he lamented the cancerous secularization and materialism in decadent Rome: "One of the cancers (δαπανῶν) of the spiritual life in souls born into the present generation is the low spiritual tension (ῥαθυμίαν) in which all but a few chosen spirits among us pass their days. In our work and in our recreation alike our only objective is popularity and enjoyment. We feel no concern to win the true spiritual treasure."[9] Nevertheless, while mysticism and metaphysics are at their strongest in the stark conditions of deserts, they did flourish in Alexandria in the late Roman time, and in defence of the West they are flourishing today in both North America and Europe among alternative New-Age groups, despite the prevailing affluence and materialism.

The "alternative" New-Age movement of coteries has been inspired by the growing American Light. It has also been inspired by the occult vision of the 1776 Freemasonic Illuminati, the heresy which encourages "one world" and therefore (though it is opposed to religion) a drawing together of all world religions as we have seen (pp507-508). As the heresy that anticipates stage 17 of the North-American civilization, the New-Age movement is both the successor to American New Thought and the forerunner of a coming Universalism (stage 44 of the European civilization); it anticipates stage 27 of the North-American civilization, when Universalism will be grafted onto the American Central Idea. The New-Age movement is full of people who have been illumined or who are on the verge of illumination. They are in New-Age groups rather than within the Christian fold because they have (perhaps prematurely) seceded from a tradition they regard as having been enfeebled by three and a half centuries of Humanism and materialism and by the secularization of the traditional Christian vision of the 14th-century mystics, whom they admire. The British Archbishop of Canterbury (in November 1989) warned against the dangers of the New-Age movement, which (he claimed) concentrates on personal survival and self-preservation, and on "the idea of a shift from the Age of Pisces, which corresponds roughly to the Christian era, to the Age of Aquarius, which is to dawn, so I am told, between now and 2062". He called on Christians to "engage" the New Age rather than condemn it, but his statement had the effect of making the New-Age movement a heresy from the Anglican point of view. *The Light of Civilization* records that the New-Age thinker David Spangler, rejecting Christianity, has written, "Something else must take its place, perhaps theosophy, perhaps esotericism..., perhaps one of the Eastern disciplines," and it is as if the New-Age groups are groping towards the idea of an American-led worldwide religion. In fact, from the point of view of the coming American-led worldwide civilization the New-Age groups have been doing excellent work in preparing for the world-wide culture ahead. By drawing on the metaphysical cultures of India, Tibet, Japan, and Islam, they have made possible a Counter-Renaissance against the senses-dominated Humanism which they find irrelevant, and they have begun the syncretistic mixing of traditional cultures which a world-wide culture will be able to inherit.

Out of their efforts may grow a world-wide religion which will unify and dominate the American-led world-wide civilization of the 21st-22nd centuries as early Christianity unified and dominated the new Roman Christian and Byzantine Empires. Just as Christianity absorbed elements from the other metaphysical systems – the Druid Yesu or Esus, the Eleusinian grain, the Roman Isis (who became the Virgin Mary) and so on (see *The Light of Civilization*) – so a new American-led Universalist religion of the Light, adopted from Europe's stage 44, may absorb the Tradition we have examined, including Christianity, but blend all systems, devise new forms that prefer meditation and contemplation to hymn-singing, combine practices we have considered. Christianity could be a dominating element in this blend, especially if it undergoes reunification through the American-led Ecumenical Movement.

The burden of creating a world-wide culture and religion which can bring in such an American-led world-wide civilization (stage 15 of the North-American civilization's development) will fall initially, to some degree, on the growing North-American civilization's metaphysical vision. In the very early stages of its growth this may be dominated by Christianity. To preserve its integrity, the North-American civilization will need to retain its religion free from foreign contamination, whereas to cement its world role it will inevitably blend its religion with other religions and adopt a Universalist vision. It may be that Christianity would in fact prefer to remain independent and avoid syncretistic mergings with other religions while strengthening links with them. This is certainly the attitude of contemporary Popes and of the Archbishop of Canterbury's British Inter-Faith Consultants Group. But whether the Christianity of the 21st-22nd centuries remains independent or merges, for the common good of all world citizens Christians will need to redefine Christianity to emphasise the Light, and thus give it a meaning which can be shared by the metaphysical visions of the world's traditional cultures. This has already begun to happen: Christianity is in a dialogue with the other religions, and in October 1986 it was possible for the leaders of several different religions to pray together (open themselves to the one Light?) in Assisi. More than ever the Light seems to belong to a world spiritual order.

THE NEXT MOVE: A METAPHYSICAL REVOLUTION TO RENEW THE GROWTH OF AMERICA'S STAGE 15 AND EUROPE'S STAGE 44

Let us return from the 22nd century to the present. Universalism sees the whole and expresses a timeless truth that encompasses all civilizations – indeed, the truth from the point of view of the whole. Civilizations throw up Universalist awareness in stages 15, 29, 34 and 44. Civilizations entering stage 15 perceive the Universalist vision and project it onto civilizations they conquer or influence when those civilizations enter stage 44. North America is now in stage 15 but until Europe reached stage 44, the Universalist view, although fundamentally true, was obscured in the West by Christianity, whose integrity Westernizers will seek to preserve. Whatever is ahead, whether we are looking at the coming European Resurgence or a future American world hegemony, whether Christianity renews itself or prepares for a world-wide religion, we need to consider the next move, the immediate practical way forward for Western (European and American) civilization.

The immediate goal is for Christianity to reunite itself, which means that the Ecumenical Movement will have to go forward. There will have to be a reunification of Christendom, in which Rome, Protestant and Orthodox leaders and the heirs to the early Celtic Church and Church of Jerusalem present themselves as one movement which includes all sects and overrides all doctrinal squabbles. This will require far-sighted leadership on the part of the Pope and Church leaders. In this connection it is encouraging that in October 1989 the Archbishop of Canterbury stood on the spot in Rome where St Gregory the Great dispatched St Augustine to reconvert the Anglo-Saxons, and called for the Pope to be recognised as a "universal" leader of all Christians.

However, the success of the Ecumenical Movement largely hinges on the attitude of Orthodoxy, the religion of the originally Greek Byzantine-Russian civilization; which is growing in strength following the changes in the ex-USSR. Orthodoxy claims to represent the true uninterrupted line from the time of the Apostles and therefore reveres the Celtic saints (including the Cornish saints). Orthodoxy maintains that Catholicism split away from the trunk in the schism of 1054, and that Catholicism is therefore a Protestantism; and that as the Catholic defectors were corrupt there had to be a Reformation. The Russians regarded Constantinople as the second Rome, which was occupied by the Islamic Ottomans in 1453, and it was principally to retake Constantinople that the Russians fought the Crimean War. The Pope's claim to infallibility in 1870 has meant that Orthodoxy maintains that there can be no *rapprochement* between Orthodoxy and Roman Catholicism until the claim to infallibility is withdrawn by the contemporary Pope, and until Orthodoxy's orthodoxy is acknowledged. Such claims, together with the purity of the Orthodox liturgical tradition and the Orthodox emphasis on the Transfiguration and illumination, have drawn a number of Anglicans to convert to Orthodoxy in recent times. Indeed, in the 19th century a movement from Anglo-Catholicism to Roman Catholicism, which Cardinal Newman began, is now parallelled by an equivalent movement from Anglicanism to Orthodoxy in the late 20th century. Ecumenism will not be achieved until the Protestants, Catholics and

Orthodox leaders agree to acknowledge their similarity in the Light, on which Christendom can be reunified at a time when it is being opposed by Islam, while agreeing that there can be separate interpretations as to whether the Orthodox or Catholic tradition goes back to the Apostles.

The Ecumenical Movement has had to come to terms with the formerly Soviet-based Christian "front" movements. Since Lenin, and certainly since the Second World War, Christianity, especially Protestantism, has been heavily infiltrated from Moscow, and one Jesuit priest who has made a study of the problem reckons that no fewer than 10,000 Christian Ministers, eager to bring justice to the poor, were trained behind the (now breached) Iron Curtain. One strand of "international" Christianity has been strongly Marxist, and reflects the revolutionary socialism of the Prague-based Christian Peace Conference. The groups involved can be tracked back to the spate of Soviet Front organizations, like the Prague-based World Marxist Review, that were created around 1958 by Krushchev, following the model of a "solar system" of Fronts created in 1926 by the aged 1917 veteran Otto Kuusinen. The World Council of Churches' funding of the African revolutionary liberation movements was one consequence of this infiltration, and the penetration has reached the Vatican. The Second Vatican Council was under pressure from the subversive forces and it is significant that from 1958 until Cardinal (later Pope) Ratzinger's statement in 1986, the Vatican has refused to condemn atheistic Communism.

Revolutionary organizations which use Christianity as a front to undermine Christendom have nothing to do with the metaphysic of the Light. The Ecumenical Movement that will reunite Christianity is not an internationalist ex-Soviet-based movement, but the "Christian Unity" movement to which Pope John Paul II was committed, which would reunify Christendom in both the West and East, so that Catholics, Protestants and Orthodox Christians would share one faith from the Baltic to the Aegean and from the Atlantic to the Urals. This is the movement that helped Gorbachev break down the barriers between West and East and that can prepare the ground for the world-wide religion that is approaching in stage 15 of the North-American civilization (America's current stage).

To achieve this there will have to be a new Movement – a "Light of the World Movement" or "Brotherhood of Light" – that will focus attention on the central experience of Christianity and of all religions (the experience of the transforming

Light) at the expense of the myths and the doctrine, the dogma, the old forms of worship or the hymn-singing. This "Light of the World Movement" will focus on the Orthodox Light of the Transfiguration, the Catholic "*lumen gentium*" (i.e. "Christ is the light of all nations") of the Second Vatican Council document, and the Protestant Light of the World, which form the common ground of the Christian metaphysical experience (the Christian encounter with Being). There are signs that such a Movement is not far ahead. It is very exciting that Laurence Freeman OSB, who became prior of the Benedictine Priory of Montreal which was founded from Ealing Abbey in London, has headed a world-wide network of Christian meditation groups that look back to the Desert Father John Cassian. In his book *Light Within* Freeman writes of the freedom "to see the light of our real self and to know that we are that light", "that light shining at the centre of our self" which is "there in every-thing".[10] Attempts to reconcile the Christian and New-Age outlooks may have a long-term significance in this regard, such as the work of Canon Peter Spink, author of *Spiritual Man in a New Age*, who founded the Omega Order which takes its inspiration from F. C. Happold, the authority on mysticism, and Teilhard de Chardin, and who promoted contemplative meditation at Kent House, Tunbridge Wells (a reclaimed ruin in the Findhorn style).[11] In Britain there has been an upsurge of Evangelical-inspired devotional pop street songs, and on Battle of Britain day in September 1990 200,000 people took part in 59 marches for unity, carrying banners proclaiming "Jesus is Light" and singing the songs of Graham Kendrick, such as "Let the flame burn brighter/Let it shine", "Shine, Jesus, shine/Fill this land with the Father's glory,/Set our hearts on fire" and "We walk the land/With us on fire,/Let it shine." The Battle *for* Britain movement is changing the Church and has brought Catholics and Protestants together in Northern Ireland on the Light. The Archbishop of Canterbury spoke of the importance of this popular movement which is not afraid to proclaim the Light in the marketplace.

There will have to be a return to fundamentals within Christendom, and a rein-terpretation of the essence of Christianity to focus attention on the common Light it shares with the metaphysical visions of the world's other traditional cultures. There will inevitably have to be a Western (European and American) Mystic Revival within the framework of Christianity, and a Metaphysical Revolution across the Western culture, which will in fact be a Metaphysical Restoration. Because it will break with the immediate past it will be experienced as a Revolution rather than as a Restoration. How dominant Christianity will be in the American-led world-wide civilization will depend on the mystical and metaphysical performance of Christianity in the coming decades – on whether it can put its metaphysical house in order and renew itself by readmitting the Light. This can be expected to happen in stage 45 of the European civilization when a revival of cultural purity coexists with the Universalism of stage 44, creating a new Classical/Baroque Age in which man is again defined as body, mind, soul, spirit and divine spark.

Metaphysics, the study of Reality, its meaning and structure, traditionally includes ontology, the study of Being; epistemology, or what can be known with certainty about Being; and philosophical cosmology, which is based on astronomical cosmology and relates the physical structure of the universe to ontological Being. From Plato to Leibniz and Kant metaphysics has been theoretical and speculative, but today, especially under Husserl and Heidegger, and with American space probes sharpening our knowledge of cosmology, metaphysics has become more empirical and practical.

Each age reinterprets the metaphysical vision it inherits, finds new meaning in it, and transmits it so that the intuitive intellect feels life has a meaning, a purpose. Contrary to what we often hear, our age is no exception. Western metaphysics has been reinterpreted in Husserl's *Ideas* (1913), Marcel's *Metaphysical Journal* (1927), Whitehead's *Process and Reality* (1929), and Heidegger's *Being and Time* (1927) and *Introduction to Metaphysics* (1935). The foundations for a reinterpretation and reunification of Eastern and Western metaphysics have been laid by René Guénon (in works such as *East and West*) and Frithjof Schuon (whose titles include *The Transcendent Unity of Religions* and *Gnosis, Divine Knowledge*). Marco Pallis writes in his Foreword to W. N. Perry's 1,143 page *A Treasury of Traditional Wisdom,* "This century of ours, for all its vast and various discontents and because of them, has been productive of some of the most clear-sighted and heart-searching commentaries that the West has ever known, among which those of René Guénon and, more especially, Frithjof Schuon, provide pre-eminent examples: it is indeed a long time since anything of this intellectual order has been heard in Europe."

Guénon (1886-1951) and later Schuon (born 1907) have extended the approach of Robert Ballou's *Bible of the World* (1940), Lin Yutang's Asian-based *The Wisdom of India and China* (1942), Coomaraswamy's *Hinduism and Buddhism* (1943), and Aldous Huxley's personal and eclectic *The Perennial Philosophy*

(1946).[12] Guénon was more than an Orientalist; he is usually described as a traditionalist – an interpreter of tradition – or as a metaphysician. After flirting with Martinists and Gnostics he was converted to Islam in 1912, and in 1930 left France and lived in Egypt where he spent the last 21 years of his life. His metaphysical work *The Multiple States of Being* includes a chapter on *The Spiritual Hierarchies*, which goes beyond the boundaries of traditional metaphysical philosophy. Schuon was born in Basel, Switzerland, of German parents, and he studied in Paris. He read widely in his search for metaphysical truth, came upon the writings of Guénon, corresponded with Guénon for six years and in 1938 went to Cairo to meet him. He saw him again in 1939. In recent years he has become identified with the Plain Indians, who feature in his oil paintings. His fundamental perception in comparative religion came when a Senegalese *marabout* (Mohammedan hermit or monk) visited Basel and drew a circle with radii on the ground and said, "God is the centre, all paths lead to Him." Schuon's position is "fundamentally that of metaphysics" (his Preface to *From the Divine to the Human*) and T. S. Eliot remarked of *The Transcendent Unity of Religions* (1948), on which he advised Fabers c.1951, "I have met with no more impressive work in the the comparative study of Oriental and Occidental religions."[13] Schuon's approach is rational-intellectual and is concerned with ontological and cosmological proofs for the existence of God. Both Guénon and Schuon focus on the *sophia perennis* or the *religio perennis*, the timeless metaphysical truth which underlies the different religions. They concentrate on the *tradition* of this truth and the intellect rather than on the direct experience of the metaphysical Light, and neither really deals with the *experience* of the vision of God, the direct mystical experience that forms the basis of this book, although Schuon hints at it. For example: "the Heart-in-intellect is the seat, not only of knowledge, but also of Love, that is both Light and Heat."[14] Again: "There is nothing but Light.... The Light shines for itself, then it radiates to communicate itself, and by radiating, it produces the Veil and the veils.... Gnosis, being the science of Light, is thereby the science of veilings and unveilings."[15]

The metaphysical view is now to be found in a number of disciplines. Today comparative religion is dominated by Schuon's metaphysical approach. This can be gleaned by glancing through the back numbers of the impressive *Studies in Comparative Religion*. Every issue since 1971 leads with a contribution from Schuon, who is called "the greatest writer of our time" by Martin Lings, and whose

Logic and Transcendence is described by Seyyed Hossein Nasr as "one of the most important philosophical works of this century if philosophy be understood in the traditional sense of love of wisdom". In the field of philosophy, not religion, the metaphysical approach is to be found in the works of E. W. F. Tomlin, whose first philosophical work was *The Approach to Metaphysics* (1947) and whose *Philosophers of East and West* unites the philosophical traditions of the metaphysical East and the empirical West and paves the way for the coming Universalism. A reinterpretation of the metaphysical vision, and of what is sacred in culture, was organized by Kathleen Raine, the Neoplatonist scholar and poet who edited a fat metaphysical magazine, *Temenos*, and was influenced by Guénon's "law of correspondence" which makes possible "a plurality of meanings" in the literary symbol.[16] Raine attempted to revive Plato's Academy in London. Plato's Academy lasted from 385 BC to AD 529, and was revived in Florence during the Renaissance, when it was associated with Ficino, and its return in our time should have heralded (had Raine been more illumined) the preservation of the knowledge of the metaphysical Light through a group of people rather than one person working in isolation (such as Thomas Taylor the Platonist in the 18th century). In the field of psychoanalysis, Gaston Bachelard in *The Psychoanalysis of Fire* reinterpreted "the metaphysics of fire" or "inner fire" by dwelling on Novalis's treatment of the "inward light".[17]

We have already remarked that the new American-led biology and physics has a world-view that is close to that of the metaphysical vision. Twentieth-century physics has brought us to the brink of metaphysics. Einstein said, "Anyone who studies physics long enough is inevitably led to metaphysics," and ever since Einstein physicists have sought a Theory Of Everything (or TOE) that will explain all known forces: gravity, electro-magnetic fields, and subatomic events. Just as historians have unsuccessfully sought the unifying factor in history, so physicists have sought it in the events of physics – again so far without success. A number of possibilities have been put forward, including the idea that multi-dimensional strings account for everything that is known. According to this theory, everything in our universe – all matter, gravity and space itself – is a manifestation of tiny events, to see which would require the magnification of subatomic particles into the size of galaxies. It is largely because such magnification has so far proved impossible that physicists have failed to see the strings, which therefore remain theoretical.

The metaphysical vision can provide physicists with the unifying factor they seek. It is likely that the unifying principle that explains everything and provides a "theory of everything" (or TOE) will also explain historical patterns and trends, and I have argued in my Grand Unified Theory (GUT) that the presence or absence of the Light provides a context which explains all historical patterns and trends. Is it not then possible that the energy of the Light (which presumably has a – hitherto unknown – physical vehicle and counterpart) is the missing principle which the physicists seek, and that they have missed it because it is no more to be found in physics books than it is in history books? According to the evidence of our mystics (see *The Light of Civilization*), the Light contains properties of wisdom and healing, and probably other qualities as well, just as a ray of light is a spectrum and just as a rainbow has bands. Could not the Light also contain an organising band that includes gravity, electro-magnetism and the strong and weak forces which physicists have posited to account for subatomic events? Could not the "Fire", in Heraclitus's sense, pervade the universe and all that can be known, set matter dancing and images whirling in minds? If it can lodge ideas in our mystics' minds, can it not expand and contract atoms? The physicist David Bohm proposed in *Wholeness and the Implicate Order* that the cosmos has manifested from a "nothingness", unfolding into explicitness from implicateness, and Schwarz and Green, recent defenders of the string theory, have in a sense developed Bohm's idea. Regardless of whether there are strings or chains of events, could not the Light be the latent, implicate superforce which manifests into the phenomena of creation – trees and stars and waves – and in that case would it not be wonderful that mental events can coincide with physical events through the experiences of mystics, who see the organising principle of the cosmos (i.e. the Light of God, the Whole)? Could not the Light be the invisible power or One known to the Romantic poets and painters that holds all four physical forces in place, organizes our cellular division and breathes through our lungs, that shoots the acorn and blows through the oak, that ripples the waves and pulls the tides? Is it not the force van Gogh showed burning through trees? All such events can be explained in terms of biology and physics up to a point, but in an academic application of the Metaphysical Revolution all can be given unity by the miraculous action of the mysterious Light which spirals through all galaxies and minds as through one subatomic particle and which would then be seen to unify history, physics, biology, and all human life within its creative power. To the Western mind this unity restates and redefines the traditional view of God. To the Eastern mind that knows the Ryoanji stone garden in Kyoto, Japan, the unifying principle can be found in the Oneness of the rocks and pebbles which are variously rocks from the sea, mountains and clouds, and mountains and earth, the essential oneness within the four elements of earth, air, fire and water.

I can go further and ask if this unifying Light is associated with, i.e. manifests in, cosmic background radiation, the radiation left over from the Big Bang which created the universe 18 billion to 15 billion years ago. Discovered in New Jersey, America, in 1964/5 by Arno Penzias and Robert Wilson, this radiation, which is now being regarded as proof that the universe had a fiery birth in a Big Bang, is received on a receiver as a perpetual hiss akin to radio interference or snow on a TV set. This perpetual echo of the primeval fireball is dispersed and is a diffuse glow at constant microwave frequencies throughout the known universe. It corresponds to matter only 3 degrees above zero, and is being investigated by the American NASA (National Aeronautics and Space Administration) satellite Cobe (Cosmic Background Explorer), which was launched in November 1989 and which is also looking for the seeds from which the galaxies were born. According to one of its discoverers, Arno Penzias, anyone standing under the stars experiences this cosmic background radiation as a slight cosmic warmth which warms the head. This may be the source of the healing energy. (Compare the rays with healing hands which Akhenaton worshipped.) The 92-inch Hubble space telescope which was launched into space in April 1990 and named after the famous American astronomer Edwin Hubble who discovered in the 1920s that there are other galaxies besides ours and that they are expanding in accordance with a Big Bang theory, has received images of light from near the time of the Creation and can also eventually help us to understand this cosmic background radiation. Indeed, the conditions that immediately followed the Big Bang are being recreated in an SSC (Super Conducting Super Collider), which is being developed with American government approval in a tunnel 54 miles in circumference beneath the plains of Waxahachie, south of Dallas in the USA. There eventually two beams of protons, hurled by powerful magnets in opposite directions and with velocities approaching the speed of light or an energy of 20 trillion electric volts (TeV), will collide and create a subatomic fireball and the conditions that existed in the millionth of a second after the Big Bang. American "inner space" scientists may then understand the origin and structure of cosmic background radiation and of matter, and the secrets of the creation of the universe, thus complementing the observations of astronomers looking at outer space.

A sceptical Materialist would say that this radiation is the Light, i.e. that the Light is no more than temporal, finite radiation which did not exist before the Big Bang and whose echo is dying. However, if this radiation from the time of creation is seen as a *manifestation*, via the vacuum or Void that preceded the Big Bang, of our original metaphysical Light, whose properties include wisdom and guidance as *The Light of Civilization* shows, then our perpetual, eternal, silent Light *manifests* in a perpetual (albeit temporal) physical hissing radiation which cooled into matter when hydrogen separated and which can be expected to organize gravity, electromagnetism and strong (nuclear) and weak forces, and to provide the Theory of Everything (TOE) which the physicists are seeking. A Theory of Everything is impossible without cosmic rays because two of the three families of elementary particles (strange and charmed quarks, leptons called muons, muon neutrinos, bottom and top quarks, tau leptons and tau neutrinos) can only exist naturally on earth in cosmic rays because the universe has cooled since the Big Bang. (All three families existed naturally a fraction of a second after the Big Bang, and the first family, which *is* found naturally on earth today, consists of up and down quarks, the fundamental particles of matter which make up the protons and neutrons found in the nuclei of atoms and two leptons: electrons which orbit the nuclei of atoms and electron neutrinos which are produced by exploding stars.)

A manifestation of the Light in cosmic background radiation makes possible a Theory of Everything that reconciles cosmology and ontology, physics with metaphysics, time and eternity. This manifestation from Light to Void to cosmic background radiation after the Big Bang, and to matter, mirrors the four worlds of the occult Kabbalah, and the overall structure of the Theory of Everything can be expressed as follows:

Four layers of Reality	Religious interpretation	Four Kabbalistic worlds	Metaphysical discipline
Infinity, Timelessness, Eternity:			
1. Infinite/Supreme Being/Reality/	God	divine	ontology/

Light/the One/absolute Good (& Ontic realm above intellect)			mysticism
2. Non-manifestation/Non-Being/ Vacuum (before Big Bang)/ Void/implicate order/ Nonduality (*advaita*)/Idea/ Archetypes/Forms/*Logos*/*Tao*/ Superspace/sea of Light/ Alchemists' *unus mundus*/ metaphysical Zero/Divine Mind/ Intellectual Principle (or *Nous*)/ Totality of Possibilities of Being/Holy Spirit/Heaven	Holy Spirit known by spirit	spiritual	intellectual Idealism/ transper- sonal psychology/ transformation to new centre

Time:

3. Manifestation after Big Bang/ Being/Totality of Possibilities of Existence/invisible cosmic background radiation/Ocean of Being/Unity of Being known by soul	Oneness of creation known by individual soul illumined by Light through spirit	psycho- logical	epistemology/ psychology
4. Existence/matter/organism/ world of senses	world known by social ego/ body	physical	cosmology/ physics

The above table assumes that Supreme Being, the Light and its *alias*es, envelops the Void or vacuum or Non-Being, the sum total of everything unmanifested, which is also known by many aliases (see 2 above); which in turn envelops Being the sum total of all manifestation to which it gives rise; which in turn envelops Existence or the world of the senses. Existence (matter) is thus permeated by Being (perhaps the cosmic background radiation and imaged in the pebbles in the Zen-Ryoanji stone garden in Kyoto, Japan) which together with Non-Being (the Void) make up the Infinite Supreme Being (the Light).

This is a hugely important idea. If perpetual, healing cosmic background radiation spreads out from the beginning of creation 13.7 billion years ago, permeating all living things which congealed from it (for our bodies are composed of material which emanated from the Big Bang), manifesting from implicate "nothing" (Non-Being, the Void, and ultimately the Light) into something and influencing souls as the physical manifestation of an eternal God who is experienced within as a healing vision of Light, a vision which (as we have seen) has inspired the genesis of the world's 25 civilizations, then our Universalism is indeed inextricably associated with the universe, the exploration of which is one of the great rational and intellectual achievements of the North-American civilization.

Philosophers have long sought the meaning and purpose of the cosmos. Our proposal takes us to a unity that Plato would have approved, judging from his famous image of the fire in the shadowed cave; it restores a synoptic view to philosophy: a view that the philosopher who is open to wisdom, which manifests from the "Fire" or Light, can unify (some would say reunify) all the academic disciplines in a truly whole "Theory Of Everything" (or TOE). (It is interesting that even an anti-metaphysical philosopher can open to this wisdom. In 1988 the late A. J. Ayer's heart stopped for four minutes when: "I was confronted by a red light, exceedingly bright. I was aware that this light was responsible for the government of the universe.")

If a world-wide religion is to grow, the next move is for the active souls to reverse the trend of the last three hundred and fifty years in Europe and restore the traditional metaphysical vision of the Christian Western culture, but in a new form that is appropriate for the coming American-led world-wide civilization. There will have to be one metaphysical vision for all the world's groups, classes and races. It will have to offer rituals that give all citizens of the world significance, meaning, and symbolic analogies in their everyday life. The way forward is through meditation, for when the body and mind are calmed the spirit emerges and the Light is eventually seen. The world's artists, poets, scientists, politicians and labourers can find meaning in the Tradition I have outlined. In a very real sense the Light completes the Metaphysical Revolution begun by Guénon and Schuon. The metaphysical vision of the Light in meditation adds a new layer to their rational-intellectual statement of their tradition. It offers direct experience of metaphysical Reality and therefore a Metaphysical Existentialism (or Existential Metaphysics) in which Being can be directly known as both ontological and cosmological truth. The metaphysical vision of the Light makes the systems of Guénon and Schuon more immediate, restores the sacred to world culture, and offers a new sacredness for the arts, which will undergo a new renaissance as they take account of man's metaphysical stature as a being who is more than his body and senses. This book attempts to show that the metaphysical vision allows for the return of sacred history. To create this new sacredness and meaning will require a world-wide missionary effort on a huge-scale, of the kind that St Bernard organized at the time of the Second Crusade, but the effort will be worth-while as every human being in the world is a citizen of the Light. This is the true egalitarianism: we are all Light-centred creatures, and the tragedy is that at present so few know it.

It is another dream that man has long awaited, that we are moving towards a world in which racism and war will seem irrelevant, a world from which the threat of a new nuclear-triggered Dark Age, which is only twenty minutes away, is removed. It is to be hoped that the Eastern-European countries have now officially returned from their superficial, secular Communism to their traditional, profound metaphysical culture which has continued unofficially. The signs are that they have: Christianity is thriving behind the Iron Curtain, where oppression has created a spiritual intensity not found in the materialistic, affluent West and *glasnost* has brought a new tolerance of the Russian Orthodox religion. (One of the prophecies apparently made by the Virgin Mary to three Portuguese children at Fatima in May 1917 was that the world's civilizations will collapse if Russia does not again fully embrace Christianity, a revelation Pope John Paul II apparently took very seriously. He was reported to wish to make a Papal Crusade to Moscow.) It is to be hoped that both West and the East can soon meet on the common Light of their traditional cultures. Both sides need to undergo transformations in their values before this can happen, and an easing of the secular, ideological conflicts between the two can promote peace and pave the way for such a development.

I have looked deep into history and although I have excluded what lies outside my phenomenological method it may now seem that we have perhaps glimpsed the will of God as Light at work in the emergence of one world-wide civilization. Such a noble, truly internationalist vision of peace, even though it would be under

American leadership and is at present entrammelled in the machinations of the corrupting Syndicate, anticipates the millennium, the reign of Christ on earth. It is what man has dreamt of for thousands of years, and never more so than in times of war and famine. So much famine is caused by wars waged by leaders with Lightless values. A renewed widespread acceptance of the Light by the masses and their leaders could bring in the impossible millennium in the unlikely form of American world hegemony. AIDS has given the world a chance to draw back or even turn away from the senses; can a new Light of the World Movement be established at the start of our new millennium?

CLOSING VISION

Such a prospect may seem excessively idealistic to many, but it is predicted in my 61 stages. Turning our eyes back to the immediate reality of Western civilization (the European and North-American civilizations), I have in the end to ask this realistic and practical question: will the illumined few continue the Tradition of the Light in Europe as they have done for five thousand years so that the metaphysical vision of the European West can be saved, and will the American masses return to the Light in sufficient numbers, as did the British masses in the early 17th century, so that the American West can be strengthened?

Western civilization is at a turning-point. Europe for all the expansion of its coming conglomerate (stage 43) is declining, America (now at stage 15) growing. One period of history is ending and a new period is beginning. Just as the Middle Ages passed into the Renaissance, a new millennium has begun in which Europe and North America – and Christianity – will expand, and a Counter-Renaissance (i.e. Counter-Humanism) is with us. Will it revive the West? Will it renew decaying Europe and energise growing America? Our interpretation of our 61 stages predicts that it will.

What is crucial is that we in the West should make a start. The common Light is there. Whether Christianity remains independent in a close network of world religions or whether syncretistic merging does take place to create one world-wide religion (European civilization's stage 44), the Light is common to all the world's religions. All times relate to all cultures through the Light. The *fana* of the Sufi in ecstasy is the burning heart of the Christian and the glow of the Buddhist. We need to change our values so that we can bring in a better world. We need a renewal of Christian mysticism in an inter-faith context. My reinterpretation of history in terms of the Light has rediscovered a vision of a universal metaphysical Reality that is shared by all religions and cultures, and has made possible a Metaphysical Revolution in our time. We need a Metaphysical Revolution in the West, a Metaphysical Restoration, *now*.

The options are clear. Either American-inspired visions of the Light will renew Christianity and the European West (into the European Resurgence of stage 43) and will in turn influence the American West so that through American hegemony the North-American civilization can develop a world-wide religion (in stage 15) in which Christianity is dominant. Or European civilization will be violently occupied (at the beginning of stage 43) and will fall, and there will be a new (possibly Islamic-caused) Dark Age in Europe.

Thomas Merton seems to have had a similar view: "The world of our time is in confusion. It is reaching the peak of the greatest crisis in history.... Mankind stands on the brink of a new barbarism, yet at the same time there remain possibilities for an unexpected and almost unbelievable solution, the creation of a new world and a new civilization the like of which has never been seen. We are face to face either with Antichrist or the Millennium, no-one knows which."[18]

Willy-nilly, I find myself cast in the role of the *Old Testament* prophet. I can see the future clearly, but, a product of the secularized, declining European civilization of stages 41 and 43, I can do little on my own except write this book – my *"prolegomena"* to a vast work of several thousand pages – to warn the Western (European and American) world. Like Isaiah or Ezekiel or Jeremiah in Jerusalem, I see the American dream ahead, I see the Light in the stones of past cultures, but if there were to be no coming American/European-inspired European conglomerate I would also see the fall of Western Europe before an occupying power (possibly Islam) as inevitable (at the beginning of stage 43) unless there is a widespread return within our Christian civilization to the Tradition of the Light which is the European civilization's Central Idea (not capitalism). Mercifully I do see an American/European-inspired European conglomerate (a United States of Western and Eastern Europe), and I can see a return to the Light happening by inspiration from a stage-15 North-American civilization and its accompanying Universalism, and from a liberated Eastern Europe, which can be expected to enter the European conglomerate, and through something akin to a Universalist "Light of the World Movement".

A new "Light of the World Movement" would devise a new Universalist terminology and would have three aims, which would correspond to the three levels on which the Tradition of the Light can be read: to bring individuals to an existential confrontation with the Light; to bring to pass a Metaphysical revival within all societies, cultures and civilizations, but particularly within the European and North-American civilizations, so that university syllabuses contain metaphysical as well as secular texts; and to show that the Light is the common ground for all civilizations, whose central idea it is, that the Light provides the common ground for the coming world-wide culture, and that it is an impetus for world peace. It is time to establish a Foundation in the US – a Foundation of the Light – which will further these aims and safeguard the Metaphysical Revolution. This is an idea whose time has come.

I can see the North-American civilization break free from the influence of the Satanic, Illuminatist Syndicate and inspire a world-wide culture whose common ground is the Light: a New World Order that is more akin to Christ's outlook than Satan's. Within the context of this North-American globalist influence, and although a new European constitution will superimpose a new European superstate on individual nation-states, I can see Europe's stage 43 being a glorious, albeit American-led, European Resurgence lasting 150 years, *provided the Light of the European civilization's Central Idea is renewed.* What the lucid contemplative eye sees let the active life now perform, for the Light also unites the *vita contemplativa* and *vita activa* and translates contemplative vision into action.

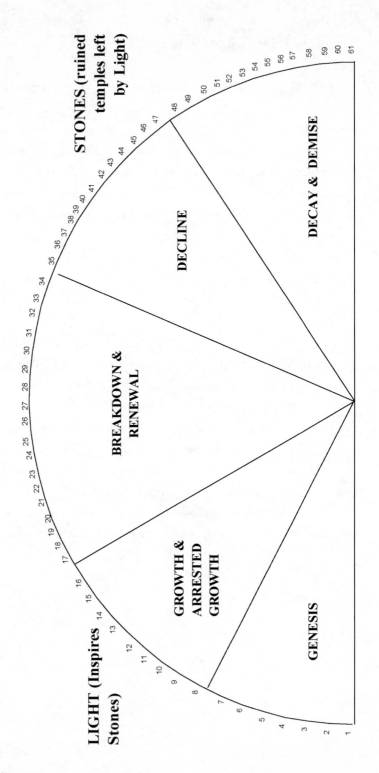

CHART 1: THE RAINBOW-LIKE PARABOLA
61 STAGES IN A CIVILIZATION'S LIFE CYCLE

LIGHT (Inspires Stones)

STONES (ruined temples left by Light)

GENESIS

GROWTH & ARRESTED GROWTH

BREAKDOWN & RENEWAL

DECLINE

DECAY & DEMISE

1. Light originates in earlier civilisation
2. Light migrates to new culture
3. Light absorbs new culture
4. Light creates new religion through religious unification
5. Light precedes genesis
6. Light creates Central Idea amid 16 alternatives
7. Light attracts, converts & unifies peoples round Central Idea
8. Light strong during growth
9. Light inspires stones
10. Doctrinal controversy round Light
11. Political unification
12. Schism between supporters of rival gods
13. Foreign military blow
14. Arrest in growth of secularized civilisation (50 years)
15. Counterthrust: expansion into Empire, Light-led renewal of growth
16. Heroic epic literature with god of Light-led growth
17. Creation of Light-based heretical sect
18. Persecution of heretical sect
19. Decline of religion as a result of heretical sect & foreign influence
20. Mystics resist decline
21. Foreign military blow
22. Breakdown of civilisation (100 years)
23. Secularization in response to foreign threat
24. Revival of past culture of another civilisation
25. Civil War: Rulers v heretical New People
26. New People in limelight
27. Heresy grafted on to Central Idea as new religious focus
28. New people's heretical renewal of Light and Central Idea
29. Geographical expansion of New People
30. Secession from New People's God
31. New People persecute sceders and become New Orthodoxy

32. Scientific materialism weakens religion
33. Artistic reaction
34. Further expansion into Empire over-extends civilisation
35. Light weakens as energy is dispersed abroad
36. Light disappears from official religion
37. Breakdown of certainties after military event
38. Central Idea/Religion weaken, Arts become secular
39. Rationalism & scepticism weaken religion
40. Industrial decline as civilisation over-extends itself
41. Colonial conflict ending in decolonisation & occupation
42. Proletarianisation & egalitarianism
43. Loss of national sovereignty to secularizing conglomerate
44. Syncretism & Universalism round Light
45. Revival of lost past of civilisation
46. Counterthrust under foreign federal influence
47. Economic decline & inflation, class conflict
48. Light ceases to be publicly recognised by religion
49. Invaders undermine Lightless religion
50. Foreign invaders destroy Stones
51. Loss of Central Idea as peoples secede to foreign invaders' culture
52. Final independent phase
53. Further occupation by foreign power
54. Contemplative mystics turn from decaying religion to foreign cults
55. Civilisation resists occupier
56. Occupier persecutes defectors from its cults
57. Coteries continue Light & Central Idea in mysteries
58. Further occupation
59. Occupier's religion suppresses & kills Lightless religion
60. Sudden final conquest or religionless civilisation
61. Demise of civilisation which now passes into a successor civilisation

CHART 2: YEARS BETWEEN SEVEN NODAL POINTS OF GROWTH AND DECLINE

Civilization	Genesis	Years Between	Unification	Years Between	Arrest of Growth	Years Between	Breakdown	Years Between	Decline/Loss of National Sovereignty	Years Between	Decay/Occupation	Years Between	Demise	Full Span of Years So Far
1. Indo-European Kurgan Old European	c.3700BC	1000	c.2700BC	100	c.2600BC	600	c.2000BC	550	c.1550BC	350	c.1200BC	400	c.800BC	3100
2. Mesopotamian	c.3500BC	1150	c.2350BC	346	c.2004BC	414	c.1590BC	1051	c.539BC	398	c.141BC	783	642AD	4142
3. Egyptian	c.3100BC	414	c.2686BC	526	c.2160BC	486	c.1674BC	1149	c.525BC	332	c.193BC	835	642AD	3742
4. Aegean-Greek	c.2200BC	400	c.1800BC	100	c.1700BC	500	c.1200BC	863	c.337BC	122	c.215BC	844	629AD	2829
5. Roman	c.800BC	291	c.509BC	119	c.390BC	277	c.113BC	589	476AD	92	c.568	219	c.787	1587
6. Anatolian	c.2000BC	300	c.1700BC	180	c.1520BC	295	c.1225BC	679	c.546BC	268	c.278BC	904	626AD	2626
7. Syrian	c.3000BC	1000	c.2000BC	480	c.1520BC	295	c.1225BC	687	c.538BC	319	c.219BC	855	636AD	3636
8. Israelite	19th-18th BC	550	c.1250BC	60	c.1190BC	349	c.841BC	303	c.538BC	340	c.198BC	834	636AD	2536
9. Celtic	c.1200BC	750	c.450BC	63	c.387BC	329	c.58BC	598	c.540AD	298	c.838	333	c.1171	2371
10. Iranian	c.850BC	300	c.550BC	220	c.330BC	444	c.114AD	526	c.640	415	c.1055	456	c.1511	2361
11. European	5th C AD	300	c.800	100	c.900	553	c.1453	544 544	c.1997/c.2008?	–	–	–	–	1500
12. North-American	1494 AD	293	c.1787	74	1861		–		–		–		–	600
13. Byzantine-Russian	c.395AD	145	c.540	86	c.626	728	c.1354	564	c.1918	–	–	–	–	1660
14. Germanic-Scandinavian	c.500BC	350	c.150BC	138	c.12BC	282	c.270BC	502	c.772AD	139	c.911	303	c.1214	1741

Civilization	Genesis	Years Between	Unification	Years Between	Arrest of Growth	Years Between	Breakdown	Years Between	Decline/Loss of National Sovereignty	Years Between	Decay/Occupation	Years Between	Demise	Full Span of Years So Far
15. Andean	c.1200BC	200	c.1000BC	600	c.400BC	900	c.500AD	1072	c.1572		–		–	3190
16. Meso-American	c.1500BC	400	c.1100BC	700	c.400BC	600	c.200AD	1342	c.1542		–		–	3490
17. Arab	c.325AD	297	c.622	118	c.740	518	c.1258	623	c.1881		–		–	1380
18. African	c.2000BC	1250	c.750BC	430	c.320AD	320	c.640	1260	c.1900		–		–	3990
19. Indian	c.1500BC	1175	c.325BC	395	c.70AD? (or 240)	1080	c.1150	668	c.1818		–		–	3490
20. South-East-Asian	1st C AD	300	c.300-400	400	c.800	377	c.1177	663	c.1840		–		–	1950
21. Japanese	c.250BC	670	c.420	243	c.663	611	c.1274	671	c.1945		–		–	2240
22. Oceanian	c.400-500AD	300	c.400-500	300	c.800	300	c.1100	770	c.1870		–		–	1590
23. Chinese	c.2205/1766BC	1545	c.221BC	525	c.304AD	967	1271	678	c.1949		–		–	3756
24. Tibetan	c.200BC	808	c.608AD	599	c.1207	358	c.1565	386	c.1951		–		–	2190
25. Central-Asian (including Mongolia)	c.500BC	280	c.220BC	520	c.300AD	825	c.1125	519	c.1644		–		–	2690

CHART 3: DATE-BASED SUMMARY OF THE 61 STAGES IN THE LIFE CYCLE OF

Civilization		1. Light Originates in Earlier Civilization.	2 & 3
1. Indo-European Kurgan	b.c.4500 BC	"C-Asian/Altaic"	c.3700 BC
2. Mesopotamian	b.c.3500 BC	Indo-European Kurgan	c.3500 BC
3. Egyptian	b.c.3400 BC?	Indo-European/Mesopotamian	c.3400-3100 BC
4. Aegean-Greek	b.c.3500/c.2200 BC	Indo-European/Anatolian	c.2200 BC
5. Roman	b.c.1200 /c.800 BC	Indo-European/Greek	c.1200/c.800BC
6. Anatolian	c.6000/c.2000 BC	Indo-European	c.2000 BC
7. Syrian	c.8500/c.3000 BC	"Neolithic/Mesopotamian"	c.3000 BC
8. Israelite	b.19th-18th C BC	Indo-European/Mesopotamian	19th-18th C BC
9. Celtic	b.c.1200 BC	Indo-European	c.1200/c.700 BC
10. Iranian	b.c.2250 BC	"Indo-European/Mesopotamian"	c.2250-1700BC
11. European*	b.1st C	Israeli/Celtic/Roman	1st-5th C
12. North-American	b.c.1494	"Central-Asian"	frm c.1494-1650
13. Byzantine-Russian	b.324-330	Roman	330-395
14. Germanic-Scandinavian	b.c.500 BC	Indo-European	c.500 BC
15. Andean	b.c.2600 BC?	C-Asian/Indo-E/Mesopotamian	c.2600?-1200 BC
16. Meso-American	b.c.2600 BC?	C-Asian/Indo-E/Mesopotamian	c.2600?-1150 BC
17. Arab	b.c.721 BC	Israelite	c.721BC-AD325
18. African	b.c.2000 BC	C-Asian/Egyptian	c.2000 BC
19. Indian	c.2250/b.c.1500 BC	"Iranian/Indo-European"	c.1500 BC
20. South-East-Asian	1st C	Indian	1st-4th C
21. Japanese	b.c.250 BC	Chinese	c.250 BC
22. Oceanian	c.3000/c.1300 BC	C-Asian/Indo-European/Indian	c.1000 BC-1st CAD
23. Chinese	b.c.2205 BC?	C-Asian/Indo-European	c.2205 BC?
24. Tibetan	b.c.200 BC	Indian/Chinese	c.200 BC
25. Central-Asian	c.50,000 BC	unknown	c.500 BC
*European Peoples:			
11A.British	b.1st C	Israelite/Celtic/Roman	1st C-670
11B.French	b.1st C	Israelite/Celtic/Roman	1st-5th C
11C.German	b.1st C	Israelite/Celtic/Roman	1st-5thC
11D.Spanish	b.1st C	Israelite/Celtic/Roman	1st C-c.500
11E.Italian	b.1st C	Israelite/Celtic/Roman	1st-5th C
11F.Low Countries	b.1st C	Israelite/Celtic/Roman	1st C-c.500
11G.Portuguese	b.1st C	Israelite/Celtic/Roman	1st-6th C
11H.Austro-Hungarian	b.1st C	Israelite/Celtic/Roman	1st-6th C

Abbreviations: bt.= between, f.= from, b.= before, a.= after, c.= circa (around), esp. = especially, beg.= began

25 CIVILIZATIONS (INCLUDING PROJECTIONS FOR LIVING CIVILIZATIONS)

4. Light Creates New Religion.		5	6. Light of New Religion Creates Central Idea	
c.3700 BC	Magna Mater/Sky Father	c.3700 BC	c.3700-2700 BC	Dyaeus Pitar
c.3500 BC	Sumerian Anu/Utu	c.3500 BC	c.3500-2350 BC	Anu/Sumerian gods
c.3100 BC	Horus(Nth)/Seth (Sth)	c.3100 BC	c.3100-2686 BC	Ra
c.2200 BC	Zeus	c.2200 BC	c.2200-1800 BC	Zeus/Apollo
c.800 BC	Etruscan Tin	c.750 BC	c.800-509 BC	Jupiter
c.2000 BC	Tarhun/Teshub	c.2000 BC	c.2000-1700 BC	Tarhun/Teshub
c.3000 BC	El/Dagon	c.3000 BC	c.3000-2000 BC	El/Dagon/ Hadad/Baal
19-18th C BC	El Shaddai	19th-18th C BC	19th C-c.1250 BC	El Shaddai/Yahweh
a.c.1200 BC	Du-w/Lug	c.1200 BC	c.1200-450 BC	Du-w
c.2250-1700 BC	Mithras	c.1300 BC	c.1700-550 BC	Mithras
5th-6th C	Church of Rome	5th-6th C	5th C-800	Catholic God/Christ
c.1620-1649	Protestant Christ	1607 c.1650	c.1620-1787	Puritan God/Christ
c. 395	Gr Orthodox Christ	c.395	c.395-540	Orthodox God/Christ
c.500 BC	Tiwaz/Tiw	c.500 BC	c.500-150 BC	Wodan/Odin
a.c.2600 BC	Sun-god	c.1200 BC	c.2600-1000 BC	Sun-god
a.c.2600 BC	Sun-god	c.1150 BC	c.2600-1100 BC	Sun-god
bt c.721BC/c.325	Dhu-Samawi	c.325	c.721 BC-AD 622	Allah/ Dhu/El or Illah
c.2000 BC	Shamanistic African gods	c.2000 BC	c.2000-750 BC	African gods
c.1500 BC	Vedic Brahmanism	c.1500 BC	c.1500-325 BC	Agni, Siva
1st C	Mahayana Budd/ Saivism	1st C	1st C-c.400	Buddha
c.250 BC	Shinto	c.250 BC	c.250 BC-AD 420	Kami
bt c.1000 BC/1st C	Mana/Buddha	c.1st C	c.1000 BC-AD 500	Buddha?/Andean sun-god?
c.2205 BC	Ti	c.1766 BC	c.2205-221 BC	Ti/Heaven
c.200 BC	Tibetan Buddhism	c.200 BC	c.200 BC-AD 608	Buddha
c.500 BC	Shamanism	c.500 BC	c.500-220 BC	Shamans/Buddha
5th-6th C	Celtic/Catholic Christ	5th-6th C	5th-6th C	God/Christ
5th-6th C	Frankish Catholicism	5th-6th C	5th-6th C	God/Christ
5th-6th C	German Catholicism	5th-6th C	5th-6th C	God/Christ
5th-6th C	Spanish Catholicism	5th-6th C	5th-6th C	God/Christ
5th-6th C	Papal Catholicism	5th-6th C	5th-6th C	God/Christ
5th-6th C	Low Countries Catholicism	5th-6th C	c.5th-6th C	God/Christ
5th-6th C	Portuguese Catholicism	5th-6th C	c.5th-6th C	God/Christ
5th-6th C	Austrian Catholicism	5th-6th C	c.5th-6th C	God/Christ

	7	8	9	10
1.	c.3700-2700 BC	c.3700-1750 BC	c.3500-1750 BC	c.3000 BC
2.	c.3500-2350 BC	c.3500-11th C BC	c.3500-11th C BC	c.2750 BC
3.	c.3100-2686 BC	c.3100-11th C BC	c.2700-11th C BC	c.2800 BC
4.	c.2200-1800 BC	c.2200-5th C BC	c.2200-5th C BC	c.1800 BC
5.	c.800-509 BC	c.800 BC-3rd C AD	c.500 BC-3rd C AD	c.550 BC
6.	2000-1700 BC	c.2000-700 BC	c.2000-700 BC	c.1750 BC
7.	3000-2000 BC	c.3000-700 BC	c.2000-700 BC	after c.2500 BC
8.	19th C-c.1250 BC	c.1800-600 BC	c.950-2nd C BC	c.1275 BC
9.	c.1200-450 BC	c.1200 BC?/-2nd C AD	9th C BC-2nd C AD	c.5th C BC?
10.	c.1700-550 BC	c.2250 BC-4th C AD	c.1700 BC-4th C AD	c.720 BC
11.	5th C- 800	5th-17th C	5th-17th C	c.727
12.	1607/c.1620-1787	c.1620-present	17th C -present	c.1725-1750
13.	c.395-540	c.395-19th C	6th-19th C	c.400-451
14.	c.500-150 BC	c.500 BC-5th C AD	1st-5th C	c.200 BC
15.	c.2600- 1000 BC	c.1200 BC-AD 1300	c.900 BC-AD 1300	c.1100 BC
16.	c.2600-1100 BC	c.1150 BC-AD 1200	c.900 BC-AD 1200	c.1150 BC
17.	c.721 BC-AD 622	5th-17th C	5th-17th C	c.610-632
18.	c.2000-750 BC	c.2000 BC-16th C AD	c.2000 BC-16th C AD	c.1000 BC
19.	c.1500-325 BC	c.1500 BC-16th C AD	c.1500 BC-16th C AD	4th C BC
20.	1st C- c.400	1st-16th C	1st-16th C	3rd C
21.	c.250 BC-AD 420	4th-19th C	4th-19th C	c.400
22.	c.1000 BC- AD 500	c.380-1680	c.300-17th C	c.380
23.	c.2205-221 BC	c.2000 BC-17th C AD	18th C BC-17th C AD	6th-5th C BC
24.	c.200 BC-AD 608	8th-18th C	7th-18th C	6th C
25.	c.500-220 BC	500 BC?-C.14th C AD	c.3rd C BC-14th C AD	3rd C BC
*European Peoples:				
	2nd C- c.900	5th-17th C	5th-17th C	from 727
	5th C- c.900	5th-17th C	5th-17th C	from 727
	5th C- c.900	5th-17th C	5th-17th C	from 727
	c.500-711	5th-17th C	5th-17th C	from 727
	5th C- c.900	5th-17th C	5th-17th C	from 727
	500-c.900	5th-17th C	5th-17th C	from 727
	c.550-711	5th-17th C	5th-17th C	from 727
	568-c.900	5th-17th C	5th-17th C	from 727

11 Political Unification		12	13	14
c.2700 BC	European megaliths	2650 BC	c.2600 BC	c.2600-2550 BC
c.2350 BC	Sargon's Akkad	c.2300 BC	c.2004 BC	c.2004-1950 BC
c.2686 BC	Old Kingdom	c.2400 BC	c.2160 BC	2160-2110 BC
c.1800 BC	Minoan Empire	c.1750 BC	c.1700 BC	c.1700-1650 BC
c.509/475 BC	Latin League's Italy	c.430 BC	c.390 BC	c.390-341 BC
c.1700 BC	Old Hittite Kgdom/Empire	c.1600 BC	c.1520 BC	c.1520-1471 BC
from c.2000 BC	Amorites' Syria	c.1600 BC	c.1520 BC	c.1520-1471 BC
c.1250 BC	Moses' Covenant League	a. c.1230 BC	c.1190 BC	c.1190-c.1140 BC
c.450 BC	La Tene culture	c.400 BC	c.387 BC	c.387-337 BC
c.550 BC	Persian Empire of Cyrus	c.500 BC	c.330 BC	c.330-280 BC
c.800	Frankish Empire	867	c.900	c.900-951
c.1787	US Federal Constitution	c.1835	c.1861	c.1861-1913
c.540	Justinian's Empire	c.638	c.626	c.626-677
c.150 BC	Germanic tribes	c.75 BC	c.55 BC	12 BC-AD 38
c.1000 BC	Chavin	bt. c.900 & 600 BC	c.400 BC	c.400-350 BC
c.1100 BC	Olmec-San Lorenzo	bt. c.900 & 600 BC	c.400 BC	c.400-350 BC
c.622	Ummah/Caliphate	f. c.661	740	c.740-790
c.750 BC	Kush/Meroe in Egypt	a. 656 BC	c.320	c.320-370
c.325 BC	Mauryan Empire	1st C	c.70 or c.240	c.70-120 or c.240-290
c.300-400	Mon/Hindu kingdoms	c.500	c.800	c.800-850
c.420	Yamato unification	a. c.550	c.663	c.663-710
c.400-500	Marquesas	c.600?	c.800	c.800-850
c.221 BC	Ch'in under Shih Huang Ti	b. c.300	c.304	c.304-354
c.608	Creation of Tibet	8th C	c.1207	c.1207-1247
c.220 BC	Confed. of Hsiung-nu	c.100 BC	c.51 BC	c.51 BC-AD 1
c.886	Kingdom of Wessex	867	c.900	c.900-950
c.800	Franks	867	c.911	c.911-962
c.800	Frankish Empire	867	c.900	c.900-962
756	Galicia	867	711	from 711
c.800	Frankish Empire	867	c.880	c.880-950
800	Frankish Empire	867	c.911	c.900-962
c.756	Galicia	867	711	from 711
c.800	Frankish Empire	867	c.900	c.900-950

1.	2550-2200 BC	Funnel-Neck Beaker Folk	c.1500 BC
2.	c.1950-1750 BC	Old Babylonian Empire	c.1900 BC
3.	2110-1786 BC	Empire of Middle Kingdom	c.2345-a. c.1570 BC
4.	c.1650-1450 BC	Minoan Empire on mainland Greece	c.800 BC
5.	c.341-218 BC	Roman Empire in Italy	c.29-19 BC
6.	c.1471-1300 BC	Hittite Empire in Syria/Canaan	from c.1700 BC
7.	c.1471-1360 BC	Ugaritic hegemony in Canaan	early 2nd mill. BC
8.	c.1140-960 BC	Israelite Empire to David	c.1000-5th C BC
9.	c.337-250 BC	Celtic La Tene expansion	from 1st C
10.	c.280 BC-AD 10	Parthian Empire	c.550
11.	c.951-1244	Europe's expansion into Mediterranean	c.1100-1240
12.	c.1913-present/c.2250?	America's world expansion	21st C?
13.	c.677-1071	Byzantine Empire (including Balkans)	10th C
14.	c.38-170	Expansion of Germanic tribes	8th C- c.1270
15.	c.350 BC-AD 300	Expansion of Nazca/Moche	Oral
16.	c.350 BC-AD 100	Post-Olmec expansion	Oral
17.	790-1055	Abbasid Caliphate's expansion	11th C
18.	c.370-540	Aksum Empire	Oral
19.	c.120 or c.290-750	Gupta Empire	c.1500 BC-AD c.200
20.	c.850-1100	7 S-E Asian Empires	from 1st C
21.	c.710-1000	Imperial state ruled from Nara/Kyoto	c.712/c.720
22.	c.850-950	Polynesian expansion	Oral
23.	c.354-907	Sui/Tang Empires	c.5th C BC
24.	c.1247-1481	Tibetan Expansion	Oral
25.	c.1-950	Expansion under Hsiung-nu etc	Oral
	*European Peoples:		
	c.962-1244	Conquest of Danes/Crusaders/Ireland	c.1190-1225
	c.962-1244	Norman Empire	c.1100/c.1190-1225
	c.962-1244	Holy Roman Empire	c.1190-1225
	c.1000-1212	Reconquista	c.1000-1150
	c.962-1244	Holy Roman Empire	c.1310/c.1581
	c.962-1244	Holy Roman Empire	
	c.1000-1212	Reconquista	c.1570
	c.962-1244	Holy Roman Empire	c.1190-1225

17. Creation of Light-based Heretical Sect of :		18	19
c.2250 BC	Ogma	c.2200-2150 BC	c.2200-2000 BC
c.1800 BC	Ashur	c.1800-1650 BC	c.1750-1595 BC
c.1991 BC	Amon	c.190-1850 BC	1786-1674 BC
c.1500 BC	Apollo	c.1400 BC	c.1450-1200 BC
c.250 & c.204 BC	Deified leader's "genius"	c.186 BC	c.218-113 BC
c.1350 BC	Cybele/Attis	c.1300 BC	c.1300-1225 BC
c.1450 BC	Melqart or Baal Hammon/Astarte	c.1360 BC	c.1360-1225 BC
after c.1050 BC	Elohim from Canaan	1050-900 BC	c.960-841 BC
from 3rd C BC	Esus (Yesu)	3rd C BC	c.250-58 BC
1st C BC	Ahura Mazda	1st-2nd C AD	c.10-114
from c.1130	Templars, Cathars, Lollards, Hussites	c.1244-1430	c.1244-1453
?	Universalist God	–	c.2250?
from c.988	Byzantine Christ of Moscow	1204-1261	c.1071-1354
c.120	Human Christ	c.150	c.170-270
c.200 BC	Doorway god	c.200 BC	c.300-500
AD c.50	Kinich Ahau (or Itzamna)	AD c.50	c.100-200
c.900-1000	Theosophical Sufism	c.900-1000	c.1055-1258
before c.540	Pre-Islamic Allah	c.540	c.540-640
8th C	Islamic Allah	8th C	c.750-1150
c.1056-1100	Theravada Buddha	c.1056-1150	c.1100-1177
from c.750	Ch'an/Zen Enlightenment	9th C	c.1000-1274
c.850	Doorway god or precursor of Inti	c.900?	c.950-1100?
8th C	Neo-Confucianism	from 8th C	c.907-1271
after c.1409	Atisan Tantric Tibetan Buddhism	c.1430	c.1481-1565
after c.900	Tibetan Buddha	c.925	c.950-1125
from c.1130	Templars,Cathars,Lollards,Hussites	c.1244-1430	c.1244-1453
from c.1130	Templars,Cathars,Lollards,Hussites	c.1244-1430	c.1244-1453
from c.1130	Templars,Cathars,Lollards,Hussites	c.1244-1430	c.1244-1453
from c.1130	Templars,Cathars,Lollards,Hussites	c.1244-1430	c.1244-1453
from c.1130	Templars,Cathars,Lollards,Hussites	c.1244-1430	c.1244-1453
from c.1130	Templars,Cathars,Lollards,Hussites	c.1244-1430	c.1244-1453
from c.1130	Templars,Cathars,Lollards,Hussites	c.1244-1430	c.1244-1453
from c.1130	Templars,Cathars,Lollards,Hussites	c.1244-1430	c.1244-1453

	20	21	22 Breakdown of Civilization at hands of:		23
1.	c.2200-2000 BC	c.2000 BC	c.2000-1900 BC	Battle-Axe Kurgans	c.2000-1900 BC
2.	c.1750-1595 BC	c.1595-1590 BC	c.1590-1490 BC	Kassites	c.1590-1490 BC
3.	c.1786-1674 BC	c.1674 BC	c.1674-1576 BC	Hyksos	c.1674-1576 BC
4.	c.1450-1200 BC	c.1200 BC	c.1200-1100 BC	Sea Peoples, Dorians	c.1200-1100 BC
5.	c.218-113 BC	c.113 BC	c.113-30 BC	Germanic tribes	c.113-30 BC
6.	c.1300-1225 BC	c.1225 BC	c.1225-1125 BC	Sea Peoples, Phrygians	c.1225-1125 BC
7.	c.1360-1225 BC	c.1225 BC	c.1225-1125 BC	Sea Peoples (Luwians/Philistines)	c.1225-1125 BC
8.	9th C BC	c.841 BC	c.841-732 BC	Assyrians	c.841-732 BC
9.	c.250-58 BC	58 BC	58 BC-AD 52	Romans	c.58 BC-AD 52
10.	c.10-114	c.114	c.114-226	Romans	c.114-226
11.	c.1244-1453	1453	1453-1555	Ottomans	c. 1453-1555
12.	_	c.2400?	c.2400-2500?	_	_
13.	c.1071-1354	1354	c.1354-1462	Ottomans	c.1534-1462
14.	c.170-270	c.270	c.270-375	Romans	c.270-375
15.	c.300-500	c.500	c.500-600	Middle Horizon invaders	c.500-600
16.	c.100-200	c.200	c.200-300	Mayan invaders	c.200-300
17.	c.1055-1258	1258	c.1258-1358	II Khanate Mongols	c.1258-1358
18.	c.540-640	c.640	c.640-740	Arabs	c.640-740
19.	c.750-1150	c.1150	c.1150-1236	Islamic Turks	c.1150-1236
20.	c.1100-1177	c.1177	c.1177-1287	Chams, Mongols	c.1177-1287
21.	c.1000-1274	1274	c.1274-1391	Mongols & Koreans	c.1274-1391
22.	c.950-1100?	c.1100	c.1100-1200	S. Americans	c.1100-1200
23.	c.907-1271	1271	c.1271-1398	Mongols	c.1271-1398
24.	c.1481-1565	1565	c.1565-1642	Tumed Mongols	c.1565-1642
25.	c.950-1125	1125	c.1125-1206	Juchen-Chin	c.1125-1206
	*European Peoples:				
	c.1244-1453	1453	c.1453-1555	Ottomans' pressure on Europe	c.1453-1555
	c.1244-1453	1453	c.1453-1555	Ottomans' pressure on Europe	c.1453-1555
	c.1244-1453	1453	c.1453-1555	Ottomans' pressure on Europe	c.1453-1555
	c.1244-1453	1453	c.1453-1555	Ottomans' pressure on Europe	c.1453-1555
	c.1244-1453	1453	c.1453-1555	Ottomans' pressure on Europe	c.1453-1555
	c.1244-1453	1453	c.1453-1555	Ottomans' pressure on Europe	c.1453-1555
	c.1244-1453	1453	c.1453-1555	Ottomans' pressure on Europe	c.1453-1555
	c.1244-1453	1453	c.1453-1555	Ottomans' pressure on Europe	c.1453-1555

24	25	26	27/28. New People's Renewal of the Light:	
c.2000-1900 BC	c.1900 BC?	Battle-Axe Kurgans (Bell-Beaker)	c.1900-1750 BC	Ogma
c.1590-1490 BC	c.1490 BC	Assyrians	c.1490-1000 BC	Ashur
c.1674-1576 BC	c.1580 BC	New Kingdom Thebans	c.1576-1085 BC	Amon
c.1200-1100 BC	c.1100 BC	Dorian Greeks	c.1100-750 BC	Apollo
c.113-30 BC	49-30 BC	Caesarian Principate	30 BC-AD 270	Emperor's "genius"
c.1225-1125 BC	c.1125 BC	Phrygians	c.1125-900 BC	Cybele
c.1225-1125 BC	c.1125 BC	Phoenicians	c.1125-980 BC	Melqart/Astarte
c.841-732 BC	733-732 BC	Jews of Judah	c.732-640 BC	Elohim
c.58 BC-AD 52	42-52	Christian Celts	c.52-313	Esus (or Yesu) as Jesus
c.114-226	213-226	Sasanians	c.226-364	Ahura Mazda
c.1453-1555	1546-1555	Renaissance Humanists	c.1555-1778	Protestant God/Christ
–	–	–	–	–
c.1354-1462	c.1453-1462	Russian Grand Duchy of Moscow	1462-1689	Russian Orthodox Christ
c.270-375	c.270-375	Germanic tribes displaced by Huns	c.375-476	Arian Christ
c.500-600	c.575-600	Peruvian Middle Horizon	c.600-1200	Doorway god
c.200-300	c.275-300	Mayans	c.300-900	Kinich Ahu (or Itzamna)
c.1258-1358	c.1331-1358	Ottomans	c.1358-1683	Sufi/Sunni Allah
c.640-740	c.740	Muslims	c.740-1500	African Allah
c.1150-1236	c.1206-1236	Muslims (Turkish Ghurids)	c.1236-1526	Indian Allah
c.1177-1287	c.1250-1287	Indianised S.-E. Asians	c.1287-1550	Theravada Buddhism
c.1274-1391	c.1378-1391	Ashikaga/Muromachi Shogunate	c.1391-1573	Zen Buddhism
c.1100-1200	c.1175-1200	S. American Long Ears	c.1200-1500	Sun-god
c.1271-1398	c.1368-1398	Ming dynasty	c.1398-1644	Neo-Confucianism
c.1565-1642	c.1620-1642	Dge-lugs-pa's Dalai Lamas	c.1624-1720	Tibetan Buddhism
c.1125-1206	c.1185-1206	All the Mongols	c.1206-1370	Tibetan Buddhism
c.1453-1555	c.1546-1555	Renaissance Humanists	c.1555-1778	Protestant God/Christ
c.1453-1555	c.1546-1555	Renaissance Humanists	c.1555-1778	Catholic God/Christ
c.1453-1555	c.1546-1555	Renaissance Humanists	c.1555-1778	Protestant God/Christ
c.1453-1555	c.1546-1555	Renaissance Humanists	c.1555-1778	Catholic God/Christ
c.1453-1555	c.1546-1555	Renaissance Humanists	c.1555-1778	Catholic God/Christ
c.1453-1555	c.1546-1555	Renaissance Humanists	c.1555-1778	Protestant God/Christ
c.1453-1555	c.1546-1555	Renaissance Humanists	c.1555-1778	Catholic God/Christ
c.1453-1555	c.1546-1555	Renaissance Humanists	c.1555-1778	Catholic God/Christ

#	29		30	31	32
1.	c.1900-1750 BC?	Battle-Axe in W. Europe	from c.1875 BC?	c.1850 BC?	c.1850-1750 BC
2.	c.1490-1000 BC	First & Second Assyrian Empires	c.1400 BC	c.1375 BC	c.1250-1150 BC
3.	c.1576-1085 BC	New Kingdom Empire	1379-1361 BC	c.1358 BC	c.1250-1150 BC
4.	c.1100-750 BC	Greek colonising	c.950 BC	c.900 BC	c.850-750 BC
5.	30 BC-AD 270	Roman Empire	c.30-251	c.30-251	AD c.138-235
6.	c.1125-900 BC	Phrygian Empire	c.1100 BC	c.1050 BC	c.1000 BC
7.	c.1125-980 BC	Phoenician colonising	c.1100 BC	c.1075 BC	c.1050-980 BC
8.	c.732-640 BC	Judah's counterthrust	c.720 BC	from c.715 BC	from c.697 BC
9.	c.52-313	Celtic Christian Empire	from c.90	c.150	c.170-270
10.	c.226-364	Sasanian Empire	c.240-274	c.274-300	c.280-360
11.	c.1555-1778	Colonising/Mercantile Empire	c.1600-1680	c.1620-1700	c.1680-1778
12.	_	_	_	_	_
13.	1462-1689	Russian Empire	1596-1620	from c.1620	from c.1630
14.	c.375-476	Germanic hegemony on Roman frontier	c.380-410	from c.392	c.400-500
15.	c.600-1200	Huari & Tiahuanaco Empires	c.800	c.800	c.900-1000
16.	c.300-900	Mayan Empire	c.600	after c.600	c.900-1000
17.	c.1358-1683	Ottoman Empire (including Balkans)	c.1502-1514	c.1502-1554	c.1560-1660
18.	c.740-1500	Muslim trading Empires in Africa	c.1200	c.1300-1350	c.1350-1450
19.	c.1236-1526	Muslim/Hindu Empires	c.1290-1316	1316-1320	c.1400-1500
20.	c.1287-1550	Empires in S.E. Asia	c.1350-1480	c.1400	c.1450-1550
21.	c.1391-1573	Ashikaga/Muromachi Empire	after 1400	from c.1420	c.1470-1570
22.	c.1200-1500	S. American colonising	14th C	14th C	c.1375-1475?
23.	c.1398-1644	Ming Empire	c.1500-1529	from c.1500	c.1540-1640
24.	c.1642-1720	Dala Lamas' expansion	c.1696-1705	c.1720	c.1650-1720
25.	c.1206-1370	Mongol Empire	c.1230-1396	1260-1294	c.1270-1370

*European Peoples:

29		30	31	32
c.1555-1778	Empire, union with Wales & Scotland	c.1600-1680	c.1620-1700	c.1680-1780
c.1555-1778	European colonising	c.1600-1680	c.1620-1700	c.1680-1780
c.1555-1778	European colonising	c.1600-1680	c.1620-1700	c.1680-1780
c.1555-1778	Spanish Empire	c.1600-1680	c.1620-1700	c.1680-1780
c.1555-1778	European colonising	c.1600-1680	c.1620-1700	c.1680-1780
c.1555-1778	European colonising	c.1600-1680	c.1620-1700	c.1680-1780
c.1555-1778	Portuguese Empire	c.1600-1680	c.1620-1700	c.1680-1780
c.1555-1778	European colonising (including Bohemia)	c.1600-1680	c.1620-1700	c.1680-1780

c.1760 BC?	c.1750-1625 BC	Further Battle-Axe Empire in Europe & Britain	c.1750-1625 BC
from c.1150 BC	c.1000-626 BC	Third Assyrian Empire	c.1000-626 BC
from c.1150 BC	c.1085-730 BC	Egyptian Empire under Tanite & Libyan dynasties	c.1085-730 BC
c.760 BC	c.750-431 BC	Further Greek colonising in Mediterranean	c.750-480 BC
from c.230	c.270-410	Recovery of Roman Empire	c.270-410
c.950 BC	c.900-696 BC	Phrygian Kingdom/Lydian Empire	c.900-696 BC
c.1000 BC	c.980-710 BC	Further Phoenician colonising (including Carthage)	c.980-710 BC
c.650 BC	c.640-597 BC	Josiah's restoration of David's Empire	c.640-597 BC
c.260	c.313-446	Christian Celtic expansion as Romans withdrew	c.313-446
c.350	c.364-572	Further Sasanian expansion to east	c.364-572
from c.1770	c.1778-1914	Empires (British, German, Dutch, Belgian, French)	c.1778-1918
–	–	–	–
from c.1650	c.1689-1853	Expansion of Westernised Petrine Empire	c.1689-1855
c.450	c.476-596	Germanic Arian kingdoms,(including Saxons)	c.476-596
c.1175	c.1200-1460	Peruvian Chimu Empire & Inca Empire	c.1200-1460
c.1175	c.1200-1428	Mexican Toltec Empire & Aztec Empire	c.1200-1428
c.1650	c.1683-1798	Ottoman Empire/Iranian Muslim Empire	c.1683-1798
c.1450	c.1500-1835	Rise of African states	c.1500-1835
c.1490	c.1526-1749	Moghul Empire	c.1526-1749
c.1540	c.1550-1786	Empires in Burma, Siam & Cambodia	c.1550-1786
c.1560	1573-1863	Empires of Hideyoshi (in Korea) & Tokugawas	c.1573-1863
c.1470	c.1500-1850	Further expansion of Oceanian culture to islands	c.1500-1840
c.1630	c.1644-1840	Empire of Manchus or Juchen as Ch'ing dynasty	c.1644-1840
c.1720	c.1720-1903	Empire of Dalai Lamas	c.1720-1903
from c.1370	c.1370-1543	Empire of Eastern Mongols	c.1370-1543
c.1770-1840	c.1778-1914	Second British Empire; union with Ireland	c.1778-1914
c.1770-1840	c.1778-1914	French Empire	c.1778-1914
c.1770-1840	c.1778-1914	German Empire	c.1778-1914
c.1770-1840	c.1778-1914	Spanish expansion	c.1778-1914
c.1770-1840	c.1778-1914	Italian expansion	c.1778-1914
c.1770-1840	c.1778-1914	Dutch Empire	c.1778-1914
c.1770-1840	c.1778-1914	Portuguese expansion	c.1778-1914
c.1770-1840	c.1778-1914	Austro-Hungarian Empire	c.1778-1914

1. c.1650 BC?	c.1625 BC	Battle-Axe invasion	c.1660-1600 BC?
2. c.648 BC	c.626 BC	Chaldean occupation of Assyrian Babylon	c.658-597 BC
3. c.760 BC	c.730 BC	Fall of Egypt to Kushites	c.770-210 BC
4. c.510 BC	c.480 BC	Persian victory over Greeks at Thermoplyae	c.510-450 BC
5. c.380	c.410	Visigoth sack of Rome	c.370-420
6. c.730 BC	c.696-5 BC	Cimmerian sack of Gordium	c.725-665 BC
7. c.750 BC	c.710 BC	Assyrian rule in Neo-Hittite states	c.760-700 BC
8. c.620 BC	c.597 BC	Neo-Babylonians captured Jerusalem	c.630-587 BC
9. c.410	c.446	Celtic British flight before Saxons	c.400-460
10. c.542	c.572	War with Turks & Byzantines	c.532-592
11. c.1880	c.1914	First World War	c.1870-1930
12. _	_	_	_
13. c.1812	c.1855	Crimean defeat by English & French	c.1800-1860
14. c.568	c.596	Arab conquest of Visigothic Kingdom in Spain	c.588-618
15. c.1430	c.1460	Incas overran Chimu Empire	c.1420-1480
16. c.1400	c.1428	Aztecs overran Toltec Empire	c.1390-1450
17. c.1770	1798	European French in Egypt	c.1760-1820
18. c.1806	c.1835	Great Trek of Boers	c.1795-1855
19. c.1710	c.1749	Anglo-French struggle for India	c.1700-1760
20. c.1760	c.1786	British occupation of Penang	c.1750-1810
21. c.1840	c.1863	US/French/British defeat of Tokugawas	c.1830-1890
22. c.1810?	c.1840	British colonisation of New Zealand	c.1800-1860
23. c.1810	c.1840	European British: Opium War	c.1800-1860
24. c.1880	c.1903	British conquered Tibet	c.1870-1930
25. c.1490	c.1543	Mongols of the Ordos	c.1480-1540

*European Peoples:

c.1880	1914	First World War	c.1870-1930
c.1880	1914	First World War	c.1870-1930
c.1880	1914	First World War	c.1870-1930
c.1880	1914	First World War	c.1870-1930
c.1880	1914	First World War	c.1870-1930
c.1880	1914	First World War	c.1870-1930
c.1880	1914	First World War	c.1870-1930
c.1880	1914	First World War	c.1870-1930

39	40	41	42
c.1660-1600 BC?	c.1625-1550 BC	c.1625-1550 BC	from c.1550 BC
c.658-597 BC	c.626-539 BC	c.626-539 BC	from c.539 BC
c.770-710 BC	c.730-664 BC	c.730-664 BC	from c.664 BC
c.520-460 BC	c.460-404 BC	c.460-404 BC	from c.404 BC
c.370-430	c.410-476	c.410-476	from c.476
c.725-665 BC	c.696-546 BC	c.696-546 BC	from c.546 BC
c.730-670 BC	c.710-538 BC	c.710-538 BC	from c.538 BC
c.630-587 BC	c.597-538 BC	c.597-538 BC	from c.538 BC
c.400-460	c.446-540	c.446-540	from c.540
c.532-592	c.572-642	c.572-642	from c.642
c.1870-1930	c.1916-1997?	1914-1997	from c.1997
–	–	–	–
c.1800-1860	c.1855-1918	c.1855-1918	from c.1918
c.558-618	c.596-687	c.596-687	from c.687
c.1420-1480	c.1460-1572	c.1460-1572	from 1572
c.1390-1450	c.1428-1542	c.1428-1542	from c.1542
c.1760-1820	c.1798-1881	c.1798-1881	from c.1881
c.1795-1855	c.1835-1914	c.1835-1914	from c.1914
c.1700-1760	c.1749-1818	c.1749-1818	c.1818-1997
c.1750-1810	c.1786-1876	c.1786-1876	c.1876-1947
c.1830-1890	c.1868-1945	c.1868-1945	c.1945-present
c.1800-1860	c.1840-1900	c.1840-1900	from c.1900
c.1800-1860	c.1840-1949	c.1840-1949	1949-present
c.1870-1930	c.1903-1951	c.1903-1951	1951-present
c.1480-1540	c.1543-1644	c.1543-1644	c.1644-1911
c.1870-1930	c.1914-1997?	c.1914-1997?	c.1997-present
c.1870-1930	c.1914-1997?	c.1914-1997?	c.1997-present
c.1870-1930	c.1914-1997?	c.1914-1997?	c.1997-present
c.1870-1930	c.1914-1997?	c.1914-1997?	c.1997-present
c.1870-1930	c.1914-1997?	c.1914-1997?	c.1997-present
c.1870-1930	c.1914-1997?	c.1914-1997?	c.1997-present
c.1870-1930	c.1914-1997?	c.1914-1997?	c.1997-present
c.1870-1930	c.1914-1997?	c.1914-1997?	c.1997-present

1. c.1550-1400 BC	Unetice-Tumulus Empire	f.c.1500 BC	c.1450 BC?
2. c.539-331 BC	Achaemenian Persian Empire	f.c.500 BC	c.520-482 BC
3. c.664-525 BC	Saite Empire	f.c.650 BC	c.650-595 BC
4. c.404-337 BC	Persian-backed Peloponnesian League	f.c.390 BC	c.360-337 BC
5. c.476-533	Empires of Ostrogoths/Visigoths/Vandals	f.c.485	c.493-526
6. c.546-334 BC	Achaemenian Persian Empire	f.c.530 BC	from c.500 BC
7. c.538-333 BC	Achaemenian Persian Empire	f.c.530 BC	from c.500 BC
8. c.538-333 BC	Achaemenian Persian Empire	f.c.530 BC	c.458-444 BC
9. c.540-687	Saxon Empire	f.c.560	c.630-687
10. c.642-821	Arab Empire	f.c.661	c.700-750
11. c.1997/2008-c.2150?	US-backed EU/United States of Europe	f.c.2000	a.c.2000
12. _	_	_	_
13. c.1918-1990/2050?	Marxian conglomerate of USSR	f.c.1960	after c.1987?
14. c.687-843	Frankish Pepinid Carolingian Empire	f.c.711	c.772-804
15. c.1572-1810	Spanish Empire	f.c.1600	c.1750-1790
16. c.1542-1810	Spanish Empire	f.c.1600	c.1750-1790
17. c.1881-1980	European Empires	f.c.1900	c.1956-1980
18. c.1914-1980	European Empires	f.c.1930	c.1956-1980
19. c.1818-1947	British Empire	f.c.1850	c.1885-1947
20. c.1876-1947	European Empires	f.c.1890	c.1910-1950
21. c.1945-c.2015/c.2020?	US occupation/Pacific Community	f.c.1960	from c.1989
22. c.1900-c.2015/c.2020	European Empires	f.c.1920-present	c.1945-c.2015?
23. c.1949-c.2020	Marxian Peoples's Republic of China	f.c.1960	c.2006?/c.2020?
24. c.1951-c.2015/2020	Chinese conglomerate	f.c.1970	c.2006?/c.2020?
25. c.1644-1911	Chinese Manchu conglomerate	f.c.1675	c.1890-1911
*European Peoples:			
from c.1997?	US-backed European conglomerate	f.c.2010	21st C? (c.2050?)
from c.1997?	US-backed European conglomerate	f.c.2010	22nd C? (c.2050?)
from c.1997?	US-backed European conglomerate	f.c.2010	23rd C? (c.2050?)
from c.1997?	US-backed European conglomerate	f.c.2010	24th C? (c.2050?)
from c.1997?	US-backed European conglomerate	f.c.2010	25th C? (c.2050?)
from c.1997?	US-backed European conglomerate	f.c.2010	26th C? (c.2050?)
from c.1997?	US-backed European conglomerate	f.c.2010	27th C? (c.2050?)
from c.1997?	US-backed European conglomerate	f.c.2010	28th C? (c.2050?)

46. Counter-thrust Under Foreign Federalist Influence/Foreign God to Restore Past

c.1400-1200 BC	Late Wessex culture under Unetice or Mycenaean rule (?)
c.331-141 BC	Seleucids' Empire in Babylonia
c.525-332 BC	Achaenenian Persian Empire
c.337-239 BC	Macedonian Empire & Panhellenic League
c.535-605	Byzantine reconquest of Italy & East Roman Empire of Justinian
c.334-278 BC	Empire of Alexander & Seleucid successors in Anatolia
c.323-219 BC	Ptolemies' Empire in Syria
c.333-198 BC	Ptolemies' Empire in Palestine
c.687-838	Saxon Empire in Northumbria, Mercia & Wessex
c.821-1055	Islamic Empires in Iran: Tahirids, Saffarids, Samanids, Ghaznavids & Buyids
c.2150-2250?	Federation of European nation-state?
–	–
c.1990/2050-2150?	Federalist post-Communist Russia linked to coming United States of Europe
c.843-911	Viking Empire in Britain, Ireland, Normandy, Russia, Canada & Iceland
c.1810-c.2015?/c.2020?	Pan-American federalism in Latin America under US (now through OAS)
c.1810-c.2015?/c.2020?	Pan-American federalism in Latin America under US (now through OAS)
c.1980/c.2015?-2100?	Coming Federation of Arab & Islamic states through Arab League?
from c.1980/c.2015	Coming Federation of African states (starting with OAU)?
c.1947-c.2015/c.2020?	Independent federal India under West?
c.1950-c.2015/c.2020?	Coming Federation of S.-E. Asian states (eventually Pacific Community)?
from c.2015/c.2020?	Coming Federation of Japanese Pacific territories
from c.2015/c.2020?	Coming Federation of Oceanian states?
from c.2020	Federalist post-Communist China linked to coming Federation of S.-E. Asian states?
from c.2020	Coming Federation of S.-E. Asian states (eventually Pacific Community)?
c.1911-c.2015?/c.2020?	Federalism under Russia & China, & coming Federation of Arab & Islamic states?
c.2150-2250?	Federation of European nation-states?
c.2150-2250?	Federation of European nation-states?
c.2150-2250?	Federation of European nation-states?
c.2150-2250?	Federation of European nation-states?
c.2150-2250?	Federation of European nation-states?
c.2150-2250?	Federation of European nation-states?
c.2150-2250?	Federation of European nation-states?
c.2150-2250?	Federation of European nation-states?

	47	48	49/50	
1.	c.1300-1150 BC	c.1400-1200 BC?	c.1200-1150 BC?	Bronze Age Tumulus Celts
2.	c.160-120 BC	c.331-141 BC	c.141 BC-AD 165	Parthians, Romans
3.	c.373-332 BC	c.525-332 BC	c.332-168 BC	Alexander & Successors
4.	c.250-100 BC	c.337-239 BC	c.239-146 BC	Romans
5.	c.540-620	c.535-605	c.605-652	Lombards
6.	c.300-150 BC	c.334-278 BC	c.278-220 BC	Celts
7.	c.300-150 BC	c.323-219 BC	c.219-198 BC	Seleucids
8.	c.250-180 BC	c.333-198 BC	c.198-141 BC	Seleucids
9.	c.796-851	c.687-838	c.838-896	Vikings
10.	c.983-1071	c.832-1055	c.1055-1157	Seljuq Turks
11.	bt.c.2150 & 2250?	c.2150-2250	c.2250-2325?	Non-Americans?
12.	_	_	_	_
13.	bt.c.1990/2050-2150?	c.1990/2050-2150?	c.2150-2225?	Americans?
14.	c.843-950	c.843-911	c.911-978	English
15.	1980s	c.1810-2050?	c.2050-2125?	Americans?
16.	1980s	c.1810-2050?	c.2050-2125?	Americans?
17.	bt.c.1980 & 2100?	c.1980-2100?	c.2100-2175?	Europeans, Americans?
18.	bt.c.1980 & 2100?	c.1980-2100?	c.2100-2175?	Americans?
19.	bt.c.1947 & 2050?	c.1947-2050?	c.2050-2125?	US,Europeans or Japanese?
20.	bt.c.1950 & 2100?	c.1950-2100?	c.2050-2125?	Japanese Pacific Community?
21.	bt.c.2050 & 2150?	c.2050-2150?	c.2150-2225?	Americans
22.	bt.c.2000 & 2100?	c.2000-2100?	c.2100-2175?	Japanese Pacific Community?
23.	bt.c.2020/2050 & 2150?	c.2020/2050-2150?	c.2150-2250?	Americans
24.	bt.c.2020/2050 & 2150?	c.2020/2050-2150?	c.2150-2225?	Americans
25.	bt.c.1911 & 2050?	c.1911-2050?	c.2050-2125?	Europeans, US or Pacific Community?

*European Peoples:

bt.c.2150 & 2250?	from 22nd C?	_	_
bt.c.2150 & 2250?	from 22nd C?	_	_
bt.c.2150 & 2250?	from 22nd C?	_	_
bt.c.2150 & 2250?	from 22nd C?	_	_
bt.c.2150 & 2250?	from 22nd C?	_	_
bt.c.2150 & 2250?	from 22nd C?	_	_
bt.c.2150 & 2250?	from 22nd C?	_	_
bt.c.2150 & 2250?	from 22nd C?	_	_

c.1200-1150 BC?	Celtic culture	c.1150-1100 BC?	c.1100-1000 BC	c.1100-1000 BC
c.141 BC-AD 165	Parthian & Roman gods	c.165-244	c.244-395	c.244-395
c.332-168 BC	Seleucids' Zeus	c.168-30 BC	c.30 BC-AD 395	c.30 BC-AD 395
c.239-146 BC	Roman Jupiter	c.146-27 BC	c.27 BC-AD 395	c.27 BC-AD 395
c.605-652	Lombards' Arian Christ	c.652-728	c.728-756	c.728-756
c.278-220 BC	Celtic & Hellenistic gods	c.220-133 BC	c.133 BC-AD 395	c.133 BC-AD 395
c.219-198 BC	Seleucids' Zeus	c.198-163 BC	c.163 BC-AD 395	c.163 BC-AD 395
c.198-141 BC	Seleucids' Zeus	c.141-64 BC	c.64 BC-AD 395	c.64 BC-AD 395
c.838-896	Viking Thor	c.896-1016	c.1016-1066	c.1016-1066
c.1055-1157	Seljuq Sunni Allah	c.1157-1258	c.1258-1382	c.1258-1382
c.2250-2325?	–	c.2325-2400?	c.2400-2550?	c.2400-2550?
c.2150-2225?	–	–	–	–
	–	c.2225-2300?	c.2300-2450?	c.2300-2450?
c.911-978	English Christ & God	c.978-1042	c.1042-1106	c.1042-1106
c.2050-2125?	–	c.2125-2200?	c.2200-2350?	c.2200-2350?
c.2050-2125?	–	c.2125-2200?	c.2200-2350?	c.2200-2350?
c.2100-2175?	–	c.2175-2250?	c.2250-2400?	c.2250-2400?
c.2100-2175?	–	c.2175-2250?	c.2250-2400?	c.2250-2400?
c.2050-2125?	–	c.2125-2200?	c.2200-2350?	c.2200-2350?
c.2050-2125?	–	c.2125-2200?	c.2200-2350?	c.2200-2350?
c.2150-2225?	–	c.2225-2300?	c.2300-2450?	c.2300-2450?
c.2100-2175?	–	c.2175-2250?	c.2250-2400?	c.2250-2400?
c.2150-2225?	–	c.2225-2300?	c.2300-2450?	c.2300-2450?
c.2150-2225?	–	c.2225-2300?	c.2300-2450?	c.2300-2450?
c.2050-2125?	–	c.2125-2200?	c.2200-2350?	c.2200-2350?
–	–	–	–	–
–	–	–	–	–
–	–	–	–	–
–	–	–	–	–
–	–	–	–	–
–	–	–	–	–
–	–	–	–	–
–	–	–	–	–

	55	56/57	58	59
1.	c.1100-1000 BC?	c.1100-1000 BC?	c.1000-900 BC	c.1000 BC
2.	c.244-395	c.244-395	c.395-602	c.395 (began 313)
3.	c.30 BC-395 AD (esp.22 BC)	c.30 BC-AD 395	c.395-616	c.395
4.	c.27 BC-AD 395	c.27 BC-AD 395 (esp.AD c.40-60)	c.395-602	from 395 (beg.313)
5.	c.728-756	c.728-756	c.756-774	from 756 (beg.313)
6.	c.133 BC=AD 395 (esp.c.96-66 BC)	c.133 BC-AD 395	c.395-602	c.395
7.	c.163 BC-AD 395 (esp.c.4 BC)	c.163 BC-AD 395 (esp.1st C AD)	c.395-634	c.395 (beg.313)
8.	c.64 BC-AD 395 (esp.AD c.26-135)	c.64 BC-AD 395 (esp.AD c.26)	c.395-634	c.395 (beg.313)
9.	AD c.1016-1066	c.1016-1066	c.1066-1166	c.1066 (beg.664)
10.	c.1258-1382	c.1258-1382	c.1382-1501	c.1382 (beg.6th C)
11.	c.2400-2550?	c.2400-2550?	c.2550-2700?	from c.2550?
12.	–	–	–	–
13.	c.2300-2450?	c.2300-2450?	c.2450-2600?	c.2450?
14.	c.1042-1106	c.1042-1106	c.1106-1187	c.1106
15.	c.2200-2350?	c.2200-2350?	c.2350-2500?	c.2350?
16.	c.2200-2350?	c.2200-2350?	c.2350-2500?	c.2350?
17.	c.2250-2400?	c.2250-2400?	c.2400-2550?	c.2400?
18.	c.2250-2400?	c.2250-2400?	c.2400-2550?	c.2400?
19.	c.2200-2350?	c.2200-2350?	c.2350-2500?	c.2350?
20.	c.2200-2350?	c.2200-2350?	c.2350-2500?	c.2350?
21.	c.2300-2450?	c.2300-2450?	c.2450-2600?	c.2450?
22.	c.2250-2400?	c.2250-2400?	c.2400-2550?	c.2400?
23.	c.2300-2450?	c.2300-2450?	c.2450-2600?	c.2450?
24.	c.2300-2450?	c.2300-2450?	c.2450-2600?	c.2450?
25.	c.2200-2350?	c.2200-2350?	c.2350-2500?	c.2350?

*European Peoples:

–	–	–	–
–	–	–	–
–	–	–	–
–	–	–	–
–	–	–	–
–	–	–	–
–	–	–	–

60 Sudden Final Conquest of Religionless Civilization		**61 Successor Civilization**	
c.900-800 BC	Hallstatt culture's conquest of Umfield Celts	c.800 BC	Celtic
c.602-642	Iranian/Arab conquest of Mesopotamia	c.642	Arab
c.616-642	Persian/Arab conquest of Egypt	c.642	Arab
c.602-629	Avar conquest of Greece, Byzantine reconquest	c.629	Byzantine-Russian
c.774-787	Frankish conquest of Italy (under Charlemagne)	c.787	European
c.602-626	Avar & Persian conquest of Anatolia, Byzantine reconquest	c.626	Byzantine-Russian
c.634-636	Arab conquest of Syria	c.636	Arab
c.634-636	Arab conquest of Palestine	c.636	Arab
c.1166-1171	Anglo-Norman conquest of Celtic Ireland	c.1171	European
c.1501-1511	Islamic Safavid conquest of Iran	c.1511	Arab
c.2725?	–	c.2725?	–
–	–	–	–
c.2600-2625?	–	c.2625?	–
c.1187-1214	French conquest of English Normandy	c.1214	European
c.2500-2525?	–	c.2525?	–
c.2500-2525?	–	c.2525?	–
c.2550-2575	–	c.2575?	–
c.2550-2575?	–	c.2575?	–
c.2500-2525?	–	c.2525?	–
c.2550-2575?	–	c.2525?	–
c.2600-2625?	–	c.2625?	–
c.2550-2575?	–	c.2575?	–
c.2600-2625?	–	c.2625?	–
c.2600-2625?	–	c.2625?	–
c.2500-2525?	–	c.2525?	–
–	–	–	–
–	–	–	–
–	–	–	–
–	–	–	–
–	–	–	–
–	–	–	–
–	–	–	–
–	–	–	–

NOTES AND REFERENCES TO SOURCES

PART ONE: THE 61 STAGES IN THE RISE AND FALL OF CIVILIZATIONS

1. The Light and History

1. Arnold Toynbee, one-volume edition of *A Study of History,* p97.

2. The Rise-and-Fall Pattern

1. Hagger, *Overlord,* is an American poetic epic about Eisenhower's pursuit of Hitler and the fall of Berlin (our Troy), as well as a British poetic epic.

2. See Hagger, *The Syndicate*, p18: Britain ordered $20b worth of arms on J. P. Morgan's account, on which Morgans took 2%, making $400m.

3. For the American figure, 38% weekly church attendance (the average of 32% for men and 44% for women), see http://abcnews.go.com/sections/us/DailyNews/church_poll020301.html. For the British figure of 1.7% weekly church attendance (1m out of 58.8m), see http://www.cofe.anglican.org/info/statistics.

The Light and Genesis, Growth, Breakdown and Renewal, Decline, Decay and Demise: Where Facts can be Checked

Chapter 2 traces 25 civilizations through 61 stages. The following references are for entries in *The Encyclopaedia Britannica* (15th Edition), where many of the data used in each civilization can be checked and verified. (Many other sources have also been used but it is convenient to refer the general reader to one standard work.) Also see the many notes in Hagger, *The Light of Civilization.*

Civilization	Volume of Encyclo- paedia Britannica	Pages	Heading
1. Indo-European Kurgan and	6	1059-1063	*Europe, Ancient*

	Megalithic/Old	2	611-616	*Balkans, History of the*
	European	3	193-197	*Britain, Ancient*
		3	1071-5	*Celts, Ancient*
2.	Mesopotamian	11	967-993	*Mesopotamia and Iraq,*
				History of
		11	1001-1006	*Mesopotamian Religions*
3.	Egyptian	6	464-488	*Egypt, History of*
		6	503-509	*Egyptian Religion*
4.	Aegean-Greek	1	112-122	*Aegean Civilizations*
		8	324-390	*Greek Civilization, Ancient*
5.	Roman	15	1085-1133	*Rome, Ancient*
		15	1059-1064	*Roman Religion*
		9	1076-1084	*Italic Peoples, Ancient*
		9	1114-1126	*Italy and Sicily*
		3	547-557	*Byzantine Empire*

See also Joscelyn Godwin, *Mystery Religions in the Ancient World*, 'The Imperial Cult', pp 56-58

6.	Anatolian	1	813-825	*Anatolia, Ancient*
		2	189-193	*Asia Minor, Religions of*
7.	Syrian	17	931-953	*Syria and Palestine, History of*
		2	189-193	*Asia Minor, Religions of*
8.	Israelite	17	939-951	*Syria and Palestine, History of*
		10	302-328	*Judaism, History of*
9.	Celtic	3	1071-1075	*Celts, Ancient*

	3	1068-1071	*Celtic Religion*
	3	198	*Britain, Ancient*
	3	199-208	*Britain & Ireland, History of*
	3	284-286	"
	7	960-962	*Gaul*
10. Iranian	9	829-860	*Iran, History of*
	9	867-872	*Iranian Religions*
	19	1171-2	*Zoroastrianism and Parsiism*
	11	442-447	*Manichaeism*
11. European	4	540-545	*Christianity before the Schism of 1054*
	12	139-142	*Middle Ages*
	9	1119-1112	*Italy and Sicily*
	5	298-310	*Crusades*
	15	108-120	*Protestantism, History of*
	15	1002-1019	*Roman Catholicism, History of*
12. North-American	18	946-999	*United States, History of*
	15	108-120	*Protestantism, History of*
13. Byzantine-Russian	3	548-571	*Byzantine Empire*
	16	39-88	*Russia and the Soviet Union, History of*
	6	152-162	*Eastern Orthodoxy, History of*
	5	298-310	*Crusades*
14. Germanic-Scandinavian	8	40-4	*Germans, Ancient*
	8	33-40	*Germanic Religion and Mythology*
	15	1127-1132	*Rome, Ancient*

	11	926-934	*Merovingian and Carolingian Age*
	16	304-312	*Scandinavia, History of*
15. Andean	1	839-854	*Andean Civilization, History of*
	9	259-261	*Inca Religion*
16. Meso-American	11	935-954	*Meso-American Civilization, History of*
	2	548-552	*Aztec Religion*
17. Arab	1	1043-1051	*Arabia, History of*
	3	623-645	*Caliphate, Empire of the*
	9	926-937	*Islam, History of*
	1	1057-1059	*Arabian Religions*
18. African	1	206-209	*Africa*
	17	274-298	*Southern Africa, History of*
	1	285	*African Peoples and Cultures; Religions*
19. Indian	9	336-428	*Indian Subcontinent, History of the*
	8	908-920	*Hinduism, History of*
	3	403-414	*Buddhism, History of*
20. S.-E.-Asian	17	231-3,	*Southeast-Asian Peoples, Arts of*
		250-271	"
	3	510-515	*Burma, History of*
	16	718-723	*Siam and Thailand, History of*
	3	681-689	*Cambodia, History of*

	19	120-131	*Vietnam, History of*
	3	412-413	*Buddhism, History of*

21. Japanese	10	57-91	*Japan, History of*
	10	109-115	*Japanese Religion*
	16	671-676	*Shinto*
	3	409-410	*Buddhism, History of*
	4	1101-1102	*Confucianism, History of*

22. Oceanian	13	443-448	*Oceanian, History of*
	6	130-132	*Easter Island*
	14	777-784	*Polynesian Cultures*
	11	864-870	*Melanesian Cultures*
	2	412-421	*Australia, History of*
	13	50-55	*New Zealand, History of*

23. Chinese	4	297-402	*China, History of*
	4	422-428	*Chinese Religion*
	4	1099-1103	*Confucianism, History of*
	3	403-413	*Buddhism, History of*
	17	1044-1050	*Taoism, History of*

24. Tibetan	18	378-382	*Tibet, History of*
	3	386-388, 397,401	*Buddhism*
	3	1141	*Central-Asian Peoples, Arts of*

25. Central-Asian	3	1118-1122	*Central-Asian Cultures*
	12	370-376	*Mongols*
	3	1122-1143	*Central-Asian Peoples, Arts of*
	3	407-408	*Buddhism, History of*

PART TWO: LESSONS AND PREDICTIONS

3. Civilizations as Light-Bearers: The Process of Growth, Breakdown and Decay

1. E. W. F. Tomlin in conversation with Nicholas Hagger; in *The Tall Trees of Marsland*, unpublished; and in *Philosophers of East and West*.

4. Illumined Mystics and the Renewal and Decline of Civilizations

1. For an idea of societies within civilizations that have been strong through visions of the Light, see this table and the one on p394; and the table for stage 8 on p64; the table for stage 20 on p144; and the table for stage 28 on p187.

5. Predictions

1. See ch 2, note 3.

2. For the US figure see http://www.cia.gov/cia/publications/factbook/geos/us.html; for the Japanese figure, the same website ending ja.html; for the German figure, the same web-site ending gm.html.

3. Harry Beckhough, *Germany's Four Reichs*, warns against the dangers of a Fourth Reich. Beckhough helped break Rommel's codes for the 8th Army before El Alamein.

6. The Future of Western Civilization

1. T. S. Eliot, *Notes Towards the Definition of Culture*, pp29, 122.

2. Bishop Kenneth Kirk, *The Vision of God*, pp174-175.

3. Clark, Kenneth, *Civilisation*, p347.

4. J. M. Roberts, *The Triumph of the West*, p428.

5. Arnold Toynbee, *A Study of History*, vol. 12, *Reconsiderations*, p559 ('A Re-survey of Civilizations').

6. Nigel Pennick, *Hitler's Secret Sciences*, pp5-6.

7. See Hagger, *The Secret History of the West*, chs 5 and 6. The sources are set out in the Notes in that work.

8. For full coverage, see Hagger, *The Syndicate*.

9. *Sublimity in Style*, last chapter, quoted in Toynbee, *op. cit.*, vol 9, p608.

10. Laurence Freeman, *Light Within*, p87.

11. Canon Peter Spink, *Spiritual Man in a New Age*. See also *The Path of the Mystic*. See my poem on Kent House in *Collected Poems, 1958-2005* and my accompanying note.

12. See the *Bibliography* for these works.

13. Quoted in *Studies in Comparative Religion*, vol 17, numbers 1 & 2, contribution by Martin Lings, p112.

14. Schuon, *From the Divine to the Human*, p14.

15. *The Essential Writings of Frithjof Schuon*, ed. Seyyed Hossain Nasr, p333.

16. Kathleen Raine, *Defending Ancient Springs*, pp112-114.

17. Gaston Bachelard, *The Psychoanalysis of Fire*, pp38-39, 111.

18. Thomas Merton, *The Silent Life*, p173. Quoted in Waterfield, *René Guénon and the Future of the West*, p213.

BIBLIOGRAPHY

Adams, Brooks, *The Law of Civilization and Decay*, Vintage, New York, 1955.

Al-Biruni, *Chronology of Ancient Nations*, ed. and trans. by C. E. Sachau, London, 1879.

Ancrene Riwle, The, trans. by M. B. Salu, University of Exeter Press, 1990.

Bachelard, Gaston, *The Psychoanalysis of Fire*, Beacon, USA, 1964.

Bagby, P., *Culture and History*, Longmans, London, 1958.

Ballou, Robert, *Bible of the World*.

Barraclough, Geoffrey, ed., *The Times Concise Atlas of World History*, Times Books Ltd., London, 1982.

Bohm, David, *Wholeness and the Implicate Order*, Routledge and Kegan Paul, 1980.

Cassian, John, *Conferences*, trans. by Edgar Gibson, 1894, re-issued by Eerdmans, USA, 1973. See also Cistercian Publications.

Clark, Kenneth, *Civilisation*, John Murray, London, 1969.

Collins, *Atlas of World History*, The, Guild Publishing, London, 1987.

Coomaraswamy, Ananda, *A New Approach to The Vedas*, Luzac, London, 1933.

Coomaraswamy, Ananda, *Hinduism and Buddhism*, Prologos Books, USA, 1976.

Easton, Stewart C., *A Brief History of the Western World*, Darren and Noble, USA, 1965.

Eliot, T. S., *Notes Towards the Definition of Culture*, Faber, London, 1957.

Eliot, T.S., *The Idea of a Christian Society*, Faber, London, 1939.

Frankfort, Henri, *The Birth of Civilization in the Near East*, 1951.

Freeman, Laurence, *Light Within*, Darton, Longman and Todd, London, 1986.

Fukuyama, Francis, *The End of History?*, article in *National Interest* magazine, USA, 1989.

Fukuyama, Francis, *The End of History and The Last Man*, Hamish Hamilton, 1992.

Guénon, René, *The Multiple States of Being*, Larson, USA, 1984.

Hagger, Nicholas, *The Light of Civilization*, O Books, 2006.

Hagger, Nicholas, *The Secret History of the West*, O Books, 2005.

Hagger, Nicholas, *The Syndicate*, O Books, 2004.

Heidegger, Martin, *Being and Time*, 1927.

Husserl, Edmund, *Ideas, General Introduction to Pure Phenomenology*, Allen and Unwin, London, 1969.

Huxley, Aldous, *The Perennial Philosophy*, Chatto and Windus, 1946/Fontana Books, 1958.

Jaspers, Karl, *The Origin and Goal of History*, trans. from *Vom Ursprung und Zeit der Geschichte* (1949) by Michael Bullock, London, 1953.

Kennedy, Paul, *The Rise and Fall of the Great Powers*, Unwin Hyman, London, 1988.

Kirk, Bishop Kenneth, *The Vision of God*, James Clarke, UK, 1977.

McEvedy, Colin, *The Penguin Atlas of Ancient History*, Penguin, London, 1978.

McForan, Dr. D. J., *The World Held Hostage*, Oak-Tree Books, London, 1986.

Marcel, Gabriel, *Metaphysical Journal, 1913-23*, Paris, 1927.

Merton, Thomas, *The Silent Life*, London, 1957.

Nasr, Seyyed Hossain ed., *The Essential Writings of Frithjof Schuon*, Amity House, New York, 1986.

Nye, Joseph S., *Bound to Lead*, Basic Books, New York, 1990.

Pennick, Nigel, *Hitler's Secret Sciences*, Neville Spearman, London, 1981.

Perry, Whitall N., *A Treasury of Traditional Wisdom*, Allen and Unwin, London, 1971.

Raine, Kathleen, *Defending Ancient Springs*, Golgonooza, UK, 1985.

Roberts, J. M., *The Triumph of the West*, BBC, 1985.

The Penguin Atlas of Medieval History, Penguin, London, 1961.

Schuon, Frithjof, *From the Divine to the Human*, World Wisdom, USA, 1981.

Schuon, Frithjof, *The Transcendent Unity of Religions*, Faber and Faber, London, 1953.

Secret of the Golden Flower, The, trans. by Richard Wilhelm, Harcourt, Brace and World, New York, 1962.

Snow, C. P., *The Two Cultures: and a Second Look*, Cambridge, UK, 1964.

Spink, Canon Peter, *Spiritual Man in a New Age*, Darton, Longman and Todd, London, 1981.

Tomlin, E. W. F., *Philosophers of East and West*, Oak-Tree Books, 1986.

Toynbee, Arnold, *A Study of History*, Oxford University Press 12 vols, U.K., 1934, 1939, 1954, 1961.

Toynbee, Arnold, revised one volume edition of *A Study of History*, OUP/Thames and Hudson, London, 1972.

Van Buren, Elizabeth, *The Secret of the Illuminati*, Neville Spearman, U.K., 1982.

Waterfield, Robin, *René Guénon and the Future of the West*, Crucible, London, 1987.

Whitehead, Alfred North, *Process and Reality*, in *Whitehead, An Anthology*, Sel. by Northrop and Gross, Cambridge University Press, London, 1953.

Yutang, Lin, *The Wisdom of India and China*, Random House, New York, 1942.

BOOKS

O books
O is a symbol of the world, of oneness and unity. In
different cultures it also means the "eye", symbolizing
knowledge and insight, and in Old English it means "place
of love or home". O books explores the many paths of
understanding which different traditions have developed
down the ages, particularly those today that express
respect for the planet and all of life.

For more information on the full list of over 300 titles
please visit our website
www.O-books.net

SOME RECENT O BOOKS

The Last Tourist in Iran
From Persepolis to Nuclear Natanz
Nicholas Hagger

The first book on Iran to combine travelogue with in-depth historical reflection/ getting to the heart of the Iranian Islamic mind, this is a reflective look at the cultural heritage and present nuclear crisis in Iran – Iran's cultural and spiritual heritage is now threatened by policies that may trigger international intervention. Iran, a source of Western civilization, may be destroyed by its main beneficiary, Western civilization.
9781846940767 272pp **£11.99 $22.95**

Light of Civilization
Nicholas Hagger

A sweeping overview work in which Hagger looks at the underlying, long-term patterns in the history of civilisations. This one is highly recommended. **Odyssey**
1905047630 672pp **£24.99 $49.95**

Secret History of the West
Nicholas Hagger

If you think that the history of Western civilization is all about progressive leaps and bounds, with Utopian visions often ending in wars, then think again. Nicholas Hagger has produced an enticing narrative analysing the roots and histories of large and small revolutions since the Renaissance. He courageously covers a broad territory with a stunning array of "heretical" sects that have shaped and continue to shape our world behind the scenes. **Nexus**
1905047045 592pp **£16.99 $29.95**